Elements of Sociology

Sociology

A Critical Canadian Introduction

▶ John Steckley ▶ Guy Kirby Letts

OXFORD
UNIVERSITY PRESS

OXFORD

UNIVERSITY PRESS

70 Wynford Drive, Don Mills, Ontario M3C 1J9
www.oup.com/ca

Oxford University Press is a department of the University of Oxford.
It furthers the University's objective of excellence in research, scholarship,
and education by publishing worldwide in

Oxford   New York

Auckland   Cape Town   Dar es Salaam   Hong Kong   Karachi
Kuala Lumpur   Madrid   Melbourne   Mexico City   Nairobi
New Delhi   Shanghai   Taipei   Toronto

Oxford is a trade mark of Oxford University Press
in the UK and in certain other countries

Published in Canada
by Oxford University Press

Statistics Canada information is used with the permission of Statistics Canada.
Users are forbiddento copy this material and/or redisseminate the data, in an original or
modified form, for commercial purposes, without the expressed permission of Statistics Canada.
Information on the availability of the wide range of data from Statistics Canada can
be obtained from Statistics Canada's Regional Offices, its World Wide Web site at
http://www.statcan.ca, and its toll-free access number 1-800-263-1136.

Every effort has been made to determine and contact copyright owners.
In the case of any omissions, the publisher will be pleased to make
suitable acknowledgement in future editions.

Library and Archives Canada Cataloguing in Publication

Steckley, John, 1949–
Elements of sociology : a Canadian introduction / John Steckley,
Guy Letts.

Includes bibliographical references and index.
ISBN 978-0-19-542999-2

1. Canada—Social conditions—Textbooks. 2. Sociology—Canada—
Textbooks. I. Letts, Guy Kirby, 1961– II. Title.
HM586.S84 2007   301.0971   C2007-900792-9

3 4 5 6 - 11 10 09 08
Cover image: Gerard Launet/PhotoAlto/Getty Images
Cover design: Brett J. Miller
Text Design: Sherill Chapman
This book is printed on permanent (acid-free) paper ∞.
Printed in the United States of America

Brief Contents

Contents

PART THREE   SOCIAL INSTITUTIONS

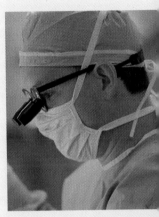

PART FOUR   SOCIAL DIFFERENCE

PART FIVE   GLOBAL PERSPECTIVES

List of Boxes

(Canadian) Sociology in Action

In Other Words, In Our View

Quick Hits

List of Tables

To C. Wright Mills,
our sociological hero.

Preface

Why Write a Sociology Text?

Why write a Canadian introductory sociology textbook when there are so many out there already? Our journey began with what we perceived as an inability among introductory texts on the Canadian market to give proper voice to Aboriginal and South Asian perspectives. We don't pretend we can claim to have corrected the deficiency. We have only begun a change, by incorporating more than ten authors from each group. We acknowledge that this is not enough, but we feel this marks a significant change from earlier Canadian sociology textbooks.

A Narrative Approach

At the same time, we realized that other voices needed to be heard as well. While we have touched on, and cited the work of, authors from a broad variety of groups, representing different ethnic backgrounds, cultures, and sexualities, we felt that the best way to make different voices heard was in narratives, which we have incorporated in each chapter. These feature a variety of perspectives informed by a variety of social locations: Black, Chinese, Italian, Lesbian, Muslim, Palestinian, and Portuguese. We strongly believe that the narratives constitute one of the most important features of this textbook.

An Inclusive Approach

The narrative approach is a fairly obvious way in which we think our textbook is a little different, but it's not the only way. We are fairly radical in our thinking and were tired of the dry, conservative bent of other textbooks, and their general failure to include much or anything about the heroes of our discipline, the ones who have inspired us: Dorothy Smith, Michel Foucault, Franz Fanon, Antonio Gramsci, Albert Memmi, and (apart from a perfunctory nod to his sociological imagination) C. Wright Mills. We decided to aim to be much more inclusive in covering theories and theorists. We have also made a point to acknowledge women and people of colour who have influenced and redirected the discipline.

Breaking Out of the Mould

Another problem affecting introductory sociology texts is the market imperative within the broader political economy of publishing itself. There is little interest in doing something different than what has already been done, and a repetition of the same becomes the predominant modus operandi. It wasn't until we began the publishing process that we realized how the conservative elements found within the market were a factor in what materialized as the final product. There is little tolerance for difference only because there is little appetite for risk, which results in reproducing what is known to have worked before. We were fortunate that Oxford, constrained by its own market imperative and logic, has been as supportive as it has of this project.

up, as a text for Canadian students, to teach them about what we—Canadian sociologists—have done, are doing, have failed to do, and hope to do in the future.

Written by Canadians for Canadians

Then there is the Canadian nature of the textbook. The idea of a textbook being Canadian or expressing a Canadian perspective is rarely dealt with in any real way. In many respects, texts are considered Canadian when they use Canadian figures, Canadian data, and Canadian research; however, they may entirely overlook the history and emergence of sociology in this country. Canadian sociology, with its unique perspective, is quite different from the sociology found in Europe and the US. For instance, the focus of early Canadian sociology was on rural life and the resource economy, which speaks to a society that is not highly urbanized or industrialized. Moreover, the influence of the social gospel movement and social work orientates Canadian sociology, more than its counterparts elsewhere, around issues of social justice. Even today, we can still see this influence in the research that sociologists do in Canada.

We are confident that this is the most Canadian introductory sociology textbook on the market. It is not an adapted American textbook with Canadian extensions, nor is it a North American textbook co-written by American and Canadian authors. We designed this book, from the ground

Qualitative Methods—Not Just Questionnaires Anymore

While contemporary sociology still engages in foundational methods, there has been an expansion of qualitative methodological approaches that have been influenced by feminism, queer theory, poststructuralism, postcolonialism, and cultural studies, many of which had been ghettoized into other disciplines, such as anthropology, comparative literature, and women's studies. And while none of these methods are new, they have not been part of the methodological lexicon in sociology. In order to represent contemporary sociology and the current methods being used in the discipline, we thought it necessary to expand our methods section by incorporating and reflecting some of theses practices. Beyond a conventional discussion on both quantitative and qualitative methods we have included ethnographic research, case studies, and narratives, as well as content and discourse analysis, psychoanalysis, semiotics, and genealogy. The idea behind incorporating methods not found in most introductory sociology texts was to introduce students to concepts, ideas, and themes that will be recurring throughout their education. We hope, by presenting these methodological approaches, to inspire their imagination.

Contemporary Theory and Shifting the Canon

In terms of what is relevant within the discipline itself, it becomes necessary to stress what is current, what is being done, and who is being studied. The discipline generally and the theory specifically are exciting, yet we feel that this is not being conveyed to our students, who often see sociology as boring—and why wouldn't they. Sociological theory today has shifted immensely, with theoretical influences from queer theory, feminist psychoanalysis, postcolonialism, and poststructuralism, as well as people like Foucault, Lacan, Spivak, and Said. Whether the exclusion of these influences and figures is the result of the status quo or the belief that they are too complex for our students to comprehend, it is a misrepresentation that in the end benefits no one, and one that we have tried to correct.

A Visual Approach

A casual flip through the pages of this text will reveal an abundance of photographs and other illustrations. The photos are not just pretty distractions to keep students looking at the book. They serve a purpose. We have chosen photos

In Our View

It takes a number of people to put together a book of this size and scope. First, I would like to thank the people at Oxford University Press who made major contributions to this project. David Stover I thank for suggesting (twice) that I write this book. Lisa Meschino, who signed us on and contributed greatly to the first steps on this path with her constant enthusiasm, should be acknowledged, as should Eric Sinkins, who, with amazing effort and diplomatic skill, got us to the finish line.

I would also like to thank several of my colleagues at Humber. Les Takahashi, Jim Jackson, John Metcalfe, and Joey Noble all contributed to this work with their support and helpful ideas. Librarians Jennifer Rayment and Marlene Beck worked major feats of magic to make obscure articles and books appear.

Closer to home, there is my good friend Bryan Cummins, who saw to it that my pub life at the Toby Jug kept me sane and on track in this project. My dogs, Egwene and Cosmo, proved, as always, to be useful distractions and sources of constant emotional support.

Then, finally, there is my wife, Angie. She supported me through the highs and lows of this project, when I was not the easiest person to live with. When the sands of my life shift, there is always a rock I can depend on.

John Steckley
February 2007

and have written captions that we hope will encourage students to adopt a sociological perspective. The same objective is served by the numerous critical-thinking questions scattered throughout the chapters.

At the same time, we are aware of the power of illustrations, and that they can unconsciously give messages the authors of a sociology book do not intend. For example, if you argue for inclusion and diversity while featuring pictures that predominantly portray blond-haired, blue-eyed White folks, then your words and your picture choices are clashing with each other. And if you include a picture of a Native person who is homeless, actively protesting the high rate of homelessness in Canada, you can be serving conflicting purposes as well. Yes, the face of homelessness in Canada is often Aboriginal—history and systemic racism are major contributors to this problem—and you are being accurate in representing that. And it is good to show Aboriginal people taking an active role in fighting for a better position in Canadian society. However, if it is one of only a few pictures you show of Aboriginal people, then, like the Canadian media generally, you are merely reinforcing the stereotypes of Native people as being homeless (the vast majority are not) and as doing nothing but protest, rather than 'getting jobs like normal people.'

In Our View

I have used numerous texts throughout my teaching career and have always been at odds with both the representation and the pedagogy that was being advocated. In many ways, the sociology that I read, that my colleagues do, and that I myself practise looks nothing like the sociology found in introductory textbooks. I often wondered why a discipline would represent itself to young adults as something conservative, parochial, and, well, boring, given that the discipline itself is liberating, dynamic, and exciting.

I would like to thank Oxford University Press for giving us the opportunity to attempt something different, new, and—I believe—exciting. I would like to thank Lisa Meschino, at Oxford, who believed in the value of what we were trying to do and shared our enthusiasm, and, also at Oxford, Eric Sinkins, for his patience, creativity, and input. I would also like to thank my family, Angela Aujla, Anushka Luna, and Indigo West, for tolerating my always 'present absence'. I would like to acknowledge all those who, both real and imagined, helped me formulate a particular perspective that has allowed me to think critically about sociology specifically and society in general, to which I am eternally grateful. And finally, I would like to acknowledge my students for whom I wrote this text, so we might better understand together this strange thing called life.

Guy Kirby Letts
February 2007

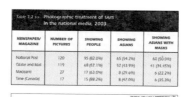

Written by Canadians for Canadians

Landmarks in Canadian sociological research are highlighted in *Canadian Sociology in Action* boxes.

A Visual Approach

Boxes, tables, and illustrations engage the student reader.

Case Studies and Groundbreaking Research

Sociology in Action boxes present case studies and highlight important contributions to sociological research, past and present.

Coverage of Canada's First Nations

Issues that have affected and continue to affect Canada's Aboriginal communities are given thorough and detailed coverage.

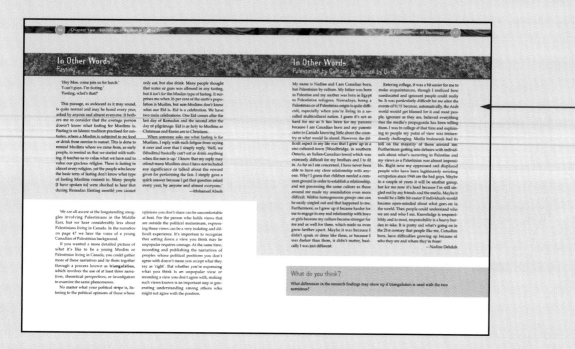

Qualitative Methods

Discussion of research methods covers ethnographic research, case studies, and narratives, as well as content and discourse analysis, psychoanalysis, semiotics, and genealogy, in order to expose students to concepts, ideas, and themes that will recur throughout their education.

A Narrative Approach

First-person narratives give voice to a variety of perspectives informed by a variety of social locations: Black, Chinese, Italian, Lesbian, Muslim, Palestinian, and Portuguese.

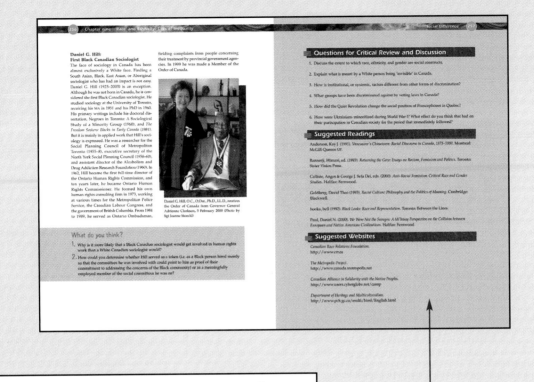

Thought-Provoking Pedagogy

Carefully chosen photographs, critical-thinking questions, and end-of-chapter review questions encourage students to adopt a sociological perspective and see the sociology in everyday life. The same objective is served by the numerous critical-thinking questions scattered throughout the chapters.

Introduction to Sociology

Contents

Key Terms

archaeology of knowledge
conflict theory
critical sociology
cultural mosaic
discourse
dramaturgical approach
ethnography
folk society
functionalism
impression management
macro-sociology
melting pot
micro-sociology
narratives
objective
political economy
professional sociology
protestant (work) ethic
public sociology
relations of ruling
social gospel
sociological imagination
sociological poetry
sociology
standpoint theory
staples
subjective
total institution
totalitarian discourse
vertical mosaic

Boxes and Tables

Sociology in Action Herbert Spencer: An Early Sociological Contribution
Canadian Sociology in Action Applying Goffman to Research
Sociology in Action Abandoning Inuit Elders: An Archaeology of Knowledge
Sociology in Action The Sociologist as Hero: C. Wright Mills

Learning Objectives

After reading this chapter, you should be able to

- outline the differences and similarities between sociology and other disciplines.
- describe what the sociological imagination is.
- identify some of the key ideas of the foundational thinkers Durkheim, Marx, and Weber.
- distinguish the different 'functions' identified by Robert Merton.
- outline the differences between, on the one hand, structural-functionalism, conflict approaches, and symbolic-interaction, and on the other hand, professional, critical, policy, and public sociology.
- articulate the basic ideas of Michel Foucault and Dorothy Smith.
- outline the origin and development of sociology in Canada.

>>> # For Starters
Doughnut Shops, Drive-Throughs, and the Value of Sociology

As I am from Ontario, it isn't surprising that I am a big fan (physically and emotionally) of doughnut shops. I consider it part of my culture. When I go to a doughnut shop, I park my car, walk in, chat with the server, and generally enjoy the social aspect of the transaction. I have never used—and will never use—a drive-through. I feel that using the drive-through limits the overall experience—the socializing, the ritual of surveying and choosing the doughnut. For that matter, it doesn't save any time (I've done an informal study) and increases the local pollution level.

You can tell I have strong views on the subject. So you probably won't be surprised to learn that I've spent a fair bit of time contemplating why some people use the drive-through. Just who are these people who would rather interact over an intercom and receive their orders through a pickup window? I'd always thought it was either young men whose

most significant relationships were with their cars, or lazy, fat, older men who drive everywhere rather than walk.

My opinion changed, however, because of a student in one of my sociology classes. This is the value of sociology—it can change your opinion. The student carried out a 'Pilot Assessment of Donut Shop Patronage' in Newmarket, a bedroom community north of Toronto. He spent approximately an hour one morning in the doughnut shop observing who used the drive-through, and who were 'walk-ins'. Over that period he saw 91 people walk in, and 95 people drive through. He noticed a gender difference in the two groups: for the counter sales, 49 of the customers were men and 42 were women, while of the drive-through patrons, 70 were women and only 25 were men. He also noted that young women were much more likely to use the drive-through than were middle-aged or older

Photo © John Steckley

women (he reckoned the ratio was 7 to 1). This was different from the group of male drive-through customers, where there was roughly a 1:1 ratio of the two age-determined groups. Another statistic enabled the student to come up with a hypothesis to account for the results of his research: he observed that the cars going through the drive-through were more likely to have child-seats in them than the parked cars of the walk-in clientele. Further, he often saw young children among the passengers of the drive-through cars.

The student's hypothesis, which would apply to that time (between approximately eight and nine o'clock a.m.) and location, was that young mothers with babies and toddlers used the drive-through significantly more because it was easier than going through the often complicated work of taking their children into the restaurant. To be really convincing, his hypothesis would have to be tested for other times and locations, but it presented a sociological profile that I would not otherwise have guessed.

Introduction to the Textbook

We hope that you'll notice, from this first example on, that this textbook is not like the others. There will be humour and lots of stories told from the perspective of the writers. In keeping with contemporary sociological terminology, we are calling these stories **narratives**. Narratives make up an important branch of sociological literature, one recognizing that understanding a person's situation requires input from the words, the 'voice', and the narratives of that person him- or herself. Every chapter will make use of narratives to illustrate key points and concepts.

There are two basic strategies that textbook writers can take. One is to create a kind of reference book that touches on pretty much every conceivable subject within the discipline. This sort of book can be good for students that need support outside of the classroom or away from the professor. The other approach is to write a book that engages the student as a reader and as a student of the discipline (even if only for one semester), and that's what we are trying to do here. Our aim is to hook you on the subject of sociology, make you interested in reading about it. We feel that—to use a baseball analogy—if

you try to round the bases too quickly, you'll get picked off. We'd rather get you safely on base. You may not touch all the bases this inning, but there's a better chance you will in your next at-bat. In other words, we've tried to avoid writing a text you will lose interest in because it tries to introduce you to too much, too quickly.

There are precedents for our approach in introductory sociology textbooks. In 1980, Elliott Krause published *Why Study Sociology?*, which he said was

designed as a bridge between your every-day understanding of social life and the kind you can develop through the study of sociology. If you do not have a broad overview of all that sociology is doing, by the time you finish this book, I hope that you will have a strong sense of some of the ways that sociology can be relevant to your life. Think of this as the appetizer. Think of any full introductory sociology course you are taking as the main entree. Think of this as the *why*, the full course as the what. (Krause 1980: xi)

The book only had six chapters, and was less than 200 pages long. This book is longer and more comprehensive. Think of it as a large, hopefully tasty snack—say a box of Timbits.

Introduction to Sociology

Sociologists notice social patterns. For example, things tend to happen differently to you depending on your gender, age, class, ethnicity ('race'), religion, and sexual orientation. If you are a woman, you pay more in Canada for a haircut and to have your shirt dry-cleaned than you would if you were a man (Dunfield 2005). It's not that you're getting more for your money; it's just that your hair and your shirt, because they are designated as 'female', are more expensive to cut and to clean (respectively). If you are a young black man driving in Canada, you are more likely than a white male driver to be pulled over at night by the police (even if you are famous, as in the case of Canadian Olympic boxer Kirk Johnson). You are guilty of the offence known facetiously as 'driving while black'.

What if you are a young, white, heterosexual male? If you belong to that group, you might think that all the 'other groups' are ganging up on you. Take the education system, for instance. It has a policy of zero tolerance for 'fighting', which covers behaviour you would have thought of as just 'fooling around'. You didn't have a male teacher until you were in your middle grades. When you studied English literature in high school, your teachers asked you 'girl' questions about things like relationships and feelings, questions you couldn't possibly have answered as your female classmates could. Insurance companies make it very expensive for you (and your parents) to pay for your driving. You

Based on this picture, why is the classroom setting more comfortable for male students than for female students? (© Photodisc)

read and hear that white males have privilege in terms of getting jobs, but it is often difficult for you to find the jobs that privilege is supposed to help you with. If your aim is to be a police officer, you might be discouraged by rumours that only women and visible minorities are being hired. (Such rumours are not true, and say something about the older white males who often spread them.)

If any of these scenarios describes you, take heart: sociology can help you understand your situation. Sociologists investigate and challenge the social patterns that other people perceive. Why do so many people, even those in the medical profession, assume that male nurses are gay? It has never been demonstrated statistically (in part because it would be unethical to ask a male nurse about his sexual preferences). Sociologists studying the subject would have to investigate the effects of movies like *Meet the Fockers*, where characters played by well-known and well-respected actors (Robert de Niro, in this case) articulate their belief that male nurses are either gay or sissies. Sociologists would look at how nursing is thought of as 'naturally feminine' because it involves care-giving and is a chronically underpaid profession involving duties culturally considered less important than the work of (typically male) doctors. They might also look at how male nurses and nursing students might act out their heterosexuality (e.g. by bragging about the women they have had sex with) in order to combat the perception that they are gay. In short, sociologists would look carefully at the patterns of social behaviour associated with male nurses.

Consider another example: politicians that promote conservative social policies often talk about the 'liberal media'. Sociologists can test whether this assumption about the left-leaning media is true or false by doing a statistically based content analysis of the political views recorded in popular media. Sociologists might conclude that with the number of tabloid-style papers that exist in Canada, the very opposite position could very well be demonstrated. We'll talk more about statistical analysis and other kinds of quantitative and qualitative research in the next chapter. What is important to understand here is that sociologists use these kinds of tools to assess and challenge the social perceptions that people hold.

Sociology and Issues

Sociology can help students understand the issues facing society today. One of the most divisive social issues in Canada is the debate surrounding same-sex marriage. What can sociologists tell us about this issue? Sociology can't say what is moral or 'right'. There really isn't a 'scientific' way of doing that. What sociology can do is enable us to be well informed about this and other current issues. For example, sociology can tell us about who *tends* to be in favour of same-sex marriage—younger people, those with more education, women more than men, French Canadians more than English Canadians. As well, sociology can speak about who *tends* to be against same-sex marriage: those with more fundamentalist religious views as opposed to the more liberal members of Canada's many faiths, and people from rural rather than urban communities. Beyond this, sociology gives us the perspective to document and discuss the various ways that marriage is defined in contemporary cultures across the world, or in Canadian cultures over time, and it can inform a discussion about changes in the relationship that marriage has had with religious institutions through the centuries. In this way, it can help a sociology student avoid making uninformed, universal statements beginning with 'Marriage has always . . .' or 'I can't understand how someone can think that . . .'. Sociology might also help students understand the impact that socializing influences like parents, the media, and sociology professors have on their own opinions concerning same-sex marriage. You can have more choice in forming your own opinion when you know what has influenced it in the past.

All of this relates to a question that sociology students often ask: 'How come I received a low mark when it's just an opinion and there are no right or wrong answers?' Ideally, sociology helps students distinguish between a well-argued, informed opinion and an uninformed opinion spouted off without careful thought. While students often say, justly, that everybody has a right to an opinion, it is likewise true that everyone owes it to themselves to become well informed on the issues before offering their opinions. Sociology gives us the means to achieve considered opinions on social issues.

Sociology as a Discipline

Academic disciplines such as sociology are artificial creations. There is nothing 'natural' about the borderlines that separate sociology from such other well-established disciplines as, say, anthropology, business economics, history, psychology, philosophy, or political science.

These various fields of interest have much in common, as Table 1.1 shows, and there is a lot of cross-referencing in the books and articles written by specialists in each discipline. Health professionals often engage in sociological research that is published in medical journals. Students will notice, if they have taken courses in psychology, anthropology, or philosophy, that sociology regularly encroaches on their territory, just as those disciplines often 'poach' on sociology's turf. The people who teach such varied subjects as Canadian studies, communication, criminology, cultural studies, education, Native studies, international relations, and women's studies often have degrees in sociology.

Still, artificial or not, the discipline of sociology does exist and is unique. It has its own history, a distinct vocabulary and set of tools (although some are borrowed from or lent out to other disciplines), and a separate department in most colleges and universities. In order to understand sociology, its weaknesses and strengths, and the ways in which its perspective

Table 1.1 >> Sociology and related disciplines

DISCIPLINE	EMPHASIS
anthropology	the comparative study of human societies and cultures and their development
economics	the production and consumption of wealth, including the distribution of goods and services among individuals and groups
philosophy	major thinkers and trends of thought in particular societies (usually Western)
political science	systems of government and how they serve citizens
psychology	the human mind, the social and biological influences on it, and its functions, especially those affecting behaviour
social work	the application of our understanding of society and individuals in order to improve peoples' well-being
sociology	the development, structure, and functioning of human society: group interaction, social relations, social institutions, and social structures

has broadened over the last few decades, it needs to be understood as a discipline.

So, What Is Sociology?

By now you may have noticed that so far we have cleverly avoided defining what sociology is. That's because it's not a straightforward thing to do. We could give a simple (but not terribly useful) definition by saying that sociology is 'the systematic or scientific study of society'. Can you imagine the type of multiple-choice questions that could come from that?

> Sociology is:
  a) the systematic study of society;
  b) the unsystematic study of society;
  c) 'statistical stuff and heavy-duty theoretical bullshit' (Mills, see below);
  d) all of the above.

The answer could easily be the final one, 'all of the above'.

The truth is that giving a precise, all-encompassing explanation of what sociology *is* is much more difficult that explaining what sociology *does*. This is why we've begun our introduction to sociology by highlighting some of its uses. At this point it is enough to know that **sociology** involves looking for and looking at patterns in social variables such as age, gender, race, ethnicity, religion, and sexual orientation; in social institutions such as education and justice systems, religions, and family; and in social interactions. By the time you've reached the end of this textbook, you will have formed your own idea of what sociology really *is*.

So, Why Study Sociology?

It is useful to study sociology in order to achieve for oneself and to generate among others a greater understanding of the social world. Studying sociology will also enable you to better understand yourself in terms of whether you follow or do not follow predictable pat-

terns created by sociological variables. And it will help you develop an understanding (sometimes more than one valid interpretation is possible) about others around you in our multicultural and generally diverse social world that we call Canada, as well as in the small worlds of neighbourhoods, chat groups, classrooms, pubs, and the workplace.

During a strike by Ontario public-school teachers in the 1990s, some strike supporters sported a bumper sticker that read, 'If you think education is expensive, just try ignorance'. In a similar vein you could say, 'If you think sociology is hard to understand, just try understanding society without it.'

The Heart of Sociology: The *Sociological* Imagination

While we've managed to excuse ourselves from defining sociology itself, we would be remiss if we avoided defining one of the discipline's key terms: the **sociological imagination**. Developing a sociological imagination is a goal that practitioners and students of the discipline strive for. **C. Wright Mills** (1916–1962), who coined the term, sums it up nicely as

> the capacity to shift from one perspective to another—from the political to the psychological; from examination of a single family to comparative assessment of the national budgets of the world. . . . It is the capacity to range from the most impersonal and remote transformations to the most intimate features of the human self—and to see the relationship between the two. (Mills 1959:4)

Mills argues that when we create and communicate sociological knowledge, it must show not only 'how society works' but 'how society works in terms of my personal life'. If you go to buy rubber boots, and the only pair you can get is relatively flimsy and comes only in yellow, then you are a woman, and your shopping experience reflects how society thinks of and treats women.

The Origins of Sociology

Who Was the First Sociologist?

It might be fair to say that for nearly as long as humans have lived, there have been people who have contemplated social systems and looked for patterns in human relationships. Indeed, many of the great classical philosophers were social thinkers. Perhaps the earliest person who at least in some ways was a sociologist, and whose words were written down, is the Chinese philosopher Confucius (*c.* 551–479 BCE). He theorized about, among other things, role-modelling, a topic discussed often in sociology. Confucius believed it was better for a leader to engage in moral practices that modelled the principles he wanted his citizens to follow than to overuse laws to enforce morality. In his words:

> If you use laws to direct the people, and punishments to control them, they will merely try to evade the laws, and will have no sense of shame. (Kaizuka 2002:126)

We can all think of politicians that would have benefited from following the wise sociological advice of Confucius.

Perhaps the first person to carry out a systematic study of sociological subjects and set down his thoughts in writing is the Arab scholar Ibn Khaldun (1332–1406), whom some contemporary writers consider the first social scientist. In his book *Al Muqaddimah* (*An Introduction to History*), Ibn Khaldun examines various types of societies—tribes, cities, countries, and dynasties—and their histories, cultures, and economies. Many of his ideas and much of his research are still relevant today. For instance, in *Al Muqaddimah*, he gives us insight

Confucius emphasized socialization over social control and stressed that a country's leaders must engage in moral practices which model the type of behaviour that would be desirable in its citizenry. Are politicians, or even celebrities and corporate CEOs, good role models? (Photo © Archivo Iconagrafico, S.A./Corbis)

into how the power and status of desert tribes in the Middle East would rise and fall in cycles:

> [W]hen a tribe has achieved a certain measure of superiority with the help of its group feeling, it gains control over a corresponding amount of wealth and comes to share prosperity and abundance with those who have been in possession of these things. It shares in them to the degree of its power and usefulness to the ruling dynasty. If the ruling dynasty is so strong that no one thinks of depriving it of its power or of sharing with it, the tribe in question submits to its rule and is satis-

fied with whatever share in the dynasty's wealth and tax revenue it is permitted to enjoy. . . . Members of the tribe are merely concerned with prosperity, gain, and a life of abundance. [They are satisfied] to lead an easy, restful life in the shadow of the ruling dynasty, and to adopt royal habits in building and dress, a matter they stress and in which they take more and more pride, the more luxuries and plenty they acquire, as well as all the other things that go with luxury and plenty.

As a result the toughness of desert life is lost. Group feeling and courage weaken. Members of the tribe revel in the well-being that God has given them. Their children and offspring grow up too proud to look after themselves or to attend to their own needs. They have disdain also for all the other things that are necessary in connection with group feeling. . . . Their group feeling and courage decrease in the next generations. Eventually group feeling is altogether destroyed. . . . It will be swallowed up by other nations. (109)

Ibn Khaldun is considered the first sociologist to systematically study the sociohistorical nature of societies. According to Khaldun, as societies acquire more affluence they also become more senile and fall into demise. (Drawing by Hatem El Mekki/Tunisian Stamp Authority)

Replace 'tribe' with 'country' or 'empire', and Ibn Khaldun's observations could have been written any time in the past century.

What do you think?

1. Why do you think that Ibn Khaldun has only recently been recognized and connected to the ideas of sociology?

2. Change the word 'tribe' to 'country' or 'empire'. Do you think that he has a valid point?

The Development of Sociology in the West

Sociology emerged as an area of academic interest in nineteenth-century Europe, specifically in France, Germany, and Britain. It developed in response to the dramatic social changes taking place at that time: industrialization, urbanization, and dramatic population increases. The economics and especially the politics of the time were also favourable to the growth of sociology. As the American sociologist John Walton comments,

Sociology was made possible by the French Revolution. The capture of the Bastille on July 14, 1789, and the Women's March on Versailles introduced a new principle into history by demanding political action to redress mass poverty. The authority of king and church that once justified social inequality was challenged by the philosophical notion of the general will come to life among people convinced that their suffering was no longer inevitable. Public opinion became a legitimate method for expressing these social concerns. (Walton 1986:50)

In the late nineteenth and early twentieth centuries, North America—especially the United States—with the influx of millions of immigrants, the development of cities and urban life, and the greater impact of technology upon the daily lives of individuals, became an ideal location for the discipline of sociology to develop.

Table 1.2 >> Early sociologists

THINKER	NATIONALITY	KEY WORKS
Auguste Comte (1798–1857)	French	*Cours de Philosophie Positive* (1830–42), *The System of Positive Policy* (1851–4)
Harriet Martineau (1802–1876)	British	*Society in America* (1837)
Karl Marx (1818–1883)	German	*The German Ideology* (1846), *The Communist Manifesto* (1848), *Das Capital* (1867)
Herbert Spencer (1820–1903)	British	*Social Statics* (1851), *First Principles* (1862) *The Study of Sociology* (1880)
Fredrick Nietzsche (1844–1900)	German	*Human, all too Human* (1878), *The Gay Science* (1882), *The Genealogy of Morals* (1887), *Will to Power* (1901)
Émile Durkheim (1858–1917)	French	*The Division of Labour in Society* (1893), *The Rules of Sociological Method* (1895), *Suicide* (1897), *The Elementary Forms of the Religious Life* (1912)
Georg Simmel (1858–1918)	French	*On Social Differentiation* (1890), *The Philosophy of Money* (1900), *Sociology: Investigations on the forms of Socialization* (1908)
Max Weber (1864–1920)	German	*The Protestant Ethic and the Spirit of Capitalism* (1904–5), *Economy and Society* (1914)
Thorstein Veblen (1857–1929)	American	*The Theory of the Leisure Class* (1899), *The Theory of Business Enterprise* (1904)
George Herbert Mead (1863–1931)	American	*Mind, Self, and Society* (1934)
Robert Park (1864–1944)	American	*Introduction to the Science of Sociology* (& Burgess, 1921), *The City* (& Burgess, 1925)

What do you think?

1. Do you think that sociology would have developed differently as a discipline if the early thinkers had been African, Middle Eastern, Chinese, or South Asian?

2. Why do you think that sociology developed in Europe, not in Africa, the Middle East, China, or South Asia?

3. Why are most of these people men?

>> Sociology in Action
Herbert Spencer: An Early Sociological Contribution

You've probably heard the phrase 'survival of the fittest'. Most people attribute it to biologist Charles Darwin (1809–1882), who, in his pioneering theory of evolution through natural selection, claimed that only those organisms 'fit' enough—that is, those individuals or species that have adapted to be most suitable in a particular environment—are destined to survive.

What most people don't know is that the saying itself was coined not by Darwin but by the early English sociologist Herbert Spencer (1820–1903). Heavily influenced by Darwin, Spencer was one of a number of scholars who tried to extend the theory of natural selection by applying it to human society in order to describe the competitive struggle for power, wealth, and general well-being brought about by European industrialization and colonization. Using evolutionary theory in this way to describe social inequalities became known as **social Darwinism**.

Social Darwinists held up natural selection as the basis for claims of European superiority—societies in Africa, Asia, and the Pacific Islands were seen as more 'primitive' and less evolved—and as justification for colonizing and even enslaving peoples in parts of the world outside Europe. By the same token, they argued that governments should not intervene to help the sick and the poor in their own societies, as these people were 'naturally selected' to fail. Social Darwinism was used to justify discriminatory practices, such as sterilization, against a variety of groups including women, people of colour, and various ethnic groups. For Spencer in particular, evolution guided social change (a notion that runs counter to Marx's idea of class struggle and Innis's notion of technology, which we will examine later in this chapter).

Poverty, as we will see later, is in fact a social problem, not a problem of one's 'fitness'. Notions of superiority and inferiority, and of who should have access to resources, create inequalities and are the byproducts of culture and social history.

Max Weber: A Founder of Modern Sociology

No one better illustrates the intellectual force and impact of early sociology than German sociologist **Max Weber** (pronounced VAY-ber; 1864–1920). One of his most important and famous contributions was his identification of a set of values embodied in early Protestantism that he believed led to the development of modern capitalism; he called this set of values the **protestant (work) ethic**.

Weber's theory was based on a number of related ideas. One is the notion, popular among early Protestants, that there is a predestined 'elect' that will be 'saved' during the time of reckoning, at the Second Coming of Jesus. Naturally, it was important to early Protestants to be seen as part of this select group. Success through hard work was considered one proof of membership. Another was the accumulation of capital (money and money-producing possessions) through thriftiness. Working hard ('idle hands are the devil's tool'), making profitable use of your time, and living a materially ascetic life (self-denying) through property acquisition rather than lavish expenditure were all principles of the Protestant work ethic. As Weber explained,

> The span of human life is infinitely short and precious to make sure of one's own election. Loss of time through sociability, idle talk, luxury, even more sleep than is necessary for health . . . is worthy of absolute moral condemnation. . . . [Time] is infinitely valuable because every hour lost is lost to labour for the glory of God. Thus inactive contemplation is also valueless, or even directly reprehensible if it is at the expense of one's daily work. For it is less pleasing to God than the active performance of His will in a calling. (1904/1930:157–8)

In a later work, Weber elaborated on how demonstrating these values represents proof of being one of God's chosen few, and how these values supposedly fuelled the rise of capitalism:

> The religious valuation of restless, continuous, systematic work in a worldly calling, as the . . . surest and most evident proof of rebirth and genuine faith, must have been the most powerful conceivable lever for the expansion of . . . the spirit of capitalism (1946/1958:172).

It's important to note that although the phrase 'Protestant (work) ethic' entered popular speech, it was never sociologically demonstrated that capitalism developed primarily in Protestant rather than Catholic countries, or that the work ethic Weber associated with Protestantism was somehow missing from Catholicism, or from any religion for that matter. Latin American scholars, for instance, argue that the rise of capitalism began with colonialism, a movement in which Catholic Spain and Portugal were early major players. Weber paid little attention to the role that colonialism played in the rise of capitalism through exploiting and amassing foreign wealth. Further, Weber seems to have been justifying the relatively 'recent' historical superiority of European Protestants by attributing the development of capitalism to the power of their own will. At the same time he was implying that Chinese and Indian societies somehow lacked a work ethic, a fact that negatively affected their economic success.

What do you think?

Do you think that Weber would have advanced this theory if he had been a devout Catholic, Muslim, or Buddhist, rather than a liberal Protestant?

The Emergence of Different Kinds of Sociology

As modern sociology developed in nineteenth-century Europe, it did not take on a uniform appearance. Asking 'What is sociology?' was no simpler then than it is today, and even its best uses were in dispute. Different social thinkers had their own ideas about what sociology was, what it could do, and how it should be applied. Consequently, sociology developed into several different schools that varied according to the particular applications and perspectives (historical, political-economical, feminist, and so on) of those who were using it.

In this chapter we will explore two ways of distinguishing the various kinds of sociology. The first is based on the approach used; the second is based on the audience and how reflexive or critical the sociologist is. These are by no means the only two ways of viewing sociology, but in our view they are the most useful.

1. Structural Functionalism, Conflict, and Symbolic Interaction

The traditional way of representing different kinds of sociology in Canadian introductory sociology textbooks is to break sociology into three different approaches: structural functionalism, conflict, and symbolic interaction. These terms are generally presented in introductory chapters and then repeated throughout most, if not all, of the subsequent chapters. The linguist Edward Sapir said, 'all grammars [i.e. explanations of language] leak.' As a way of illustrating the differences between sociologists, we feel that this particular grammar of sociology leaks too much (imagine a flooded basement) to sustain using it throughout the text. Nevertheless, these distinctions do reveal some key differences, so they are worth explaining and illustrating here.

Structural Functionalism

The **structural-functionalist** approach has deep roots in sociology, especially American sociology. As the name suggests, the approach contains two elements. Functionalism focuses on how social systems, in their entirety, operate and produce consequences. The work of Émile Durkheim, Talcott Parsons, and Robert Merton represents the functionalist approach.

Activists roll out their banner at the site of the North Star squat, an abandoned single-room occupancy hotel in Vancouver's Downtown Eastside neighbourhood. Is homelessness a social consequence produced by our economic system? (Photo © M.J. Milloy)

The functionalist approach was fused with structuralism (grounded in the anthropological work of Bronislav Malinowski and A.A. Radcliffe-Brown) as a way of explaining social forms and their contributions to social cohesion. It uses an organic or biological analogy for society. How? Nursing students, when they take the dreaded Anatomy and Physiology course, have to learn all the different *structures* of the human body as well as the *functions* they perform. The structural-functionalist approach treats society in a similar way: 'This is religion, and this is how it functions . . .'; 'This is the family, which functions like so . . .'

While the structural-functionalist approach was popular for much of the history of sociology as a discipline, it has lost favour during the last few decades. It is too much of a stretch, for example, to talk about the *functions* of poverty or inequality. After all, poverty and inequality don't really serve the interests of society at large, just the narrow class interests of those who profit from others' misfortunes. In addition, functionalism is not usually very good at promoting an understanding of conflict or social change. While sociologists still draw on the works and concepts of structural functionalism, very few contemporary sociologists are committed to the theoretical practice itself.

To get a better sense of the functionalist approach, we'll look at the work of **Émile Durkheim** (1858–1917), who is considered one of the founders of sociology. Presenting the highlights of Durkheim's career would fill a chapter. Instead of doing that, we'll focus on one of his works in order to illustrate functionalism. Let's begin, though, with Durkheim's notion of the **social fact**, a term he coined. Social facts are patterned ways of acting, thinking, and feeling that exist outside of any one individual but exert social control over all people. Think about how social characteristics such as gender, age, religion, ethnicity, 'race', sexual orientation, your role as sister or brother, or as student or teacher, all exert a compelling social force over you and lead you to act in sociologically predictable ways. These ways of acting based on social characteristics are social facts.

There are three main characteristics of every social fact:

- It was developed prior to and separate from you as an individual (in other words, you didn't invent it).
- It can be seen as being characteristic of a particular group (young Canadian males, for instance, like to watch sports while drinking beer).
- It involves a constraining or coercing force that pushes individuals into acting in a particular way.

You can see how looking for social facts would be a particularly good way for a sociologist like Durkheim to get away from the focus on individuals to examine larger social forms and how different parts of society function. Hence the birth of functionalism, and in many ways sociology as we know it.

In his groundbreaking book *Suicide* (1897), Durkheim treated suicide as a social fact. Recalling that social facts exist outside of any one individual, you might find this approach strange given the intensely personal nature of the act. But Durkheim found that in late nineteenth-century France, certain groups were more likely to commit suicide than others: officers as opposed to enlisted men, Protestants as opposed to Catholics, unmarried over married people, and the rich over the poor and the middle-class. He correlated suicide with the degree to which individuals were connected with or committed to society, finding that those having a stronger dedication to society were more likely to commit suicide. Officers are responsible for their men; an intense sense of honour might make them suicidal when they make a mistake that results in death. According to Durkheim, having too weak connections with society also could produce suicide. Protestants were then in the minority in France, and thus had weaker bonds to both country and culture.

Unmarried adults were—as they generally are now—not as connected to family as are married ones. And the wealthy were more aloof, much less concerned than others with becoming involved in the affairs of the larger society.

In Canada today, men commit suicide more often than women do. This is a social fact. Why men commit suicide more often than women do is a complicated matter. It has to do in part with the fact that women are more likely to share their problems with other people than to 'suck it up' and remain silent. Women are more likely to have a network of friends with whom they can communicate about serious matters, and they are more likely to go to a therapist with an emotional problem, which lowers their likelihood of committing suicide. Women attempting suicide are also more likely to use less efficient means: pills and slashed wrists over the more deadly male choice of guns.

American sociologist **Robert K. Merton** (1910–2003) identified three types of functions:

- **Manifest functions** are both intended and readily recognized, or 'manifest' (i.e. easily seen).
- **Latent functions** are largely unintended and unrecognized.
- **Latent dysfunctions** are functions that are unintended and produce socially negative consequences.

This last group is sympathetic to the conflict approach, as we will see, making Merton's brand of functionalism something of a bridge to conflict theory. Table 1.3 provides three examples to illustrate the differences among Merton's three functions.

Conflict Approach

The **conflict approach** is based on the four 'C's': *conflict, class, contestation,* and *change*. This approach is predicated first on the idea that *conflict* exists in all large-scale societies. The stress lines are major sociological factors, such as gender, race, ethnicity, religion, age, and class. Second, it asserts that *class* has always existed in every society. Third, it contends that the functions of society, as laid out in traditional structural-functional theory, can be *contested* or challenged based on the question 'What group does this function best serve?' Finally, the approach involves the assumption that society either will or should be *changed*.

A major figure early in the history of sociology was the German economist and political philosopher **Karl Marx** (1818–1883), who with Friedrich Engels founded modern communism in the mid-nineteenth century. For Marx, conflict was all about **class**: the division of society into a hierarchy of groups, with each group's position determined by its role in the production of wealth. Beginning with Marx, conflict theory looks at how conflict between the different groups, or classes, leads to change. Marx saw class conflict as the driving force behind all major socio-historical change. He believed that conflict between the class of capitalists (the **bourgeoisie**) and the class of workers (the **proletariat**) would initiate a socialist revolution that would produce a classless or **egalitarian** society. A classless society has never really existed in more complex societies, but many of Marx's insights about class conflict and capitalist production are still valid. This is particularly true if you think of transnational corporations in Western societies as the 'owning class' and underpaid workers in the poorer countries as the ultimate 'working class' (for more on this, see Chapter 11, on globalization).

The limits of the conflict approach now stretch beyond just Marxism to incorporate themes from feminist sociology, international political science, personal relations and interaction, and many other fields of study that fit rather neatly into the category of 'critical sociology'. We'll look at critical sociology in greater detail later in this chapter.

Symbolic Interaction

The **symbolic interaction** approach looks at the meaning (the symbolic part) of the daily social interaction of individuals. For example,

Table 1.3 >> Examples of Robert Merton's three functions

EXAMPLE 1

Post-Secondary Education

manifest functions	– provides necessary skills and knowledge
latent functions	– provides social network that will make aid the search for employment and a marriage partner easier
latent dysfunctions	– reinforces class distinctions (from a left-wing perspective)
	– exposes students to socialist ideas (from a right-wing perspective)

EXAMPLE 2

Religion

manifest functions	– fulfills spiritual and emotional needs, answers important existential questions
latent functions	– creates a social network and marriage market
latent dysfunctions	– provides justification for judging non-believers negatively

EXAMPLE 3

Canadian Doughnut Shops

manifest functions	– provide coffee and food quickly
latent functions	– provide a meeting and socializing place
latent dysfunctions	– provides late night location for drug dealing

What do you think?

1. Could you challenge, amend, or add to any of the functions presented? How?

2. What would be the three different functions for organized sports for Canadian children?

two male students approach each other and say, 'What up?', lightly bringing their fists together in greeting. What are they communicating to each other about their relationship, their shared interests, and the role models that they identify with?

The symbolic interaction method was pioneered by American social psychologist **George Herbert Mead** (1863–1931), who examined how the self is constructed as we interact with others and how the self allows us to take on social roles, reflect on ourselves, and internalize social expectations (1912–13). Another important figure in the movement was **Herbert Blumer** (1900–1987), a pupil of Mead's and the one who coined the term 'symbolic interaction'. Blumer (1969) argued that social systems are simply abstractions and do not exist independently of individual relations and interactions. In other words, social systems (e.g. friendship, education, economy) are simply by-products of our personal dealings with one another. The American sociologist **Harold Garfinkel** (b. 1917) founded a method associated with symbolic interaction and known as **ethnomethodology**. Garfinkel developed ethnomethodology (which means the 'people's method', referring to its focus on practical reasoning or common-sense knowledge) to explain how people use social interaction to maintain a sense of reality in any given situation. While symbolic interaction examines *what* kind of meaning is generated through social interaction, ethnomethodology looks at *how* meaning is generated through social interaction.

You might have observed that the symbolic interaction approach, with its focus on individuals rather than larger social structures, differs from the approaches described earlier in the chapter. In this way it represents one part of another distinction used to differentiate various kinds of sociology, the distinction between **macro-sociology** and **micro-sociology**. When a sociologist engages in research and writing that focuses primarily on the 'big picture' of society and its institutions, he or she is involved with macro-sociology. Weber, Durkheim, Merton, and Marx were all primarily macro-sociologists. When the focus is more on the plans, motivations, and actions of the individual or a specific group, then we are looking at micro-sociology. A good example of how micro-sociology is used to understand people's actions comes from Erving Goffman. Goffman's work also serves as an example of symbolic interactionism.

Born in Alberta, **Erving Goffman** (1922–1982) received his BA from the University of Toronto and his MA and PhD from the University of Chicago. Goffman was a pioneer in micro-sociology. His work constantly bore the stamp of originality, as evidenced by the many terms he introduced to the discipline of sociology. One example is **total institution**, a term he coined in his book *Asylums* (1961). A total institution is any of 'a range of institutions in which whole blocks of people are bureaucratically processed, whilst being physically isolated from the normal round of activities, by being required to sleep, work, and play within the confines of the same institution' (Marshall 1998:669–70). The term is used to describe mental hospitals, prisons, army barracks, boarding schools, concentration camps, monasteries, and convents—institutions whose

In this conversation, how is meaning being generated? Words are simply one aspect of constructing meaning in our day-to-day interactions. (© Photodisc)

residents are controlled, regulated, or manipulated by those in charge.

Goffman carried out his research for *Asylums* in 1955–6, when he engaged in fieldwork in a mental hospital in Washington, DC. He was ahead of his time in stating the importance of learning the subjectivity of people, and especially in the way he denied both objectivity and neutrality in his research methodology. He unequivocally sided with the patients as opposed to the professionals that managed them in the hospital. He wanted to learn about the day-to-day social world of the inmate. He did this by pretending to be an assistant to the athletic director, and passing his days with the patients:

[A]ny group of persons—prisoners, primitives, pilots, or patients—develop a life of their own that becomes meaningful, reasonable, and normal once you get close to it, and . . . a good way to learn about any of these worlds is to submit oneself in the company of the members to the daily round of petty contingencies to which they are subject. (Goffman 1961: x)

2. Professional, Critical, Policy, and Public Sociology

Structural functionalism, conflict theory, and symbolic interaction are all different *approaches* to sociology practice and research. The second way of categorizing sociology that we'll pres-

A group of inmates start boot camp at Sumter County Correctional Institute in Bushnell, Florida. In what ways do you see these men being controlled by a total institution? Could there be similar pictures for elementary school children? soldiers? hospital inmates? (Photo © Bettmann/Corbis)

>>> Canadian Sociology in Action
Applying Goffman to Research

I have long been a fan of Goffman's research and writing. His books are straightforward, readable, and engaging. His concepts seem readily adaptable to research. When I was writing my honours thesis (fourth-year major paper, 1972–3), I was studying a religious group in downtown Toronto. I needed a theoretical base for my research, and so I turned to Goffman's *Presentation of Self in Everyday Life* (1959). It was an example of what has been called Goffman's **dramaturgical approach**, a way of approaching research as if everyday life were taking place on the stage of a theatre. According to an often-told sociological anecdote, Goffman was on the Hebrides Islands off of the coast of Scotland, looking in vain for a topic for his doctoral dissertation, when, sitting in a restaurant, he noticed that the people working there acted differently when they were on the '**front stage**'—that is, in the public eye—than when they were on the '**back stage**', in the kitchen, away from the customers. They presented themselves differently depending on which stage they were on, an example of what Goffman called **impression management**. Impression management refers to the ways in which people present themselves in specific roles and social circumstances. His thesis and his best-selling book were born that day, or so the story goes.

In my research, the religious group was managing their impressions for two different audiences. One included street kids and other youthful lost souls who they thought were in need of spiritual guidance. For this audience, representatives of the religious group put on a hip, anti-establishment face. However, in order to obtain food donations from supermarket chains to feed their flock, and to achieve respectability in the eyes of both corporate sponsors and the neighbouring businesses in their rather exclusive downtown area, they had to present a more conservative face.

I predicted in my honours thesis that the group would split according to the two stages, the two audiences to which they were presenting themselves. This in fact happened just a year later. Thanks to some inspiration from Erving Goffman, I managed to get a pretty good mark in the course.

---

ent in this chapter is based on the *audience* and how reflexive or critical the sociologist is. The particular distinction we'll present is based on the work of American sociologist Michael Burawoy, who in a recent paper (2004) divided sociology into four types: *professional*, *critical*, *policy*, and *public*.

Professional Sociology

Professional sociology has as its audience the academic world of sociology departments, academic journals, professional associations (such as the American Sociological Association), and conferences. The research carried out by professional sociologists is typically designed to gen-

erate highly specific information, often with the aim of applying it to a particular problem or intellectual question. Consider the following list of articles printed in the spring 2005 editions of the *Canadian Journal of Sociology* and the *Canadian Review of Sociology and Anthropology*:

Canadian Journal of Sociology, **Spring 2005**
Asymmetric Hybridities: Youths at Francophone Games in Quebec
Seeing Beyond the Ruins: Surveillance as a Response to Terrorist Threats
How Closed-circuit Television Organizes the Social: An Institutional Ethnography

Canadian Review of Sociology and Anthropology, **Spring 2005**

La question de la symetrie dans les enquetes sur la violence dans le couple et les relations amoureuses [The question of symmetry in surveys on violence amongst couples and amorous relations]

No longer 'One of the Boys': Negotiations with Motherhood, as Prospect or Reality, among Women in Engineering

The NDP Regime in British Columbia, 1991–2001: A Post Mortem

Breast-feeding, Bottle-feeding and Dr Spock: The Shifting Context of Choice

'Canada's Most Notorious Bad Mother': The Newspaper Coverage of the Jordan Heikamp Inquest

As you can see from the titles, these articles address specific sociological questions. They tend to be written in technical or specialized language, targeting an academic or professional readership.

Critical Sociology

The main role of **critical sociology**, according to Burawoy (2004), is to be 'the conscience of professional sociology'. It performs this role in two ways:

> Critical sociology reminds professional sociology of its raison d'etre, of its value premises and its guiding questions. It also proposes alternative foundations upon which to erect sociological research. In other words, critical sociology is critical in two senses, first in bringing professional sociology into alignment with its historical mission and second in shifting the direction of that mission. (Burawoy 2004)

Critical sociology, then, addresses the same audience that professional sociology does. Its aim is to make sure that professional sociologists do not become so lost in esoteric debates that they lose sight of the issues of fundamental importance to the discipline.

As we stated earlier, much of what can be termed conflict theory in sociology would fit into this category. Two of the giants of critical sociology, Michel Foucault and Dorothy Smith, have examined the production of knowledge and how that involves conflict. Foucault discussed the conflict between 'scientific experts' and other producers of knowledge, while Smith discussed the conflict in terms of gender relations.

The French philosopher and historian **Michel Foucault** (1926–1984) was a major intellectual force in the sociological world. In his seminal article 'Two Lectures' (1980), Foucault talked about the misleading nature of what he termed **totalitarian** (what other writers call 'global', 'universalizing', or 'totalizing') **discourse**. A totalitarian discourse is any universal claim about how all knowledge and understanding can be achieved. Western science is at the centre of a totalitarian discourse engaged in by those who claim that it is the only path to discovering 'truth'.

'Totalitarian' in this context should be easy enough to understand: it describes a set of beliefs or ideas that dominates all others. The other part of the term, 'discourse', is not as easily understood. **Discourse** can be defined in the following way:

> A conceptual framework with its own internal logic and underlying assumptions that may be readily recognizable to the audience. A discourse involves a distinct way of speaking about some aspect of reality. [Use of the term] also suggests that the item under discussion is not a natural attribute of reality but socially constructed and defined. (Fleras and Elliot 1999:433)

Calling something a discourse is not necessarily accusing it of being wrong. It is just a way of describing a treatment of a topic that has a given set of assumptions, logic, and vocabulary, and that has been created. However, to call something a *totalizing* discourse is to condemn it as flawed or incorrect. Consider the commonly made statement that the brain is like a computer. It is possible to create a discourse comparing the functions and capabilities of the brain to those of a computer. Both store memories, both acquire and process data. I think we can all relate to times when we felt our brains have 'crashed'. You can see, though, how this discourse fails when you consider how poorly computers handle translation. (If you haven't experienced this aspect of computers, go to a website in which the text is written in a language other than English; click on 'Translate This', and what you will get is not anywhere near what a native speaker of English would produce.) Computers cannot translate well—not as well as humans—since they cannot deal with the input of social and cultural context. Very few words or phrases from any given language can be translated directly and perfectly into another. Our discourse, then, is flawed: the brain may be similar to a computer in certain ways, but it would be wrong to say that the human brain is just like a computer.

In *The Archaeology of Knowledge* (1994), Foucault spoke about the importance of discovering how individual discourses developed in order to outline their strengths, weaknesses and limits. He calls this process of discovery an **archaeology of knowledge**. The sociologist must dig down or excavate from a presentation of information considered to be factual (a discourse, in other words) in order to discover how that supposed fact or truth was established or constructed. In this process the sociologist may find that there has been some distortion along the way, which has affected how people have interpreted and acted upon the discourse. Box 1.2 offers an example of how an archaeology of knowledge can lead us to reassess our understanding of a supposed historical fact.

Foucault's challenge to students of sociology is to understand that knowledge is constructed, and that it is important to investigate the question '*How do we know what we know?*' There may be other constructions of knowledge on a particular subject that are just as valid or even more valid than our own.

While she was doing graduate work at the University of California in Berkeley, **Dorothy Smith** (b. 1926), as a woman involved in sociology, experienced first-hand the systemic discrimination that became the subject of her first work. Fortunately for the discipline in general and for Canadian sociology in particular, departments of sociology in this country were (in her words) 'scraping the bottom of the barrel'. Smith moved to Canada in the late 1960s when she was given a teaching opportunity at the University of British Columbia. Her distinguished academic career also includes a tenure of more than twenty years at the University of Toronto.

Smith developed what is known as **standpoint theory** directly out of her own experience as a woman discriminated against by male colleagues in the academic community. Smith's standpoint theory challenged traditional sociology on two fronts, both relating to sociology's preference for **objective** (depersonalized and distanced from everyday life) as opposed to **subjective** (personalized and connected to everyday life) research and analysis. Her first criticism attacked the traditional position that the objective approach is more scientific and therefore truthful, while the subjective position is **ideological**, based on biases and prejudices, and therefore distorted. According to Smith, knowledge is developed from a particular lived position, or 'standpoint'. Sociology, having developed from a male standpoint, denied the validity of the female standpoint and overlooked the everyday lives of women.

Smith's second criticism concerns traditional sociology's tendency to reinforce what she calls the existing **relations of ruling**. She believes that

Sociology in Action
Abandoning Inuit Elders: An Archaeology of Knowledge

Many introductory sociology textbooks assert that among Inuit populations, it was customary to abandon the elders when times got tough (for instance, when there was a shortage of food). By conducting an archeological excavation of this discourse, we can find out where the textbook authors found that 'fact'.

The first step is to check the relevant footnotes and the bibliographies contained in the textbook. Most of the sociology textbooks in question obtained the information from three earlier studies: one on the Inuit (Weyer 1932), one on suicide (Cavan 1928), and one on primitive law (Hoebel 1954). When you look at these books, none of the writers actually did their own research on the Inuit; they were merely referring to other scholars who did.

Next, you would track down the works written by those earlier scholars to find out what they actually said. Some of these ethnologists assumed that the practice took place, but did not actually observe it. Others report that when elders or the very sick were dying, forms of euthanasia were practiced. (This discourse has also proven to be flawed.) A few mention times when elders were temporarily left behind while those more fit looked for food.

Ultimately you find that the custom did not really ever exist. Your archaeology of knowledge has proven a supposed 'fact' to be a distortion.

denying the subjective standpoint further entrenches the dominance of the rulers over the ruled. For example, the Oka crisis of 1990 pitted members of a Quebec Mohawk community against some non-Native members of the community and provincial authorities, represented by the Sureté de Quebec (SQ), the Quebec provincial police force. The emotional standoff between the French-Canadian police and the Mohawk needs to be understood in the context of the long history of conflict in the region. But when conventional sociologists deny the subjectivity of the SQ, characterizing the police as 'neutral' agents of society performing their duty to control and punish 'troublemakers', they effectively legitimize the standpoint of the SQ while de-legitimizing the standpoint of the Mohawk (Steckley 2003).

Policy Sociology

Policy sociology is a relatively new term. To a certain extent it replaces the category of 'applied sociology', which is the application of

What do you think?

1. How does Smith's standpoint theory fit with Mills' notion of the sociological imagination?

2. Do you agree with Smith's view that sociology developed from a male standpoint? Why or why not?

sociological research to social change through various means, including public policy. Policy sociology is about generating sociological data to be used in the development of social policy for governments or corporations. Education, health, and social welfare are three main areas that policy sociology serves.

Policy sociology has a long tradition in Canada. A classic work of Canadian policy sociology is the *Report on Social Security for Canada*, prepared by **Leonard Marsh** (1906–1982) and issued in 1943. Based on research Marsh had done in the 1930s while acting as research director for the McGill Social Science Research Project, it set the stage for a number of major social policy initiatives that we now take for granted. When you read the following description of the ideas in the report, keep in mind that none of the social policies referred to here existed in Canada at that time. The report, as Antonia Maioni explains, offered

> a dense and detailed plan for comprehensive social programs, constructed around the idea of a social minimum and the eradication of poverty. The realization of this ideal, according to Marsh, meant the recognition that individual risks were part of modern industrial society, and that they could be met by collective benefits throughout the lifecycle. . . . 'Employment risks' were to be met through income-maintenance programs, such as unemployment insurance and assistance, accident and disability benefits, plus paid maternity leave. . . . 'Universal risks' were addressed through national health insurance, children's allowances, and pensions for old age, permanent disability, and widows and orphans.
>
> Significantly, practically all of these programs were to be contributory and under . . . federal . . . administration, with the exception of provincial workmen's compensation and medical care. . . . Also significant was Marsh's holistic view of social security that considered health as a central part of the welfare state, rather than a separate item and expense. (Maioni 2004:21)

The first person to introduce one of Marsh's policy initiatives, health insurance, was Saskatchewan Premier Tommy Douglas, who held a degree in sociology from McMaster University.

Public Sociology

Public sociology addresses an audience outside of the academy. Herbert Gans, in his 1988 address as the president of the American Sociological Association, identified three key traits of public sociologists:

> One is their ability to discuss even sociological concepts and theories in the English of the college-educated reader. . . . Their second trait is the breadth of their sociological interests, which covers much of society even if their research is restricted to a few fields. That breadth also extends to their conception of sociology, which extends beyond research reporting to commentary and in many cases social criticism. To put it another way, their work is intellectual as well as scientific. A third, not unrelated, trait is the ability to avoid the pitfalls of undue professionalism [e.g. an overly cautious style, a tendency to footnote everything and bury analysis in statistics]. (Gans 1987:7)

Our nominee as the ideal public sociologist is C. Wright Mills, whom we introduced earlier in this chapter.

Professional, Critical, Policy, and Public Sociology: Review

Distinctions between the four types of sociology are not watertight. It is common for individual sociologists to engage in more than one area, often while doing the same work. Criticisms can flow easily from people who see themselves as practitioners of one form only. Professional sociologists criticize critical sociologists for low professional standards and for being little more than 'trouble-making radicals'. Critical sociologists accuse professional sociologists of being overly conservative and of taking small bites of data and over analyzing it. But the opposite is to take big chunks of data and try to swallow them whole, an equally

Sociology in Action
The Sociologist as Hero: C. Wright Mills

In my first year of university, I was an English major. I wanted to be a writer. But studying English did not appeal to me the way I hoped it would. Sociology did. The sociologist that captured my imagination that first year was the American C. Wright Mills. He took on the rich and the powerful and challenged his conservative colleagues and his country's government in the staid 1950s. His public critique of American society caught the attention of the FBI, who started a file on him. He rode a motorcycle to work, and he wore plaid shirts, old jeans, and work boots. Mills became my first sociologist hero. I can also say that I am two degrees of intellectual separation from him: a teacher of mine was a student of his. (This makes students I've taught his intellectual great-grandchildren.)

During his lifetime Mills published seven of his own books (in addition to others that he co-authored). These include two trilogies and a seminal stand-alone volume that gave its name to a key characteristic of the very best sociologists and sociology students: *The Sociological Imagination* (1959; see above). His first trilogy, a study of the three main classes in the United States, comprises *The New Man of Power: America's Labor Leaders* (1948), *White Collar: The American Middle Classes* (1951), and *The Power*

Consider this photo of C. Wright Mills: does he look like an educator to you? Why (not)? (Photo © Yaroslava Mills)

Elite (1956). It was the last of these that was the most influential of the three. Original entitled 'The High and Mighty: The American Upper

untenable approach. Public sociologists could accuse professional sociologists of speaking only to a very small audience made up exclusively of peers; at the same time they accuse the policy sociologists of selling out their values to corporate and government 'pimps'. But policy and professional sociologists can counter-accuse the public sociologists of being in it just

for the publicity, of being no more than 'media whores', 'pop-sociologists', or mere popularizers—a dirty term among many in academia.

It is important to point out, however, that this level of competition is rare among sociologists, most of whom see beyond such narrow perspectives and have respect for their colleagues who pursue other strategies.

Classes' before being given its less incendiary title, it found a wide and varied audience that included Cuban revolutionary Fidel Castro, who, after he had overthrown the American-backed dictator Batista, invited Mills to visit so they could discuss his ideas—something few Americans, sociologists or not, have ever done. After the book was translated into Russian, Mills was asked to visit Moscow.

Mills' second trilogy consists of three best-selling, mass-marketed paperbacks. The first of these was *The Causes of World War Three* (1958), an impassioned plea for an end to the nuclear arms race. The second, and most successful, was *Listen Yankee* (1960). The product of two weeks of interviewing in Cuba and six weeks of writing, it was written in the style of an open letter to Americans from a Cuban revolutionary trying to communicate what life had been like under Batista, what harm American policies were having on the people of Cuba, and what accomplishments in education and health care Castro had achieved during his short term in power. Of the more than 450,000 copies printed, over 370,000 were sold in Mills' lifetime. The third book of the trilogy, *The Marxists* (1962), though it was less popular, was nevertheless translated into four languages. Collectively, Mills' works have been translated into 23 different languages.

Mills coined the term **sociological poetry** in 1948 while writing a letter in praise of a book he had read:

It is a style of experience and expression that reports social facts and at the same time reveals their human meanings. As a reading experience, it stands somewhere between the thick facts and thin meanings of the ordinary sociological monograph and those art forms which in their attempts at meaningful reach do away with the facts, which they consider as anyway merely an excuse for imagination construction. (Mills and Mills 2000:111)

A few years later, Mills recast this statement as more of a challenge to sociologists. Responding to a question about whether or not you can get sociologists to write decently, Mills wrote:

It doesn't look good for two reasons: First, there is no real writing tradition in sociology, as there is, for example, in history. It just doesn't exist. Second, the field is now split into statistical stuff and heavy duty theoretical bullshit. In both cases, there's no writing but only turgid polysyllabic slabs of stuff. So, because that is now the field, no men get trained, have models to look up to; there is no aspiration to write well. (Mills and Mills 2000:154–5)

While Mills himself, and a handful of others, have disproved the first point, the second critique stands. Sociologists (and sociology students), your duty is clear: prove him wrong!

The Development of Canadian Sociology

While there is no definitive Canadian way to carry out sociological research and practice, sociology's development and primary focal points in this country are distinctive. The relationship between French and English, the development of the Canadian West, the connection between class and ethnicity, and a close working relationship with anthropology have all been key to the development of a uniquely Canadian branch of sociology.

As we will see in later chapters, sociology began in this country long before the establishment of departments of sociology in Canadian universities and colleges. Herbert Ames, Leon Gérin, James S. Woodsworth, Carrie Derick, and Colin McKay are just a few of those who practised sociology in Canada before it became firmly established as an academic discipline. However, we will begin here with Canadian sociology as it developed in post-secondary institutions across the country.

McGill: Dawson, Hughes, and Miner

The first professional, institutionalized sociologist in Canada was **Carl Addington Dawson** (1887–1964). Born in Prince Edward Island, Dawson completed his MA and PhD at the University of Chicago. Shortly after joining the faculty at McGill University, he founded the Department of Sociology, an accomplishment that was not achieved without opposition. Senior administrators worried about the left-wing political leanings of sociologists (they still do), and academics in other departments did not want their scholarly territory infringed upon. Dawson succeeded in spite of these objections, and McGill's remained the only independent department of sociology until 1961.

Dawson's work reflected two elements of early Canadian sociology: the **social gospel movement** and social work. The social gospel movement developed as an attempt by people trained for the ministry to apply Christian principles of human welfare to the treatment of social, medical, and psychological ills brought on by industrialization and unregulated capitalism in Canada, the United States, Britain, Germany, and other European countries during the late nineteenth century. Out of the social gospel movement came, among other things, the Social Service Council of Canada (1912), which through various churches engaged in the first sociological surveys of Canadian cities, and, in 1914, sponsored the first national meeting to address various social problems.

Dawson's affinity with the social gospel movement was natural—his first degree from the University of Chicago was in divinity—but his inspiration to become involved in the early development of social work in Canada came as well from the methods of and philosophy of the Chicago school of sociology. The Chicago school put an emphasis on going out into communities—what University of Chicago sociologist Robert Park called 'living laboratories'—to observe them. Dawson took this approach and, with his students, applied it to the living laboratory of Montreal. Their research was given a jump-start in 1929, when they were awarded a $110,000 Rockefeller Foundation grant to study unemployment in the city.

That same year, Dawson and Warren E. Gettys became the first Canadians to write a sociology textbook. The text was an instant success: it was adopted by over 150 colleges and universities across North America within a year, and went through three editions (1929, 1935, 1948). While there was not a great deal of Canadian content, it helped legitimize sociology in Canada. Dawson went on to study and write extensively on settlement patterns on the frontier in western Canada.

Another figure vital to the development of sociology at McGill was **Everett C. Hughes** (1897–1983), whose influence was felt not just in Quebec but also in the rest of Canada and in the United States. Another graduate of the University of Chicago, Hughes joined the sociology department at McGill in 1927 a firm believer in the Chicago school's commitment to community research. For more than the ten years that he spent in Canada Hughes focused on what he termed the 'ethnic division of labour', a situation that enabled English Canadians to rise above French Canadians, creating a disparity that he badly wished to correct. Out of this research came his classic work, *French Canada in Transition* (1943; see the chapter on 'Race and Ethnicity'). By this time, Hughes had already returned to the States to take a position in the faculty of his alma mater. In recognition of his important role in the development of Canadian sociology Hughes was made an Honorary Life President of the Canadian Sociology and Anthropology Association.

Horace Miner (1912–1993) was another American sociologist that put the study of French Canada at the forefront of the Canadian sociology movement. As a graduate student at the University of Chicago, he came to Quebec to study the parish of St Denis. His book *St Denis: A French-Canadian Parish* (1939) shows the blurred distinction between sociology and anthropology in Canada. His work is best described as an **ethnography**, a study of a community based on extensive fieldwork, whose primary research activities include direct observation and talking and listening to people. Ethnography is the main research method used in social anthropology. Miner describes the rural peasants and farmers of his study as a **folk society**, following the model of University of Chicago anthropologist Robert Redfield, who coined the term. The close connection between sociology and anthropology can still be seen today in some Canadian universities where the two disciplines are joined in the same department.

The University of Toronto: Harold Innis and S.D. Clark

As sociology was developing along a particular line at McGill, a very different tradition, **political economy**, was emerging at the University of Toronto. Political economy is an interdisciplinary approach involving sociology, political science, economics, law, anthropology, and history. It began in the eighteenth century and looks primarily at the relationship between politics and the economics of the production, distribution, and consumption of goods. It is often Marxist in nature, pointing to the tensions that arise in the extraction and distribution of goods.

A Canadian pioneer in this field was **Harold Innis** (1894–1952), who joined the Department of Political Economy at the University of Toronto in 1920. Innis was more an economic historian than a sociologist, but his work has exerted a strong influence on Canadian sociology. He argued that the availability of **staples**—resources such as cod, fur, minerals, and wheat—shaped the economic and social development of Canada.

Innis was also a mentor to the first person hired at the university specifically as a sociologist, **Samuel Delbert Clark** (1910–2003). Born in Alberta, S.D. Clark received his first two degrees from the University of Saskatchewan before joining the Department of Political Economy at the University of Toronto in 1938. Sociology remained a branch of that department until 1963, when it became its own department with Clark as chair. In a statement accompanying the publication of a book in his honour, Deborah Harrison wrote:

> The importance of S.D. Clark within the development of Canadian sociology is universally recognized. Clark's publications span more than forty prolific years, with at least the first fifteen occurring when almost no other sociologists were writing in Canada; he is generally acknowledged as the father of the Canadian approach to the discipline. . . . For reasons of both his scholarly engagement and his articulation of a 'Canadian' sociology, Clark is the most important sociologist Canada has yet produced. (1999)

Clark can be called a sociological historian. To get a sense of what we mean by this, consider the chapter headings of his book *The Developing Canadian Community* (1962):

I   Social Organization and the Changing Structure of the Community

II   The Farming-Fur-Trade Society of New France

III The Rural Village Society of the Maritimes

IV   The Backwoods Society of Upper Canada

V   The Gold-Rush Society of British Columbia and the Yukon

VI   The Prairie Wheat-Farming Frontier and the New Industrial City

As you can see, Clark, like others who would be considered sociological historians, traced the development of different societies, looking in particular at how the resources available to early settlers shaped the growth of regional communities.

Fundamentally missing from both Innis and Clark are the themes of class and ethnicity, which are so persistent in much of Canadian sociology. These themes received their definitive treatment in what is generally recognized as the best-known work of Canadian sociology, *The Vertical Mosaic: An Analysis of Social Class and Power in Canada* (1965), by **John Porter** (1921–1979). Porter joined the faculty of Carleton University in 1949, becoming the university's first full-time appointment in sociology; he remained at Carleton for most of his career. The title of his book plays on the term **cultural mosaic**, a metaphor frequently used to characterize

In 1995, three patrons of this tavern in the agricultural Yakim valley in Washington State were ejected for speaking Spanish. The sign hanging above the door clearly states the position of the tavern's management: 'IN THE U.S.A. IT'S—ENGLISH, OR ADIOS AMIGO. Is this attitude more characteristic of a cultural mosaic or a cultural melting pot? (AP Photo/Kirk Hirota)

Canada's multicultural society, especially when compared with the **melting pot** found in the United States. A mosaic, of course, is a type of artwork composed of many small tiles that lend different colours to the picture. A society that is a cultural mosaic is therefore one 'in which racial, ethnic, and religious groups maintain a distinct identity, rather than being absorbed into a "melting pot"'(Lundy and Warme 1990:583). By contrast, a melting pot, Lundy and Warme explain, involves the 'rapid assimilation of recent immigrants into their new society. This concept has been a long-standing ideal underlying immigration policy in the United States' (Lundy and Warme 1990:586).

Porter coined the term **vertical mosaic** to describe a situation in which systemic discrimination produces leads to there being a hierarchy of racial, ethnic, and religious groups. To stay within the metaphor of the mosaic, we can say that Porter's study found that the different tiles were stacked and not placed evenly. White, Anglo-Saxon, Protestant tiles were on top, followed by French-Canadian tiles, Aboriginal tiles, and finally those of everyone else. Porter concluded that ethnicity and ranking were linked. The impact of Porter's seminal work can be seen in the number of sociology books and articles that draw upon the title. These include such books as Roberta Hamilton's *Gendering the Vertical Mosaic: Feminist Perspectives on Canadian Society* (1996) and *The Vertical Mosaic Revisited*, edited by Richard Helmes-Hayes and James Curtis (1998), as well as articles such as 'The vertical mosaic in later life: ethnicity and retirement in Canada', from *The Journals of Gerontology* (1986) by Yameen Abu-Laban.

The Growth of Sociology in Canada

In 1958, there were fewer than twenty sociology professors in Canada, teaching in just nine universities (Clark 1976:120). Sociology did not become a significant area of study and teaching in Canada until the 1960s and 1970s, as baby-boomers entered universities and colleges. The growth of sociology during that time is astounding. Hiller and Di Luzio, for example, report that 'the University of Alberta had no sociology majors in 1956–57, but a year later had nine, followed by 24 (1957–58, 44 (1959–60), and 62 (1960–61). The number of majors there reached a peak for the entire millennium at 776 in 1987' (Hiller and Di Luzio 2001:490).

During this era of growth in sociology study and research, most of the sociologists hired to teach in Canadian post-secondary institutions were from the United States and, to a lesser degree, Britain. Of those with doctorates teaching sociology and anthropology in Canada in 1967, 72 per cent had PhDs from the US, 10 per cent from Britain, and only 6 per cent from Canada (Gallagher and Lambert 1971:vii). In 1973–4, 45 per cent of the full-time sociology faculty in Canada were non-Canadians (Hofley 1992:106). This should not be surprising given that only 22 doctorates in sociology were conferred at Canadian universities between 1924 and 1967 (Gallagher and Lambert 1971:vi).

The dearth of Canadian sociologists meant that sociology textbooks, dominated by the issues close to the hearts of authors who had grown up or studied sociology outside of Canada, lacked Canadian perspectives. When John Hofley was hired to teach sociology at Carleton University in 1966, he 'found very little about Canada in the sociology texts that were available' (Hofley 1992:104). It was not uncommon that a textbook used in Canada would be exclusively American. The 1970s saw a big movement to 'Canadianize' sociology textbooks. Today most introductory sociology textbooks used in Canadian schools are either Canadian in origin or 'Canadianized' versions of American textbooks.

Summary

So what have we covered so far? We've given you a sense of what sociology looks like, enough that you could pick it out of a lineup of social sciences. You likely won't have a really good sense of what sociology is until you've reached the end of the book. You've learned a bit about what our approach to writing sociology is like, making this, ideally, a textbook not like the others. We have introduced you to some of the main players that will strut the stage of this book in the chapters that follow: Marx, Durkheim, Weber—three of the modern discipline's founders (whose views, incidentally, are often the subject of 'compare and contraste' assignments on tests and exams);

Goffman, the Canadian; Foucault and Smith (two more subjects for comparative questions); and Mead. Others we have merely mentioned here, but you will be more fully introduced to them in later chapters.

In addition to familiarizing you with some of the discipline's key figures, we've shown you two different ways of categorizing sociology. References to these categories turn up frequently throughout the book. Finally, we have added some Canadian flavour to the overall look at sociology. Expect plenty more back bacon and maple syrup in the chapters to come.

Questions for Critical Review and Discussion

1. Outline the differences and similarities between sociology and other social science disciplines.

2. Identify the key ideas of Durkheim, Marx, and Weber as outlined in this chapter.

3. Distinguish between the structural-functional, conflict, and symbolic-interactionist approaches to sociology.

4. Distinguish between professional, critical, policy, and public sociology.

5. Articulate the basic ideas of Erving Goffman, Michel Foucault, and Dorothy Smith as outlined in this chapter.

Suggested Readings

Gunew, Sneja, ed. (1991). *A Reader in Feminist Knowledge*. London: Routledge.

Gutting, Gary (2005). *Foucault: A Very Short Introduction*. Oxford: Oxford UP.

Johnson, Allan G. (1997). *The Blackwell Dictionary of Sociology: A User's Guide to Sociological Language*. Oxford: Blackwell.

Kivisto, Peter, ed. (2001). *Illuminating Social Life: Classical and Contemporary Theory Revised*, 2nd edn. London: Pine Forge P.

Robinson, Dave (1999). *Nietzsche and Postmodernism*. New York: Totem Books.

Turner, Stephen P., ed. (1996). *Social Theory and Sociology: The Classics and Beyond*. Oxford: Blackwell.

Suggested Websites

C. Wright Mills.
http://www.genordell.com/stores/maison/CWMills.htm

Émile Durkheim (Robert Alum, University of Illinois).
http://www.relst.uiuc.edu/durkheim/

Karl Marx.
http://www.marxists.org/archive/marx/

Max Weber (Albert Benschop, University of Amsterdam).
http://www.pscw.uva.nl/sociosite/topics/weber.html

Sociological Research Methods

Key Terms

absolute poverty
age group
anomie
best practices
case study approach
content analysis
discourse analysis
disjuncture
epistemological
ethnography
fact
Frankfurt School
free-floating statistic
genealogy
hypothesis
informant
insider approach
institutional
ethnography
Low Income Cutoffs
Low Income Measure
Market Basket
Measurement (MBM)
narrative
ontological
operational definition
Orientalism
outsider approach
participant observation
poverty
poverty line
psychoanalysis
qualitative research
quantitative research
relative poverty

rhetoric
ruling interests
ruling relations
semiotics
semi-structured
interview
sign
signified
signifier
spurious
reasoning
statistics
third variable
theory
triangulation
voice

Boxes and Tables

In Other Words Fasting
In Other Words Palestinian by Culture, Canadian by Birth
Sociology in Action So You Think You Know What A Single Parent Is?

Table 2.1 Independent and dependent variables: three examples
Table 2.2 Direct correlation of independent and dependent variables: three examples
Table 2.3 Inverse correlation of independent and dependent variables: three examples
Table 2.4 Correlation between divorce and suicide rates in four countries, 1870–1889

Learning Objectives

After reading this chapter, you should be able to

- contrast and compare fact, theory, and hypothesis.
- distinguish between qualitative and quantitative social research.
- distinguish between the various qualitative research methods.
- discuss the importance of identifying the individual informant in ethnographic research.
- explain the significance of narratives in sociological research.
- identify the importance of operational definitions in quantitative research.
- explain and give examples of spurious reasoning.
- discuss the connection between statistics and rhetoric.

For Starters
Fact, Theory, Hypothesis, and Wondering Why People Speed Up When I Pass Them

It is easier to observe than it is to explain. I can observe that people speed up on the highway when I pass them, but I can't really explain why they do it. Is it because I wake them up from a semi-sleeping state? Or do I awaken their competitive spirit when I—an aging hippie in an old minivan—pass them in their shiny, high-priced, high-powered vehicles?

I believe the idea that people speed up when I pass them is a **fact**, that is *an observation that as far as can be known is true*. This doesn't mean it happens all the time, though I have observed it enough times to call it at least a tentative fact. But if I want to use important qualifiers such as 'almost all of the time' or 'most of the time', or the easier to prove 'often' or 'frequently', then I have to find a way to quantify this fact—for example, by saying 'I passed 100 vehicles and 37 were observed to speed up.' I should also be more concrete about the situation involved— on Highway 50 northwest of Toronto; while driving in the slow lane, passing someone who is in the passing lane; while driving home from work, travelling north. This is how I quantify and qualify my fact, by giving details about how often it occurs and under what conditions.

Now I need a theory. **Theory** is an attempt to explain a fact or observed phenomenon. My theory of why people speed up when I pass them is that I make them aware that they are travelling more slowly than they thought they were. My theory becomes a **hypothesis** when I set out to verify it by providing some kind of concrete test of its validity. What kind of test can I provide for my theory? Obviously, I can't pull people over on the highway and ask them why they sped up when I passed them. I might develop a questionnaire that depends on peo-

Photo © Martyn Goddard/Corbis

ple's self-knowledge. First I might ask a question such as 'Do you frequently speed up when people pass you on a highway?'. It might be followed by a multiple-choice question such as the following:

> What is the best explanation for your frequently speeding up when people pass you on a highway?

a) It makes me realize that I am driving slower than I thought.
b) I do not like people passing me.
c) I am very competitive.
d) Other (explain).

How would you test the hypothesis?

Introduction

Nothing is more contentious in sociology than **research methodology**, the system of methods a researcher uses to gather data on a particular question. There is an old joke that goes like this:

Question: How many sociologists does it take to change a light bulb?
Answer: Twenty: one to change the light bulb and nineteen to question that person's methodology.

There is no single best way to do sociological research. Many sociological researchers combine several methods in their work. In the sections that follow, we'll take a look at some of the different methods used in sociological research.

Sociology's Positivist Tradition

It was the French philosopher **Auguste Comte** (1798–1857) who coined the word 'sociology'. The basis of Comte's sociology was **positivism** (later called 'logical positivism'), which involves a belief that the methods used to study the natural sciences (including experiment, measurement, and systematic observation) and the supposed objectivity of these methods can be applied just as well to the social sciences with no accommodation made for the biases, or any other aspects of the personal life (gender, age, ethnicity, etc.) of the social scientist. Although the positivist mode of thinking had a long run, many sociologists today do not

believe it possible for an 'outsider' to study a group objectively.

Insider versus Outsider Perspective

One way to contrast the different methods of sociology research is to look at the ways researchers treat the **insider** and **outsider** views. In Comte's approach the outsider was the 'expert' and was given a privileged position. Most of sociology's history reflects this privileging. Of the four types of sociology mentioned in the last chapter, policy sociology is the one tied most closely to the outside expert ideal.

By contrast, critical sociology, particularly feminist sociology, rates the insider view highly while questioning the presumed objectivity of positivism. Dorothy Smith's standpoint theory, referred to in the opening chapter, states that attributes of the sociologist, including such social characteristics as gender, race, ethnicity, age, and sexual orientation, will strongly condition the questions he or she asks as well as the answers he or she will receive. Michel Foucault, in the first volume of *The History of Sexuality* (1978), criticized the outsider approach in his discussion of the intellectual model of the 'sexual confession'. According to this model, the subject being studied provides information that comes from his or her subjective experience. But this information is marginalized: it is not recognized as authentic knowledge until it has been interpreted by an 'objective' outsider who, by virtue of being an expert, is in the privileged position of deciding which parts of the account are true and which are fabricated or imagined. The subject is therefore not allowed to have a voice that is heard without translation from the outsider/expert. That means that important sociological messages get lost.

To get a better sense of how an outsider perspective can be flawed, imagine you are a sociologist studying a First Nations reserve. Taking an outsider approach, you conduct your study by looking only at various statistics, covering subjects such as unemployment, housing, and crime rate. Not including the voice of the people who live there means that you will miss key elements of interpretation. First, some definitions could be problematic. Is a person who hunts, traps, fishes, gathers plants for food and medicine, and cuts wood for home heating and cooking unemployed? How do you define 'overcrowding' without looking at cultural definitions and strategies used by the people themselves to cope with this issue (e.g. being 'home' in more than one relative's house and spending a lot of time 'in the bush', the former an aspect of cultural practices of family sharing, the latter a traditional way of obtaining food and other needed supplies)? Second, typical statistical surveys of Aboriginal reserves leave unanswered the question of why so many people choose to live on reserves if there is so much unemployment, crime, and overcrowding compared with lower rates in non-Native communities of comparable size. You need to observe the people you're studying in order to properly answer these questions; you need to hear the people's voice.

Brian Maracle is a Mohawk who left his home reserve when he was five years old but returned as an adult. *Back on the Rez: Finding the Way Back Home* (1996) is his account of the first year of his return to the Six Nations reserve near Brantford, Ontario. This reserve is very different in certain respects from the more troubled reserves— Davis Inlet and Grassy Narrows, for example— that are commonly cited in sociology textbooks. The people of the Six Nations reserve have lived there for over 200 years, since the time when it was given to them as a reward for siding with the British during the American Revolution. It includes good farmland, something that the Six Nations Iroquois, who were farmers long prior to European contact, were able to take full

Mohawk boys play lacrosse on a Six Nations reserve. Do you notice a difference in 'play' when it is constituted as a community activity versus a competitive sport? (Photo © Michael S. Yamashita/Corbis)

advantage of. In the introduction to *Back on the Rez*, Maracle points out that reserves can be considered homelands because they function as refuges from non-Aboriginal society:

> The reserves mean many things. . . . On one level, these postage-stamp remnants of our original territories are nagging reminders of the echoing vastness of what we have lost. On another, they are the legacy and bastion of our being. They are a refuge, a prison, a madhouse, a fortress, a birthplace, a Mecca, a resting-place, Home-Sweet-Home, Fatherland and Motherland rolled into one. (Maracle 1996:3)

Maracle speaks of the importance of the reserve as the home of the elders, who interpret past traditions and adapt them to the present, thus stressing that the home of Aboriginal culture is the reserve.

Of course, it is important to see that reserves are not always homeland to everyone. Reserves can be places where men with physical strength and political power can oppress women and sexually abuse children. While recognizing the insider's view is key, it's important to remember that different voices have to be heard.

Our position here is that complete objectivity is impossible whenever one human being studies others. However, complete subjectivity can be blind. A judicious balance of insider and outsider vision is the ideal.

Qualitative versus Quantitative Research

An ongoing debate in sociological research concerns the relative merits of **qualitative** and **quantitative research**. Quantitative research focuses on social elements that can be counted or measured, and therefore used to generate statistics. It often involves working with questionnaires and polls. Qualitative research involves the close examination of characteristics that cannot be counted or measured. Unlike quantitative research, which is typically used to find the patterns governing whole structures or systems, communities, and so on, qualitative research may be used to study those individual cases that don't fit into the larger model.

And so the debate begins. Proponents of quantitative research accuse qualitative researchers of relying on data that is 'soft', 'anecdotal', 'too subjective', or 'merely literary'. In turn, those favouring the qualitative approach refer to quantitative researchers as soulless 'number crunchers' who delude themselves into believing that a human can ever be objective in studying other humans. Of course, it's wrong to think that the two methods are mutually exclusive. Good quantitative researchers know that, despite its close historical connection with positivism, their research always has a subjective component to it, always involves choice and some personal bias. Qualitative researchers, similarly, can learn to benefit from using quantitative data occasionally.

Qualitative Research

When we think of qualitative research, we think of its subjectivity. Qualitative research connects more closely than quantitative research to the subjectivity of both researchers and research subjects. Among the various qualitative methods are **ethnography** and the **case study approach**, two techniques that differ in their breadth of field. The former is typically broader than the latter, attempting to describe the entirety of a culture, while the latter has a narrower focus.

Ethnography

Gephart captures the essence of ethnography when he describes it as relying on

> direct observation and extended field research to produce a thick, naturalistic description of a people and their culture. Ethnography seeks to uncover the symbols and categories members of the given

culture use to interpret their world. . . . (Gephart 1988:16)

A classic example of the ethnographic approach in sociology is William Whyte's *Street-Corner Society: the social structure of an Italian Slum*. Beginning early in 1937, Whyte spent three-and-a-half years living in the neighbourhood he called 'Cornerville', following a standard research practice of renaming for writing purposes the community studied in order to make the subjects more anonymous. During that time he lived for 18 months with an Italian-American family. His methodology involved **semi-structured interviews**—informal, face-to-face interviews designed to cover specific topics without the rigid structure of a questionnaire but with more structure than an open interview—and **participant observation**, which entails both observing people as an outsider would and actively participating in the various activities of the studied people's lives. Participant observation enables the researcher

to achieve something resembling an 'insider's view'. Researchers engaged in ethnography typically depend as well on **informants**, people who act as insider interpreters and who help the researcher become accepted by the community studied. Whyte's informant was a gang leader in his late twenties who went by the name 'Doc'. Whyte was introduced to Doc by the latter's social worker. Whyte describes their first meeting:

I began by asking him if the social worker had told him about what I was trying to do.

'No, she just told me that you wanted to meet me and that I should like to meet you.'

Then I went into a long explanation. . . . I said that I had been interested in congested city districts in my college study but had felt very remote from them. I hoped to study the problems in such a district. I felt I could do very little as an

Boston in the late 1930s. (Prints & Photographs Division, Library of Congress)

outsider. Only if I could get to know the people and learn their problems first hand would I be able to gain the understanding I needed. (Whyte 1955:291)

When Whyte stated his research needs, Doc replied:

'Well, any nights you want to see anything, I'll take you around. I can take you to the joints—gambling joints—I can take you around to the street corners. Just remember that you're my friend. That's all they need to know. I know these places, and, if I tell them that you're my friend, nobody will bother you. You just tell me what you want to see, and we'll arrange it.' (Whyte 1955:291)

Doc and Whyte would discuss Whyte's research interests and findings to the point where Doc became 'in a very real sense, a collaborator in the research' (Whyte 1955:301). Whyte learned to speak Italian so that he could talk directly to the older generation from Italy. He participated in the second generation's activities of going to 'gambling joints', bowling, playing baseball and cards. He called his work 'participatory action research' because he wanted his research to lead to actions that improved the lives of the people studied.

Whyte's ethnography was typical of the sociology work then being done at the University of Chicago (where he earned his PhD). John Dollard adopted this approach for a five-month study of a small Mississippi town, the results of which he presented in *Caste and Class in a Southern Town* (1937). In Canada, Whyte's study influenced Carl Dawson's work with Prairie communities, and the Quebec community studies of Everett Hughes (*French Canada in Transition*; 1943) and Horace Miner (*St Denis: A French-Canadian Parish*; 1939 and 1963).

Institutional Ethnography
Institutional ethnography is a relatively new method of research, based on the theories of Dorothy Smith. This method of research, as outlined by Marie Campbell and Frances Gregor in *Mapping Social Relations: A Primer in Doing Institutional Ethnography* (2002), is different from traditional sociological research in that it does not reflect the view that a neutral stance is necessarily more scientific than an approach that explicitly involves 'taking sides' (Campbell and Gregor 2002:48).

Institutional ethnography recognizes that any institution or organization can be seen as having two sides, each associated with a different kind of data. One side represents **ruling interests**: the interests of the organization, particularly its administration, or the interests of those who are dominant in society. The data associated with this side are text-based, comprising the written rules and practices of the institution. When the workers in the institution follow these rules and practices they are activating **ruling relations**—that is, they are helping to serve the needs of the organization, often at the cost of their clients and/or themselves.

The other side is that of the informant. In this context, an informant may be anyone who works for the institution. The data associated with this side is *experiential*, based on the experience of the informant. Institutional ethnography recognizes that there is a **disjuncture**, or separation, between the knowledge produced from the two perspectives. In pointing out this disjuncture, institutional ethnographers generate information that they hope will lead to institutional change.

Schools offer a good example of the kind of organization institutional ethnographers study. Alison Griffith asserts that teachers rely on parents, specifically mothers, to get school children to do the work and acquire the skills necessary to succeed in school. Campbell and Gregor refer to this as 'downloading educational work' (2002:43), a practice that serves the ruling interests—boards of education and provincial governments—who can then spend less on schools and teachers. Teachers and parents, by complying with the demands of school administrators, are activating ruling relations. At the same time, they are also biasing the system in favour of students from middle-class households, whose parents are more likely to have the resources (including books, a good study space, and time) to best serve this end. Lower-class students are poorly served by the system, as they are more dependent on the school alone. This is the kind of useful finding that institutional ethnography can produce.

Another frequently studied institution is hospitals. Campbell and Gregor have examined the 'unofficial' hospital work carried out by nurses. This work includes tasks that are officially the responsibility of doctors. When nurses take responsibility for performing these tasks, it helps to make the system work while serving the patients' needs more efficiently. But as the authors point out, nurses who rise to meet the ruling interests may be putting themselves at risk:

> They go round in circles fixing the flaws in abstracted (textual) organization of patient care and then cover their tracks in accordance with the traditional gender regime [i.e. in which doctors are typically male and nurses typically female]. When the work they do is not part of the official and textual organization of nursing, it tends to be overlooked, thus not attributable to them as their knowledge, judgement or action. . . . [T]his may create even more trouble for nurses. When it appears that 'the system' runs efficiently on the basis of abstract information, they may find their jobs being cut. (Campbell and Gregor 2002:21)

Parents with greater access to services and resources are more likely to give their children an edge in a system that already favours them. (© Photodisc)

What do you think?

1. What 'sides' are involved in institutional ethnography? Which side do institutional researchers typically take?

2. According to the Campbell and Gregor, how does the extra work nurses do make it more likely that nursing jobs might be lost?

Case Study Approach

British sociologist Gordon Marshall describes the case study approach as

[a] research design that takes as its subject a single case or a few selected examples of a social entity—such as communities, social groups, employers, events, life-histories, families, work teams, roles, or relationships—and employs a variety of methods to study them. . . . Case-studies include descriptive reports on typical, illustrative, or deviant examples; descriptions of good practice in policy research; evaluations of policies after implementation in an organization; studies that focus on extreme or strategic cases; the rigorous test of a well-defined hypothesis through the use of carefully selected contrasting cases; and studies of natural experiments. (Marshall 1998:56)

The case study approach is often used to identify and describe **best practices**—strategies with a proven history of achieving desired results more effectively or consistently than similar methods used in the past by a particular organization or currently by other organizations in the same industry. The case study typically introduces the organization demonstrating best practices before describing why it is considered successful and how it achieved its success. The case study is often geared to finding out whether certain best practices can be applied with comparable success elsewhere in the organization or industry.

The following example of a case study describes policing in a First Nations community. Aboriginal communities generally did not police themselves until the early 1990s, when the federal government put enabling legislation in place to allow band councils of individual Aboriginal communities to establish their own police services, once they had signed a tripartite agreement with the federal and provincial or territorial governments.

Case Study of a Best Practice: Kitigan Zibi Anishnabeg First Nation Policing

Located about 130 kilometres north of Ottawa, Kitigan Zibi, with an estimated band population of 2,350 people, is the largest of the nine communities that make up the Algonquin Nation in Quebec. The community first had its own policing services in 1981, when they, like other Quebec First Nations, began operating a community police force under the auspices of the Amerindian Police Service (the APS). The APS is usually seen as a failure by First Nations in Quebec, owing mainly to the fact that Aboriginal officers were given limited, second-class roles as 'special constables'. In 1985, the Kitigan Zibi community moved ahead of other Aboriginal communities by transferring police services to its own independent force.

Following the introduction of the federal First Nation Policing Policy in April 1992, the community entered into a three-year tripartite agreement that allowed the Kitigan Zibi Anishinabeg Police Department (KZAPD) to become a fully functional force, the equivalent of any non-Native force in Canada. This agreement was renegotiated in March 1995. By 2002, the KZAPD had a chief of police, five full-time officers, and one part-time officer. Community satisfaction with their work has been high. In a survey conducted in 2002, 91 per cent of the members of the community surveyed felt that the KZAPD was the best police organization to meet the needs of the community. This compares favourably to the 55 per cent of community stakeholders who, in a First Nations Chiefs of Police Association survey, felt the self-administered police services in their communities were effective.

There are four keys to the success of the KZAPD. Unfortunately, two of these keys are unique to the Kitigan Zibi community and cannot be replicated in most other First Nation communities. First, Kitigan Zibi has a very stable political environment. At the time of the study, the chief councillor of the band had been in the position for over twenty years, and during that time there had been few changes in the makeup of the band council. Further, there were no apparent political factions in the community, making it unlike many First Nations communities. Second, there have been no major clashes between the provincial government and Kitigan Zibi, putting it in the minority in Quebec. Largely because of this lack of conflict, the KZAPD has a reasonably harmonious relationship with the Quebec provincial police, a rarity for a First Nations force in Quebec.

Two remaining keys to the KZAPD's success offer lessons for other police forces operating in Native (and non-Native) communities to learn from. One is the strong relationship between the KZAPD and the youth of the community. In 1995, the KZAPD took part in a pilot project with Aboriginal youths aged between 12 and 24, who were paired with police officers to ride in cruisers, observe police duties first-hand, and visit the homes of their police mentors. Commenting on the mentoring experience, one officer said, 'I took great pride in seeing the bar-riers fall and the sense of openness that developed in our communication' (First Nations Policing Update, July 1995, #3). In 1996, Chief of Police Gordon MacGregor stressed

> [t]he importance of being among the people, being visible and approachable especially to the youth and young children. . . . people see you as being human and as a father, not just as a police figure. (Stewart 1996)

The final key is the KZAPD's dedication to training. One condition of the 1992 tripartite agreement signed with Ottawa and the Quebec provincial government was that constables already in the force would earn the basic training equivalency diploma. This would enable the officers to assume powers equal to those of any other officer in the province. All the KZAPD's officers successfully completed the training. The chief of police even went beyond the qualifications required in the agreement, taking managerial courses for senior officers and additional courses offered at the Police College in Ottawa. When the Quebec Police Act was amended to include more training for provincial officers, the chief of police prepared a five-year forecast of the training needs of his force.

Narratives

Perhaps the purest form of the insider view is the **narrative**. Narratives are the stories peoples

What do you think?

1. What indicates that the KZAPD is a good choice for a best practice?

2. What factors in its success cannot be readily replicated in other First Nation communities in Quebec?

3. What factors can be readily replicated in other First Nation communities in Quebec?

4. The case study approach combines quantitative and qualitative research. How is that evident in the case study presented here?

tell about themselves, their situations, and the others around them. They have long been part of sociology. They appeared in W.I. Thomas and Florian Znaiecki's five-volume *The Polish Peasant in Europe and America* (1918–20). Of the 2,200 pages of that work, 800 were dedicated to letters, autobiographical accounts, and other narrative documents. Still, the positivism of early sociology and the more recent emphasis on statistical evidence kept narrative study in a minor role in sociological research until the last twenty years. In 1993, H.R. Maines referred to the growing interest in narratives in a number of different disciplines, including sociology, as 'narrative's moment'. He saw in this trend a dual focus for sociological study, aimed both at examining the narratives of the usual subjects of study and at the same time 'viewing sociologists as narrators and thereby inquiring into what they do to and with their and other people's narratives' (Maines 1993:17). He suggested 10 propositions on which narrative sociology would be based:

1. Since all socialized humans are storytellers, they are always in a potential storytelling situation when interacting with or encountering others.

2. The vast majority of all speech acts and self-representations contain at least some elements of narratives.

3. Variation in situation, audience, individual perspective, and power/authority relations will produce the universal condition of multiple versions of narrated events.

4. Narratives and narrative occasions are always potential sites of conflict and competition as well as of co-operation and consensus.

5. All narratives are potentially rational accounts, but because of inherent human ambiguity and variation in linguistic competence, all narratives are ultimately incomplete.

6. Narratives exist at various levels of scale, ranging from the personal to the institutional to the cultural; they exist for varying lengths of time; and they inevitably change.

7. All social science data are already interpreted data; the uninterpreted datum does not exist.

8. All sociological facts are narrated facts insofar as they have been processed through some form of story structure that renders events as factual.

9. The act of data collection is an act of entering respondents' lives that are partly formed by still unfolding stories. Therefore, in the name of honesty, research subjects will likely tell different stories about the same thing at different times and to different people.

10. A major implication of the above nine propositions is that sociology can only be a science of interpretations and to some extent must constitute itself as an interpretive science. (Maines 1993)

The inclusion of narrative in research is important because it can give **voice** to people who do not usually get to speak directly in research. Voice is the expression of *a* (not *the*) viewpoint that comes from occupying a particular social location (determined by factors including gender, 'race', ethnicity, sexual orientation, class, status as a student, and so on).

Consider the following two narratives. Both give voice to viewpoints that are not often heard. In the first, we hear a young Muslim college student talk about life in Canada. His voice is different from the voice of an older person born in another country, or that of a Muslim religious leader. It is not 'the official view', normal or abnormal, representative or strange, but it speaks a truth because it is what the speaker thinks, and it does reflect his life's experience. And it gives the non-Muslim reader a sense of what it is like to be a young Muslim in Canada.

In Other Words
Fasting

'Hey Moe, come join us for lunch.'

'I can't guys. I'm fasting.'

'Fasting, what's that?'

This passage, as awkward as it may sound, is quite normal and may be heard every year, asked by anyone and almost everyone. It bothers me to consider that the average person doesn't know what fasting for Muslims is. Fasting is an Islamic tradition practised for centuries, where a Muslim is subjected to no food or drink from sunrise to sunset. This is done to remind Muslims where we came from, as early people, to remind us that we started with nothing. It teaches us to value what we have and to value our gracious religion. There is fasting in almost every religion, yet the people who know the basic term of fasting don't know what type of fasting Muslims commit to. Many people [I have spoken to] were shocked to hear that during Ramadan [fasting month] you cannot only eat, but also drink. Many people thought that water or gum was allowed in any fasting, but it isn't for the Muslim type of fasting. It surprises me when 26 per cent of the earth's population is Muslim, but non-Muslims don't know what our Eid is. Eid is a celebration. We have two main celebrations. One Eid comes after the last day of Ramadan and the second after the day of pilgrimage. Eid is as holy to Muslims as Christmas and Easter are to Christians.

When someone asks me what fasting is for Muslims, I reply with such fatigue from saying it over and over that I simply reply, 'Well, we (Muslims) basically can't eat or drink anything when the sun is up.' I know that my reply may offend many Muslims since I have not included any significance or talked about the reward given for performing the fast. I simply gave a quick answer because I get that question asked every year, by anyone and almost everyone.'

—Mohamed Abseh

We are all aware of the longstanding struggles involving Palestinians in the Middle East, but we hear considerably less about Palestinians living in Canada. In the narrative on page 47 we hear the voice of a young Canadian of Palestinian background.

If you wanted a more detailed picture of what it's like to be a young Muslim or Palestinian living in Canada, you could gather more of these narratives and tie them together through a process known as **triangulation**, which involves the use of at least three narratives, theoretical perspectives, or investigators to examine the same phenomenon.

No matter what your political stripe is, listening to the political opinions of those whose opinions you don't share can be uncomfortable at best. For the person who holds views that are outside the political mainstream, expressing those views can be a very isolating and difficult experience. It's important to recognize that setting down a view you think may be unpopular requires courage. At the same time, recording and publishing the narratives of peoples whose political positions you don't agree with doesn't mean you accept what they say as 'right'. But whether you're expressing what you think is an unpopular view or recording a view you don't agree with, making such views known is an important step in generating understanding among others who might not agree with the position.

In Other Words
Palestinian by Culture, Canadian by Birth

My name is Nadine and I am Canadian born, but Palestinian by culture. My father was born in Palestine and my mother was born in Egypt to Palestinian refugees. Nowadays, being a Palestinian or of Palestinian origin is quite difficult, especially when you're living in a so-called multicultural nation. I guess it's not as hard for me as it has been for my parents because I am Canadian born and my parents came to Canada knowing little about the country or what would lie ahead. However, the difficult aspect in my life was that I grew up in a one-cultured-town [Woodbridge, in southern Ontario, an Italian-Canadian town] which was extremely difficult for my brothers and I to fit in. As far as I am concerned, I have never been able to have any close relationship with anyone. Why? I guess that children needed a common ground in order to establish a relationship, and not possessing the same culture as those around me made my assimilation even more difficult. Within homogeneous groups one can be easily singled out and that happened to me. Furthermore, as I grew up it became harder for me to engage in any real relationship with boys or girls because my culture became stronger for me and as well for them, which made us even grow farther apart. Maybe it was because I didn't speak or dress like them, or because I was darker than them, it didn't matter, basically I was just different.

Entering college, it was a bit easier for me to make acquaintances, though I realized how uneducated and ignorant people could really be. It was particularly difficult for me after the events of 9/11 because, automatically, the Arab world would get blamed for it and most people, ignorant as they are, believed everything that the media's propaganda has been telling them. I was in college at that time and explaining to people my point of view was tremendously challenging. Media brainwash had its toll on the majority of those around me. Furthermore getting into debates with individuals about what's occurring in Palestine and my views as a Palestinian was almost impossible. Right now my oppressed and displaced people who have been legitimately resisting occupation since 1948 are the bad guys. Maybe in a couple of years it will be another group, but for me now it's hard because I'm still singled out by my friends and the media. Maybe it would be a little bit easier if individuals would become open-minded about what goes on in the world. Then people could understand who we are and who I am. Knowledge is responsibility and to most, responsibility is a heavy burden to take. It is pretty sad what's going on in the 21st century that people like me, Canadian born, have difficulties growing up because of who they are and where they're from!

—Nadine Dahdah

What do you think?

What differences in the research findings may show up if triangulation is used with the two narratives?

Alternative Qualitative Research Methods

Psychoanalysis as Theory and Method

When we think of **Sigmund Freud** (1856–1939), we generally think of psychology and the theory of **psychoanalysis**. You will recall from Chapter 1 the difference between psychology and sociology: psychology focuses on the individual, while sociology generally deals with larger aspects of society. Psychoanalysis, though, despite being psychological and highly theoretical, has become a useful research tool for sociologists.

What makes the work of Freud and contemporary neo-Freudian psychoanalysts interesting to sociologists is its potential universality. Freud believed that childhood developmental stages (the oral, anal, phallic, latency, and genital stages) and the formation of *self* (comprising id, ego, and super ego) were culturally universal concepts. And, while they focus on the individual, they also consider the individual's relationship to society. Sociologists, rather than looking at the individual, use psychoanalytic categories and concepts to examine society at a cultural level (Chaitin 1996).

As an example of how psychoanalysis can be used to examine broader social and cultural institutions, we will turn our attention to architecture. Ian Craib notes that 'crucial aspects of psychoanalysis are concerned with areas of human life that are often manifested in art, literature and religion' (1989:11), and architecture is no different. Using psychoanalysis as a methodological tool, we can examine various buildings within a larger cultural context. For instance, Toronto's CN tower is often viewed as a phallic symbol—the conscious or unconscious representation of a penis. In Freudian terms, phallic symbols represent not just 'sex' but patriarchy—the domination of society by men, and the exclusion of women from positions of power. The question arises: why would a symbol representing the municipal pride of Toronto also symbolize the subordination of women? In this example psychoanalysis is used to 'read' the underlying symbol found in cultural institutions. In this respect, it is similar to semiotics or, as we will see, discourse analysis, though it is much more specific.

Early feminists dismissed Freud's theories because of ideas like 'penis envy', the supposed desire among women to have a penis, which Freud felt accounted for certain aspects of female behaviour. But in the late 1970s and 1980s, there was a feminization of psychoanalysis, which invigorated the theory and turned it into a method that could be used for feminist research. Among those leading the movement was Nancy Chodorow, who has been using feminist psychoanalysis in sociological research on gender, sexuality, and the family for thirty years. In *The Reproduction of Mothering* (1978), her pioneering study of psychoanalysis and the sociology of gender, she wrote that 'Freud's accounts of the

Toronto, as the centre for finance and trade, erects a monument to its own greatness. Why do you think this has been identified as a symbol of male hegemony? (iStockphoto)

psychological destructiveness of bourgeois marriage, gender differentiation, and child-rearing practices remain unsurpassed, and both psychoanalysts and feminists since Freud have deepened and extended his critique' (1978:40).

Among others who have made noteworthy use of psychoanalysis in sociology research are members of the **Frankfurt School** of social philosophers. Adherents of the Frankfurt School, which began in the 1920s, applied the work of Nietzsche, Marx, and Freud to their analyses. They were generally critical of fascism, communism, and capitalism as systems that produce social domination. Principal figures of the Frankfurt School include Theodor Adorno, Max Horkheimer, and Herbert Marcuse.

In *One Dimensional Man* (1964), Marcuse used a psychoanalytic approach to argue that, at a cultural level, society had institutionalized elements of the id (which drives us to pursue pleasure in order to satisfy instinctual desires); these elements, he believed, had come to displace the superego (our conscience, reflecting social standards learned from parents) and the ego (which controls the id's pleasure-seeking activities in order to meet the demands of civilized society). As a result, contradictory messages are brought together—progress and exploitation, satisfaction and drudgery, freedom and oppression—and made 'normal', producing what Marcuse called the *happy consciousness*. For Marcuse, the happy consciousness subordinates human freedom, promotes aggressive and immoral social activity, and lays the political foundation for new forms of fascism (1964:76–9). Here, fascism is not simply a political ideology but an ideology that links erotic pleasure and violence.

We will discuss psychoanalysis and its applications in sociology further in Chapter 4.

Content Analysis

Content analysis involves studying a set of **cultural artifacts** or **events** by systematically counting them and then interpreting the

Marcuse might have argued that video games like *Doom* and *Grand Theft Auto* are the extension and internalization of fascist ideals, encouraging us to take part in the domination of our own consciousness. (Ivy Images)

themes they reflect. Cultural artefacts include children's books, billboards, novels, newspaper articles, advertisements, artwork, fashion, clinical records, and even introductory textbooks like the one you're reading. Cultural artifacts have two distinct properties not found in other types of qualitative methodology. First, they have a natural or 'found' quality because they are not created specifically to be studied. Second, they are non-interactive in that there are interviews used or behaviour observed to gather the data (Reinharz 1992:146–8).

A feminist approach to content analysis attempts to expose pervasive patriarchal and misogynist culture. Elaine Hall's article *One Week for Women? The Structure of Inclusion of Gender Issues in Introductory Textbooks* (1988) demonstrated how women's issues are treated as an afterthought in introductory-level text, while Judith Dilorio (1980) used content analysis to examine scholarly articles on gender role research and found that their methods naturalized (i.e. made to seem natural or normal) social facts that diminished women and promoted conservatism (Reinharz 1992:147, 361).

In *Gender Advertisements* (1976), Goffman undertook a content analysis of commercial pictures depicting gender in print media. He demonstrated that women in advertisements were overwhelmingly depicted as subordinate and submissive. The magazines Goffman used in the study represent both mass media and popular culture, having been selected based on their availability and on the size of their circulation. Taken together, these magazines, available in every supermarket, drugstore, bookstore, and corner store, act as a cultural object, which reflects or mirrors the social world. This relationship, however, is not unidirectional but bi-directional: cultural objects reflect the social world, and the social world in turn reflects the cultural objects (Griswold 1994:22–3). Thus, with massive distribution and wide circulation, these most popular magazines give us both a snapshot of the social world and also an indication of how the social world is being constructed through mass media.

It is important to point out that 'social reflections' are only partial representations, as Sut Jhally (1990) notes in his discussion of gender. Magazine advertisements, he argues, are neither true nor false reflections of social reality. Ads depicting gender therefore don't give true or false representations of real gender relations

Would you say the men and women depicted in this ad are presented as equals? (© Images.com/Corbis)

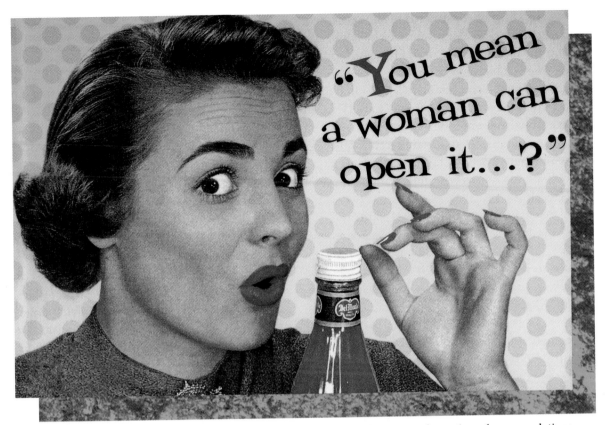

Ritualized displays of gender often assert stereotypes and speak more to the notion of power relations than to reality. What notions of power relations are expressed in this ad from the 1950s? Are those same notions evident in advertising today? (Ivy Images)

or ritualized gender displays. Rather, for Jhally, they are 'hyper-ritualizations' that emphasize certain aspects of gender display and de-emphasize others (1990:135).

Semiotics

Coined by the Swiss linguist Ferdinand de Saussure, **semiotics**, or semiology, refers to the study of signs and signifying practices; to use Saussure's words, it is 'the science of signs'. A **sign** is made up of two parts: a **signifier**, which carries meaning, and a **signified**, the meaning that is carried. Put another way, the signifier refers to the meaningful form while the signi-fied designates the concept that the form evokes. The interrelationship between the sig-nifier and the signified constitutes a sign.

Signs act together with other signs in a sys-tem. It is through the interaction of a system's component parts that meaning is formed. Language is a system of signs (words) that express ideas and create meaning when used in relation to one another. All words, after all, are signs. The word *apple*, for instance, is a signifier: it stands for a particular type of fruit that grows on a tree (this definition is the signified).

There are a number of problems with the semiotic approach. Leiss (1988), for instance, argues that semiotic studies of advertising depend too heavily on the skill of the individ-ual analyst. Too often, unskilled analysts state only the obvious, though Leiss names a few exceptions—Roland Barthes, Judith Williamson, and Erving Goffman—whose work uncovers deeper levels of meaning in the construction of ads. This discrepancy in the skill of various analysts makes it impossible to establish consistency or reliability in the results. Leiss cites other limitations of semiotic research, including its inability to derive an overall sense of constructed meanings from a survey of even a large number of messages, and the fact that, contrary to the assumptions of some, semiology cannot be applied to all ads with equal success. Notwithstanding these critiques, Leiss cites Goffman's study as an example of semiology demonstrating its capacity to dissect and examine cultural codes with a sensitivity to the subtle nuances and oblique references within the cultural system (1988:165–6).

For Leiss, Kline, and Jhally, the limitations of semiotics as a method can be overcome with the help of **content analysis**. Combining a semiotic approach with content analysis reduces concerns about reliability, sample size, and generalizability. Leiss, Kline, and Jhally (1988:169) identified four main *descriptors* of a content analysis, criteria by which any legitimate study may be judged:

- **objective description**: an acceptable level of agreement among analysts
- **systematic description**: the same criteria are applied to all data
- **descriptive categories**: a specific quantitative procedure permitting a degree of precision in measurement
- **deliberate restriction**: only the manifest or 'surface' content of the message is measured

Like semiotics, content analysis has limitations when used on its own to examine things like advertisements. The implication of 'deliberate restriction' is that content analysis, while it can measure what is actually going on in an ad, cannot truly measure 'meaning'. In other words, it cannot examine the impact of signs on the audience (Leiss, et al. 1988:174). What distinguishes Goffman's work is that although his categorization of like images appears to demonstrate all the qualities of a content analysis, he sets aside the deliberate restriction criteria and looks at the underlying *ritualization* of the images. A rough grouping of

Goffman's categories surrounding women— lying down, body cant, disassociated gaze, child-like innocence—support an interpretative 'reading' of female subordinate and submissive posturing. It is in this way that he might be considered a semiotician.

Discourse Analysis

There are two types of **discourse analysis** used by sociologists. The first analyzes discourse as it is traditionally defined—that is, as a conversation, a speech, or a written text. A sociologist may examine the 'discourse' found in a given ethnography, in an open-ended interview, or in a narrative. He or she might also focus on things like court transcripts, newspaper stories, and advertisements. As well as applying observational techniques, ethnomethodologists analyze everyday discourse to determine how, through language, people construct, make sense of, and generate meaning about their social world. Foucault's work on totalitarian discourse, which we touched on in Chapter 1, can be considered in terms of this definition of discourse. Foucault himself, you'll recall, defined discourse as *'a conceptual framework with its own internal logic and underlying assumptions that are generally recognizable'*.

The second type of discourse analysis focuses more on the methodological practices of genealogy and deconstruction, which we will discuss in the next section. As it is defined in this context, *discourse* is broader and more encompassing. Instead of referring merely to texts or authors, it refers to entire 'fields', such as economics, natural history, or political philosophy, and how they are constructed and constituted in particular periods—something **Foucault** did as well as part of his genealogical analysis. A 'field', then, would comprise all known discourse on a particular cultural concept or idea, such as *masculinity*. It is the role of the researcher to trace the discourse through time and space looking at the representation, naturalization, change, and influence of the discursive field. An example of this kind of study would be a discourse analysis of changing popular cultural representations of masculinity in Hollywood films over the past 50 years.

Genealogy

Genealogy in its everyday use refers to the study of heredity for the purposes of genetic or social history, or the study of pedigree. In the context of discourse analysis, genealogy is a method of examining the history of the second type of discourse, as defined above. Foucault, in his later works, used a genealogical method to study the 'heredity' of discourses, to trace the origin and history of modern discourses as they collide, fragment, and adhere to other cultural practices and discourses over time. Foucault's genealogical work captures the dynamic nature of such discourses as mental illness (1961), the penal system (1975), and sexuality (1978).

To understand the genealogical method, we will consider as our discourse the colour bar in South Asian culture. Any study looking at the social system in South Asia will observe a valuing of skin colour. Darker skin is less desirable, while a lighter skin colour is seen as more desirable. This cultural valuing of skin colour leads to prejudice and discrimination. In its origin, this cultural practice reproduced and reinforced a caste and class hierarchy in which those who were wealthier stayed inside, and those who were poorer worked in the fields and were, as a result, darker. Skin colour, then, reflected one's social status within society.

However, a contemporary study of this discourse requires an examination of the role British colonialism played in formulating current constructions of this cultural value. The discourse surrounding skin colour initially involved caste, class, social stratification, religion, inequality, gender, and colour, all of which operated within a particular field with its own history and logic. With the advent of colonialism, a new discourse of skin colour, with its own history and logic, was introduced into the culture. These two discourses, while distinct and different, grafted onto one another to become a new discourse, one that values and, in turn, privileges those with lighter skin above those with darker skin (Aujla, 1998:1–5).

Edward Said's classic study of Western attitudes towards Eastern culture, *Orientalism* (1979), offers another example of genealogical research. In the book Said (b. 1935) acknowledges Foucault's influence, in particular his notion of discourse, which allowed him to conceive of the genealogy of Orientalism. For Said, Orientalism cannot be studied or understood without the concept of discourse:

> My contention is that without examining Orientalism as a discourse one cannot possibly understand the enormously systematic discipline by which European culture was able to manage—and even produce—the Orient politically, sociologically, militarily, ideologically, scientifically, and imaginatively during the post-Enlightenment period. (1979:3)

Orientalism, in this sense, refers to 'a corporate institution for dealing with the Orient—dealing with it by making statements about it, authorising views of it, describing it, by teaching it, settling it, ruling over it: in short, Orientalism as a Western style for dominating, restructuring, and having authority over the Orient' (Said, 1979:3). As well as being a form of academic discourse, Orientalism is a style of thought based on the **ontological** and **epistemological** distinctions between East and West, the Orient and the Occident respectively. Here, we take Orientalism to mean the process by which the 'Orient' was, and continues to be, constructed in western European thinking.

Quantitative Research

Statistics

People have mixed feelings about **statistics**, a science that, in sociology, involves the use of numbers to map social behaviour and beliefs. Many of us, particularly the social scientists and politicians in our number, like quoting them. And yet, we are also suspicious of them (particularly other people's statistics). There are more jokes about statistics than there are about any other kind of sociological research method—and we can prove that statistically. But here is some anecdotal evidence:

- 'It shames me some to hear the statistics about us in class. The shame burns holes in whatever sympathy I may have for Indians, not my mom though.' —the Native protagonist of Aboriginal writer Lee Maracle's novel *Sun Dogs*, on how sociological statistics portray her people (Maracle 1992:3).
- 'There are three kinds of lies: lies, damned lies, and statistics.' —Benjamin Disraeli
- 'USA Today has come out with a new survey: apparently, three out of every four people make up 75 per cent of the population.' —David Letterman
- 'There are two kinds of statistics: the kind you look up, and the kind you make up.' —Rex Stout
- 'An unsophisticated forecaster uses statistics as a drunk man uses lamp-posts—for support rather than illumination.' —Andrew Lang
- 'Smoking is one of the leading causes of statistics.' —Fletcher Knebel
- 'Statistician: A man who believes figures don't lie, but admits that under analysis some of them won't stand up either.' —Evan Esar, *Esar's Comic Dictionary*
- 'Statistics: The only science that enables different experts using the same figures to draw different conclusions.' —Esar

Operational Definition

A key area of quantifiable research, and one in which a sociology student can learn to chal-lenge the research of professionals, is that of **operational definitions**. These are definitions that take abstract or theoretical concepts—'poverty', 'abuse', or 'working class', for example—and transform them into concepts that are concrete, observable, measurable, and counta-ble. This is difficult to do well.

The *Handbook for Sociology Teachers* (1982), by British sociologists Roger Gomm and Patrick McNeill, contains a brilliant exercise that illus-trates one of the difficulties of using operational definitions. Students are presented with a table showing the number of thefts that have occurred at each of a series of schools. Included in the table are the following potential inde-pendent variables: size of school, social class of the students, and whether the schools are sin-gle-sex or co-educational. Students are asked to try to determine whether there is causal rela-tionship between any of the variables and the number of thefts at each school. Once they have arrived at some tentative conclusions, the teacher gives them an additional handout showing that each school defined 'theft' differ-ently. With no consistency in the operation def-inition, their efforts to compare schools were sociologically worthless (although pedagogi-cally rewarding).

To get a sense of how operational definitions are used, let's consider poverty, a common focus of sociological study. There is no standard definition for 'poverty' or 'poor'; definitions of these terms vary across the globe. There are, however, various conventional methods of defining poverty. One is to establish a **poverty line**, an income level below which a household is defined (for statistical or governmental pur-poses) as being poor.

How is a poverty line established? Again, there is no universally accepted procedure, though a few methods are prevalent. One is to link it to the provision of basic material needs—food, clothing, and shelter. Anything below the minimum income level needed to secure these necessities is considered **absolute poverty**. But

Sociology in Action
So You Think You Know What A Single Parent Is?

Whenever you're gathering or interpreting data from questionnaires, it's critical that you understand the exact meaning—the operational definition—of key terms being used. Take a category as seemingly self-evident as 'single parent'. In the following exercise, say who you would count as a single parent, then address the questions below.

Who Would You Include?

a) a mother whose husband is dead   _____

b) a 41-year-old separated mother who lives with her 22-year-old son   _____

c) a father whose 4-year-old daughter sees her mother every weekend   _____

d) a mother whose 10-year-old son lives with his father every summer   _____

e) a father whose two daughters live with their mother every other week   _____

f) a mother whose husband lives in the same house but contributes nothing financially or in services to the raising of her children from a previous marriage   _____

g) a gay man who, along with his live-in partner, is raising his two sons (his ex-wife is completely out of the picture)   _____

h) a mother who along with her son is completely supported by her ex-husband   _____

i) a mother whose husband is away at work most of the year   _____

What do you think?

1. How would you define 'single parent'?

2. Do you think that 'single-parent family' is an independent variable that would be easy to do research with? Why or why not?

this, too, will vary even within countries. Consider how housing costs vary across Canada.

Since 1997 Statistics Canada has used the **Market Basket Measure** (MBM) to establish a poverty line for different regions across the country. As Giles explains,

The MBM estimates the cost of a specific basket of goods and services for the reference year, assuming that all items in the basket were entirely provided for out of the spending of the household [i.e. that parents, other family or friends aren't providing it].

Any household with a level of income lower than the cost of the basket is considered to be living in low income. (Giles 2004)

The 'basket' includes five types of expenditures for a reference family of two adults and two children: food, clothing, shelter, transportation, and 'other' (which includes school supplies, furniture, newspapers, recreation and family entertainment, personal care products, and a telephone). Different levels are calculated for 48 different geographical areas in Canada (StatsCan 2003).

Another way to define 'poor' is to use a **relative poverty** scale, which defines poverty relative to the average, median, or mean household incomes. One such measure used in Canada involves **Low-Income Cut-Offs**. These are calculated based on the percentage of a family's income spent on food, clothing, and shelter. So for instance, according to Statistics Canada, in 1992 the percentage of total income (before income tax) spent on these three items by Canadians was 34.7 per cent. Any household that spent at least 20 per cent more of its total income (i.e. 54.7 per cent) on these three items could be classified as poor.

Another relative poverty measurement used in Canada employs a mode of calculation that is commonly used across the world for comparative purposes. The **Low Income Measure** (LIM-IAT) is calculated by identifying those households with total incomes (after taxes) half that of the median income in Canada (with some adjustments made for family size and composition).

What we've seen, then, is that there are three legitimate ways to achieve an operational definition of poverty: the Market Basket Measure, the Low-Income Cut-Off, and the Low-Income Measure. According to Statistics Canada, the three methods yield similar results:

The Market Basket Measure (MBM) establishes a regional poverty line for Canada. What does poverty mean to you? (© Photodisc)

Using the MBM, in 2000, the incidence of low income for all children in Canada was 16.9%. This number is very similar to the number using the pre-income tax LICOs (16.5%), and slightly above the incidence using the post–income tax LICOs (12.5%) and the LIM-IAT (13.5%).

Note, however, that while the results are similar, the difference of a mere percentage point is a big deal to a statistician, underlying again the importance of knowing the precise meaning of any operational definition you use.

What do you think?

All ways of making an operational definition of poverty have strengths and weaknesses. What do you see as the strengths and weaknesses of the three systems discussed here?

Variables and Correlations

There are a few terms that are key to understanding and carrying out quantifiable research (and even certain forms of qualitative research). The first one is **variable**. A variable is a concept with measurable traits or characteristics that can vary or change from one person, group, culture, or time to another. One variable can cause another variable to change or it can be affected by another. The average temperature of Iqaluit can be a variable, as can the average amount of clothing a resident of Iqaluit wears. Clearly the first variable can affect the second one.

Sociologists commonly use two different types of variables: **independent variables** and **dependent variables**. The first are variables presumed to have some affect on another variable. In the example given above, the average temperature of Iqaluit is the independent variable. Dependent variables are those that are assumed by the sociologist to be affected by an independent variable. In the example given above, the average amount of clothing worn by the Iqalungiut would be the dependent variable. The following is a list of possible independent and dependent variables from examples presented in this chapter:

STUDY	INDEPENDENT VARIABLE	DEPENDENT VARIABLE
Opening narrative	car passing another car	the second car speeding up
Schoolwork	parental participation in schooling	reinforcement of better schooling results for middle-class children
Aboriginal policing	stable political environment commitment to training	successful police force increased competency of managers and officers* good relationship to the Quebec police*
	mentorship program	good relationship with local youth

Table 2.1 >> Independent and dependent variables: three examples

* This has not been measured; it has been assumed by the lack to problems with the band police.

Another key term is **correlation**. A correlation exists when two variables are associated more frequently than could be expected by chance. Both variables might increase together, or one might increase while the other decreases. A **direct correlation** (sometimes referred to as a **positive correlation**) exists when the independent variable and the dependent variable increase or decrease together. Table 2.2 shows some examples.

An **inverse correlation** (sometimes referred to as a negative correlation) exists when the two variables change in opposing directions—in other words, when the independent variable increases, the dependent decreases, and vice versa. Table 2.3 shows examples of inverse correlation.

Table 2.2 >> Direct correlation of independent and dependent variables: three examples	
VARIABLE	**DEPENDENT VARIABLE**
smoking	lung cancer
education level	income level
	tolerance for difference in humans (e.g. regarding race, ethnicity, sexual orientation, etc.)
parents' income level	likelihood of child becoming a doctor or lawyer

Table 2.3 >> Inverse correlation of independent and dependent variables: three examples	
INDEPENDENT VARIABLE	**DEPENDENT VARIABLE**
average temperature	average amount of clothes worn
a woman's education	the number of children she has
age (of an adult)	support for same-sex marriages

Spurious Reasoning: Correlation is *Not* Causation

You may have noticed that in the correlations above we've said nothing about **causation**, the attributing of effects to causes. We may observe that people shed layers of clothing as the temperature rises, but we can't assume, based on that correlation, that people wear fewer clothes *because* the temperature rises. That is something we have to prove.

It should be stated clearly that while correlation is relatively easy to prove, causation is not. One of the curses/challenges of teaching sociology is trying to explain and demonstrate what **spurious reasoning** is. It is one of those concepts that's hard to grasp by the definition alone. You need examples and lots of them. First the definition, then the examples. Spurious reasoning exists when someone sees correlation and falsely assumes causation. Remember that correlation is easy to determine; causation is not. The journey from one to the other is far. It involves proving—or else disproving—the existence of the critical **third variable**, the outside factor that influences both correlating variables.

Here are the examples. Some of them are silly, some serious.

Example #1 Birds and Leaves

There is a correlation in Canada between birds flying south (except for the fat Toronto geese, which seem to travel from York University only as far south as Lake Ontario) and leaves falling. Both take place roughly at the same time. It would be spurious reasoning to say that the birds see the leaves falling and therefore decide to leave. If we look for a the third factor, we'll find that the angle of the sun's rays affects both dependent variables.

Example #2 Fire Trucks and Fire Damage

This is a classic, perhaps the most often taught example of spurious reasoning. There is a direct correlation between the number of fire trucks that go to a fire and the amount of damage that takes place at the fire. The greater the number of fire trucks, the greater the damage the fire causes. It would be spurious reasoning to say that a large number of fire trucks *causes* the great damage done at the site of the fire (though think of how some budget-conscious municipal politicians would love us to believe this—they could save a lot of money on fire trucks). Seek out the third variable: the seriousness of the fire affects both the number of fire trucks that appear and the damage that is caused.

Example #3 Older Men and Younger Wives

Older men who marry significantly younger women tend to live longer than the cohort of jealous men their own age. Spurious reasoning would lead us to conclude that marrying frolicsome young women keeps old men active and healthy. But before declaring that we've found the solution for men who want to live long and happy lives, we must look for a third variable. That's when we discover that if the older man is already relatively strong and healthy for his age, then he is both more likely to attract and keep a younger woman and more likely to live longer.

Example #4 Cohabitation and Divorce

There is a direct (but not strong) correlation between living together prior to marriage and the likelihood of divorce. People who live together first are more likely to divorce than those who go from living apart to living together in marriage (perhaps the latter are also more likely to die of shock). It would be spurious rea-

Spurious reasoning leads us to conclude that this man will live long. What do *you* think? (Photo © PNC/Brand X/Corbis)

soning to say that a couple's greater likelihood of divorce comes from the fact that they lived together first (e.g., they are disillusioned because they find no greater bliss in lawful marriage than in mere cohabitation). Seek out the third variable and we find social liberalism and social conservatism (the latter possibly a cause or effect of that strange social factor 'religiosity'). People who are socially liberal are more likely *both* to live together *and* to leave a marriage if they feel it is a bad one. People who are more socially conservative are *both* more likely to begin living together with marriage, *and* more likely to stay in a marriage, even if it is horrible (our sympathies).

Example #5 Aboriginal Deaths and Christianity

In the seventeenth century some Aboriginal people living in present-day Canada—the Huron (Wendat), the Montagnais (Innu), the Algonquin, and the Ottawa—came into contact with French explorers and missionaries. At that time, there was a definite correlation between Native exposure to European religion (primarily through the Jesuits) and Native deaths from European diseases such as smallpox and influenza. It would be spurious reasoning to say, as some of the Aboriginal people did, that it was the religion that was causing the death. Seek out the third variable: exposure to priests carrying European diseases to which the Aboriginal people had not naturally developed any antibodies.

Example #6 Divorce and Suicide

Durkheim recorded the following direct correlation between divorce rates and suicide rates during a ten-year period from 1870 to 1880:

Table 2.4 >> Correlation between divorce and suicide rates in four countries, 1870–1889		
	DIVORCE RATE (PER 1,000 MARRIAGES)	**SUICIDE RATE (PER 1 MILLION PEOPLE)**
Italy	3.1	31.0
Sweden	6.4	81.0
France	7.5	150.0
Switzerland	47.0	216.0

Source: Spaulding and Simpson (1951).

It would be spurious reasoning to say that greater rates of divorce produced higher suicide rates during this time. Durkheim sought out a third variable, found it, and called it **anomie**, a societal state of breakdown or confusion, or a more personal one based on an individual's lack of connection or contact with society. Anomie, concluded Durkheim, was the real cause of higher divorce and suicide rates.

Critical Thinking and Statistics

Sociologist Joel Best, author of *Damned Lies and Statistics: Untangling Numbers from the Media, Politicians, and Activists* (2001), begins an article excerpted from his book with an example that well illustrates why we should approach statistics with a critical mind. He was on the PhD dissertation committee of a graduate student who began the prospectus of his dissertation with a questionable statistic meant to grab the attention of the reader. The student wrote the following, which was obtained from an article published in 1995: 'Every year since 1950, the number of American children gunned down has doubled.'

This would certainly gain the attention of those Canadian readers who already think of Americans as gun-toting, trigger-happy rednecks. But wait a minute, said Best: do the math. Say the 1950 figure was the unbelievably low figure of 1. Here is how it would add up to 1995:

1950	1
1951	2
1952	4
1955	32
1957	128
1959	512
1960	1,012
1961	2,058
1965	32,768 (there were 9,960 homicides that year)
1970	1 million +
1980	1 billion (approximately; that's more than four times the total population of the United States at the time)
1983	8.6 billion (nearly two times the world's population)
1995	3 trillion

What the author of the original article had done was mistakenly repeat a 1994 document that stated the number of American children killed each year by guns had doubled since 1950; the number itself had not doubled *each year*. If the original number had been one, that would make the 1994 figure two.

After presenting to us this cautionary tale, Best warns the reader that bad statistics come to support all political stripes, from the political right wing (the Conservative Party) to the left wing (the New Democratic Party), from wealthy corporations to advocates for the poor, the sick, and the powerless. To cite an extreme Canadian examples, the Mike Harris Conservative govern-

ment of Ontario officially stated in the late 1990s that the number of people on welfare in the province had gone down, suggesting that the situation for poor people had improved under their administration. It hadn't. The welfare numbers were down because the agencies run by the government had closed the welfare door on a number of people. Rather than assume that all of the people off the welfare rolls got jobs, included in that number were people who had committed suicide (in part because of their poverty), had become homeless, had moved out of the province to one that was not so tough-minded, had moved in with family members or friends, or had resorted to criminal activity for a living.

Best advises us to approach statistics critically. To be critical is to recognize that all statistics are flawed to some extent, but that some flaws are more significant than others. While he admits that no checklist of critical questions is complete, he does present the following useful series of questions for sociology students to consider when encountering a news statistic in a news report, magazine, newspaper or, conversation:

What might be the sources for this number? How could one go about producing the figure? Who produced the number, and what interests might they have? What are the different ways key terms might have been defined, and which definitions have been chosen? How might the phenomena be measured, and which measurement choices have been made? What sort of sample was gathered, and how might that sample affect the result? Is the statistic properly interpreted? Are comparisons being made, and if so, are the comparisons appropriate? Are there competing statistics? If so, what stakes do the opponents have in the issue, and how are those stakes likely to affect their use of statistics? And is it possible to figure out why the statistics seem to disagree, what the differences are in the ways the competing sides are using figures. (Best 2001)

Abuse Statistic or Statistical Abuse?

We can apply Best's critical thinking to the following example. In 1980, Linda McLeod produced a controversial book, *Wife Battering in Canada: The Vicious Circle*. In it she cited a statistic that has since become what some call a **free-floating statistic**. A free-floating statistic is a figure that is frequently reproduced without presenting the context—the time, set of assumptions, operational definition, or sample size relevant to how and why the statistic was calculated. McLeod's claim was that 'Every year, 1 in 10 Canadian women who are married or in a relationship with a live-in lover are battered' (McLeod 1980:21). This was a stunning claim, and commendable as one of the first real attempts to gauge the level of domestic violence against women in Canada. But it's important to look at just how McLeod arrived at this figure.

Two things should be noted from the beginning. First, McLeod clearly stated, as a good sociological researcher often has to, 'no *definitive* statement about the incidence of wife abuse can be made' (i.e. largely due to the lack of reporting; McLeod 1980:16). Second, her figures were for the year 1978.

Next, we have to take a look at her operational definition is of wife battering:

Wife battering *is* violence, physical and/or psychological, expressed by a husband or a male or lesbian live-in lover toward his wife or his/her live-in lover, to which the 'wife' does not consent, and which is directly or indirectly condoned by the traditions, laws and attitudes prevalent in the society in which it occurs. (McLeod 1980:7)

She generated her statistic first by requesting annual statistics from 71 transition houses or hostels for women. She received data from 47 of these, on a total of 9,688 women (McLeod 1980:16). She estimated that about 60 per cent of these women would go to these shelters because they were 'physically battered', producing a figure of roughly 5,800 (rounded off from 5,813). She then rounded off the number of shelters that supplied data (47/71) as 2/3, and multiplied her estimated number of battered women from these shelters by 3/2 to get roughly 9,000 (the actual figure would be 8,700). She then used a rough statistic that the transition houses could not house 1/3 of the women who contacted them, raising her figure to 12,000. This figure was multiplied by two, as she estimated (from 1976 statistics) that about 45 per cent (which she rounded off to 50 per cent) of the Canadian population was not served by a transition house. Using all these calculations, she arrived at her first major conclusion:

If transition houses existed across Canada, we can estimate that at least 24,000 Canadian women would request help from them because they were battered by their husbands. (McLeod 1980:17)

She next went to the divorce statistics for 1978. One of the grounds that could be cited for divorce at that time was 'mental or physical cruelty'. She found 2,800 applications for divorce on that basis only, with physical cruelty also included in 17,116 cases where multiple grounds were listed. This gave a combined figure of roughly 20,000.

She acknowledged some flaws with this figure, namely that some of the physical cruelty figures would have come from applications from men, and that 'there is no doubt some overlap between women who stayed in transition houses and those who applied for divorce' (McLeod 1980:20). Still, she added her two numbers together to say that:

40,000–50,000 women in Canada in 1978 suffered sufficient physical and mental abuse to seek outside help. (McLeod 1980:20)

She then estimated that there were roughly 5 million couples existing in Canada at that time (no source given), leading her to state that

> One out of every hundred women in Canada married or living in a common-law relationship is battered and has filed for a divorce on grounds of physical cruelty or has approached a transition house for help (given the extrapolation discussed above). (McLeod 1980:20)

From an examination of what she called 'Miscellaneous Canadian Sources', she concluded that the number of domestic violence calls was 'far above' the cases she had discussed. She then took an estimate from a University of Windsor study of 1976 to say that

> There are *ten* unreported cases for every call by a battered wife to the police. (McLeod 1980:21)

Multiplying her previous figure of 1/100 by ten, McLeod arrived at the often quoted statistic that

> Every year, 1 in 10 Canadian women who are married or in a relationship with a live-in lover are battered. (McLeod 1980:21)

Think of how often the term 'estimate' appeared in the discussion above, and how many times figures were rounded off. This is a good example of how the misuse of statistics can be used for social good (i.e. the recognition of the profound problem of spousal abuse). It should also be noted that more recent Canadian studies (Minister of Supply and Services Canada, 1993, and Minister of Industry, Science and Technology, 1993) suggest a figure even higher than the one produced here. Nevertheless, the flaw in McLeod's calculation of the statistic is evident, and to cite it without understanding or explaining how one arrived at that figure is irresponsible research.

Abuse of a Statistic

Unfortunately, this statistic was seized upon and used out of context over the next two decades. Here are a few examples, obtained from the Internet on 4 January 2005:

- 'It is currently estimated that wife assault involves one in ten women in Canada.' British Columbia Hansard, 1993
- 'One in ten women in Canada are victims of violence by conservative estimates.' The Student Union at the University of Alberta
- 'One in ten women is physically and/or sexually assaulted by her spouse or live-in partner.' The Canadian Labour Council
- 'This year one in ten women in Canada will be hit, kicked, punched or threatened by their husbands or boyfriends.' The ATIRA Women's Resource Society
- 'The National Clearinghouse on Family Violence suggests that Canada-wide, one in ten women is physically abused by her husband or partner.' Peter McFarlane

What do you think?

What have these quotations changed from the original operational definition?

Sociological Research Methods: A Final Word

In this chapter we've introduced a number of ways to carry out sociological research. In all the talk about quantitative and qualitative methods, independent and dependent variables, correlation and statistics, it's easy to lose sight of an important point: the subjects under investigation are people, and the moment you begin to study them, you start a relationship that will not always be equal. Students, soldiers, and inmates of prisons and asylums are often studied because they have little power to say 'no'. If I can ask questions about your life but you can't ask questions about mine, then I have a kind of power over you that you do not have over me. People who are poor, who belong to racialized (Blacks) or colonized (Aboriginal people) groups when studied by White middle-class researchers have often been studied for purposes that serve more to control or exploit the subjects of research than to give them power over their lives. In an important work by Maori researcher Linda Tuhiwai Smith, *Decolonizing Methodologies: Research and Indigenous Peoples* (1999), she writes the following:

> From the vantage point of the colonized . . . the term 'research' is inextricably linked to European imperialism and colonialism. The word itself, 'research', is probably one of the dirtiest words in the indigenous world's vocabulary. When mentioned in many indigenous contexts, it stirs up silence, it conjures up bad memories, it raises a smile that is knowing and distrustful. . . . The ways in which scientific research is implicated in the worst excesses of colonialism remains a powerful remembered history for many of the world's colonized peoples. . . . It galls us that Western researchers and intellectuals can assume to know all that it is possible to know of us, on the basis of their brief encounters with some of us. It appals us that the West can desire, extract and claim ownership of ways of knowing, our imagery, the things we create and produce, and then simultaneously reject then people who created and developed those ideas and seek to deny them further opportunities to be creators of their own culture and own nations. (Tuhiwai Smith 1999:1)

If your interest in sociology comes from a desire to effect positive social change, the bitter tone of this statement might shock you. Let it serve as a reminder: treat research subjects with respect and represent the data fairly, and you will go a long way towards sociology's goal of bringing clarity to social issues.

Questions for Critical Review and Discussion

1. Distinguish between qualitative and quantitative research. Give examples.

2. Explain the significance of narratives in sociological research.

3. Explain and give examples of spurious reasoning.

4. Outline the different methods of sociological research.

5. Identify the importance of operational definitions in quantitative research.

Suggested Readings

Bourdieu, Pierre, et al. (1999). *The Weight of the World: Social Suffering in Contemporary Society*. Stanford: Stanford UP.

Brown, Gillian, & George Yule (1983). *Discourse Analysis*. Cambridge: Cambridge UP.

Feyerabend, Paul (1975). *Against Method*. London: Verso.

Grosrichard, Alain (1979). *The Sultan's Court: European Fantasies of the East*. London: Verso.

Hoffer, Lee D. (2006). *Junkie Business: The Evolution and Operation of a Heroin Dealing Network*. Belmont: Thomson/Wadsworth.

Vinitzky-Seroussi, Vered (1998). *After Pomp and Circumstance: High School Reunion as an Autobiographical Occasion*. Chicago: U of Chicago P.

Suggested Websites

Canadian Sociology & Anthropology Association.
http://artsci-ccwin.concordia.casocanth/csaa/csaa.html

Doing Research in Sociology (University of Waterloo Library).
http://129.97.58.10/discipline/sociology/research.html

Semiotics (Martin Ryder, University of Colorado at Denver, School of Education).
http://carbon.cudenver.edu/~mryder/itc_data/semiotics.html

Statistics Canada.
http://www.statcan.ca/start.html

Culture

Contents

Key Terms

authenticity
contested
counterculture
cultural capital
cultural studies
cultural relativism
culture
dialect
dominant culture
dominants
ethnic entrepreneurs
ethnocentrism
exoticism
folkways
high culture
hijab
indigeneity
mass culture
mores
negative sanctions
noble savage
norms
patriarchy
positive sanctions
potlatch
primordiality
reverse ethnocentrism
Sapir-Whorf Hypothesis
simulacrum/simulacra
sociolinguistics
subculture
subordinate culture
symbol
taboos
values
victimology
Xenocentrism

Boxes and Tables

In Our View The 'Native' Expert Confesses
Quick Hits Mind Traps in Understanding Culture
Canadian Sociology in Action Are You Excluded from the Dominant Culture?
Sociology in Action Aragorn and the Arabs
Sociology in Action The Jackrocks Story: A Narrative about the Power of Symbols
In Other Words The Hijab as Worn by Young Canadian Muslim Women in Montreal
In Our View A Sociologist Sees Beauty in Taiwan: Reverse Ethnocentrism

Table 3.1 Percentage of respondents agreeing with the statement 'The father of the family must be master of his own home'
Table 3.2 Percentage of respondents agreeing with the statement 'Men are naturally superior to women'
Table 3.3 Religious differences as reflected in dialect: two examples

Learning Objectives

After reading this chapter, you should be able to

- distinguish between
    - dominant cultures and subcultures/countercultures;
    - high culture and popular culture;
    - mass culture and popular culture;
    - reading and decipherment; and
    - folkways, mores, and taboos.
- identify the intellectual traps of
    - Eurocentrism,
    - victimology,
    - exoticism, and
    - the biases of Western medicine.
- explain what it means for culture to be 'contested'.
- discuss how ethnocentrism has affected the mainstream sociological interpretation of the potlatch.
- discuss the roles played by wearing the hijab in Canada.
- contrast the linguistic expectations of speakers of Algonquian and Indo-European languages.

For Starters
Culture and Claiming Space

It was all about culture. I saw the conflict coming, but I could do nothing to stop it. I was in Edinburgh, Scotland, in 1981, in one of the few decent (according to my North American bias) hamburger places in the city. It was a popular spot, both for locals and for tourists, commanding a beautiful full view of the castle on the top of the hill across the street. I was waiting in line with my Scottish friends when I saw the incident that would precipitate the conflict.

A pair of American tourists set their jackets on two of four chairs attached to a table, and then slowly proceeded the short distance to the lineup. I knew they were asking for trouble. As I stood there in line I saw a Scottish couple looking for a place to sit with their meals. Their eyes fixed on the chairs opposite the ones with the tourists' jackets. They went over, sat down at the unoccupied chairs, and innocently began to eat their hamburgers.

The tourists had been distracted by the view of the castle. When then turned around and saw the couple at the table, they reacted instantly.

'What are you doing? That's our table. Didn't you see the jackets?' The Scots looked up at them, dumbfounded, but unprepared to move. This was their country, and they felt that they were in the right. My Scottish friends asked me (as a Canadian 'Translantic', an obvious expert in things North American):

'What's wrong with them? Do they think they bought the table? Bloody tourists!'

The tourists continued to argue with the Scots before storming out of the place.

A few months earlier, I might have sided with the tourists, sympathizing with their typically North American sense of space. But having spent time in Scotland, I understood why the Scots were surprised. In Canada, when two people in a bar are sitting at a table with four chairs, and someone asks them, 'Are these seats taken?', the unseated patrons will take the two extra chairs and sit at a vacant table. In Scotland, they will sit down right at 'your' table, and then either join you in conversation or ignore you altogether.

It's all about culture.

Joseph Sohm/Getty Images

Culture

What is culture? It is not the meaning used in the punchline of the old joke, 'What's the difference between yogourt and Dullsville [or the neighbouring town of your choice]? Yogurt has culture.' The culture referred to in the joke can more properly be called **high culture**. It's what we have in mind when we think of opera, ballet, theatre, fine restaurants. And it's from that idea of culture that we get the adjectives 'cultured'—as in having a sophistication of manners and taste—and 'uncultured'—as in 'I never met a beer I didn't like.'

The word **culture** as we mean to use it here is a system involving behaviour, beliefs, knowledge, practices, values, and material such as buildings, tools, and sacred items. In calling it a system, we don't mean to suggest that there is total agreement concerning any one culture by those who belong to it. In other words, culture is **contested**. As we will see below, the veil is a contested part of Muslim culture. To illustrate this point, let's talk about hockey. Probably just about everybody would say that hockey is part of Canadian culture, but that's where the agreement would end. Does success by Canada's national teams in international hockey mean we've succeeded as a culture? Not everyone would agree there. Is fighting an integral part of the Canadian game? You don't have to be Don Cherry to get into an argument there. There is no consensus.

One of the points of contestation is **authenticity**. Culture involves traditions but is not confined by them. It is dynamic: it changes over time. Authenticity suggests being true to a particular culture (think of 'authentic' Italian cuisine as opposed to North American pizza). Sometimes the word 'traditional' is used to imply that only those practices that have been carried on for generations can be true to the culture (i.e., authentic), while new cultural forms that may involve features from other cultures are not.

Authenticity becomes a problem when a colonial society studies a colonized culture and claims, having studied that culture's traditions, to hold the key to its authenticity. One of Said's main points in *Orientalism* is that Western intellectuals formed their impressions of the Middle East and central Asia from nineteenth- and twentieth-century scholarship. Once they had defined what 'the Orient' was and is, these same scholars and intellectuals negatively compared their somewhat romanticized (think Aladdin) notion of the Eastern world's traditional with their negative perceptions of its present. In effect they said, 'You are a corruption of what you used to be. You are no longer authentic.' That would be as infuriating as someone saying to you, 'I understand you better than you do, and you are not as good as you used to be.' A similar situation occurs when non-Native scholars invoke the stereotype of the noble savage to compare the 'authentic past' of Native culture with what they consider its corrupted, degenerated present state. We'll have more to say about the noble savage myth later in this chapter.

It should be noted that it is a common mistake to think of one's own culture as being contested while thinking that someone else's culture has complete agreement. 'Canadians differ on many issues, but all Americans carry guns, hate foreigners, and make obnoxious tourists.' In short, all culture is contested.

What Kinds of Cultures Are There?

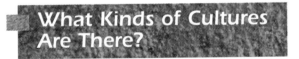

The different kinds of cultures that exist within a society can be seen in terms of two oppositions:

dominant culture *vs*
subculture and **counterculture**

high culture *vs*
popular culture and **mass culture**

As we examine each of these oppositions, you will understand why we say that culture is contested.

>>> **In Our View**
The 'Native' Expert Confesses

I am a white guy who is a 'Native expert'. That has given me a lot of power: I often find myself in the position to declare whether something is or is not 'authentic Indian'. I tend to use 'traditional' rather than 'authentic', but the issue is still the same.

The problem is that I, and outsider experts like me, have too much control over the word 'traditional', and therefore over judging authenticity. What we know are details about the past. But we have no intellectual right to claim that something (for instance, an Ojibwa jingle dress dance performed by a Mohawk) is inauthentic because it isn't how it was done in the past. If the Mohawk does the dance in a way that brings honour to herself and her people, then it is authentic.

A book I read recently helped me work out this problem. It was called *'Real' Indians and Others: Mixed-Blood Urban Native Peoples and Indigenous Nationhood* (2004). In it, author Bonita Lawrence, a Mi'kmaq woman of mixed heritage, avoids the term 'traditional culture', using two other terms instead. The first is **primordiality**, which she defines as 'a state of existence in contradistinction to modernity, whereby language, ways of living, and cultural knowledge as manifested by distinct beliefs, traits, and practices, [are] transmitted in relatively unbroken lines from a distant past . . .' (Lawrence 2004:1). Such a static (i.e. unchanging) construct of culture is what outsider academic 'experts' like me have authority in. It's like knowing the 'letter of the law'. According to a strict primordialist view, a Mohawk performing an Ojibwa dance is not 'traditional', and is therefore inauthentic.

The second, and opposing, term she uses is **indigeneity**, which 'refers less to precolonial states of existence and identity than to a future, postcolonial refashioning of Indigenous identities that are truer to Indigenous histories and cultures than those identities shaped by the colonial realities that continue to surround Native people at present' (Lawrence 2004:14). This is where the insiders have primary authority. It's a more dynamic view, in which a practice can be informed by traditional culture, but it's not an exact replica. It's like knowing the spirit of the law. From this perspective, a Mohawk performing an Ojibwa dance is honouring traditional Aboriginal culture.

Authenticity is like a river formed by the joining of the two streams of primordiality and indigeneity. Both are authentic. Primordiality tends to be outsider-defined and deals primarily with the details of the past. Indigeneity is mostly insider-defined and deals primarily with the present as reflecting the spirit of the past

—J.S.

Dominant Culture versus Subculture and Counterculture

It is not difficult to see that there is a **dominant culture** in Canada. The dominant culture is the one that through its political and economic power is able to impose its values, language, and ways of behaving and interpreting behaviour on a given society. The people most closely linked with it are sometimes referred to in the literature as **dominants**. In Canada it is fairly safe to say that the dominant culture is English-speaking, European-based, White, and Christian. It is also fair to say that the dominant culture is middle-class. How do we know what the dominant culture looks like? Think of what culture is typically represented in Canadian morning shows like *Canada AM*, in commercials, and in television programs generally. Think of the expectations they express about what people own, what their concerns are, and how they live.

>> Quick Hits
Mind Traps in Understanding Culture

Try to avoid the following common mind traps in understanding culture:

- thinking that 'culture' refers only to high culture
- thinking that total agreement can be or should be achieved in a culture
- thinking that culture is locked into one time period (as with popular ideas of Aboriginal culture)
- thinking that 'our' culture is contested whereas other cultures have total agreement (e.g., the false but popular notion that Christians differ but that all Muslims, Hindus, Sikhs or Buddhists think alike)

We can further narrow our picture of Canada's dominant culture by looking at the issue from a regionalist perspective. People living in the Atlantic provinces have good reason to suspect that the dominant culture lies in central Canada, where most big companies have their head offices, and where the greatest share of the national population is situated. Likewise, Western Canada has several times produced political parties (Social Credit and the Reform Party, for instance) to protest the West's alienation from the dominant culture and its unfair treatment at the hands of central Canadian institutions.

Feminists (both female and male) argue that Canada's dominant culture is male. Think of our most powerful politicians—prime ministers, premiers, cabinet ministers, mayors of large cities. Of the 308 members of Parliament in 2004, only 65, or 22 per cent, were women. Next, think of the country's most powerful and influential businesspeople, our 'captains of industry'. The majority of these are also men. It seems the feminists have a valid point.

We could add age to our portrait of Canada's dominant culture as well. Those who are just starting or have just ended their careers often feel marginal to the dominant culture. Other factors to consider are sexual orientation, level of education, and overall health (since those with disabilities or chronic medical conditions might feel outside the dominant culture). To summarize, our portrait of Canada's dominant culture looks something like this: English-speaking, White, heterosexual male university graduate of European background between the ages of 25 and 55, in good health, who owns a home in a middle-class neighbourhood in

Which of the people in this picture belong to the dominant culture? (© Photodisc)

Ontario or Quebec. How many people do you know who fit this description?

Subcultures are commonly discussed in the culture chapter of sociology textbooks, where they are defined in terms used to describe cultures generally. The beliefs, values, behaviour, and material culture of subcultures are presented and then contrasted with those of a vaguely defined 'larger society' or 'larger culture'. In this way, the term 'subculture' might seem to represent an intellectually 'soft' and socially benign or harmless notion of size difference: a subculture is merely a smaller version of the dominant culture. But this may downplay the imbalance of power—the ability to make political, economic, and social decisions that affect not only oneself and one's family, but a good number of others as well—

between the dominant cultures and subcultures. For this reason, we find it useful to use the term **subordinate cultures** for those groups who feel the power of the dominant culture and exist in opposition to it, and to reserve *subculture* for those involved in the more neutral cultural contrast often referred to in introductory sociology textbooks: computer nerds, lawyers, sociologists, stamp collectors, and so on. We would then define *subculture* in terms of a set of minor cultural differences possessed by groups organized around occupations or hobbies, engaged in no significant opposition or challenge to the dominant culture.

Counterculture

Countercultures are defined oppositionally. That is, they are usually described as groups

Canadian Sociology in Action
Are You Excluded from the Dominant Culture?

Are you excluded from dominant culture? Here is a simple, informal test.

1. How likely is it that political leaders (prime ministers, premiers, cabinet ministers, opposition leaders, mayors of major cities) are like you in gender, religion, clothing style, language, and parentage?
2. How likely is it that the homes portrayed in most television series look like your home?
3. How likely is it that the lead character in a movie lives a life like yours?
4. How likely is it that your boss is of the same gender, ethnicity, and age as you?
5. How likely is it that in an introductory sociology textbook, there are people like you discussed in every chapter?
6. How likely is it that the authors of an introductory sociology textbook are like you culturally?
7. How likely is it that on 'reality-based' police television shows the people that are arrested look like you and your neighbours?
8. How likely is it that people like you are seen demonstrating or protesting something on the TV news or the front page of a newspaper?
9. How likely is it that there are a lot of derogatory slang terms that refer to people like you?
10. How likely are people like you to be called a 'special interest' or a 'designated' group?
11. How often are people like you called 'too sensitive' or 'pushy'?
12. How likely are you to be asked 'Where did you come from?'

For questions 1–6, 'low likelihood' equals exclusion from the dominant culture; for questions 7–12, 'high likelihood' equals exclusion from the dominant culture.

that reject selected elements of the dominant culture (for instance, clothing styles or sexual norms). Examples of counterculture range from the relatively harmless (i.e. not fundamentally challenging to social order) beatniks of the 1950s and hippies of the 1960s and early 1970s to the dangerous biker gangs that flourish today. A counterculture that has emerged more recently is that of the **Goths**. Descriptions of this counterculture abound on the Internet, from which the following brief description is summarized.

What are Goths? Most people will be able to summon a rough image: dyed black (less often blue) hair, dark clothes, and white makeup that contrasts sharply with clothing and hair colour. When we think of Goths we may think of their supposedly typical fascination with death and with art—especially music and film—that reflects this fascination. But who are the people who belong to this counterculture? What can we add to this picture?

First, they tend to be young. Goth seems to be a phenomenon that is invented and re-invented by the youth cohort of the time. Some bloggers claim that there are three generations of Goths, each not so aware of its predecessors or reincarnations; the 'generation gap' seems a perpetual feature. Second, they are typically White. There are Internet references to Black and Asian Goths, but it appears their numbers are very small. Third, although there has been, to the best of our knowledge, no significant sociological study done of this, they seem to be mostly from middle-class families.

While there is some reason to consider the beatniks the earliest generation of Goths, the oral/Internet history places the origins of the Goth subculture in the late 1970s. The Goth of that period is associated with the song 'Bela Lugosi's Dead', released in 1979 by Bauhaus, and with the look and music of bands such as the Cure and Siouxsie and the Banshees, to mention just two.

The opposition of Goths to dominant culture is expressed most clearly in their dress and overall appearance, but it goes well

Can clothing alone constitute a counterculture or do other values, beliefs, and ideals have to be present? (Photo © Waltraud Grubitzsh/dpa/Corbis)

beyond this visual aspect. The early Goths rejected the Yuppie world of financial self-indulgence and the conservative politics of Ronald Reagan, Maggie Thatcher, and Brian Mulroney; they pursued a life concerned with less world-exploitive politics and cultish small-market arts. Succeeding generations of Goths have taken up different causes, but they carry on the traditional appearance and connection to the arts that their predecessors established.

A Theoretical Matter

Just as it is meaningful to distinguish between the dominant culture and subordinate cultures within a single society, it might also be worthwhile to distinguish among a society's countercultures. We could, for instance, draw a distinction among countercultures based on the way each is treated by the dominant culture, as expressed particularly in mainstream media. What we propose to call **dominant countercultures** (i.e. those drawn from the dominant culture) are usually treated with lighthearted criticism and mild restrictions. Think of how Goths are portrayed on television. Different from those are countercultures drawn as subordinate cultures, comprising groups whose class and ethnic background set them apart from the dominant culture. Examples here include the 'gangsta' culture of Black youth and, from an earlier time, the zoot-suit culture (see Chapter 5, on deviance).

High Culture versus Popular Culture

The second of our two major oppositions has risen to prominence over the last quarter century or so. **High culture** is the culture of the elite, a distinct minority. High culture is associated with such cultural elements as European-based opera, classical music and ballet, 'serious' works of literary fiction and non-fiction, 'artsy' films that may be difficult to appreciate without having taken post-secondary courses on the subject, and a 'cultivated palate' for various high-priced foods and alcoholic beverages. It is sometimes also referred to as elite culture. Canadian sociologist Karen Anderson defines high culture as follows:

> Elite culture is produced for and appreciated by a limited number of people with specialized interests. It tends to be evaluated in terms of 'universal' criteria of artistic merit and to be seen as a sign of prestige. Appreciation of elite culture usually entails a process of learning and the acquisition of specific tastes. (Anderson 1996:471)

French sociologist Pierre Bourdieu coined the term **cultural capital** to refer to the knowledge and skills needed to acquire the sophisticated tastes that mark someone as a person of 'high' culture. The more cultural capital you have, the 'higher' your cultural class.

Popular culture, on the other hand, is the culture of the majority, particularly of those people who do not have power (the working class, the less educated, women, and racialized minorities). Academic discussion of popular culture has developed with the rise of **cultural studies**. This relatively recent field draws on both the social sciences (primarily sociology) and the humanities (primarily literature and media studies) to cast light on the significance of and meanings expressed in popular culture, topics that before this development were mostly neglected by academics.

Mass Culture and Popular Culture

While the terms *popular culture* and *mass culture* are sometimes presented as if they were more or less synonymous, there is a crucial distinction: the two differ in terms of **agency**, the ability of 'the people' (i.e. the masses) to be creative or productive with what a colonial power, a dominant culture, or a mass media has given them. Sociologists disagree on how much agency people have. Those who believe that people take an active role in shaping the culture they consume (in terms of the items they buy, the music they listen to, the TV shows and movies they watch) use the term **popular culture** to describe the majority of those who fall outside the world of the cultural elite. Those who believe people have little or no agency in the culture they consume are more likely to use the term **mass culture**. They tend to believe that big companies (Walmart, McDonald's, Disney, and Microsoft, for instance) and powerful governments dictate what the people should buy, watch, value, and believe. Members of countercultures are predisposed to thinking those outside their group belong to mass culture.

One feature of mass culture is what French sociologist Jean Baudrillard calls **simulacra**. Simulacra are cultural images, often associated with stereotypes, that are produced and reproduced like material goods or commodities by the media and sometimes by scholars. For example, the Inuit are often represented by simulacra of described practices (e.g., rubbing noses, abandoning elders [see Steckley 2003], and wife-sharing) and in physical objects (e.g., igloos and kayaks). These images tend to distort contemporary Inuit 'reality'. Consider, for instance, the way the inukshuk, the Inuit stone figure, has developed as a Canadian cultural symbol, with models of these stone figures sold in tourist shops across the country. It has even been incorporated into the logo for the 2010 Winter Olympics in Vancouver, BC (a province that has no Inuit community).

Baudrillard describes simulacra as being **hyperreal**—that is, likely to be considered more real than what actually exists or existed. If someone were to say to you, 'Don't bother me with the facts; *I* know how it *really* is—I saw it on television!', you can assume he or she is heavily influence by simulacra. Baudrillard illustrates the principle with an analogy of a map. Imagine that you are on a canoe trip and your map indicates that there is a river in a particular place. You paddle your canoe to that place and find only mud. If you keep paddling in search of the promised river because you believe that what the map says is 'more real' than what your eyes see, then the map is a simulacrum.

When sociologists encourage their students to be critical of what the media presents, they are hoping their students will be able to detect simulacra. The famous 'weapons of mass destruction' that were never found in Iraq are a classic example: governments operated as though these weapons actually existed. The weapons in fact were hyperreal.

The 'Orient', the Western portrait of East Asia and the Middle East described by Edward Said, is a simulacrum. Evidence of Orientalism frequently appears in Western media, and notably in Hollywood representations of the East. A recent example is the 2004 movie *Hidalgo*, discussed in the box on page 76.

British sociologist John Fiske takes the popular culture position. He believes that there is no mass culture, that the power bloc—the political and cultural institutions with the greatest influence on society—just provides resources that the people resist, evade, or turn to their own ends. He recognizes agency and warns about the dangers of left-leaning sociologists presenting people as mere dupes of mass media. Without using the word, he expresses his concern about the dangers of **victimology**. Victimology has two contrasting meanings in sociology. The first, more general meaning is the study, within criminology, of people who are victims of crime. The second is an outlook that undervalues the victims of crime by portraying them as people who

An inukshuk stands before a nursery in southern Ontario. Why do you think the inukshuk is fast becoming a universal Canadian symbol? (Photo © John Steckley)

Sociology in Action
Aragorn and the Arabs

In March 2004 my wife and I saw the movie *Hidalgo*. Set in the late nineteenth century and starring Viggo Mortensen, the movie tells the supposedly true story of Frank Hopkins, an aging American cowboy and dispatch rider for the US cavalry, who rides his mustang against some of the finest Bedouin thoroughbreds in a 3,000-mile race across the Arabian Desert. We had admired the work of the movie's lead actor in *The Lord of the Rings*, and the trailers for *Hidalgo* made it seem like the type of adventure movie we both enjoy. What we weren't prepared for was the Oriental simulacrum promoted relentlessly throughout the movie. All of the stock features of a romanticized portrait of Arabia were on display: an omnipotent sheik, the Arabs' insatiable thirst for vengeance and callousness concerning the lives of others,

Islamic fanaticism and intolerance for non-Muslims, and a veiled Muslim woman willing to be threatened (and rescued) by the heroic Westerner and to be freed from the 'oppression' of her veil. She closely resembled the stereotype—another simulacrum—of the Indian Princess (see chapters 9, on race and ethnicity, and 10, on gender inequality.).

We appreciated that the hero acknowledged and drew upon his Aboriginal roots, even if his character embodied a few too many clichés. However, the movie was like an old Western, pitting cowboys against Indians—only in this case, the cowboy was part Indian, and the Indians were really Arabs. Note to the director: Muslims, unlike Orcs, cannot be depicted, one and all, as villains without creating waves in the 'real world' of contemporary politics.

---

cannot help themselves, who cannot exercise agency. It is in this sense that the term victimology captures Fiske's concerns about the mass culture position of some sociologists.

An important distinction between the two positions involves the contrast, identified by de Certeau (1984), between **decipherment** and **reading**. Decipherment is the process of looking in a text for the definitive interpretation, the intent (conscious or unconscious) of the culture industry in creating the text. For sociologists who believe that mass culture predominates, decipherment is about looking for the message that mass media presents people with, without allowing them to challenge it or reject it by substituting their own.

Sociologists who believe that popular rather than mass culture predominates tend to talk not about decipherment but about reading. Reading is the process in which people treat what is pro-

vided by the culture industry as a resource or text to be interpreted as they see fit, in ways not strictly intended by the creators of the text. The sociological study of reading involves the analysis of narratives of those who are using or have used the text as a cultural resource.

E. Michaels (1986), in a description of the reception by the Aborigines of central Australia of the Sylvester Stallone movie *Rambo*, offers a good example of the difference between decipherment and reading. A mass culture interpretation of the movie would be that it delivers a propaganda message about the triumph of good over evil, of the capitalist West over the communist East. But the Australian Aborigines, who loved the movie, had their own reading of the film:

> [T]hey understood the major conflict to be that between Rambo, whom they saw as a representative of the Third World, and the

white officer class—a set of meanings that were clearly relevant to their experience of white, postcolonial paternalism and that may well have been functional in helping them to make a resistant sense of their interracial relationships. . . . The Aborigines also produced tribal or kinship relations between Rambo and the prisoners he was rescuing that were more relevant to their social experience than any nationalistic relationships structured around the East–West axis . . . . (Fiske 1994:57)

Norms

Norms are rules or standards of behaviour that are expected of a group, society, or culture. There may not always be consensus concerning these standards: norms may be contested along the sociological faultlines of ethnicity, race, gender, and age. Norms are expressed in a culture through various means, from ceremonies that reflect cultural mores to symbolic articles of dress. In the following sections, we'll have a look at how norms are expressed or enforced through these various means.

Sanctions

People react to how others follow or do not follow the norms of their culture or subculture. If the reaction is one that supports the behaviour, it is called a **positive sanction**. It is a reward for 'doing the right thing'. Positive sanctions can be small things such as smiles, a high five, or a supportive comment, or they can be larger material rewards, such as a bonus for hard work on the job or a plaque for being the 'Innovator of the Year' at college. A hockey player who gets into a fight is positively sanctioned by teammates at the bench banging their sticks against the boards.

The opposite of a positive sanction is a **negative sanction**. It is a reaction designed to tell offenders they have violated a norm. It could be anything from a 'look' with rolling eyes or a mild joke (I hear 'It's Santa Claus' directed towards me, a middle-aged, well-proportioned sociologist with a big beard) to a nasty note left on the windshield of a car taking up two parking spaces on a crowded street, to the fine you pay at the library for an overdue book.

Sanctions for 'inappropriate' behaviour can range from an informal dirty look to formal charges involving the police and the courts. (© Photodisc)

Folkways, Mores, and Taboos

William Graham Sumner (1840–1910) distinguished three kinds of norms that differ in terms of how seriously they are respected and sanctioned. He used the term **folkways** for those norms governing day-to-day matters; these are norms that in the normal course of things you 'should not' (as opposed to 'must not') violate, and they are the least respected and most weakly sanctioned. The term *etiquette* can often by applied to folkways. If you want to think of folkways with an example from popular culture, think of George Costanza from the TV show *Seinfeld*. He continually violates folkways: double-dipping chips and fetching a chocolate eclair out of the garbage come immediately to mind.

Mores

Mores (pronounced like the eels—*morays*) are norms that are taken much more seriously than folkways. They are rules you 'must not' violate. Some mores, against rape, killing, vandalism, and most forms of stealing, are enshrined in the criminal code as laws. Violation of some mores, even if they are not laws, will meet with shock or severe disapproval. Booing the national anthem of the visiting team prior to a sporting event is likely to cause offence among supporters of the visiting team and even anger or embarrassment among fans of the home side. Violations of this kind can be complicated and contested. For example, some fans at Toronto Blue Jay home games did not stand during the playing of 'God Bless America', which was mandatory at all Major League Baseball ballparks for a short period during the US's 'War on Terror'. Is this an unforgivable breach of mores or a justifiable negative sanction of American foreign policy?

Mores of cleanliness, too, are in the cultural eye of the beholder. In Britain, dogs are allowed in pubs; in Canada, they are not. This does not mean that bars in Canada are more sanitary than those in Britain. Many readers of this textbook will be able to think of bars restricted to human rather than canine patrons that have appallingly unsanitary conditions, particularly in the washrooms. Differences in cleanliness mores can lead to serious problems when an overly developed sense of cleanliness as a Western medical more can jeopardize the health of a patient (see the example of the Hmong study in Chapter 8, on medical sociology).

Like folkways, mores can change over time. A young woman sporting a tattoo would once have been seen as violating the mores of acceptable behaviour for a lady. Today, many women have tattoos and display them without arousing the kind of shock or condemnation generally produced when mores are violated.

Taboos

A taboo is a norm so deeply ingrained that the mere thought or mention of it is enough to arouse disgust or revulsion. The taboos against cannibalism, incest, and child pornography are examples that come immediately to mind. Taboos affect our dietary habits: for instance, eating dogs, cats, or other animals that might be considered family pets is taboo in North American culture, and religious taboos ban the consumption of certain foods—pork by Jews and Muslims, beef by Hindus. Some cultures recognize gender taboos, such as those aimed at women 'interfering' with male activities. Consider the following speech by a character in Anna Reid's novel *The Shaman's Coat* (2002). She is an older woman of the Nivkh people of Siberia:

> Everything about men was sacred; everything about women was dirty. If a man was sitting down it was wrong to step over his legs—it would bring bad weather when he was out hunting. If I or my sisters just touched a gun, we'd get such a scolding. I remember once, my father went out to check his traps, and didn't come back for a long time. We all sat there holding our heads, wondering what we'd done wrong. (Reid 2002:155)

Sociology in Action
The Jackrocks Story: A Narrative about the Power of Symbols

In the fall of 1989, I went to rural Virginia on a short lecture tour, invited by staff and students of Southwest Virginia Community College who had attended a lecture of mine during their spring break. I spent the first night of my stay at the home of the college president. It was elegant, finely furnished, with everything in its place. While there, I noticed something that surprised me. In a glass case—the kind normally used to hold curios and objets d'art, such as glass and china figurines—I saw two 6-pointed objects, each one made of three nails. They reminded me of the jacks I had played with as a child. Why had these mean-looking items been placed on display?

The next night I stayed with a coal-miner's family. It was a fascinating evening. Among the things I learned from them are that moonshine drunk from a mason jar can disconnect your brain from your feet, and that the term *cakewalk*, meaning a surprisingly easy task, comes from a kind of musical chairs in which the winner receives a cake as a prize. During a more serious conversation I learned about the dynamics of a months-long miner's strike in a one-industry area. I was taken on a tour of the strike centre, where bunk beds were being built to accommodate the families of striking workers who were thrown out of their homes for failing to pay the rent. The people I met there were friendly, but the long strike cast a shadow across their spirits.

The mining company was owned by people from outside the area, foreigners in the eyes of the locals. But then, even the state capital of Richmond was considered foreign, much like Halifax is by people who live in Cape Breton. The company owners had circumvented the picket lines by trucking the coal out at night, but striking miners in camouflage had found ways to thwart their efforts. One of my souvenirs of the trip is a camouflage shirt with 'Holding the Line in 1989'. I wore it with pride during the most recent Ontario community college strike.

The next day, at the college, I spoke to a sociology class about symbols. Near the end of the class, I asked whether there were any local symbols. One student piped up, 'Jackrocks.' When I asked what 'jackrocks' were, I got a description of the 6-pointed objects I had seen in the president's glass case, as well as a bag full of jackrocks handed to me by a student who went to his car to get them. I was told that one of the methods used to keep the coal trucks from shipping out the coal was to toss these jackrocks underneath the tires. The jackrocks had become symbols of resistance. They appeared in store windows in the town nearest the mine, and I was given a pair of small, aluminum jackrock earrings—another souvenir. I then understood why the college president kept the two jackrocks in the glass case. He was from Florida, and therefore a 'foreigner' to the area. By keeping the jackrocks in a place of honour, he was expressing solidarity with his students and their community.

What do you think?

1. What meaning did the jackrocks have for the local people of southwest Virginia?

2. Why did the college president keep jackrocks in his glass case at home?

Symbols

Symbols are aspects of a culture that come to take on tremendous meaning within a culture or within a subculture of a society. Symbols can be material objects, as illustrated in the narrative on page 79, or non-material objects such as songs or the memory of events.

Symbols of Ethnic Identity

Canadians travelling abroad often wear pins with little Canadian flags on them or display the Maple Leaf on their backpacks. A flag is one symbol of ethnic identity. For Americans the symbolic significance of the flag is even more firmly entrenched: it is the subject of their national anthem; in schools, they pledge allegiance to it; and many support a law that makes it illegal to burn or otherwise desecrate it. In Zimbabwe, the coins bear the symbol of a bird carved in stone. The image represents the birds found in the Great Zimbabwe, the large stone ruins after which the country was named. Scottish people show a great emotional attachment to songs about battles fought in the early fourteenth century against the English. These are all **symbols of ethnic identity**: elements that contribute to a people's sense of national or ethnic identity.

The Veil as a Symbol for Canadian Muslim Women

Few clothing symbols have a greater power to evoke emotions than the Muslim veil, or (in Arabic) *hijab*. For many in the West, it is a symbol of patriarchal domination by weapons-waving misogynist young men of the Taliban, similar in effect to the full-length, screen-faced *burqa* that hides Afghani women from the world of opportunities and freedom, and to the *chador* that Iranian women are forced by law to wear. British Prime Minister Tony Blair has gone on the record with his views of the veil, which he calls a 'mark of separation' that makes others feel uncomfortable and that discourages the integration of Muslims with mainstream British society.

A Muslim woman wearing a hijab passes a Paris clothing store, as symbols of beauty and identity face each other. (Graham Bibby/CP Photo)

In Other Words
The Hijab as Worn by Young Canadian Muslim Women in Montreal

1. Narrative of a 19-year-old Palestinian-Canadian Woman

The veil has freed me from arguments and headaches. I always wanted to do many things that women normally do not do in my culture. I had thought living in Canada would give me that opportunity. But when I turned fourteen, my life changed. My parents started to limit my activities and even telephone conversations. My brothers were free to go and come as they pleased, but my sister and I were to be good Muslim girls. . . . Life became intolerable for me. The weekends were hell.

Then as a way out, I asked to go to Qur'anic classes on Saturdays. There I met with several veiled women of my age. They came from similar backgrounds. None of them seemed to face my problems. Some told me that since they took the veil, their parents know that they are not going to do anything that goes against Muslim morality. The more I hung around with them, the more convinced I was that the veil is the answer to all Muslim girls' problems here in North America. Because parents seem to be relieved and assured that you are not going to do stupid things, and your community knows that you are acting like a Muslim woman, you are much freer. (Hoodfar 2003:20–1.)

2. Narrative of a 17-year-old Pakistani-Canadian Woman

Although we did not intermingle much with non-Indian-Canadians, I very much felt at home and part of the wider society. This, however, changed as I got older and clearly my life was different than many girls in my class. I did not talk about boyfriends and did not go out. I did not participate in extracurricular activities. Gradually, I began feeling isolated. Then my cousin and I decided together to wear the veil

and made a pact to ignore people's comments, that no matter how much hardship we suffered at school, we would keep our veils on.

One weekend we announced this to our surprised parents. They . . . consented, though they did not think we would stick with it. . . . At first it was difficult. At school people joked and asked stupid questions, but after three months they took us more seriously and there was even a little bit of respect. We even got a little more respect when we talked about Islam in our classes, while before our teacher dismissed what we said if it didn't agree with her casual perceptions. (Hoodfar 2003:28–9.)

3. Narrative of Mona, an Egyptian-Canadian Woman

I would never have taken up the veil if I lived in Egypt. Not that I disagree with that, but I see it as part of the male imposition of rules. . . . The double standard frustrates me. But since the Gulf War, seeing how my veiled friends were treated, I made a vow to wear the veil to make a point about my Muslimness and Arabness. I am delighted when people ask me about my veil and Islam, because it gives me a chance to point out their prejudices concerning Muslims. (Hoodfar 2003:30)

4. A Muslim Female Student from Montreal Reacts to the Examples

The young women in these articles claim that wearing the hijab, overall brought them joy and happiness. However, look at the reason they decided to wear the hijab. In the first example, it was because her parents were not letting her go out and be free like her brothers. So she wore it to gain her own freedom, not to appreciate anything about the culture. In the second, it was because they did not talk about going out or boyfriends. Big deal! Many people do not talk about those things. It was their own minds that made them feel isolated, not the culture surrounding them. And the third example, I feel she did it for more right reasons than any of the others. Nevertheless, to prove a point???

I do not wear this 'veil', but have relatives that do. It does not make me a 'poor' Muslim woman. Even if a girl has this 'veil' on she can still do bad things and be persuaded to do bad things just like anyone else.

—Ferita Haque

It is important for readers of this textbook to understand some of the reasons why women of different cultures—especially in Canada—choose to wear the veil. One point must be emphasized: for a significant number of women in Canada, as for those women in France opposing a law that would ban the veil in schools, the veil is a matter of choice, not command.

To hear the perspective of Canadian Muslim women on this subject we are drawing upon a ground-breaking study by Iranian-Canadian anthropologist Homa Hoodfar (2003), carried out in Montreal during the mid-1990s. The voices Hoodfar recorded speak compellingly of choosing to wear the veil as a way of opposing restrictions placed on them (and not their brothers) as teenagers by parents concerned that their daughters will fall prey to the irreligious sex-, alcohol-, and drug-related behaviours of North American culture. Some saw veil-wearing as a step, together with Qu'ranic study and banding together with Canadian Muslim women of different cultural backgrounds, down a path of opposition to some of the patriarchal mores of their specific cultures. In addition, taking the veil gave some of them the opportunity to defend their faith against the ignorance and ethnocentrism of some of their fellow Canadians. The three examples in the box on page 81 are particularly instructive.

Values

Values are the standards used by a culture to describe abstract qualities such as goodness, beauty, and justice, and to assess the behaviour of others. Values have long been a topic of great interest to sociologists. Max Weber's identification of the Protestant work ethic is but one early example of a sociological study of values. But in spite of these studies, values remain difficult to understand and to represent accurately. What makes the issue especially puzzling is that the values that people claim to have are not always acted upon. Do we then recognize the value that is professed or the value that is reflected in human action? Is the person who preaches a value but fails to honour it in his or her daily life necessarily a hypocrite?

The issue revolves around the distinction between **ideal culture** and **real culture**, the former more talked about, the latter more acted upon. A person might speak passionately about environmentalism at a community meeting (a statement of Canadian ideal culture), then drive three blocks home in a gas-guzzling SUV. The same person might not always put recyclable garbage in the recycling bins because he or she is 'in a hurry'. And sometimes we feel we don't have a choice. We might hate the idea of driving to work, but if we live in a small town with no bus or train service to the big city we work in, we have no option but to drive. Do we?

There can be value contradictions in what people say and do that are different from the contradictions of ideal and real culture. Holding a double standard can be a value contradiction. We can see this in examples of racism. Nineteenth-century Canadian governments, whose members doubtless believed strongly in individual freedom, created policies that put tight restrictions on Native people and limited the freedom of Black refugees who fled slavery after the War of 1812 to come to supposed freedom and opportunity in Nova Scotia (see Chapter 9, on race and ethnicity). Patrick Henry, the American patriot and revolutionary who bravely said 'Give me liberty or give me death', owned slaves.

Canadian and American Values

Canadians will regularly compare themselves with Americans on anything from foreign policy to international hockey. In fact, some Canadians define themselves by what an American is not, making statements like 'A Canadian is an unarmed American with health insurance.' But how much do these two neighbouring societies really differ in their values?

Michael Adams, of the Environics Research Group, has been conducting and publishing polls since the early 1980s. In this work he has tried to measure and track 100 'social values' of Canadians. In *Fire and Ice: The United States, Canada and the Myth of Converging Values* (2003) he follows his own work, as well as the work of American sociologist Seymour Martin Lipset (1990), to contrast the values of Canadians and Americans. His thesis is that Canadians and Americans are becoming more different rather than more alike in their values. It certainly seemed so in 2003, when the American military was heading into Iraq and Canada was not,

and when a slight majority of Canadians were supportive of gay marriage and the liberalization of marijuana laws, two social changes that were not on the radar screen of American values. The following discussion deals with a number of the divergent trends Adams claimed were taking place.

Adams based his findings not on informal research or anecdotal evidence but on data from polls conducted by Environics in the US and Canada in 1992, 1996, and 2000. Still, it's always important to look at the data critically. For one thing, the polls prompted respondents to 'talk' about their values. Remember the difference between professed and real values. Are these kinds of responses likely to yield data accurate enough to identify actual cultural differences? Another point: is the time period—from 1992 to 2000—long enough to produce evidence of what he calls 'long-term shifts'? Remember, too, that all of this data was gathered before 11 September 2001; Adams is quick to point this out, though he argues that the events of that day

Even Canadian and American flags reflect different cultural values. The Canadian flag, handed down by the government in the 1960, features a leaf that is not native to most of the country. First sewn by Betsy Ross, the American flag emerged as a powerful symbol during the American Revolution and is still the subject of the country's national anthem. (© Photodisc)

would only make the differences he identified greater. We will look at one of the value clusters Adams identified—**patriarchy**—leaving out his interpretation and leaving you, the reader, to put in your own.

Adams used two statements to measure patriarchy:

1. 'The father of the family must be master in his own home.'
2. 'Men are naturally superior to women.'

Respondents were asked whether they agreed with these two statements. The following table presents the results:

Table 3.1 >>   Percentage of respondents agreeing with the statement 'The father of the family must be master of his own home'

YEAR	CANADA	UNITED STATES	DIFFERENCE
1992	26	42	16
1996	20	44	24
2000	18	49	31

Source: Adams 2003:50–1.

Note the difference in increase after each four-year period. It's worth noting that even the ranges of the two countries do not intersect: agreement with this statement among Canadian respondents ranged from a province-wide low of 15 per cent (in Quebec) to a high of 21 per cent (in the Prairie provinces) in the 2000 poll; among US respondents, the range started at 29 per cent (in New England) all the way to 71 per cent (in the Deep South) (Adams 2003:87).

The percentage of difference between Canadian and American agreement on the second question was less than on the first, but note how the difference increased over each four-year period:

Table 3.2 >>   Percentage of respondents agreeing with the statement 'Men are naturally superior to women'

YEAR	CANADA	UNITED STATES	DIFFERENCE
1992	26	30	4
1996	23	32	9
2000	24	38	14

Source: Adams 2003:51.

What do you think?

1. These findings appear to support Adams's thesis that American and Canadian social values are becoming less alike. How convincing do you find them?

2. What do you think the cause of the difference might be?

3. Could the difference be caused by the greater involvement of Americans in organized religion?

4. Is using religious-influenced values a fair way to measure Canada–US social difference or does it skew the results?

Ethnocentrism

Ethnocentrism occurs when someone holds up one culture (usually, but not always, the culture of the ethnocentric individual) as the standard by which all cultures are to be judged. It follows a simple formula: 'All cultures like the standard culture are good, praiseworthy, beautiful, moral, and modern; Those that are not are bad, ugly, immoral, and primitive.' Ethnocentrism can manifest itself in many forms. It can entail saying that business should be run in only one way—the way of the cultural model—that policing should take only one form, or that progressive policies should concentrate only on certain ideas.

Ethnocentrism is often the product of ignorance. For instance, there are North American websites that report that Chinese people eat aborted fetuses. This idea, which has become something of an urban legend, may have its origins in the idea that in some cultures, a mother who has just given birth eats a piece of the placenta, in an act that combines symbolism and

Using a story cloth, Chau Vue, multicultural outreach coordinator for the Minneapolis-area chapter of the American Red Cross, points out some of the dangers of a Minnesota winter to a group of Hmong immigrants who have never experienced snow or sub-zero temperatures. (Beth Schlanker/AP Photo)

tradition with beliefs about the nutritive value of placenta.

Hmong refugees living in the United States have had to contend with such ethnocentric ignorance. They have been targeted because of their supposed practice of stealing, killing, and eating dogs. Lack of evidence or truth does not deter an ethnocentric public from spreading these stories about a 'foreign' culture. According to Roger Mitchell the false stories follow particular themes:

[Rumored] methods of [dog] procurement vary. Some are coaxed home by Hmong children. Some were adopted from animal shelters (until those in charge noted a high rate of adoption). Others are strays. The most common accusation is theft, often from backyards, sometimes leaving the head and collar as mute testimony to Rover's passing. . . . The dog is usually an expensive one, often owned by a doctor. The theft is observed, the license plate number is marked down. When the police check, the dog is already in some Hmong family's pot.

The supposed proof varies. That fixture in the urban legend, the garbage man, reports the presence of canine remains in Hmong garbage cans. Carcasses are seen hanging in the cellar by meter readers, salesmen, or whomever. Freezers are said to be full of frozen dogs. A bizarre touch is that the dogs are supposedly skinned alive to make them more tasty.' (as reported in Fadiman 1997:190–1)

On a larger scale, ethnocentrism has played a role in the colonizing efforts of powerful nations that have tried to impose their political, economic, and religious beliefs on the indigenous populations of lands they 'discovered'. European missionaries arriving in present-day North American found a large Native population they regarded as uncivilized, uneducated, and badly in need of Christianity to replace their pagan spirituality. Their ideas stemmed from the belief that their god—the Christian God—was the only true god. This kind of ethnocentric treatment of North American Aboriginal people did not end there, as succeeding generations of religious, government, and social leaders laboured to impose European values on the Native population. The church-run residential schools for Native children are a well-know example of how misguided such ethnocentric beliefs can be and what tragic results they can produce. The following discussion highlights another example of how Canada's First Nations were forced by an ethnocentric government to abandon a traditional custom.

What do you think?

While in Canada dogs are seen as pets, in other cultures they are seen as edible meat. Western ethnocentrism informs the protests to stop the consumption of dog meat in other cultures; it is called 'barbaric' and an 'insidious industry'. But is there any difference between eating a dog and eating a chicken, pig, lamb or cow?

The Potlatch Act of 1884

The Potlatch is a traditional ceremony of the Northwest Coast Native people. It centres around the acquiring or affirmation of hereditary names. During the ceremony, the host of the potlatch demonstrates his social, economic, and spiritual worthiness to be given the hereditary name. An important aspect of the event is the telling, singing, and acting out of stories. In this way, potlatches affirm the possession of the stories, songs, dances, carved and painted images, masks, and musical instruments used by the hosting group to celebrate the cultural history of the name and those identified with it. These hereditary names carry more than just symbolic significance: they are connected with rights to fish, hunt, or forage for plants in a particular territory, and with the responsibility to conserve the living entities within that territory. Potlatches go a long way in maintaining the strength and social unity of the group.

Another important aspect of the potlatch is the giving away of gifts and possessions. One way for a high-ranking man to prove he was worthy of his position was to give away many gifts. The hierarchical nature of Northwest Coast culture made this very competitive, as those holding or aspiring to high rank gave away as much as they could afford. The level of competition rose after European contact, in part because of the availability of European manufactured goods, but also because of the toll European diseases took on the Native population. The population of the Kwakiutl, for example, dropped from roughly 8,000 in 1835 to around only 2,000 in 1885. When diseases decimated lineages entitled to important names, more distant relatives would vie for prestigious family names. In some cases, competition could become socially divisive, and there were even incidents in which property was destroyed as a show of wealth ('I am so rich, that this property means nothing to me'). Such incidents appear to have been rare, but over-reported in the literature. And by its very nature, the potlatch encouraged the circulation of wealth throughout the community, for one could be a host on the giving side at one potlatch, a guest on the receiving side of the next.

In 1884, the Government of Canada, under pressure from church leaders opposed to 'pagan practices' and fearful of the Native population because of rumoured Métis hostility on the prairies, made the potlatch illegal:

> Every Indian or other person who engages in or assists in celebrating the Indian festival known as the 'Potlatch'. . . is guilty of a misdemeanour, and shall be liable to imprisonment for a term of not more than six nor less than two months in any gaol or other place of confinement, and any Indian or other person who encourages, either directly or indirectly, an Indian or Indians to get up such a festival or dance, or to celebrate the same, or who shall assist in the celebration of same, is guilty of a like offense, and shall be liable to the same punishment.

In 1921, 45 of the highest ranking Kwakiutl were arrested, and 22 were sentenced to prison terms of two to three months. For the community, the tragedy was twofold: first, they had lost their leaders; second, they lost many sacred potlatch items that were taken as a condition for the release of community members arrested but not charged. The items became the property of the Minister of Indian Affairs, who distributed them to art collectors and museums.

In 1951, the potlatch ban was repealed. But it wasn't until 1975 that the National Museum declared it would return the sacred items, provided they be kept in museums. The Royal Ontario Museum returned the items it had in 1988, and the National Museum of the American Indian in New York repatriated some of its holdings in 1993. Some items will never be recovered.

We see ethnocentrism here at several levels. Northwest Coast ceremonies were not respected because of their difference from Western Christian ceremonies. They involved dance, drums, masks, and other elements not typically found in churches. If there were parallels in Western culture, they were not recognized.

Ethnocentrism is not a phenomenon confined to the West, or to White people. When the Japanese seized control of its northern islands from the Ainu, the indigenous people of those islands, they developed and implemented ethnocentric policies that rival any laws enacted by the governments of Canada and the United States to limit the freedoms of the North American Native people.

Eurocentrism

It is easier, and perhaps more enlightening, to say what **Eurocentrism** involves than what it is. It involves addressing others from a broadly defined 'European' (i.e. western and northern European, and North American) and assuming that the audience is or would like to be part of that 'we'. It can be seen in historical references to the 'known world'—that is, the world as it was known by Europeans—and, of course, to Christopher Columbus 'discovering' in 1492 continents in which millions of people lived, and which their ancestors had settled more than 12,000 years earlier. It involves a tendency to foreground discoveries and contributions that are Western, and background those that are not. It involves promoting the cause of historical heroes and heroines who are European or who acted to benefit a European cause. For example, it would be Eurocentric to downplay or ignore the fact that Native agriculture gave the world many crops, arguably the most, by volume, of all the crops currently grown: corn, squash and pumpkins, most beans, peppers (hot and sweet), potatoes, tomatoes and sunflowers, to mention just some.

Reverse Ethnocentrism

Not to be confused with **xenocentrism**—a preference for foreign goods and tastes based on the belief that anything foreign must be better than the same thing produced domestically—**reverse ethnocentrism** involves assuming, often blindly, that a particular culture that is not one's own is better than one's own in some way. Reverse ethnocentrism sets an absolute standard that one's own culture does not or cannot match. In the United States, liberal Americans who blame their own country's cultural values and foreign policy for terrorist attacks on Americans at home and abroad are sometimes accused of reverse ethnocentrism and anti-Americanism by more conservative thinkers. Sometimes the myth of the **noble savage** is seen as an instance of reverse ethnocentrism. The term 'noble savage' refers to any idealized representation of primitive culture that symbolizes the innate goodness of humanity when free from the corrupting influence of civilization. It was a theme especially popular in literature of the seventeenth and eighteenth centuries, when European explorers were encountering the indigenous populations of foreign lands. The image of the noble savage, which is frequently invoked today by opponents of globalization, is largely drawn by

matching the perceived flaws of Western civilization—pollution, consumerism, exploitation, warfare—with their opposites: environmental balance, subsistence economy, fair trade, peace.

A strong sense of reverse ethnocentrism can be experienced by the children of immigrants, who may turn their backs on their parents' cultural roots in an attempt to fit into their adoptive culture. Children of families that have immigrated to the West can be bombarded by messages implying that the cultural ideal is not their own, not the one of their parents or grandparents. When these first-generation Canadian children achieve positions of linguistic power by having 'better English' than their parents, and when peer pressure makes them want to be like 'real Canadian' children, preteens, and teens, they can easily succumb to reverse ethnocentrism.

Cultural Relativism

Cultural relativism, which is an approach to studying the context of an aspect of another culture, can be spoken of as existing at two levels. One is the level of **understanding**. Because of the holistic nature of culture, because everything is connected in a system, no single thing can be understood outside of its social, historical, and environmental context. Every aspect of culture has strings attached. Just as you can't understand a single part of a car without understanding the system of which it is a part, so you must understand aspects of culture within their cultural context.

Unlike what Spock used to say in the original *Star Trek*, logic (as a pure entity) does *not* dictate. Logic is a cultural construct. Each culture has its own cultural logic. Any explanation of a cultural practice or belief must in some way incorporate this logic. This is especially important in medicine. Western medicine is dominated by a kind of ethnocentric logic that states that nothing worth knowing comes from non-Western traditions. Yet in order to cure or to heal, it's important to respond to the way the patient envisions the healing process. This point comes across with striking clarity in the award-winning book *The Spirit Catches You and You Fall Down: A Hmong Child, Her American Doctors and the Collision of Two Cultures*, by Anne Fadiman (1997). The book shows American doctors and nurses failing to respect, among other things, the Hmong people's spiritual connections to medicine, the importance of encouraging their belief that a cure is available, and the role this belief plays in the curing process.

The second—and more contested—level at which cultural relativism operates is that of *judging*. One viewpoint suggests that individuals should not be judged by the practices of their culture. They have relatively little choice in what they do. After all, they no more invented those customs that might be objectionable than they invented their more laudable practices. Consider the Maasai, an African people with a strong warrior tradition, who have a custom in which boys, at the onset of puberty, are circumcised. It is frightening and painful, but it is an important initiation ceremony: only once he has gone through the ceremony is a Maasai boy treated as a man, and permitted to have sex with women. It is easy for Canadians to judge this custom negatively, to be critical of those who perpetuate what they consider a cruel and barbaric ritual. But is that right?

Cultural Relativism, Ethnocentrism, and Smell: Two Stories

Our senses are conditioned to a certain extent by our culture. Our perception of beauty is affected by culture. Many North Americans have a skinny model (or skinny models) in their minds when they think of female beauty. And, if sales and commercials are anything to judge by, they set a great deal by the whiteness of a person's teeth. What we hear as either 'music' or 'noise' is conditioned by our experience. Our ears are not totally our own. The same applies to our noses.

Describing his experience working in the Peace Corps, an organization of volunteers working in developing countries, Tom Bissell noted how difficult he found it to share a bus in the central Asian country of Uzbekistan with people who were overdressed for the weather, and smelly. He made the following observation:

Is this model beautiful? What characteristics are meant to appeal to a North American perception of beauty? Are these characteristics universal? (iStockphoto)

In Our View
A Sociologist Sees Beauty in Taiwan: Reverse Ethnocentrism

It was my first trip to Asia, and not a moment passed when I wasn't aware I was no longer in Canada. The streets of Taipei, capital of Taiwan, buzzed with the sound of scooters; small feral dogs roamed the sidewalks; rooftop gardens crowned many of the buildings with lush greenery; and everywhere my whiteness drew gawks and stares from the locals. A group of school kids in the museum pointed to me more often than to the exhibits. A young girl, brimming with fragile self-confidence, walked up to me, and with her best English looked at the painting I was viewing and said, 'Beautiful, isn't it?'

I think it was late, the third night we were there, that we decided to go to the Shilin night market, where food and clothing is sold at hundreds of stalls. For a special price, you could have the tourist special: 'freshly killed snake'. Being over 200 pounds (*well* over), I often find it hard to get appropriately sized clothes in Canada, and in the night market, where I was something of a curiosity because of my size, it was even more difficult. It was fascinating, nevertheless, to visit the clothing stalls, where entire families would be there to encourage me to buy from their family stall.

During the tour I saw something strange, and my sociological spider senses began to tingle. After noting it once I started to look for it, and I saw it again and again. The mannequins in the clothing stalls were modelled after Europeans. I did not see one 'Chinese' man-

A mannequin displays current fashions in a shop in Toronto's Chinatown. What culturally loaded ideas of beauty does this mannequin teach you? (Bill Ivy/Ivy Images)

When I was in the Peace Corps, one of my least favorite things was when my fellow volunteers complained about Central Asian body odor, even though most people in Central Asia did indeed smell really bad. But Gandhi probably smelled bad. Surely Abraham Lincoln smelled, as . . . did . . . King George, and Henry IV. William Shakespeare was, in all likelihood, rank. . . . Most certainly Jesus and Julius Caesar and the Buddha all smelled terrible. People have been smelly for the vast majority of human

nequin, either there or anywhere I went the entire week-and-a-half I was in Taiwan.

What does a sociologist make of this? While I was in Taipei I read an article in one of the English-language newspapers questioning whether the Taiwanese people admired the West too much. What I had found was an example. Mannequins, which I believe set the standard for beauty, are in Taiwanese terms 'not us'. Beauty is 'not us'. It couldn't be economics dictating this move. These couldn't be spares for the Western market. They must be for the domestic market.

Then I remembered a beautiful young Italian-Canadian woman, a former student of mine, who made money in Japan as a model. She had remarked to me that she met a good number of White models in Japan. I also remembered reading about how, during the war in Vietnam, South Vietnamese prostitutes would have eye operations on their epicanthic folds (the technical term for the distinctive skin and fat tissue that makes most Asian people distinctive) to make themselves look 'more White'. I thought of Japanese animé characters with big eyes—Sailor Moon comes first to mind.

Are these examples of 'beauty is not us', of a prevailing belief that standards of beauty come from another culture, of reverse ethnocentrism? I think so, but some of my students do not agree with me (particularly the White students, which is interesting in itself). What do you think?

—J.S.

What do you think?

1. What was the example of reverse ethnocentrism that the writer alleged existed in Taiwan?
2. To what standard did this relate?
3. Do you think that Canadians sometimes subscribe to reverse ethnocentrism?

history. By gooping up our pheromonal reactors with dyed laboratory gels, could it be that we in the West are to blame for our peculiar alienation? Might not the waft from another's armpit contain crucial bio-erotic code? Could it be by obscuring such code we have confused otherwise very simple matters of attraction? (Bissell 2003:98)

In a completely different setting, Emma LaRoque, a Métis writer from northeastern Alberta, came to a similar conclusion:

Several summers ago when I was intern-teaching in a northern reserve, one of the teachers told me how she 'had to get used to' the smells of the children. She insisted it was not just stuffiness, but a 'peculiar odor'.

It was a beautiful summer, a summer northern Natives enjoy. There were fishes to be caught and smoked. There was moosehide to be tanned, and as always pesky mosquitoes to be repelled with smudge [smoke]. Oddly enough, the 'peculiar' smell was a redolent mixture of spruce, moosehide, and woodsmoke. All the while this teacher was complaining about the smell of the children, the children reported a 'strange' odor coming from the vicinity of some of the teachers and their chemical toilets. And it never seemed to occur to the teacher that she could be giving off odors.

More to the point, both the teacher and the children attached value judgements to unfamiliar odors. As a friend of mine noted, 'to a person whose culture evidently prefers Chanel No. 5 or pine-scented aerosol cans, moosehide and woodsmoke can seem foreign.' The converse is true, I might add. (LaRoque 1975:37)

As we have seen, ethnocentrism and cultural relativism are opposing ways of looking at cultures (our own and those of others). The former is laden with negative judgement, the latter with a greater appreciation for context in understanding and evaluating culture. This is not to say that everything is relative, or that there are no standards, as some sociology students seem to conclude after learning about the two concepts. Some things, such as female genital mutilation, land mines, and the torturing of political prisoners can be considered universally bad.

The point to take from this is that it's important to realize how easy it is to make an ethnocentric assessment of a different culture. It is also worthwhile to try to understand why dif-ferent cultures do what they do. And, while true appreciation of aspects of other cultures might not always be possible, it is worth the trip to take a few steps down that path.

Sociolinguistics

Sociolinguistics is the study of language as part of culture. Language exists at the centre of communication between individuals and between groups. It is a source both of understanding and of misunderstanding. It is also the main vehicle for transmitting culture, and a culture cannot be understood without some sense of the language(s) spoken and the fit of language with other aspects of culture. Sociolinguistics thus looks at language in relation to such sociological factors as race, ethnicity, age, gender, and region.

Dialect as a Sociological Term

A **dialect** is a variety of a language, a version that is perhaps different from others in terms of pronunciation, vocabulary, and grammar. To the sociologist, the distinction between dialect and language is interesting because it can be as much a product of social factors as of linguistic ones. Dutch and German, for instance, are considered separate languages, although based strictly on linguistic criteria they could be called dialects of the same language. For some German speakers living near the Netherlands, Dutch is easier to understand than dialects of German spoken in Austria or Switzerland. Dialects, unlike languages, are often evaluated according to whether they represent proper or improper, casual or formal, even funny or serious versions of a language; these judgements usually depend on the social status of the dialect's speakers. In Britain, the 'Queen's English' is an upper-class dialect, more highly valued in written and formal communication than are regional dialects like that of the city of Manchester. The latter is often heard spoken by characters of TV shows like *Coronation Street*, where it signifies that the characters using it are 'real people' rather than aristocrats. A current commercial for a Nissan SUV features a voice-over spoken in a Newfoundland accent. The accent here is used to put the audience in a receptive mood by evoking the famed good nature and affability of the people of Newfoundland and Labrador.

Sometimes differences in dialect reflect religious differences. This is generally true for the following dialect pairs:

Table 3.3 >> Religious differences as reflected in dialect: two examples				
LANGUAGE	**DIALECT**	**RELIGION**	**VOCABULARY SOURCE**	**SCRIPT**
Hindustani	Urdu	Islam	Arabic	Arabic
	Hindi	Hindu	Sanskrit	Sanskrit
Serbo-Croatian	Serbian	Orthodox	Old Church Slavonic	Cyrillic
	Croatian	Catholic	Latin	Roman

In such contexts, saying you don't understand someone when they speak can be as much a social as a linguistic commentary.

Linguistic Determinism and Relativity

The relationship between language and culture is usually discussed in terms of the **Sapir-Whorf Hypothesis**, which suggests that linguistic determinism, or causation, exists. In other words, the way each of us views and understands the world is shaped by the language we speak. Like theories of biological or social determinism, the Sapir-Whorf Hypothesis can be cast either as strongly or weakly deterministic—that is, language can be seen to exert either a strong or a weak influence on a person's worldview. We, the writers of this textbook, favour a weak determinism. We feel that linguistic relativity is a valid form of cultural relativity, that exact translation from one language into another is impossible, and that knowing the language of a people is important to grasping the ideas of a people.

Usually when sociologists discuss this topic, they drag out an old example: there are 'x' number of words for 'snow' in Inuktitut, the language of the Inuit (we say 'x' because this number changes); each one differs subtly in meaning from the others and cannot be translated exactly into other languages. That there are so many different words for 'snow' in Inuktitut reflects—supposedly—an important aspect of Inuit experience. Such references to vocabulary are not really very useful in proving the deterministic force or influence of language. They do help to make the point that there are no 'simple' languages with small vocabularies (i.e. vocabularies with less than tens of thousands of words). The Inuit have developed a sophisticated, complicated, large vocabulary without resorting to all the terms that Europeans have for their cultural features. That is important to know in terms of respecting the languages and their speakers, but it does not really help much in discussing relativity.

Noun Classes and Gender

The different noun classes that exist in various languages can reinforce the beliefs they have within their culture. English speakers in Canada have some awareness of difference in noun classes through the presence of gender exhibited by the Romance (i.e. based on Latin, the language of the Romans) languages—French, Italian, Portuguese, Spanish—to which they are exposed. Students struggling through French classes may wonder why every French noun has to be masculine or feminine. Why are the words for 'tree' (*arbre*) and tree species masculine (avoiding any Freudian interpretation), while the parts of trees—roots, leaves, branches, bark, blossoms—feminine?

While it does not have noun classes labelled as 'masculine' or 'feminine', English does have a certain degree of grammatically mandated gender, with our use of *he, him, his*, and *she, her, hers*. Take the following two sentences: *One of my sisters is called Ann. She is younger than I am, and her hair used to be the same colour as mine.* In the second sentence the words *she* and *her* are grammatically necessary but do not add any new information. We already know from the nouns *sister* and *Anne* that the person spoken about is female. English, French, all the **Indo-European** languages, the family of languages that includes almost all the languages of Europe, plus Farsi (Iranian) and the languages of Pakistan and northern India, all impose gender grammatically in some way.

Algonquian languages, which together make up the largest Aboriginal language family in Canada and the United States, have no grammatically mandated gender, either in the French or the English sense. They have no pronouns meaning 'he' or 'she'. They are not alone, nor strange in that respect. In fact, almost every Canadian Aboriginal language does not recognize gender. Interestingly, they share this feature with the non-Indo-European languages of Europe (such as Finnish, Estonian, Hungarian, and Basque). Does this mean, as some sociolinguists have suggested, that Algonquian speakers were traditionally more flexible about gender roles than their European contemporaries, that there was a greater degree of equality between the sexes? The latter was certainly true at the time of contact, but whether that can be related to the absence of grammatical gender in their language is difficult to determine.

In other cases, cultural attitudes are more strongly reflected in language. The Australian Aborigine language **Dyribal** distinguishes four grammatically recognized classes of nouns: males, females, edible fruit (and the plants that bear them), and a final, catch-all category that includes parts of the body, grass, and most trees. Included in the male category are most fish, but not the poisonous stone fish or the sharp-toothed gar fish; these are classified as female. No plants are considered male, but the short list of 'female' plants include two trees with stingers as well as the stinging nettle vine. Most insects are male, but the scorpion is female. You will probably conclude from this pattern that females were not especially well regarded in this culture. But does the language merely reflect the attitudes prevalent in the culture at the time the language developed, or has the language played a role in perpetuating those attitudes?

Questions for Critical Review and Discussion

1. Differentiate the following: *high culture, mass culture,* and *popular culture.*

2. Differentiate the following: *dominant culture, subculture,* and *counterculture.*

3. Differentiate the following: *folkways, mores,* and *taboos.*

4. Identify and give examples of Eurocentrism and ethnocentrism.

5. Contrast the linguistic expectations of speakers of Algonquian and Indo-European languages.

Suggested Readings

Adorno, Theodor W. (1991). *The Culture Industry.* J.M. Bernstein, ed. London: Routledge.

Anderson, Benedict (1983). *Imagined Communities.* London: Verso.

Benedict, Ruth (1934). *Patterns of Culture.* New York: Mentor Books.

During, Simon, ed. (1993). *The Cultural Studies Reader.* London: Routledge.

Geertz, Clifford (1973). *The Interpretation of Cultures.* New York: Basic Books.

Rose, Steven, R.C. Lewontin, & Leon J. Kamin (1984). *Not in Our Genes: Biology, Ideology and Human Nature.* Harmondsworth: Penguin Books.

Suggested Websites

Institute for Intercultural Studies.
http://www.interculturalstudies.org/IIS/index.html

Multicultural Canada.
http://www.pch.gc.ca/progs/multi/evidence/contents_e.cfm/

Postmodern Culture.
http://jefferson.village.virginia.edu/pmc/

Six Nations of the Grand River.
http://www.geocities.com/Athens/Olympus/3808

Socialization

Contents

Key Terms

agents of
  socialization
bar mitzvah
bat mitzvah
behaviourism
bopi
broad socialization
catharsis
confirmation
culture and personality
degradation ceremony
desensitization theory
ego
eros
game stage
generalized others
habitus
id
internalized
longitudinal study
narrow socialization
national character
observational learning
  theory
oversocialized
peer group
peer pressure
play stage
preparatory stage
primary socialization
relations of ruling
reproduction
resocialization
risk behaviour
rite of passage
role taking

secondary
  socialization
significant others
status Indian
superego
swaddling
  hypothesis
tabula rasa
thanatos
total institution
vision quest
warrior frame
XYY males

PART TWO
SOCIAL STRUCTURES

Boxes

In Other Words The Rajputs: Child Rearing and Personality in a North Indian Village
Canadian Sociology in Action Diamond Jenness Learns Exceptions to a 'Rule' of Inuit Family Socialization
In Our View Experiencing Peer Pressure
Sociology in Action Culture as an Agent of Socialization
Sociology in Action The Vision Quest: A Modern Aboriginal Rite of Passage

Learning Objectives

After reading this chapter, you should be able to

- outline and critique the basic ideas of Freud.
- discuss the application of *oversocialization* to the concepts of Mead and Cooley.
- compare and contrast social and biological determinism.
- contrast agency and determinism.
- discuss the roles of various agents of socialization.
- discuss critically the effects of television violence.
- contrast narrow and broad socialization.

For Starters
Resocializing the Mi'kmaq: Two Native Narratives

'I Lost My Talk':
Mi'kmaw Poet Rita Joe

I lost my talk
The talk you took away
When I was a little girl
At Shubenacadie school.

You snatched it away:
I speak like you
I think like you
I create like you
The scrambled ballad, about my word.

Two ways I talk
Both ways I say,
Your way is more powerful.

So gently I offer my hand and ask,
Let me find my talk
So I can teach you about me.

—Rita Joe

Shubenacadie school was a residential school in Nova Scotia, where Mi'kmaq suffered abuse at the hands of the staff, whose goal was to resocialize students by beating their traditional culture out of them, literally if necessary. The abuse is illustrated graphically in the words of another ex-student, anthropologist Isabelle Knockwood, who tells the following story of a little Mi'kmaq girl caught speaking in her native language:

The nun came up from behind her and swung her around and began beating her up. . . . then the Sister pinched her cheeks and her lips were drawn taut across her teeth and her eyes were wide with terror. . . . Then the nun picked the little girl clean off the floor by the ears or hair and the girl stood on her tiptoes with her feet dangling in the air . . . The nun was yelling, 'You bad, bad girl.' Then she let go with one hand and continued slapping her in the mouth until her nose bled. (Knockwood 1992:97)

The Shubenacadie Residential School. (Photo © Sisters of Charity, Halifax; Congregational Archives image #1693B)

Introduction

Socialization is an area of sociological study that brings the discipline close to psychology. The intersection of sociology and psychology is evidenced in this chapter by the fact that a good number of the socialization theorists are psychologists. Socialization is a learning process, one that involves development or changes in the individual's sense of self. This applies both in the first socialization that a child receives, generally known as **primary socialization**, and in socialization that occurs later in life, which is sometimes known as **secondary socialization**.

Determinism

Any discussion of socialization needs to address the issue of determinism versus free will, and biological determinism versus social determinism. When we speak of **determinism**, we are talking about the degree to which an individual's behaviour, attitudes, and other 'personal' characteristics are determined or caused by a specific factor. There are 'hard' and 'soft' versions of determinism, the former claiming that we are in essence programmed by our biology or our culture, the latter leaving some room for free will or the exercise of **agency** in one's life. Agency involves personal choice above and beyond the call of nature or nurture.

Biological Determinism

Biological determinism (representing 'nature' in the old 'nature *vs* nurture' debate) states that the greater part of what we are is determined by our roughly 26,000 genes. Biological determinism has become a popular subject of discussion and debate in the mainstream media, owing in large part to the rise of human genetic research generally and, in particular, the **Human Genome Project**, which involves a painstaking count of the number of genes we have and investigation into what each of those genes actually codes for.

Certain abilities seem to fall into the 'nature' category. We observe some people being 'naturally good' (or 'naturally bad') at sports, music, art, and so on. However, we have to be very careful in making even tentative statements about biological determinism. A notorious research study into the **XYY males** that began in 1962 provides a cautionary tale. Males are genetically XY in their chromosomes, females XX. The first studies were done by looking at the populations of hospitals for dangerous, violent, or criminal patients with emotional/intellectual problems, first in England, then in the United States and Australia. A certain percentage of the men were found to be XYY, and the 'criminal gene' was hastily declared. The problem was that the researchers had neglected to study non-criminals. When the study was extended to the general population, they discovered that roughly the same percentage (about one in 1,000) were XYY. There remained some well-documented associations of XYY males with above-average height, with a tendency to have acne, and with somewhat more impulsive and antisocial behaviour and slightly lower intelligence, but it is impossible to conclude that XYY males are genetically determined criminals.

Softer forms of biological determinism focus on predispositions (for shyness, for aggressiveness, etc.) that people have. These findings tend to have a stronger foundation than the '*We have found the gene for _____*' hard determinism that sometimes makes the news. What we are comes from too complex a mixture, even too close a genetic mixture, for one gene to be an absolute determinant of behaviour or personality.

Social or Cultural Determinism: Behaviourism

Behaviourism is a school of thought in psychology that takes a strong cultural determinist position. It emphasizes the causative power of learning in the development of behaviour. For the behaviourist, social environment is just about everything, while nature and free will count for very little. One cautionary statement about this school of thought is that much of the research on which it is based involves non-human animals: Pavlov and his dogs, Thorndike and his cats, B.F. Skinner and his rats and pigeons. One unkind nickname for the school is 'rat psychology'. If you were a fan of the television shows *Cheers* and *Frasier*, you would recognize that Frasier Crane's ex-wife, Lilith, was a caricature of a behaviourist. Critics say that the theory disallows the existence of choice, of agency, even for a dog, pigeon, or rat.

One of the earliest principles developed in behaviourism is the **Law of Effect**, introduced by **Edward Thorndike** (1874–1949) in his book *Animal Intelligence* (1911). The Law of Effect has two parts. The first one says that if you do something and it is rewarded, the likelihood of your doing it again increases. The behaviour is said to be **reinforced**. On the other hand, according to the second part, if you do something and it is punished or ignored, then the likelihood of your doing it again decreases. It boils down to the idea of the carrot (reward) and the stick (punishment). Accordingly, if the screaming child in the grocery store lineup is given a chocolate bar to be quiet, the reward reinforces the screaming—expect it to happen again.

There are debates about what constitutes a reward for an individual, and about what behaviour is or is not being rewarded. For example, if you punish a child who is acting out in school by making her sit in the corner, and the objectionable behaviour persists, could it be that she sees the 'punishment' as a reward? Is she getting attention, and is that her goal? If you pick up a baby who is crying, does that teach him that he can get anything he wants by crying? Or, does it reward communication, which, once he learns to speak, becomes words and not tears? Attempting to change someone's behaviour using this kind of approach is called **behaviour modification**.

Hard social determinism claims that just about any behaviour can be taught and learned. A powerful expression of this view comes from **John B. Watson** (1878–1958), the founder of behaviourist psychology, who, in his book *Behaviorism* (1925), declared:

A pigeon in a Skinner box. Behaviourism asserts that behaviour is the product of stimulus and response. Are human beings simply the byproduct of their interaction with the environment? (Photo by Robert W. Allan; reprinted with permission)

Give me a dozen healthy infants, well-formed, and my own specific world to bring them up in and I'll guarantee to take any one at random and train him to become any type of specialist I might select—a doctor, lawyer, artist, merchant, chief, yes even a beggarman and thief, regardless of his talents, penchants, tendencies, abilities, vocations, and the race of his ancestors. There is no such thing as an inheritance of capacity, talent, temperament, mental constitution and behavioral characteristics. (Watson 1925:82)

It is hardly surprising that a person who felt that manipulating humans was so easy would (after being fired for having an affair with his laboratory assistant) become involved in advertising—selling, among other things, baby powder (by playing on the guilt of young mothers)—as well as in writing articles for the popular media.

Sigmund Freud: Balancing the Biological and the Socio-Cultural

The thinking of **Sigmund Freud** (1856–1939), father of psychoanalysis, involves socialization and the balancing of biological and social aspects of human personality. He believed the mind had three parts. Think of it as a team of three players: the id, the superego, and the ego. The first two are the most involved with socialization. The **id** is motivated by two **i**nstinctive **d**rives (or **i**nner **d**emons, for those who have a difficult time remembering which of Freud's players is which) that we are born with as part of our unconscious mind: eros and thanatos. **Eros** (related to the word 'erotic') is the drive that tends to be stressed by Freud's fans and critics (and Freud, to be fair). It is a 'life drive' or instinct that involves pleasure, particularly—but not exclusively—sexual pleasure. **Thanatos**, the less celebrated of the two drives (at least by TV pundits and pop psychologists) involves a 'death drive', an instinct for aggression and violence.

The **superego**, also part of the unconscious, is your conscience. It takes in the normative messages of right and wrong that your parents, family, friends, teachers, and other socializing agents give you, and internalizes them (i.e. adopts them as a personal moral code). Picture, if you have trouble remembering this one, a caped crusader with a big 'S' on his chest, saying 'Don't hit your sister or want to have sex with your mother—that's wrong!'

Needless to say, id and superego often come to blows in conflict that can take years of psychotherapy to resolve. If one is too strong, the individual is either too unrestrained or too controlled. The **ego**, meanwhile, mediates between the conscious and unconscious while trying to make sense of what the individual self does and thinks. It can interpret well if the individual is aware of what is going on in his or her unconscious with information from dream analysis, talks about childhood, inkblot tests, hypnosis, and Freudian slips ('Today, we are going to learn about Sigmund Fraud'). If it is weak or lacks self-awareness, there will be serious problems.

The article by Dennis H. Wrong discussed in the following section began with the insights of Freud, who, like Wrong, would not have thought that socialization could control the individual.

Agency

Canadian sociologist Dennis H. Wrong, in an important article entitled 'The Oversocialized Conception of Man in Modern Sociology' (1961), stressed the importance of not seeing humans as passive recipients of socialization programming. His point was similar to the argument we made in Chapter 3: just as the culture and symbols of a society can be contested—that is, spark disagreement among groups or individuals about the nature of the former and the meaning of the latter—so, too, do individuals contest their socialization. Wrong didn't actually use the word *contest*, but he did argue that people do not naturally conform to the lessons of their socialization, automatically doing what the socializing agents of parents, peers, and media dictate. They can decide to be different, to resist their

Sigmund Freud (Archives of the History of American Psychology—The University of Akron)

socialization. This was an important point to make at the end of the 1950s, a time of relatively great conformity to norms in North America. It remains important in the branding days of the twenty-first century, when advertisers try to socialize children at younger and younger ages into social acceptance through their products. It's also worth considering this point in terms of the debate, discussed in the last chapter, between proponents of mass culture (who see individuals as passive recipients of cultural messages) and of popular culture (who view individuals as having a role in interpreting culture).

Luis M. Aguiar, who teaches sociology at Okanagan University College in British Columbia, offers another view of the conflict between agency and socialization. Born on the island of São Miguel in the Azores, off the coast of Portugal, Aguiar experienced the 'working-class socialization' of his parents, who encouraged him to adopt a trade rather than pursue a post-secondary education. The very idea of finding a 'career' was incomprehensible to Aguiar's parents (187–8). They considered boys who preferred mental to physical work 'sexually suspect' and 'unmanly', and Aguiar's father even supplied him with examples of men who 'became insane as a result of too much reading and studying' (180).

Ultimately Aguiar did go to university, demonstrating agency by overcoming his parents' attempts to socialize him into entering a trade. However, he was not unaffected by their efforts, which left him with feelings of guilt since he could not, because of his long-term education, help provide for the family until relatively late in life:

> Today I still feel terribly guilty because of my selfish educational pursuits that deprived my parents from owning a home or car or having some higher level of comfort in their retirement years. My parents never complained about my lack of financial contribution to the family, but my sense is that they are extremely disap-

pointed at not achieving the immigrant dream of owning their own home. To my mind, only immigrant students of working-class background feel this heavy load of class guilt. (Aguiar 2001:191)

Agents of Socialization

In the case of Luis Aguiar, his parents were among the most influential **agents of socialization**—the groups having a significant impact on his socialization. Among the various agents of socialization that can affect an individual, seven readily come to mind:

- family
- peer group
- neighbourhood/community
- school
- mass media
- the legal system
- culture generally

The impact of each of these agents is severely contested, both in the sociological literature and in the day-to-day conversations of people in society.

Significant Other, Generalized Other, and Sense of Self

The American psychologist and philosopher George Herbert Mead, introduced as a symbolic interactionist in Chapter 1, developed a twofold categorization of agents of socialization: significant other and generalized other. He believed that children develop their sense of self from being socialized by the 'others' in their lives. They **internalize** norms and values they observe, incorporating them into their way of being.

Significant others are those key individuals—primarily parents, to a lesser degree older siblings and close friends—whom young children imitate and model themselves after. Contrary to common usage, your spouse is not really your sole significant other. Somewhere in your mind right now there should be a picture of a mother or father doing yardwork with a young child imitating the practice (e.g., using a toy rake for clearing leaves). Later on the child comes under sway of **generalized others** and begins to take into account the attitudes, viewpoints, and general expectations of the society she or he has been socialized into. In Freudian terms, we would say that the individual's superego had internalized the norms of society.

Mead had a developmental sequence for socialization. It begins with what he called the **preparatory stage**, which involves more or less pure imitation. The next sequence is the **play stage**, where pretending is involved. The child at this stage engages in **role taking**, assuming the perspective of significant others and imag-

ining what those others are thinking as they act the way they do. The third stage is the **game stage**, in which the child considers simultaneously the perspective of several roles. In terms of baseball, for example, this is when a child, fielding the ball as a shortstop, might be able to consider what the runner and the first baseman are thinking and doing.

Significant others and generalized others continue to exert strong socialization influences later on in the life of an individual, with significant consequences for the individual's self-concept. Mentors and other role models can become important significant others for the adolescent or adult individual. Later still, a generalized other may be a social group or 'community' that has an impact on the individual's

Childhood socialization involves imitation, role playing, and role anticipation. Would you be surprised if the children in the photo were a little boys rather than little girls? (Photo © Angela Aujla)

sense of self. Think of television commercials. Whenever a star athlete, a famous actor, or any other major celebrity is chosen to endorse a product, the marketing team behind the advertising is banking on the fact that the person will be viewed as a significant other by the group the product is being marketed to. When an Old Navy commercial presents a group of young, attractive, and well-dressed people dancing and having a good time, the advertising agency is trying to tell you that this is what your cool, young community likes, and you should too.

Another symbolic interactionist, and a colleague of Mead's, **Charles Horton Cooley** (1864–1929) put forth the idea of the **looking-glass self**. This is a self-image based on how a person thinks he or she is viewed by others. In Cooley's poetic words, 'each to each a looking glass / Reflects the other that doth pass' (in Marshall 1994:374). The looking-glass self has three components:

(1) how you imagine you appear to others;
(2) how you imagine those others judge your appearance; and
(3) how you feel as a result (proud, ashamed, self-confident, embarrassed).

A good example of this is the relationship between body image and self-esteem, especially in young women. Harvard educational psychologist and respected feminist thinker Carol Gilligan noted how the self-esteem of girls falls during their teenage years (Gilligan 1990). Studies show that this happens more with girls and young women than with boys. The harsher standards of body type that we apply to women has rightfully been associated with this difference in self-esteem.

Mead's and Cooley's ideas are very much like those of behaviourism, in that they exaggerate the influence of the social environment and downplay the role of individual input into the construction of self. Wrong would speak of their sense of self as 'oversocialized'. However,

by taking a less deterministic approach to these symbolic interactionist ideas, we can find some interesting aspects about the role the environment plays in shaping behaviour.

Family

The family is the first agent of socialization, and often the most powerful one. It is important to recognize that just as the family is different across cultures, so are the means and goals of the family in socializing the child. Consider the means and goals as they are outlined in the narrative on page 105. It comes from research on the Rajput community of Khalapur in North India, carried out by anthropologist John T. Hitchcock (1917–2001) and social psychologist Ann Leigh Minturn (1928–1999) in the early 1960s. Their work was part of a classic study of cross-cultural socialization, Beatrice Whiting's *Six Cultures: Studies of Child Rearing* (1963).

Socialization and Culture: Inuit Socialization as Morality Play

In her book *Inuit Morality Play: The Emotional Education of a Three-Year-Old*, psychological anthropologist Jean Briggs records the findings of her intense six-month study of an Inuit toddler, a little girl she called Chubby Maata, in the Baffin Island community of Qipisa, a year-round camp of about sixty Inuit. She paid particular attention to how Chubby Maata's mother and other caregivers engaged in the process the Inuit call *issummaksaiyuq*, meaning 'cause (or cause to increase) thought' (Briggs 1998:5). They did this by challenging the child with difficult questions like 'Are you a baby?' and 'Who do you like?', and by prefacing instructions and explanations with the phrase 'Because you are a baby . . .'. They would also use commands such as 'Say "ungaa" [a term closely associated with baby-talk]'.

Briggs called these techniques 'morality plays', borrowing the term for the medieval drama in which the characters—personifications of abstract qualities—delivered lessons about good conduct and character. Chubby Maata's

In Other Words
The Rajputs: Child Rearing and Personality in a North Indian Village

Although Rajput infants will be picked up and attended to when they are hungry or fussing, for the most part they are left in their cots, wrapped up in blankets. . . . Except for anxieties about a baby's health, it is not the centre of attention. A baby receives attention mainly when it cries. At that time, someone will try to distract it, but when it becomes quiet, the interaction will stop. Adult interaction with babies is generally aimed at producing a cessation of response, rather than stimulation of it. Infants and children of all ages are not shown off to others. . . . Children are also not praised by their parents, who fear that this will 'spoil' them and make them disobedient.

Rajput children . . . are never left alone, yet neither are they the center of interest. The child learns that moodiness will not be tolerated. Few demands are put on Rajput children; they are not pressured or even encouraged to become self-reliant. Weaning, which generally occurs without trouble, takes place at two to three years; but if the mother does not become pregnant, a child may be nursed into its sixth year. There is no pressure for toilet training. . . . Babies are not pressured, or even encouraged to walk. They learn to walk when they are ready,

and mothers say they see no reason to rush this. . . . Village women do little to guide children's behavior by explaining or reasoning with them. There is also little direct instruction to small children. Small children learn . . . the customs and values of the group through observation and imitation. In the first five years of life, the child moves very gradually from observer to participant in village and family life.

. . . [C]hildren are not encouraged in any way to participate in adult activities. The chores a child is given are mainly directed to helping the mother. . . . There is little feeling that children should be given chores on principle in order to train them in responsibility. . . . Rajput children take little initiative in solving problems by themselves. Instead, they are taught whom they can depend on for help in the web of social relations of kin group, caste, and village. . . . Although chores increase somewhat as the child gets older, it is not a Rajput custom to require children to work if adults can do it. Children are not praised for their work, and a child's inept attempt to do an adult job is belittled. Thus children are reluctant to undertake what they cannot do well.

—J.T. Hitchcock & A.L. Minturn

What do you think?

1. How would this be interpreted by a behaviourist?
2. What values are being taught with this form of socialization?

caregivers used these techniques to teach Chubby Maata important social lessons such as the difference between -kuluk ('charming, lovable') and -silait ('undesirable, foolish') baby

behaviour, while slowly encouraging the child to grow out of being a baby. Their teaching was directed towards helping Chubby Maata develop the personal characteristic called ihuma or *isuma* (the first element of the word *issummak-saiyuq*), which relates to strong self control. This is a quality that, as Briggs argued in an earlier work (Briggs 1970), is a prized trait in adults.

What do you think?

1. How is this family socialization different from that found among the Rajputs?

2. Why might the two cultures socialize their children differently?

Culture and Personality

It is reasonable to argue that the impact of family socialization in its different forms has been over-emphasized since is became a source of interest to sociologists. During the first half of the twentieth century, sociology as well as anthropology and psychology was involved with what is called the **culture and personality** school of thought. The culture and personality school attempted to identify and describe an idealized 'personality or personality type' for different societies, both small and large, and attach to it a particular form a family socialization. During World War II and in the early years of the Cold War standoff between the United States and the USSR, the scope of these studies broadened to examine **national character**, the personality type of entire nations. David Riesman's *The Lonely Crowd: A Study of the Changing American Character* (1950) is an example of this. These studies typically drew conclusions about how the primary socialization of child raising is linked with the country's national character.

An illustrative example is *The People of Great Russia* (1949), in which authors Geoffrey Gorer and John Rickman proposed the **swaddling hypothesis**. They identified moodiness as a supposedly typical Russian character trait, citing extremes of controlled and out-of-control behaviour (evidenced, for example, in intense alco-

holic binging), and attributed it to the fact that the country's people were tightly swaddled—wrapped up—as infants. Similar theories were proposed for the Germans and the Japanese (see, for example, Ruth Benedict's *The Chrysanthemum and the Sword*, 1946). Needless to say, theories that attempt to generalize about such large populations are extremely difficult to prove.

The swaddling hypothesis and studies attempting to link child socialization practices to national character could very well be sitting on the dusty shelf of old theories that no longer affect us if it weren't for a persistent preoccupation with trying to understand overarching personality traits of certain populations. Since September 2001 there has been much focus in the media and even among American political and military leaders on the 'Arab mind'. In fact, Raphael Patai's book of this very title, first published in 1973 and revamped in 1983, was reprinted in 2002. Each edition has sold well, and *The Arab Mind* is currently enjoying considerable influence in upper military circles in the United States. It replicates all the excesses of the national character study publications, both by oversimplifying the psychological makeup of very sociologically diverse peoples (for instance, portraying them all as lazy and sex-obsessed) and by tying that broad portrait to overgeneralized childraising practices (a significant portion of the book is devoted to, in the words of the publisher, 'the upbringing of a typical Arab boy or girl'). As one critic writing on a Muslim website says,

It is hard to see how Patai's findings can apply equally to a Saudi prince and a Tunisian fisherman, to a Libyan Bedouin (a nomad in the desert) and a Kuwaiti commodities-broker, to an Egyptian soldier and Moroccan 'mulla', to a wealthy Palestinian businessman in Qatar and an impoverished Palestinian migrant-worker from Ghazzah, to a child who is growing up in the hills of Syria and the one doing so in coastal Yemen, to a woman who is an executive director of the Cairo museum and one who farms field in northern Iraq, to a Marxist in Aden and a Christian in Beirut, a 'muadhdhin' in Marrakesh and a musician in Muscat, and so on. (www.Muslimmedia.com)

Different cultures do socialize their children differently, but it is important to remember that in no culture is there complete uniformity of socialization. Think of the arguments made for and against 'spanking' or 'corporal punishment' that appear in Canadian newspaper editorials and letters to the editor. This is no different from what we know about cultures generally. We know that our own culture is not uniform, yet we easily slip into thinking that other cultures are different in that regard. The Arctic anthropologist Diamond Jenness was guilty of making this assumption in his observation of Inuit child socialization, discussed in the box below.

Canadian Sociology in Action
Diamond Jenness Learns Exceptions to a 'Rule' of Inuit Family Socialization

Early in his career of studying Northern populations, Diamond Jenness was told by his predecessor Viljamhar Stefansson that an Inuit child was considered the reborn soul of an ancestor or recently deceased family member, and that the older soul became the infant's guardian spirit, or *atka*. According to Stefansson, this belief influenced the way Inuit raised their children. As quoted by Jenness in his diary:

> The atka protects the child, guarding it from harm. A little child is wiser than an adult person, because its actions are inspired by its atka—the wise old man or wise woman who died. Consequently a child is never scolded or refused anything—even a knife or scissors. (Stuart Jenness 1991:7)

Perhaps as the tenth child of fourteen, Jenness had a hard time accepting that the latter statement could be true, because he would soon come to challenge the point. On 5 October 1913, he made the following observation:

> The boy was allowed to play with the scissors or anything else that caught his fancy. He had his father's watch and began to hammer it on the floor; the father remonstrated very mildly. (Stuart Jenness 1991:14)

The son of a watchmaker, Jenness must have found this incident particularly upsetting, since he refers to watches later on in his account.

Two days later, Jenness wrote about a young boy being called father 'apparently on the "atka" theory' (1991:17). By 25 November of that year, he was directly criticizing Stefansson's theory:

> I noticed the children were scolded several times, and twice slaps were administered severe enough to make them cry—which contradicts what Stefansson told me. (1991:63)

Three days later he develops his criticism further:

I have been watching their treatment of the children rather closely, in view of what Stefansson told us on September 27th. It is true that they are allowed to play with many things—scissors, watches, etc, which a European child would never be allowed; it is true to that their whims and caprices are often humoured and given way to; but it is not true—with these two families at least—that they are never scolded or slapped, nor that they are invariably allowed to have their own way. (1991:67)

Jenness's entry for 1 December brings more critical comment. The violence of the imagery is perhaps telling:

Stefannson's theory about little children never being hit received its death blow as far as these families are concerned. Aksiatak's baby boy (about 15 months old) was tugging at Pungashuk's hair. . . . Aksiatak hit him lightly two or three times with the stem of his long pipe, then as he [the child] did not let go, he struck him a sharp knock, which made him run screaming to his mother. Aluk's wife Qapqana also gave her son a slap, which made him cry. (Stuart Jenness 1991:70–1)

Even after the 'death blow', there is one more hit, on 11 December. It is noteworthy that Jenness criticizes not just Stefansson with this statement but also any notion that children should be treated with a light hand. His reporting betrays some cultural bias, especially with his use of the word 'deserved':

Pungasuk received rather deserved punishment this evening—three slaps as hard as Aluk's wife could inflict. Aksitak's little boy was worrying him so he gave him a slap which made him cry. Stefansson's dictum about little children not being punished does not apply here in the least. (Stuart Jenness 1991:81)

Do these episodes add up to sufficient evidence to contradict Stefansson's theory?

Peer Group

An important agent of socialization is the **peer group**, a social group sharing key social characteristics such as age, social position, and interests. It is usually used to talk about children and adolescents of the same age. In some societies the peer group of children is more formally recognized than in others. For example, among the Mbuti pygmies of the central African country of Zaire, as studied during the mid-twentieth century by anthropologist Colin Turnbull, the social world of the **bopi**, or children's playground, was almost exclusively the territory of children from the age of three to puberty, with adults and teenagers made to feel unwelcome.

The term **peer pressure** refers to the social force exerted on an individual by his or her peers to conform in behaviour, appearance, or externally demonstrated values (i.e. not appearing excited about something that isn't deemed acceptable or 'cool').

A classic sociological study that argues for the influence of the adolescent peer group is Paul E. Willis's *Learning to Labor: How Working Class Kids Get Working Class Jobs* (1977). Willis and his colleagues studied the informal culture of a group of 12 teenage boys attending a working-class, all-male school in the industrial town of Hammerstown, England. The issue Willis addressed was why working-class boys settled for labouring jobs rather than directing their

She shoots, she scores! In women's hockey what type of peer pressure exists on and off the ice? How might girls' hockey affect 'traditional' gender identity? (Photo © M-J Milloy, 2006)

energies to getting the jobs obtained by middle-class kids in their cohort. He believed the boys were not passive recipients, through socialization, of the informal working-class culture. Rather, he speculated, as an act of minority-culture resistance to the dominant culture, they were active participants both in the creation of this culture, with its belief and values systems and rules of behaviour, and in socializing newcomers into the culture. Among the evidence Willis found to support his theory were vocalized disdain for and humour directed against more conformist middle-class peers, ridicule of the 'effeminate' nature of the mind-centred work done in school and in offices, and denunciation of middle-class values in general. The minority-culture resistance also involved manipulating the classroom (by controlling attendance and the level of work done, for example) and educational figures of authority in ways that the youths would repeat in the 'shop floor' environments of factories and warehouses and with the middle-management

What do you think?

1. Did the peer group have the power it did because it was a single-gender school?

2. Did the peer group have the power it did because all of the students were from working-class families?

figures they encountered there. Their classroom behaviour prepared them for their future.

Community and Neighbourhood

Community and neighbourhood can be important agents of socialization on a child. It's one of the reasons parents debate whether they should live in the city or move their family to a town outside the big city where they work. It's also why urban planners are concerned about creating mixed-class city neighbourhoods rather than ghettoizing the poor into government-assisted housing projects. Toronto, for example, is cur-

In Our View
Experiencing Peer Pressure

Growing up, everyone is exposed to peer pressure, and how we respond to the powerful influence exerted by our peer group helps to mould us into the adults we become.

When I was ten, I had a small group of classmates I hung out with. I felt they were 'cooler' than I was, so I was fairly susceptible to peer pressure from them. I pride myself in my independence of thought, action, and appearance, but I certainly didn't show those characteristics then. I was up for anything they suggested, even when I knew they weren't the wisest things to do. We never did anything seriously wrong. We begged candy from a candy manufacturer and stole candy from a local drug store. We played 'chicken' with trains on the railroad tracks. We threw snowballs at cars passing on the road and apples at cars idling in the local lovers' lane. Peer pressure made me do things I would never have done myself, and you can probably remember petty crimes of your own youth that cause you to blush—or to chuckle—today.

But it's important to recognize that, while leading us to do some pretty silly things, peer pressure plays a vital role in forging personality. Peer pressure hits us hardest when we're insecure adolescents striving for acceptance among people outside our immediate family. By encouraging a degree of conformity, peer pressure helps children develop friendships and find acceptance among others their own age, fostering both self-confidence and independence. I belonged to a class of smart kids culled from various schools in the district, and it was easy to feel separate, different. But through our lunch-hour pranks and hijinx, my classmates and I formed a close circle from which we all gained a sense of belonging. It also gave us a safe place to test norms and values. I don't throw snowballs at passing cars anymore—I figured out then that it wasn't right. And perhaps, by remembering these stories, I will be less likely to judge younger people who do the same things.

—J.S.

rently witnessing the planned change of one of its most notorious housing projects, Regent Park, into a mixed social environment. Studies have shown that youths living outside large cities are at lower risk of becoming involved in crime and drug and alcohol abuse. J.J. Arnett's cross-cultural study of adolescents in Denmark and the United States is one such study showing a correlation between risk behaviour and city size.

Mass Media

The issue of the role mass media plays in socializing young people goes back at least as far as the ancient Greek philosopher Plato, who felt that art (in his day, plays) aroused primal instincts and stimulated violence and lust. Plato's student Aristotle believed that violence depicted in art actually produced among those viewing it an

experience of catharsis, a relief from hostile or violent emotions, leading to feelings of peace.

Does mass media today—through action movies making heroes out of vicious criminals, video games promoting war and crime, and violent TV shows—socialize young people, especially adolescent males, into committing violence, or at least into being desensitized to violence and the pain of others? Or does it provide a safe outlet for pent-up hostile emotions? The two sides of this contentious debate are taken up by contemporary writers in the following excerpts. First, arguing for a link between media violence and criminal activity, are psychologists Brad Bushman and L. Rowell Huesmann:

True, media violence is not likely to turn an otherwise fine child into a violent

Which is more likely: that these boys are becoming desensitized to violence, or that they are ridding themselves of aggression? (© Photodisc)

criminal. But, just as every cigarette one smokes increases a little bit the likelihood of a lung tumor someday, every violent show one watches increases just a little bit the likelihood of behaving more aggressively in some situation. (Bushman and Huesmann 2001:248)

Arguing for the other side is communications professor Jib Fowles, in his controversial book *The Case for Television Violence*:

Television is not a schoolhouse for criminal behavior. . . . Viewers turn to this light entertainment for relief, not for instruction. Video action exists, and is resorted to, to get material out of minds rather than to put things into them. . . . Television violence is good for people. (Fowles 1999:53 and 118)

Having whetted your appetite for the debate, we'll take a closer look at how Huesmann and Fowles arrived at their views.

Huesmann's Longitudinal Studies

Huesmann's pioneering work on the effects of television violence on children involved a **longitudinal study**, which examined data gathered on research subjects over a long period. His first was a 22-year study of 856 youths in New York State. At the beginning of his study the participants were all in grade three, about eight years of age. Huesmann followed up by looking at them again when they were 19, and then again at 30 (Huesmann et al, 1986). For male subjects, the relationship between viewing television violence and engaging in aggressive behaviour roughly ten years later was both positive and highly significant—in other words, there was a strong link. These findings were consistent for males of different class, IQ, and level of aggressiveness at the start age. When the subjects were checked again at age 30, the relationship among males between violent television habits and aggressive behaviour—both self-reported and documented in criminal records—was just as strong.

In another major study (2003), Huesmann and his colleagues studied 557 Chicago-area children from grade one to grade four in 1977. Fifteen years later they interviewed as many of them (and their spouses and friends) as they could, and also looked at public records and archival material. They were able to gather reasonably complete data for 329—roughly 60 per cent—of the original research participants (153 men and 176 women, all in their early twenties). The results of this study were similar to those of the earlier study, with the only difference being that the link between TV violence and aggressive behaviour was evident among women as well as among men. The researchers concluded their study with the following statement:

> Overall, these results suggest that both males and females from all social strata and all levels of initial aggressiveness are placed at increased risk for the development of adult aggressive and violent behavior when they view a high and steady diet of violent TV shows in early childhood. (Huesmann, et al. 2003:218)

Huesmann proposed two theories to explain the data. The first one, **observational learning theory**, states that children acquire what he termed 'aggressive scripts' for solving social problems through watching violence on television. The second, **desensitization theory**, states that increased exposure to television violence desensitizes or numbs the natural negative reaction to violence.

Fowles's Defense of Television Violence

Jib Fowles, author of the second statement cited on page 111, argued that sociologists and others who condemn violence on television are really using TV violence as a pretext to tackle other issues: class, race, gender, and generation. He calls television violence a 'whipping boy, a stand-in for other clashes':

> The attack on television violence is, at least in part, an attack by the upper classes and their partisans on popular cul-

ture. In this interpretation, . . . the push to reform television is simply the latest manifestation of the struggle between the high and the low, the dominant and the dominated. (Fowles 2001:2)

Fowles draws upon the work of **Pierre Bourdieu** (1930–2002), a French sociologist, anthropologist, and philosopher best known for his work on the connection between class and culture. In particular, he draws upon two of Bourdieu's key concepts: habitus and reproduction. **Habitus** (related in origin but somewhat different in meaning from the English word 'habits') is a set of socially acquired characteristics, as varied as opinions, definitions of 'manners' and 'good taste', leisure pursuits, ways of walking, and whether or not you spit in public. Each social class has its own set of shared characteristics. **Reproduction**, in Bourdieu's definition, is the means by which classes, particularly the upper or dominant class, preserve status differences between classes. As Fowles phrases it, 'the reproduction of habitus is the key work of a social class' (Fowles 2001:3). In one of his classic works, *La Reproduction* (1970), Bourdieu argued that educational systems reproduce the habitus distinctions of the classes.

Fowles's main point, then, is that sociologists and other academics who condemn television violence are merely fighting proxy wars aimed at reproducing the habitus of the dominant class by condemning the habitus of the dominated class. It is somewhat ironic that he uses Bourdieu's writing to do this, as Bourdieu himself was (1996) a severe critic of television.

What do you think?

1. Do you think that Fowles's arguments are valid?

2. What other criticisms of mass media might be challenged using this kind of approach?

Education

Education can be a powerful socializing agent. For example, schools often are the first source of information that children receive about a social group other than their own. Teachers, curriculum, textbooks, and the social experience of being in the classroom and the playground all play a part. We will focus here on the role teachers play in the socializing function of education.

What we call the *social location* of the teacher—his or her gender, age, ethnicity, and so on—can have an effect on the educational socialization of the student. The fact that the early years of schooling are dominated by female teachers will have a different effect on female and male students. The fact that science and math courses in high school are usually taught by men and English courses by women will also have a different effect on girls and boys. Being of the same ethnic background as the teacher can have a positive effect on a child's socialization experience, as Kristin Klopfenstein points out in her article 'Beyond Test Scores: The Impact of Black Teacher Role Models on Rigorous Math-Taking' (http://utdallas.edu/research/tsp/pdfpapers/newpaper2.pdf) She notes in the introduction to her article that:

> Poor [in terms of income] black students, amongst whom teachers are often the only college-educated people they know, are in particular need of role models who (a) are interested in their educational progress; (b) under the school system as an institution [in the sociological sense of being located in the middle class and more in 'white culture' than in 'black culture']; and (c) actively encourage academic excellence and the pursuit of challenging curriculum. Culturally similar teachers may take more interest in mentoring black students and have more credibility with those students. Given the importance of a rigorous mathematics curriculum and that math is frequently a

Girls do better at language and boys do better at math. In terms of gender differences, how much is the result of our genes and how much is the result of our socialization? (© Imageshop)

> gate-keeper subject for black students [i.e. success in math determines whether or not the will advance to post-secondary education], same-race math teachers play a potentially vital role in preparing black students for their academic and working futures. (Klopfenstein 2)

Klopfenstein's paper looks at the correlation between having a Black math teacher in grade nine and the likelihood that a Black math student will choose to enrol in a more challenging or 'rigorous' math class in grade ten. Her findings, not surprisingly, are that having either male or female Black teachers increases this likelihood, and that Black students have a greater chance of post-secondary entry and success.

Sociology in Action
Culture as an Agent of Socialization

David Elkind is an American sociologist who specializes in investigating some of the negative effects of the ways children growing up in the last 25 years or so have been socialized. In his best-known work, *The Hurried Child: Growing Up Too Fast, Too Soon* (1981, 1988, and 2001), he discusses the effects of the stress on children whose lives have been over-programmed by their parents, with little free time for spontaneous play. He calls this the **hurried child syndrome**. In 2003, he wrote an insightful article, 'Technology's impact', in which he discussed the effects of technology on child growth and development. Addressing the question 'What is it like growing up in a high-tech world, and how does that differ from growing up at an earlier time?', Elkind offers the following response, in which he expresses his concern about how the modern child's comfort with new technology is creating a **generation gap** (a significant cultural and social difference complete with an equally significant lack of understanding between generations):

> Part of the answer lies in the fact that the digital youth has a greater facility with technology than their parents and other adults. As a result, there is a greater disconnect between parents and children

Does technology change social relations and the ways in which children experience everyday life? (Photo © Angela Aujla, 2006)

The socialization effect of having Black teachers does not end there. Klopfenstein quotes P.R. Kane and A.J. Orsini's assertion that 'Teachers of color are important role models to white students, as they shape white students' images of what people of color can and do achieve' (Kane and Orsini 2003:10).

Issues of Socialization

In what follows, we will look at two issues of socialization, both involving adolescents, and both involving a complex combination of agents of socialization.

today, and some adolescents have even less respect for the knowledge, skills and values of their elders than they did a generation ago (hard as that may be to believe). . . .

Independence from parents and adults means greater dependence on peers for advice, guidance and support. The availability of cell phones and immediate access to friends through instant messaging has only exaggerated this trend and quite possibly worsened the divide between children and their parents. (Elkind 2003)

With reference again to the hurried child syndrome, Elkind in this article also expresses his concerns about how children's sense of time has changed. Digital communication enables us to do more, faster, giving us a false feeling that we can accomplish much more than before. We extend this to our children, putting pressure on them to take part in more after-school activities, play more organized sports, do more homework, and learn languages and other academic subjects at an earlier age. This, Elkind feels, adds to the stress and guilt that children feel. We could argue, as well, that this pressure contributes to the sometimes crippling apprehension that post-secondary students feel about deadlines and their career—'I'm 21 and I don't know what I want to be.'

Elkind goes on to talk about how technology is changing the 'traditional culture of children' in ways that may affect personal autonomy and originality:

[The] traditional culture of childhood is fast disappearing. In the past two decades alone, according to several studies, children have lost 12 hours of free time a week, and eight of those lost hours were once spent in unstructured play and outdoor pastimes. In part, that is a function of the digital culture, which provides so many adult-created toys, games and amusements. Game Boys and other electronic games are so addictive they dissuade children from enjoying the traditional games. Yet spontaneous play allows children to use their imaginations, make and break rules, and socialize with each other to a greater extent than when they play digital games. While research shows that video games may improve visual motor coordination and dexterity, there is no evidence that it improves higher level intellectual functioning. Digital children have fewer opportunities to nurture their autonomy and originality those engaged in free play. (Elkind 2003)

Parents reading this are nodding their head, kids are shaking their heads. Can this be considered, at least in part, like Fowles's discussion of media violence: an attack of one generation, growing older and losing power, on the habitus of a younger generation?

What do you think?

How do you think the social location of a teacher might affect a student's socialization. Give some examples. How do you think this might differ for male and female students?

Male Readers

Traditionally, boys do better in mathematics and the sciences, girls do better in writing and reading. Sociologists and educators today recognize that this is partly a result of socialization: boys have always been encouraged more in the former area of study, girls in the latter. In fact, beyond a lack of encouragement, there has been outright discouragement, as girls struggling in these supposedly male subjects have often been told, 'Don't worry, you aren't expected to do well in math,' or even 'You won't need to know it.'

A lot has been done to improve female performance in the 'male preserve' of math and science, including the institution of all-girls classes in these subjects and the conscious promotion of role models such as Roberta Bondar (who, in 1992, became the first Canadian woman in space). On average, boys still tend to perform better in these areas, but the difference has been lessened.

The same cannot be said for male–female differences in performance when it comes to reading and writing, as a 1999 federal government report, based on studies done in 1994 and 1998, makes clear. The following is an excerpt:

Girls score substantially higher than boys in language skills and this gender difference is already pronounced by the age of 13. Boys and girls do not differ in mathematics achievement at the age of 13; however a gender gap in favour of males, particularly in problem-solving skills, seems to emerge by the time students are in their last year of secondary schooling. . . . It appears nevertheless that any gender differences in numeracy are substantially smaller than such differences in literacy. Hence, with respect to skills attainment, by the end of secondary schooling, girls should be in a somewhat better competitive position than boys. (Government of Canada 1999)

This raises a number of questions. To what extent is socialization to blame for gender differences in learning? Which agents of socialization might be having the greatest effect? How might socialization be changed to diminish the gender differences in literacy skills? The following editorial, which appeared in a small-town paper, offered several intriguing suggestions:

BOYS MUST READ TO CATCH UP TO GIRLS?

So boys—are you prepared to let girls be considered smarter than you? Parents—do you know that more boys drop out of high school than girls and fewer attend post-secondary school?

Head Argo coach 'Pinball' Clemons and other Argo players joined Premier Dalton McGuinty and Education Minister Gerard Kennedy last week to publicize these disturbing trends and issue the rallying cry—boys should read more! . . . In his direct and pointed way, Pinball Clemons challenged boys to 'be champions and read to keep learning and having fun.'

Test scores from Ontario and across Canada show that boys lag behind girls in reading and writing. For example, province-wide testing of Grade 6 English-language students in 2003–4 showed only 51 per cent of boys met the provincial standard in reading, compared to 65 per cent of girls. . . .

What to do?

As research shows that positive role models can successfully encourage boys to read, the Argo team members have been enlisted to spread the message publicly. But at home, dads and older brothers can show young boys that they read themselves to keep informed and for pleasure—the newspaper, magazines, work-related manuals and novels.

Make sure your boy has available something he likes to read. Boys often like to read science fiction and fantasy, books with action and humour, and magazines, comic books or even the sports pages of the newspaper. Take him to the library or book-store and encourage him to choose his own reading materials.

Encourage the boy in your family to set aside time for reading every day. If he finds reading a struggle or a chore, try reading to him at bedtime, or alternating chapters; you reading one—him reading the next chapter himself . . .

Some parents even set up some kind of 'reward' system for reading; buying a treat after each book finished, or taking their reluctant reader to a movie based on a book he's just read.

And all parents and teachers can rely on the time-honoured 'negative reinforcement' idea to push boys to read books—they can't possibly want the girls in their class to seem smarter than they are! Get cracking, boys! Cracking open those books! (Caledon Enterprise, 26 January 2005)

What do you think?

1. What agents of socialization are stressed in this editorial?
2. What agents of socialization are not mentioned that should be?
3. What do you consider to be the most important agents of socialization in this matter?
4. What is the role of school in all of this?

Adolescents and Risk Behaviour

One of the leaders in studying the socialization of adolescents is Jeffrey Arnett. A developmental psychologist, he has extensively researched **risk behaviour** (driving at unsafe speeds, unsafe sexual activities, drug and alcohol abuse, etc.) among adolescents. While recognizing the biological component of such behaviour related to 'inherent' individual traits such as egocentrism and sensation-seeking, he stresses the importance of socialization in this area. He makes an important distinction between **narrow socialization** and **broad socialization**, describing them as follows:

> In cultures characterized by *broad socialization*, individualism and independence are promoted, and there is relatively less restrictiveness on the various dimensions of socialization. This allows for a broad range of expression of individual differences on the developmental tendencies (such as sensation seeking) that contribute to risk behavior, and leads to higher rates of risk behavior. Cultures characterized by *narrow socialization*, in contrast, consider obedience and conformity to the standards and expectations of the community to be paramount (enforced through the parents and the school as well as through members of the community), and punish physically and/or socially any deviation from the norm. The result is greater obedience and conformity, a narrower range of expression of individual differences, and low rates of antisocial adolescent risk behavior (although risk-taking tendencies may be directed by such cultures into avenues that serve a culturally approved purpose, such as warfare). (Arnett and Balle-Jensen 1993:1843)

In a cross-cultural study of adolescent socialization, Arnett and colleague Lene Balle-Jensen investigated the effects of socialization on adolescents in Denmark. While that country, like other Western countries, has a tendency towards broad socialization, the researchers noted ways in which Denmark has narrower socialization than the United States and Canada. For example, they cite the fact that the legal age for driving a car in Denmark at the time of the study was 18, reflecting, according to Arnett, narrow socialization elements in the legal system and in the cultural belief system. It reflects, too, a different cultural consensus concerning the balance between ensuring the individual autonomy of the teenager who wants to drive a car and the good of the community, through fewer traffic fatalities and fewer cars on the road. This narrower socialization means, according to Arnett, that in Denmark fewer adolescents engage in the risk behaviour of unsafe driving than in North America.

Another example of Denmark's narrower socialization is community size. As Copenhagen is the only large city in Denmark, Danish children are more likely than North American children to grow up in small cities or towns. The researchers discovered a correlation between larger city size and several types of risk behaviour, including sex without contraception, sex with someone known only casually, marijuana use, cigarette dependency, and shoplifting. However, the United States did show evidence of narrower socialization than Denmark in some areas. For instance, in the US, as in Canada, there was and is a fairly extensive anti-smoking media campaign, unlike anything that existed in Denmark at that time. Denmark has higher rates of smoking among adolescents than does North America.

In the conclusions to this study, the researchers stressed that that there significant agents of socialization (peers, school, neighbourhood/community, the legal system, the mass media, and the cultural belief system) that operate beyond the family.

Resocialization

Resocialization takes place whenever an individual shifts into a new social environment. It typically involves both unlearning and learning. In its extreme form, the individual unlearns all of the behaviours, attitudes, and values that were appropriate to the earlier social environment while learning those that make it possible to fit into the new situation.

A particularly explicit process of unlearning values was experienced by the bestselling religious author Karen Armstrong who, as a teenager in the 1960s, joined a strict order of nuns in Britain. In the following passage she recollects what the Mother Superior said to her and others who had just joined the order as postulants:

> Novices and postulants are kept in a particularly strict seclusion. They may not speak at all to seculars [i.e. to those who are neither nuns nor priests]. If a secular speaks to you, you must never reply. It is only by severing yourself absolutely from the world that you can begin to shed some of its values. Again no novice or postulant may ever speak to the professed nuns unless she is working with them and those few necessary words are essential for the job. The professed are in contact with the world, and even that indirect contact might seriously damage your spiritual progress. . . .

> You have to be absolutely ruthless in your rejection of the world, you know, Sisters. So many of its attitudes, even in really good people, are permeated with selfish values that have nothing at all to do with the self-emptying love of God. You yourselves are riddled with these ideas; you can't help it—it's not your fault. (Armstrong 1981:92–3)

Resocialization can be voluntary or involuntary. Voluntary resocialization occurs when someone starts school or moves to a new school, when someone begins a job with a new company, when someone retires from work, or when someone undergoes a religious conversion (which can also, in extreme circumstances, be involuntary, as with cults). Associated with this kind of resocialization is the **rite of passage**, which is a ritual marking a change of life from one status to another, typically following some form of training. A wedding is a rite of passage; so is a funeral. Other examples include the Christian practices of baptism and **confirmation**, and the Jewish **bar mitzvah** (for boys) or **bat mitzah** (for girls), when adolescents become 'adults in the faith' after a period of instruction.

Involuntary resocialization occurred in Native residential schools, like the one in Shubenacadie discussed at the start of this chapter, where the language, religion, and customs of First Nations children were brutally beaten out of them. Other examples include being drafted into military service, being thrown in jail, being committed to a psychiatric hospital, and being subjected to mandatory retirement. Goffman calls institutions where involuntary resocialization takes place

total institutions (1961), as they regulate all aspects of an individual's life. A significant aspect of the unlearning process associated with involuntary resocialization is what has been termed a **degradation ceremony**, a kind of rite of passage where the person is stripped of their individuality. Hazing, whether of grade nine students, first-year college or university students, or rookies on amateur and professional sports teams, is a degradation ceremony in which being made to perform acts of minor humiliation informs the initiates that they are in a new social world where they are mere beginners.

Sometimes voluntary and involuntary resocialization can occur together. Consider, for instance, programs for treating alcoholism or obesity, which begin with the sufferer's decision to change his or her lifestyle but then involve a strict and rigorous regime that is imposed for the duration of treatment.

'Incorrigible': the Resocialization of Velma Demerson

From 1913 to 1964, thousands of women in Ontario were put into reformatories under the *Female Refuge Act*. Among the 'offences' for which young women (especially teenagers and women in their early twenties) would be placed in these institutions was being sexually active outside of marriage. This kind of behaviour and the women guilty of it were branded 'incorrigible'.

In 1939, Velma Demerson, 18 years old and white, became sexually involved with a Chinese man. They intended to get married. When she became pregnant, her parents reported to the authorities that she was being 'incorrigible'. Velma was arrested and sent first to a 'home' for young girls, then to the Mercer Reformatory. The following is her account of her degradation ceremony:

> I can see that the girls ahead of me in line are getting large cotton dresses, aprons, underwear, white cotton stockings, and

A girl takes part in a college hazing ritual. How likely is it that she went through the mud and the water of her own accord? If given a chance, do you think she would inflict this ceremony on others? (O. Bierwagen/Ivy Images)

black shoes. When my turn comes, I put on a large faded old-fashioned dress. It's extremely wide and reaches my ankles. However, when I put on the full apron with its long ties I can see that it will hold the dress in, making it look like it almost fits. The thick cotton stockings are about two inches too long at the toes but are easily stuffed into the shoes, which are also several sizes too large.

Each girl has quickly been handed a bundle without reference to size. We learn that we can expect to be issued standard Mercer attire in our own size later. What we've been given is the garb provided to all new inmates, to be worn

Sociology in Action
The Vision Quest: A Modern Aboriginal Rite of Passage

A traditional rite of passage for Aboriginal peoples is the **vision quest**, which in the past was confined almost entirely to the passage from being a child to being an adult. After receiving months of informal instruction from elders, the Native individual would embark on a journey away from the home community to an isolated location. Then he or she would fast for days, and possibly go without sleep, in the process of seeking a vision. A vision could be a song that comes to mind, the appearance in dreams of an animal or other spirit who instructs the dreamer and initiates a connection with him or her that will continue until death.

More recently, adults have used the vision quest as a way of resocializing themselves with traditional ideals following a period of difficulty. The following is a generalized example of the Ojibwa vision quest as it has been practised recently in northeastern Ontario (Steckley and Rice 1997:226–7). It begins in a sweat lodge, a dome-shaped structure built around overlapping willow poles, covered with skins or tarpaulin and used as a kind of sauna. The participants throw sacred tobacco on the fire to say thanks to the Creator. They are told the story of how the sweat lodge came to the people from a little boy who was taught about healing from

the seven grandfather spirits. Water is put onto the seven stones that represent those spirits. The Elder sings ceremonial songs.

After the sweat, the participants are led to their own small lodges, where they fast and meditate. The Elder visits them and asks about their spiritual experiences.

The participants fast for three nights and four days. What they learn changes with each night:

The first is described as the night of doubt, where participants pray but are uncertain about what will happen. Hunger is mitigated by a feeling of excitement. The second night is one of fear, sometimes known as the dark night of the soul. Participants realize that their bodies are beginning to weaken, and they may question their resolve. The third night is the night of the spirit. It is often said that if something meaningful is going to happen, it will occur between the beginning of the spirit night until the fast is finished. (Steckley and Rice 1997:226–7)

After the final sweat there is a feast with gift-giving to the Elder and to those who have assisted the individuals in their resocialization.

for the first few weeks. In the months to come we are always able to recognize a new inmate by her initiation clothing. To girls already in a state of anxiety, the code of silence and humiliating dress further the subjugation. We are young women, aware of fashion. We know that large cotton dresses and wide aprons belong

to a past era of drudgery on the farm. (Demerson 2004:5)

Following this, she was led to her cell, which was seven feet long and four feet wide, equipped with one bare light bulb, a cot, a cold water tap and basin, and a covered enamel pail to be used as a toilet.

Questions for Critical Review and Discussion

1. Outline the basic ideas of Freud as they relate to socialization.

2. Outline the basic ideas of Mead and Cooley as they apply to socialization.

3. Differentiate the following: *social determinism*, *biological determinism*, and *agency*.

4. Outline the roles of various agents of socialization.

5. Contrast *narrow* and *broad socialization*.

Suggested Readings

Barthes, Roland (1972). *Mythologies*. London: Paladin.

Davis-Floyd, Robbie, & Joseph Dumit (1998). *Cyborg Babies: From Techno-Sex to Techno-Tots*. New York: Routledge.

Erwin, Lorna, & David MacLenna (1994). *Sociology of Education in Canada: Critical Perspectives on Theory, Research and Practice*. Toronto: Copp Clark Longman.

Freud, Sigmund (1953). *On Sexuality: Three Essays on the Theory of Sexuality and Other Works*. New York: Penguin.

Rousseau, Jean-Jacques (1911). *Émile*. B. Foxley, trans. London: Everyman.

Steinberg, Shirley R., & Joe L. Kincheloe, eds (1998). *Kinder-Culture: The Corporate Construction of Childhood*. Boulder: Westview Press.

Suggested Websites

FreudNet.
http://www.nypsa.org

Jean Piaget Society.
http://www.piaget.org/

Media Studies (College of Education, University of Oregon).
http://www.aber.ac.uk/media/Functions/mcs.html

National Longitudinal Study of Children and Youth.
http://www.statcan.ca/english/research/89-599-MIE/2005002/about.htm

Deviance

Contents

Key Terms

agency
assimilate
bodily stigma
conflict deviance
contested
corporate crimes
covert characteristics
delinquent subculture
dominant culture
hallucination
ideology of fag
marked terms
misogyny
moral entrepreneur
moral stigma
multiculturalism
negative sanctions
non-utilitarian
norm
normalized
occupation crimes
overt characteristics
patriarchal construct
patriarchy
positive sanctions
racializing deviance
racial profiling
reference group
relative deprivation
Other
status frustration
stigma
subculture
tribal stigma
unmarked terms
vision
white collar crimes

PART TWO SOCIAL STRUCTURES

Boxes and Tables

Learning Objectives

After reading this chapter, you should be able to

- avoid some of the leading misunderstandings of the term 'deviant'.
- distinguish between overt and covert characteristics of deviance.
- discuss how deviance can be associated with ethnicity, culture, race, gender, sexual orientation, and class.
- discuss the contested nature of deviance.

For Starters
Gordon Dias (1985–2001)

If deviance involves acting against the values of a society, then perhaps suicide is the ultimate act of deviance. It takes the gift society values most, life, and withdraws all value from it. Explaining this act of deviance has been a part of sociology ever since Durkheim's *Suicide* was published in 1897.

It has been almost four years since my nephew, Gordon Dias, committed suicide at the age of 16. He hanged himself from a tree in front of his high school. As a sociologist, and as his uncle, I need to understand why he did this.

Gordon was a young, single male. This made him part of the social group most prone to suicide. He was on the margins in several ways. He was the youngest of three children, a child whose brother and sister demanded attention by their actions and by their achievements. His older brother was the first-born grandchild and nephew on both sides of the family, a position that brought him ready attention. His older sister is simply brilliant, a very hard act to follow. In my earliest memory of Gordon talking, he is straining to be heard above his siblings.

He was a person of colour, the product of a mixed South Asian and Caucasian marriage, in a very White Canadian city. He was very close to his South Asian grandmother, so much so that when he left home for a while, he went to live with her. It could not have been easy in that city to have made that choice.

He was artistic. It is not easy for a boy to express himself artistically in our culture, not without presenting some counterbalancing signs of macho behaviour. Perhaps that is one reason why he sought the social company he did. According to his parents, my sister and brother-in-law, he had recently been hanging around with guys who regularly got into trouble. This eventually got him into trouble at school, and he was suspended. Zero-tolerance policies don't leave a lot of time for even temporary allegiances with groups of kids who act out. For him, I guess, that was the final piece of the puzzle, and the picture he was left with led him to suicide. He did care enough about his education that he left his only suicide note at school.

There was nothing inevitable about his suicide. Suicide is a personal act. Yet it reflects the society that surrounds the victim.

Gordon Dias, 1985–2001 (Photo © John Steckley)

Introduction: What Is Deviance?

Many people, when they hear the word *deviance*, think immediately of behaviour that is immoral, illegal, perverse, or just wrong. But deviance is better thought of as a neutral term. It means straying from the norm, the usual. It does not mean that the deviant—the one engaging in deviance—is necessarily bad, wrong, perverted, 'sick', or inferior in any way. These could all be qualities that characterize the norm, in which case the deviant is none of these things. Deviance, then, comes down to how we define 'the norm'. It's also about the power of those who share the norm to define and treat others as inferior or dangerous. And we must recognize that just as the norm changes—over time and across cultures, so does deviance.

Revisiting Terms from the Culture Chapter

Understanding deviance depends to a certain extent on concepts or terms learned in the culture chapter. The first is **dominant culture**, the term used for the culture most represented in the media, the one with the most power. As you read through the different sections of this chapter, keep in mind the dominant culture we asserted exists in Canada. It is White, English-speaking, European-based, Christian, male, middle-class, middle-aged and heterosexual. To a certain extent it is true that to differ from the dominant culture is to be deviant in some way.

Another term to revisit here is **subculture**. This is a group within a larger culture, often having beliefs or interests at variance with those of the dominant culture. Albert K. Cohen used this concept in his study of teenage gangs (1955). His model of what he called the **delinquent subculture** combines class and gender. In this model, young lower-class males suffer from a **status frustration**. Failing to succeed in middle-class institutions, especially school, they become socialized into an oppositional subculture in which the values of the school are inverted. For example, the youths engage in delinquent stealing that was primarily **non-utilitarian** (i.e. not done to gain possession of needed objects); rather, the objects are stolen because the act of stealing is respected by peers in the delinquent subculture. Cohen stresses that becoming a member of the delinquent subculture is like becoming a member of any culture. It does not depend on the individual psychology of the individual, nor is it invented or created by the individual. When members grow up and leave the gang (to join adult gangs or mainstream society), the subculture persists. In Cohen's terms:

> [D]elinquency is neither an inborn disposition nor something the child has contrived by himself; that children *learn* to become delinquents by becoming members of groups in which delinquent conduct is

Quick Hits
Getting Deviance Straight

- *Deviant* just means **different from** the norm, the usual.
- *Deviant* **does not mean** bad, wrong, perverted, sick, or inferior in any way.
- *Deviant* is a category that **changes with time, place, and culture**.
- *Deviance* is about **relative quantity** not quality.
- Definitions of *deviance* often **reflect power**.

Some would call this deviance, while others see is as art. What other forms of art might be considered deviant? (Alex Macnaughton/Rex Features)

already established and 'the thing to do'; and that a child need not be 'different' from other children, that he need not have any twists or defects of personality or intelligence in order to become a delinquent. (1955:11–12)

We can use this model to review other terms presented earlier. The **norms** of the subculture—the rules or expectations of behaviour—would be different, as least in part, from those of the main culture. The difference, according to Cohen, comes from inverting of norms. In other words, 'The delinquent's conduct is right, by the standards of his subculture, precisely *because*, it is wrong by the norms of the larger culture' (Cohen 1955:28). Likewise, there is an inverting of the **sanctions**, the reactions to the behaviour of the individuals. The **negative sanctions** of non-gang members—negative reactions to their behaviour—can be seen as **positive sanctions** from the delinquent gang's perspective, and vice versa.

What do you think?

Why can it be misleading to think of a delinquent subculture as being created only by opposition or inversion?

Overt and Covert Characteristics of Deviance

When looking at deviant behaviour it's important to separate the **overt characteristics** of deviance—the actions or qualities taken as explicitly violating the cultural norm—from the **covert characteristics**, the unstated qualities that might make a particular group a target for sanctions. It is like the difference between manifest and latent functions, the first being obvious and stated, the other being hidden and undeclared. Covert characteristics can include age, ethnic background, and sex. In the example about to be presented, the overt characteristics are the zoot suit clothing and hairstyle. The

Sociology in Action
Low-Level Deviance: Violating a Cultural Norm in an Antiques Barn

Sanctions are signs we receive from others to tell us we have behaved in accordance with or in violation of the norms of our culture or subculture. As you'll recall from Chapter 3, sanctions are either positive or negative, and they may be very mild or very strong, depending on how our culture values the norm and how far we've gone to meet or defy it.

On a recent drive in the country, my wife and I approached an old barn where antiques were being sold on commission, and my wife suggested that we go in. 'Antiquing' is not my thing. I don't even like to watch travelling antique shows on television, and I really don't like shopping for long periods of time (unless I'm in a book or drum store). However, I wanted to follow the cultural norm of give-and-take in marriage. We had already spent a good half-hour in a used bookstore earlier that same trip. Not wanting to receive verbal negative sanctions from my wife, I agreed that we should go in.

As we walked around the store, people spoke in whispers about what they thought of specific items and their cost. They were obeying a Canadian cultural norm of politeness or civility in not commenting about how much people were charging for these items.

I, on the other hand, sometimes have a hard time obeying that particular norm. I had behaved myself for about half an hour, but I was getting restless. Then I saw something that I felt demanded my commentary. It was a large, green, jade Buddha statute, and it carried a price tag of $3,000. Now, I have a lot of respect for Buddhism, and I thought that the statue was particularly spectacular. If I had a significantly larger disposable income, and if the statue had been priced decently, I might have bought it. But I don't have such an income, and in my opinion the statue was well overpriced. I might have kept my opinion to myself, but the price had violated a norm of my teacher subculture. I also couldn't help noticing that the vendor had misspelled the name as 'Buddah'. I applied a negative sanction of my teacher subculture and commented loudly about the error. A few people standing next to me looked away and took steps to distance themselves (both of these gestures negative sanctions). Then I began to declaim, to no one in particular, 'Buddah, wasn't he the founder of Budda-hism? I wonder if the person selling this is a Budda-hist?' (You must realize how tired I was at the time.)

The negative sanctions grew. Disapproving stares came from all corners of the room. A kindly faced older gentleman walked up to me and said, 'You know. We can't all be perfect.' He was applying a more direct negative sanction, with the clear intent of stopping my violation of the cultural norm. It was to no avail. I was on a roll. Impressed by my own clever wit, I retorted, 'Ah, but in Budda-hism, one aspires to perfection.' He walked away shaking his head (another negative sanction). For those of you who are counting, that was four different kinds of negative sanction, all of which I ignored.

What do you think?

1. What norm was violated by the author?

2. What negative sanctions were a reaction to the author's violation of the norm?

covert characteristics are age (the groups involved were mostly teens) and ethnicity (they were mostly Latino or African-American).

The Zoot Suit 'Riots' of the Early 1940s: Clothes and Ethnicity as Deviant

An unusual, and yet instructive, instance of deviance labelling and sanction is the case of the 'Zoot Suit Riots' that occurred in June 1943 in Los Angeles. The targets were racialized groups—Black and Latino males—who made convenient scapegoats for wartime tension. In the early 1940s, Los Angeles was undergoing rapid change. The population was growing and its demographics were changing, with large numbers of Mexicans and African Americans coming to the city. Teenagers made up a high percentage of the population, as older men and women were involved in the war effort, and with a surplus of well-paying jobs left available by older brothers and sisters drafted into the military, they had money to spend on music and clothes. These teens—male Latinos and Blacks in particular—adopted a unique style of dress, a distinctive haircut (the 'duck tail', also known as the 'duck's ass' or DA), and a musical style that were countercultural. The music was

jazz, rooted in the African American experience and only slowly gaining acceptance among the conservative elements of the United States. The dancing (the jitterbug) was more sexual than dancing of the 1930s. The clothing was the zoot suit: jackets with broad shoulders and narrow waists, ballooned pants with 'reet pleats', 'pegged cuffs', and striking designs. Zoot suit culture swaggered with a distinctive bold strut and posing stance, and distinguished itself from the older set with a host of new slang words unknown to parents and other adults.

How did zoot suit become deviant? Through the media. The main vehicle was the comic strip *Li'l Abner*, by Al Capp. In a time with no television, comic strips were a major part of popular media, and *Li'l Abner*, with maybe 50 million readers a day, was one of the most popular strips in this golden age. It's difficult to overstate its influence. If you ever attended a high-school Sadie Hawkins dance, when girls could ask out boys, then you've seen a small bit of the influence of *Li'l Abner*.

Al Capp identified the zoot suit as a target for his negative sanctioning humour. From 11 April to 23 May 1943, the strip told the story of the conspiracy of 'Zoot-Suit Yokum' (Yokum was the family name of the character). This

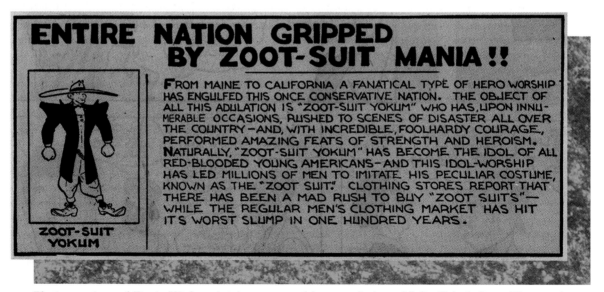

Photo courtesy of Denis Kitchen Art Agency; used by permission of Julie Cairol, Stout Thomas & Johnson NYC

strips portrayed a conspiracy of zoot-suit clothing manufacturers to take over the United States politically and economically. The plan was to create a national figure (Zoot Suit Yokum) who would perform feats of heroism while wearing a zoot-suit. But the hero had to be stupid. A gorilla-looking man with an *H* on his sweatshirt (standing for Harvard—Capp was also anti-intellectual) was an early candidate, but Li'l Abner proved to be even dumber.

This was the fictional birth of 'Zoot Suit Mania', which was soon defeated when the conservative clothing manufacturers found a Li'l Abner look-alike to act in a cowardly way. The triumph of conservative clothiers was proclaimed in the third frame of the 19 May strip, which showed the mock headline 'Governor Issues Order Banning Zoot Suit Wearers!!' (Mazón 1984:35).

Beyond the pages of dailies carrying the *Li'l Abner* comic strip a very real hostility emerged between mainstream society and the zoot suit counterculture. One LA newspaper even ran a piece on how to 'de-zoot' a zoot-suiter: 'Grab a zooter. Take off his pants and frock coat and tear them up or burn them. Trim the "Argentine ducktail" that goes with the screwy costume' (Mazon 1984:76). Whether it was intended with humour or not, instructions for the negative sanctioning of zoot suiters were carried out in a very real way by some of those opposed to the counterculture. The conflict reached a climax in early June 1943, when thousands of young white men—soldiers, marines, and sailors on weekend leave from nearby military installations—launched a campaign to rid Los Angeles of zoot-suiters by capturing them, buzzing their hair down in a military style, and tearing or burning their clothing. Still, as riots go, they were relatively harmless. As Mauricio Mazón points out in his now-classic study of this phenomenon, 'riot' is a bit of a misnomer:

They were not about zoot-suiters rioting, and they were not, in any conventional sense of the word, 'riots'. No one was killed. No one sustained massive injuries.

Property damage was slight. No major or minor judicial decisions stemmed from the riots. There was no pattern to arrests. Convictions were few and highly discretionary. (Mazón 1984:1)

The conflict lasted just under a week, and was brought to an end with two acts. First, the military reined in their troops. More significant, on 9 June, Los Angeles City Council issued the following ban:

NOW, THEREFORE, BE IT RESOLVED, that the City Council by Resolution find that wearing of Zoot Suits constitutes a public nuisance and does hereby instruct the City Attorney to prepare an ordinance declaring same a nuisance and prohibit the wearing of Zoot Suits with reet pleats within the city limits of Los Angeles. (Mazón 1984:75)

Los Angeles police round up zoot-suit suspects, 11 June 1943. Do these zoot-suiters look like troublemakers to you? (Photo © Bettmann/Corbis)

This, the culmination of a series of increasingly explicit and punitive sanctions, shows how humour with a social edge and a large audience can be used against a particular group.

What do you think?

1. Can you see parallels between zoot-suiters and any group today?

2. Why do you think the zoot-suiters were targeted?

The Importance of the Cultural Component in Deviance

It is important to note that what gets termed deviant differs across cultures. Take **vision** in Aboriginal culture. As we discussed in Chapter 4, it is traditional for Aboriginal males and often females at the time of puberty to go on a vision quest. They go off on their own, fast, often go with out sleep in the hopes of having a vision. In this vision, they might learn songs that would give them strength in difficult times. They might find objects that could connect them with spiritual power. And if they were fortunate, they would identify a guardian spirit during the experience. This important rite of passage represents the major step in becoming an adult.

In the dominant culture of North America, the experiences surrounding a vision quest might be considered 'normal' only in specially defined groups like artists (musicians, dancers, writers, and so on) or perhaps Olympic athletes in training. Otherwise the experience might strike members of the dominant culture as suspect and deviant. They might be tempted to characterize the vision as a **hallucination**, an image of something that is not considered to be 'objectively' there. They might want to label the person undergoing the experience as mentally ill. However, it is important to recognize the long-held spiritual significance of the vision in North American Native culture.

Arthur Kleinman warns students of sociology not to fall into the trap of linking what is considered a normal practice in one culture with a similar practice, deemed deviant, in another. He asks his readers to suppose that ten sociologists have interviewed ten different adult Aboriginal people who have experienced the death of a loved one. If they discover that nine out of the ten individuals interviewed reported having heard or seen the recently deceased family member in a vision, the ten researchers can conclude that their findings are reliable. However,

> . . . if they describe this observation as a 'hallucination', that is, a pathological percept indicative of mental illness, which it might be for adult non-Indian Americans, they would have an empirical finding that was reliable but not valid. Validity would require the qualifying interpretation that this percept is not pathological—in fact it is both normative and normal for American Indians since it is neither culturally inappropriate nor a predictor or sign of disease—and therefore it could not be labeled as a hallucination. Rather it would require some other categorization . . . in order for the observation to be both reliable and valid. (Kleinman 1995:73–4)

All of this is to say that what is considered deviant will differ across cultures. This has unfortunate sociological effects when one of those cultures is dominant, the other a minority, in the same country. The dominant culture's definition then might condemn as deviant not just the practice of the minority culture but the minority culture itself.

The Contested Nature of Deviance

Not only will definitions of deviance differ across culture, they will vary within cultures. It is true that the culture defines deviance—that deviance is essentially a social or cultural construct—but it is important to remember, as we mentioned earlier in this chapter, that there is seldom total or even near total agreement within a culture as to what is deviant. In other words, deviance, like other elements in a culture, can be **contested**, meaning that not everyone agrees.

When deviance is contested in any given area, we have a situation known as **conflict deviance**. Conflict deviance is a disagreement among groups over whether or not something is deviant. The legality of marijuana is a good example. Possession of marijuana is against the law, and is therefore deviant, yet results of a 2002 survey conducted by the Canadian Community Health Survey suggest that three million people aged 15 and older use marijuana or hashish at least once a year, which goes a long way towards normalizing the practice. The constant debate over whether possession of small amounts of marijuana, for medicinal

or even recreation use, should be legalized is proof that marijuana use, though deviant, is a focal point for conflict deviance.

Social Construction versus Essentialism

One of the reasons deviance is contested has to do with the differing viewpoints of social constructionism and essentialism. **Social constructionism** puts forward the idea that elements of social life—including deviance, as well as gender, race, and other elements—are not natural but are established or created by society or culture. **Essentialism**, on the other hand, argues that there is something 'natural', 'true', 'universal', and therefore 'objectively determined' about these elements of social life.

When we look at any given social element, we can see that each of these two viewpoints is applicable to some degree. Alcoholism, for

The Marijuana Party Book Store in Vancouver. The political party runs on a single platform which campaigns to legalize marijuana. If marijuana becomes legalized does it cease to be deviant? (Photo © M-J Milloy, 2006)

instance, is a physical condition, so it has something of an essence or essential nature, but whom we label an alcoholic and how we as a society perceive an alcoholic (i.e. as someone who is morally weak or as someone with a medical problem) is a social construct, one that will vary from society to society.

The interplay between social constructionism and essentialism receives excellent treatment from Erving Goffman in his study of stigma and deviance, *Stigma: Notes on the Management of a Spoiled Identity* (1963). A **stigma** is a human attribute that is seen to discredit an individual's social identity. It might be used to identify the stigmatized individual or group as deviant. Goffman believed there were three types of stigma: **bodily**, **moral**, and **tribal**. He defined them in the following way:

> First there are abominations of the body— the various physical deformities. Next there are blemishes of individual character perceived as weak will, domineering or unnatural passions, treacherous and rigid beliefs, and dishonesty, these being inferred from a known record of, for example, mental disorder, imprisonment, addiction, alcoholism, homosexuality, unemployment, suicidal attempts, and radical political behavior. Finally there are the tribal stigma of race, nation, and religion, these being stigma that can be transmitted through lineages and equally contaminate all members of a family. (Goffman 1963:4)

So while bodily stigma exist physically, definitions of 'deformed' can be and often are socially constructed—think of descriptions such as 'too fat' or 'too thin'. People in a variety of societies 'deform' their bodies (by dieting to extremes, by piercing and tattooing their bodies, or, in certain cultures, by putting boards on their children's heads to give them a sloping forehead) to look beautiful according to social standards. People who hear voices and see what is not physically there may be considered religious visionaries in some cultures, people who should be locked away in others. Racializing is another social process, national identity a social construct open to change over time, and different religions are privileged in different societies.

In this textbook, we have adopted a view of deviance that is more social constructionist than essentialist. Following Howard Becker's classic work *Outsiders* (1963), we will tend not to speak of deviance as being inherently 'bad', conformity to a norm being inherently good. Instead, we will generally follow the rule that

> social groups create deviance by making the rules, whose infraction constitutes deviance, and by applying those rules to particular people and labelling them as outsiders. . . . Deviance is *not a quality* of the act the person commits, but rather a consequence of the application by others of rules and sanctions to an 'offender'. (Becker 1963:8–10)

The Other

An important word used in contemporary critical theorizing about deviance in sociology (as well as in other disciplines), is '**other**', or 'otherness'. Difficult to define and even harder to use, it intersects with such concepts as ethnocentrism, colonialism, stereotyping, essentialism, and prejudice.

The 'other' is conjured up by the dominant culture within a society or by a colonizing nation of the colonized. When the United States took over Haiti (1915–34), Hollywood and the Catholic Church helped to make deviant the indigenous religion of the Haitians by casting it as an element of the 'other' culture. Voodoo and zombies became familiar figures of reported Haitian deviance from 'civilized' norms. The image created of the other can be mysterious, mystical, mildly dangerous, but somehow it is ultimately inferior. Edward Said, in his discussion of Orientalism, characterizes the West's image of the Middle East as the creation of an other. The dominant culture in Canada includes 'Aboriginal' as 'other'. English Canada has portrayed French Canada that way. In movies written and directed by men and aimed at young men, 'woman' seems to be constructed as an other. For Emily Murphy (see below), Chinese men were the other.

Racializing Deviance: To Be Other-Than-White Is to Be Deviant

To **racialize deviance** is to link particular ethnic groups with certain forms of deviance, and to treat these groups differently because of that connection. We see this in movies and television shows that portray all Latinos as involved with drugs, all black males as involved in street crime, and all Italians as involved with the mafia. Part of racializing deviance is making ethnic background a covert characteristic of deviance, making all people of a particular ethnic group more likely to be considered deviant.

Despite the public promotion in Canada of **multiculturalism**—the set of policies and practices directed towards the respect for cultural differences—the pressure to **assimilate** (i.e., become culturally the same as the dominant culture) is still persistent ('You're in Canada now, why don't you wear normal clothes?'). Immigrants who have experienced the embarrassment of having Canadians stumble over their names—sometimes deliberately for supposed comic effect (as when Don Cherry deliberately mispronounces French and Russian names)—may have felt pressure to Anglicize their names to make them more 'Canadian'.

A classic Canadian instance of racializing deviance comes from the 1922 book *Black Candle*, a collection of articles written by Emily Murphy, many of them originally published in *Maclean's* magazine. A journalist, activist, and self-taught legal expert, born of a prominent

and wealthy Ontario family, Murphy was a gender heroine of first-wave feminism, becoming, in 1916, the first woman magistrate not just in Canada but in the British Empire. She would later play a role in the historic 'Persons Case', a 1928 Supreme Court ruling that women were not 'persons' eligible to hold public office; the decision was appealed to the British Privy Council and overturned the following year. And her four books of personal sketches, written under the pen name Janey Canuck, were already well known when Murphy published *Black Candle* to expose the insidious details of the Canadian drug trade.

Black Candle cast Chinese Canadians as the main villains in the trafficking of illegal drugs—

When you look at this picture, do you see a man behind bars looking out or a free man looking in? What factors in society might have contributed to the way you interpreted the photo? (© Photodisc)

Canadian Sociology in Action
The Warrior Frame: How Intro Soc Texts Cast the Mohawk as Deviant 'Other'

The 1990 Oka land dispute in Quebec pitted members of several Mohawk communities against the Quebec provincial police and the Canadian army. Media reports portrayed the confrontation as a clash of interests: those of the mainstream dominant culture, represented (and upheld) by the police and the army, versus those of an 'other', deviant culture, the Mohawk. Since that time, the crisis has been dissected and analyzed in a number of introductory sociology textbooks (14 published between 1991 and 2002). What is alarming about the textbook treatment of the situation is that it differs little from media representations of the event, perpetuating stereotypes about Aboriginal people through the use of what can be called a **warrior frame**.

The warrior frame gives a narrow view of the Oka situation, making any sociological explanation partial, vague, and disconnected from any 'big picture' examination of the event. It is a good example of Dorothy Smith's **relations of ruling**: the sociological presentation essentially serves the federal government's public relations campaign to vilify the Mohawk, to defend its own inaction on the Kanesatake land question, and to downplay its failure to live up to its responsibility to stand up for Aboriginal people in conflicts with the province when it failed to call into question the highly questionable actions of the Quebec government, especially its police force.

The warrior frame, as it is reproduced in the introductory sociology textbooks, generally has seven parts:

- reproduction, without contextualization, of the famous picture of the 'Mohawk Warrior' confronting a soldier
- portrayal of the Mohawk Warriors as deviant criminal outsiders
- depiction of the Mohawk Warriors as uniformly belligerent
- exclusion from the frame of the important role of women
- presentation of a false picture of Aboriginal unity
- depiction of the Sûreté du Québec as a 'neutral' organization
- under-representation of acts of non-Aboriginal violence

The warrior frame begins with *the* picture. It appeared first on television and was often reprinted in newspaper and magazine articles; at least three textbooks include it. In shows a tough-looking masked Mohawk Warrior (often misidentified as the media darling 'Lasagna' but actually an Ojibwa university student). The 'Mohawk Warrior' is glaring at a young soldier who looks guiltless but resolute. The picture is never contextualized with a discussion of the sociological message it conveys. It is presented as if it constitutes part of a neutral or objective depiction of the events that took place, rather than being an example of how non-Aboriginal media came to distort the discourse of Oka.

Another key part of the warrior frame is that it casts the Aboriginal participants at Oka as criminal outsiders—as Americans, as Vietnam War veterans, or as criminals. In fact, the vast majority were Canadian, had never fought in a war, and had no criminal record. None of the 14 introductory sociology texts attempted to refute the outsider image; 2 actually supported this stereotype.

The warrior frame plays up a popular impression of the war-like nature of Aboriginal males. Like the Hollywood Indian, the warrior seeks out battles and does not acknowledge pain or gentler feelings. This part of the warrior frame leaves no room for contradictory images of Aboriginal maleness or any representation of women, who were important actors in the protest from beginning to end.

The warrior frame presents the Mohawk position as a unified stance. In fact, the confrontation and the events leading to it were marked by differences of opinion, both among the Mohawk and among Aboriginal people generally. Not everyone was in favour of the protest (see Monture-Angus 1995:84–5). But the textbooks manage to tie together the Mohawk and Aboriginal people generally with mystical connections of unity that appear to deny that any divisions could exist within their ranks.

You can't have Aboriginal warriors without the cavalry riding to the rescue. Our introductory textbooks all accept the role of the Quebec police as neutrally 'serving the people', in spite of the fact the Sûreté de Québec includes many Francophone officers who have been raised in a culture that views the Mohawk as the great enemy of the classical period of New France. The SQ relationship with the province's Aboriginal people in general (see Dickason 2002:332) and with the Mohawk in particular has a colonialist history forged over nearly a century. However, the SQ, by name, remains almost anonymous in the introductory sociology textbooks; most of the time they are referred to as merely the 'Quebec police', the 'provincial police', or 'the police'. There is no mention of the bad relationship between the SQ and all three Quebec Mohawk communities, and there is no discussion of role of the SQ in the long history of aggression between the province's French and Mohawk communities.

The warrior frame makes it easy to portray the Mohawk as the antagonists in the confrontation, local French residents the victims. The actions of the Mohawk appear deviant. But it's important to recognize the depth of hostility and illegal behaviour on both sides. When the Mohawk blocked the Mercier Bridge, opposition grew quickly as commuters living on the South Shore of the St Lawrence River faced a three-hour commute to bypass the barricade. The nature of the angry response reflected its multiple cause: commuter frustration, mob dynamics, and racism, but the last of these is not mentioned in the introductory sociology textbooks. Crowds of as many as 4,000 people demonstrated their anger, some yelling obscene and racist remarks. As the summer moved into August, the protesters grew more violent. At nightly demonstrations, effigies of Mohawk were burned, United Nations observers were blocked from going to the Mohawk community of Kahnawake, and journalists were threatened with violence. One night, 200 of the demonstrators stormed a local police station where one of their leaders was held; they broke windows and destroyed two squad cars. In August, a convoy of 75 vehicles left Kahnawake, evacuating Mohawk children, women, and elders who feared racial violence. A French radio station reported the convoy, and about 500 local residents came out to impede its progress. Some threw rocks at the cars, injuring at least six Mohawk.

How was this series of events represented by introductory sociology textbooks? Five make mention of it. Not one mentioned that the bridge was on Mohawk land. Not one referred to anyone being hurt. Not one used the words 'racism' or 'racist' or 'criminals' in the description. The actions of the non-Aboriginal people are dismissed merely as examples of crowd or mob behaviour, provoked by the deviant actions of the Mohawk.

particularly opium, heroin, and cocaine—although Blacks were also targeted. The main theme was that Chinese men—those bachelors who, because of the restrictive head tax on Chinese immigrants, could not be reunited with their wives or find companionship among women 'of their own race'—were corrupting White women through drug dealing, 'ruining them' and making them accomplices in their dealing. The following quotation, from the chapter on 'Girls as Pedlars', is typical:

> Much has been said, of late, concerning the entrapping of girls by Chinamen in order to secure their services as pedlars of narcotics. The importance of the subject is one which warrants our closest scrutiny: also, it is one we dare not evade, however painful its consideration. (233)

Murphy believed that the 'yellow races' could use the drug trade to take over the Anlgo-Saxon world, and she warned North American readers to be wary of these 'visitors':

> Still, it behooves the people in Canada and the United States, to consider the desirability of these visitors . . . and to say whether or not we shall be *'at home'* to them for the future. A visitor may be polite, patient, persevering, . . . but if he carries poisoned lollypops in his pocket and feeds them to our children, it might seem wise to put him out.
>
> It is hardly credible that the average Chinese pedlar has any definite idea in his mind of bringing about the downfall of the white race, his swaying motive being probably that of greed, but in the

Emily Murphy made effective use of photos to illustrate her argument that Asians and Blacks were luring White North Americans—especially women—into lives of illicit drug use. This photo from *The Black Candle* bore the ominous caption: 'When she acquires the habit, she does not know what lies before her; later she does not care' (Murphy 1922/1973:30–1).

hands of his superiors, he may become a powerful instrument to this very end.

In discussing this subject, Major Crehan of British Columbia has pointed out that whatever their motive, the [drug] traffic always comes with the Oriental, and that one would, therefore be justified in assuming that it was their desire to injure the bright-browed races of the world.

Naturally, the aliens are silent on the subject, but an addict who died this year in British Columbia . . . used to relate how the Chinese pedlars taunted him with their superiority at being able to sell the dope without using it, and by telling him how the yellow race would rule the world. They were too wise, they urged, to attempt to win in battle but would win by wits; would strike at the white race through 'dope' and when the time was ripe would command the world. (Murphy 1973:187–9)

Black Candle had a huge impact on the perception of drugs and on drug legislation in Canada. Chapter XXIII, 'Marahuana—A New Menace', was the first work in Canada to discuss marijuana use. It contained a lot of damning half-truths and anecdotes and led to the enactment of laws governing marijuana use. In fact, if you do an Internet search on the words, you will find that proponents of legalizing marijuana continue to target the book as an opponent.

Emily Murphy can be seen as an example of what is called, following Becker (1963), a **moral entrepreneur**. This is a group or individual who tries to convince others of the existence of a particular social problem as defined by the group or individual. The moral entrepreneur labours to create consensus on an issue on which there is no pre-existing consensus; at the very least, the individual or group tries to foster sufficient agreement among policy makers to ensure that the action the moral entrepreneur desires takes place. Examples of moral entrepreneurs can include opposing groups, such as the pro-life and the pro-choice movements or

the gun and the anti-gun lobbies, who compete and lobby for the most policy affecting the situation of interest.

Racial Profiling

Racial profiling is a particular form of racializing deviance. The Ontario Human Rights Commission offers the following thorough-going definition on their website:

> Racial profiling: is any action undertaken for reasons of safety, security or public protection, that relies on stereotypes about race, colour, ethnicity, ancestry, religion, or place of origin, or a combination of these, rather than on reasonable suspicion, to single out an individual for greater scrutiny or different treatment. Age and/or gender can also be factors in racial profiling.

> This type of profiling assumes that the personal characteristics of an individual are indicative of his or her actions or of a tendency to be engaged in illegal activity. This differs from criminal profiling, which relies on actual behaviour or on information about suspected activity by someone who meets the description of an individual.

> Profiling can be committed in many contexts involving safety, security, and protection issues. Some examples might be:
> - in law enforcement, such as policing and border control;
> - by security personnel, for example, private security guards;
> - by employers, for example in conducting security clearances of staff;
> - in housing accommodation, for example if landlords assume that certain applicants or tenants will be involved in criminal or other illegal activity;
> - by service providers, for instance if taxis do not stop at night for certain persons; and
> - in the criminal justice system, such as in courts and prisons.

Sociology in Action
Crossing the Border While Black

I was part of an EdD (Education doctorate) cohort in a class on community college leadership. It was a high-powered group, including faculty members, middle administrators, and presidents of three colleges. We were going on a class trip from Toronto to Monroe Community College in Rochester. It was the summer before September 11, so 'home security' was not the issue it would become in a few months' time.

The car I was in was driven by a White female administrator; the passengers were two White faculty members, one male (me) and one female. The others were dressed respectably. I looked like an extra in a Cheech and Chong movie. We passed through customs with few words said. No problems. The same could be said for all the other White travellers in our group. No delays, no problems.

There was one exception. One of our cars carried two Black males. One was an upper-level administrator, well dressed, a distinguished-looking gentleman (streaks of white in all the right places in his hair) from the Caribbean. The other was a faculty member, younger, also well dressed, very articulate, with an American accent. They were stopped and asked to get out of the car. Their trunk was searched carefully. It would be an understatement to say that they were not treated with the respect due to people of their standing in the community. It took them over half an hour to cross the border. They were guilty of crossing the border while Black.

Gender and Deviance: To Be Female Is to Be Deviant

Feminists have taught us that in a patriarchal society (one dominated by men), the concept of 'male' is treated as normal, while the concept of 'woman' is seen as inherently deviant. Male values are **normalized** (i.e. made to seem 'normal', 'right', and 'good') through customs, laws, and cultural production. Two related concepts are important here: **misogyny** and **patriarchal construct**. *Misogyny* means literally 'hating women'. In a patriarchal or male-dominated society, the images of women are constructed in ways that contain and reflect misogyny. *Patriarchal construct* refers to social conditions being thought of or structured in a way that favour men and boys over women and girls. Think, for example, of highly prized and well-paying jobs—corporate lawyer, investment banker, emergency room doctor—that have been constructed so that the job-holder is forced to place family in a distant second place to employment. This gives advantages to males, who in Canadian society are expected to fulfill fewer domestic and child-rearing duties than are women.

Casting the female as deviant is not a new phenomenon; in fact, it may be as old as human life itself. A particularly interesting example surrounds the witch hunts waged in Europe and, later on, in colonial America from about the fourteenth to the seventeenth century. Those who were identified as witches were tried and executed, and this for several reasons makes for an intriguing case for the sociological study of deviance. The deviance was fictitious: while the people tried may have committed criminal acts, their powers and connections with Satan were not real (although often believed by both accuser and some accused).

The vast majority of those accused were women (the figure usually cited by authorities on the subject is 85 per cent). The word 'witch' itself is closely associated with women, conjuring up traditional negative images of pointed black hats, old warty faces with pointed noses, and flying broomsticks: bad clothes, bad looks, and bad use of a female-associated cleaning implement. In a patriarchal society, this image of deviance is very much associated with femaleness, its opposite—normalcy—with maleness. Harley puts it well when he states that

> Women were associated with witchcraft because of the nature of Renaissance thought, which divided things into opposite categories. In the classifications that related to social order and morality (God/Devil, good/evil, normal behavior/witchcraft) the category 'female' was associated with witchcraft because it was

unthinkable not to associate the category 'male' with normal behavior.

In this context, it's worth recalling the discussion of the Australian Aborigine language Dyribal from Chapter 3. The language offers up another example of how femaleness is associated with deviance in a patriarchal culture, where nouns classified as 'feminine' include poisonous or dangerous fish, plants, and insects.

Class and Deviance: To Be Poor Is to Be Deviant

Poverty can be considered a covert characteristic of deviance. Marginally illicit activities like overindulgence in alcohol are more likely to be considered deviant in poor people than in middle-class or 'rich' people. Jeffrey Reiman, in his book *The Rich Get Richer and the Poor Get Prison* (1998), examines the ways in

Do you think that imposing negative sanctions (i.e. making homelessness illegal) is a good response to this kind of deviance? (© Ingram)

which the criminal justice system in the United States targets the poor in an attempt to deflect attention from the ruling class. Reiman outlines his thesis in the following passage:

> [T]he criminal justice system keeps before the public . . . the distorted image that crime is primarily the work of the poor. The value of this to those in positions of power is that it deflects the discontented and potential hostility of Middle America [the American middle class] away from the classes above them and toward the classes below them. . . . [I]t not only explains our dismal failure to make a significant dent in crime but also explains why the criminal justice system functions in a way that is biased against the poor at every stage from arrest to conviction. Indeed, even at the earlier stage, when crimes are defined in law, the system primarily concentrates on the predatory acts of the poor and tends to exclude or deemphasize the equally or more dangerous predatory acts of those who are well off. (Reiman 1998:4)

This is how behaviours associated with poverty and criminality become synonymous with deviance while criminal activity associated with wealth and celebrity is often labelled 'good business'. Martha Stewart, for instance, was convicted of contempt of court and yet received a standing ovation from a mostly supportive public and press following her trial.

Lower-class people are also over-represented in the statistics on criminal convictions and admission to prison. That means that per population they are more often convicted and admitted to prison than are middle- and upper-class people, and this contributes to the idea that all lower-class people are deviant. A closer look at the statistics helps us see why they do not give us an accurate picture of the lower classes.

'Lower class' is a designation that is often established by looking solely at recorded income, but it covers a broad and far from homogeneous set of individuals. Some are part of the working class, labouring for long hours with little financial reward. Others are on welfare. These two sub-groups of the lower class are probably not significantly more involved in criminal activity than are middle-class or upper-class people. In fact, it's a separate sub-group, representing a small minority of the lower class, that is responsible for a high percentage of the crimes. These people are lumped together with the first two groups statistically because of their low reported income, giving a misleading forensic picture of the working poor.

Another reason for the overrepresentation of the lower class in crime statistics has to do with **social resources**. In this context, the term refers to knowledge of the law and legal system, ability to afford a good lawyer, influential social connections, and capacity to present oneself in a way that is deemed 'respectable'. Lower-class individuals generally have access to fewer social resources than middle- and upper-class people do, and this makes them more likely to be convicted of charges people from the wealthier classes might be able to avoid. Tepperman and Rosenberg explain the importance of social resources:

> Social resources help people avoid labelling and punishment by the police and courts. For example, in assault or property-damage cases, the police and courts try to interpret behaviour and assess blame before taking any action. They are less likely to label people with more resources as 'criminal' or 'delinquent' and more likely to label them 'alcoholic' or 'mentally ill' for having committed a criminal act. (Tepperman and Rosenberg 1998:118)

The authors make use of Goffman's concept of **impression management**, which they define as 'the control of personal information flow to manipulate how other people see and treat you' (Tepperman and Rosenberg 1998:118). The upper classes are better at managing impressions than are people who belong to the lower class. Therefore, they conclude,

Official rule-enforcers (including police and judges, but also social workers, psychiatrists and the whole correctional and treatment establishment) define as serious the deviant acts in which poor people engage. On the other hand, they tend to 'define away' the deviant acts of rich people as signs of illness, not crime. They are more likely to consider those actions morally blameless. (Tepperman and Rosenberg 1998:118–19)

White Collar Crime

It was in a speech to the American Sociological Society in 1939 that Edwin Sutherland introduced the term **white collar crime**. He defined it as 'crime committed by a person of respectability and high social status in the course of his occupation' (1949:9). His article 'White Collar Criminality' was published the next year in the *American Sociological Review* (Sutherland 1940), and he would later devote an entire book to the subject (*White Collar Crime*, 1949).

Sutherland's work was an important step in the sociological study of criminology. Previous work had focused on the poor and the crimes they committed, creating at the very least a biased sample. But his definition is not flawless. Associating certain kinds of criminal behaviour with a particular class reflects a class bias and a misleading view of the situation. After all, you don't have to be a person of 'high social status' to commit identity theft (making copies of bank or charge cards), which tends to be found in the category of white collar crime. The implication in Sutherland's original definition is that only people of the higher classes are capable of planning and carrying out crimes that are essentially non-violent. In this way it fails to recognize that industrial accidents caused by unsafe working conditions that are allowed to exist by a negligent owner are in a real sense crimes of violence. Even the term itself reflects this class bias: the use of the qualifier ('white collar') to the word crime suggests that most crime, ordinary crime, is not committed by people of 'high social status', in much

the same way that the term 'white trash' carries the implication that it is unusual for whites to be 'trash', unlike other races.

More recent works have refined the definition of white collar crime to remove the class bias associated with Sutherland's original definition. Clinard and Quinney (1973) went further, breaking white collar crime into two categories by distinguishing between what they called **occupational** and **corporate** crimes. The former they defined as 'offenses committed by individuals for themselves in the course of their occupations [and] offenses by employers against their employees' (1973:188). The latter include 'offenses committed by corporate officials for their corporation and the offenses of the corporation itself' (1973:188). The difference is one of beneficiaries and victims. Occupational crimes benefit the individual at the expense of other individuals who work for the company. Corporate crimes benefit the corporation and its executives at the expense of other companies and the general public. This latter definition, by placing less emphasis on the individual, hones in on the negative aspects of corporate culture and the way that individuals and corporations work together to commit illegal acts against consumers and the common public.

The announcement in the spring of 2001 that the energy giant Enron, the seventh largest company in the United States, was declaring bankruptcy had devastating effects on the company's employees and shareholders and on the US economy as a whole. The creative legal financing and letter-but-not-principle-of-the-law accounting schemes of the executives involved, taken together with the multi-million-dollar salaries and perks they were paying themselves, constitute white collar crime of both varieties. Their crimes were occupational in that they took from the economic viability of the company, causing its bankruptcy. They also caused the personal bankruptcy and economic hardship of thousands of employees by encouraging them to sink their life savings into Enron stock. At the same time their crimes were corporate in that they had a profound negative

Table 5.1 >>   Occupational and corporate crimes

OCCUPATIONAL CRIMES	CORPORATE CRIMES
sexual harassment	industrial accidents
embezzlement	pollution
pilfering	price-fixing

impact on the American economy (particularly the financial sector) and were a major cause of the energy crisis that occurred in California.

What do you think?

Those who study linguistics distinguish between **marked** and **unmarked terms**. The unmarked term is the usual or standard one, while the marked term has a label added to it to distinguish it from the common term. 'Field hockey' (as opposed to the usual brand of hockey played in Canada), 'light beer', 'white chocolate', and 'decaffeinated coffee' are all marked terms. 'White collar crime' is another example. By distinguishing this variety of upper-class criminal activity, are we implying that most crime is committed by the lower or working class?

Sexual Orientation and Deviance

It comes as no surprise that homosexuality is defined as deviant across the world (although not in every culture). This particular social construction of deviance does differ among cultures in terms of how and what kind of social sanctions are applied. At the beginning of 2003, sex-ual activity between consenting adult homosexu-als was still against the law in 13 states (Alabama, Florida, Idaho, Kansas, Louisiana, Michigan, Mississippi, Missouri, North Carolina, South Carolina, Texas, Utah, and Virginia). In June of that year, in the case *Lawrence vs Texas*, the Supreme Court voted 6–3 against the constitu-tionality of the Texas law. In theory, the ruling means that the anti-homosexuality laws in the other 12 jurisdictions are unconstitutional, too; in practice, having the laws overturned will depend on time and changes to the conservative–liberal balance of the US Supreme Court.

In Britain, homosexuality is addressed in Section 28 of the Local Government Act. It reads:

A local authority shall not:
1) intentionally promote homosexuality or publish material with the intention of promoting homosexuality;
2) promote the teaching in any maintained school of the acceptability of homosexu-ality as a pretended family relationship.

It would interesting to find out how accurate information about homosexuality might be conceived of as 'promoting' it.

In looking at how laws concerning homosex-uality differ across the globe, it is interesting to note that former British colonies or protectorates are high on the list of those countries in which male homosexuality (and in some cases female homosexuality) is against the law: Grenada,

Guyana, Jamaica in the Caribbean; Botswana and Zimbabwe in Africa; and Bangladesh, Bhutan, Brunei, India, Malaysia, the Maldives, Myanmar, Nepal, Pakistan, Singapore and Sri Lanka in Asia. Those Asian countries appear to have carried on from colonial times with different versions of an act passed in British India in 1860. They differ from Asian countries such as China, Japan, and Thailand, which were never colonized, and countries colonized by other European nations (e.g. Cambodia, Laos, and Vietnam, colonized by France; Indonesia, colonized by the Netherlands; the Philippines, colonized by Spain). In some Muslim countries—Afghanistan, Pakistan, Saudi Arabia, Sudan, the United Arab Emirates, and Yemen—laws against homosexuality carry the death penalty, although in some of these jurisdictions (Afghanistan, for instance) it has rarely been applied. Ironically, it is not uncommon in Muslim countries for a young heterosexual man to have his first sexual experience with another young male, which, if it is discovered, is less likely to bring dishonour upon the families involved than would a sexual relationship with an unmarried woman.

In communities where homosexuality is regarded as deviant, negative sanctions can have a powerful influence on behaviour. In Canada, young men can influence the behaviour of other young men by sanctioning them with statements such as 'that's so gay', or 'you're gay'. This practice, sometimes referred to as the **ideology of fag**, is a way of influencing people to behave according to gender role expectations, particularly young males.

It is interesting to note that the attitude towards homosexuality as deviant is, on a global scale, more strict concerning men than women. There are 30 countries in the world in

Do you think that, on the whole, the men in your class would react more negatively to this picture than the women would? (© Photodisc)

which only male homosexuality is condemned (Armenia, Jamaica, Nigeria, Sri Lanka, and Uzbekistan, to name just a few).

Summary

We have tried to make several key points in this chapter. First, deviance is largely socially constructed; it can vary from culture to culture. The social construction is often contested or challenged within the culture. The dominant culture's definition of deviance (in North America, a predominantly White, male, English-speaking, middle-aged, middle-class definition) can override the definitions of deviance that come from people less powerful in the same society. This can happen in ways that socially sanction or punish members of minority cultures and people with 'alternative' lifestyles.

Skateboard decks with the images of the West Memphis Three, who were convicted of murdering three eight-year-old boys in Arkansas in 1993. Although no physical evidence or motive was ever found, the prosecution presented black hair, heavy metal T-shirts, and Stephen King novels as proof of the boys' guilt. (Photo © M-J Milloy, 2005)

Questions for Critical Review and Discussion

1. Describe with examples what is meant by the term 'deviant.'

2. Outline how deviance can be associated with ethnicity, culture, race, gender, sexual orientation, and class.

3. Explain with examples what conflict deviance is.

4. Explain how the Mohawk were cast as deviant by the Canadian media (including sociology textbooks).

5. Identify with examples what white collar crime is.

Suggested Readings

Coleman, James William (2002). *The Criminal Elite: Understanding White-Collar Crime*, 5th edn. New York: Worth Publishers.

Goffman, Erving (1963). *Stigma: Notes on the Management of Spoiled Identity*. Englewood NJ: Prentice-Hall.

Greenberg, David F., ed. (1993). *Crime and Capitalism: Readings in Marxist Criminology*. Philadelphia: Temple UP.

Hill, Stuart L. (1980). *Demystifying Social Deviance*. New York: McGraw-Hill.

Reiman, Jeffrey (1998). *The Rich Get Richer and the Poor Get Prison: Ideology, Class, and Criminal Justice*. Boston: Allyn & Beacon.

Rigakos, George S. (2002). *The New Parapolice: Risk Markets and Commodified Social Control*. Toronto: U of Toronto P.

Suggested Websites

American Society of Criminology (Critical Criminology/Feminist Criminology).
http://www.critcrim.org/feminist.htm

Kohlberg's Theory of Moral Development (Robert Barger, University of Notre Dame).
http://www.nd.edu/~rbarger/kohlberg.html

New Journal of Prisoners on Prisons.
http://www.prisonactivist.org/pipermail/prisonact-list/1995-December/000098.html

Socioweb (Criminality and Deviance).
http://www.socioweb.com/~markbl/socioweb/topical/crimedev

Family

Contents

Key Terms

cluttered nest
companionate conjugal roles
complementary conjugal
  roles
complex household
conjugal roles
crude marriage rate
dynamic
empty nest
endogamy
eugenics
evolutionary change
exogamy
extended family
fecundity
general intelligence
gender roles
gender strategy
genocide
homogamy
intelligences
nuclear family
joint conjugal roles
matrilineal
occupational segregation
patrilineal
patriarchal / patriarchy
replacement rate
residential schools
scientific classism
scientific racism
separate conjugal roles
simple household
Sixties Scoop
total fertility rate
work interruptions

Boxes and Tables

Canadian Sociology in Action The Crestwood Heights Family
In Other Words Telling Your Family You're Gay
In Other Words Italian Families and Conjugal Roles: Four Generations
Sociology in Action Blaming the Victim: Daniel Moynihan and Black Families in the United States

Learning Objectives

After reading this chapter, you should be able to

- outline the diversity of family in the Canadian context.
- describe how family in Quebec is different from family in the rest of Canada.
- discuss eight major changes taking place in the family.
- identify the different forms that conjugal roles can take.
- recognize the varying ways in which endogamy acts within different racial and ethnic groups in Canada.
- identify how immigration patterns can affect family development.
- outline the argument that Aboriginal families were 'under attack' during the twentieth century in Canada.

>>> For Starters
Family and the Negative Sanction of Humour

Wherever tension exists in a culture, there is humour. Humour gives us a way to address everyday issues that cause tension with an openness that doesn't come easily when the same issues are discussed more seriously. In North American culture, family life is often a target of humour, whether that humour comes from a stand-up comic's routine, a co-worker's rant about her mother-in-law, or one of the many sitcoms that revolve around family dynamics. That's because there is tension in the family, between people living the roles of husband and wife, parent and child, spouse and in-laws.

Looking at a culture's humour can tell us where the tension is. But remember that humour is rarely sociologically 'innocent': we can also learn about whose perspective has power. I bet if you came up with ten jokes about husbands and wives, most would take the perspective of the husband. Jokes can be, and often are, sanctions hinting that what someone is doing is not approved of. Look at each of the following jokes and see if you can find the subtle message for husbands and wives.

- If a man speaks in the forest, and his wife isn't there, is he still wrong?

  [*subtle message, from a male perspective: Don't nag your husband—he is the head of the family and should not be challenged.*]

Audrey Meadows and Jackie Gleason spar in *The Honeymooners*, one of the first television sitcoms to explore the tensions of married life. (Ivy Images)

That would depend on whether or not he's talking about sports or cars.

[*subtle message, from a female perspective: Men have a narrow scope of expertise; women are more broad-minded.*]

- A woman took her husband to the doctor. After the examination, the doctor went out to talk to the wife.

'How is he?' the wife asked.

'You're going to have to fix his meals three times a day, every day. You must keep his clothes in order, bathe him, put his pajamas on and comfort him every night, or he will die.'

So the wife went inside to see her husband. 'What did the doctor say?', the husband asked. The wife looked at him and said, 'You're going to die.'

[*subtle message, from a male perspective: wives don't work hard enough to give their husbands comfort and support.*]

'Well, the good news is that we don't have to make any changes in our lifestyle.'

[*subtle message, from a female perspective: wives work like slaves for their husbands; husbands should do more or at least recognize how much they depend on their wives.*]

- In a flashback sequence in the popular sitcom *Everybody Loves Raymond*, Raymond and Debra Barone are discussing their wedding plans. Raymond asks Debra why she's planning the wedding so soon. Debra replies that she has been planning their wedding ever since she was 12. When Ray (foolishly) comments they only met when he was 22, Debra tells him he was merely 'the last piece of the puzzle'.

[*Which gender perspective do you think this was written from?*]

Diversity of the Family

The opening line of Russian novelist Leo Tolstoy's famous, tragic romantic novel *Anna Karenina* reads, 'Happy families are all alike; every unhappy family is unhappy in its own way.' We disagree. Happy families, functional families, good families exist in many forms, and are alike only in their success at serving basic purposes: providing emotional support for family members, taking care of elders, raising the next generation, and so on. In most other respects, happy families are diverse.

Family has existed in many forms historically in Canada, as elsewhere, and still does today. Before the arrival of Europeans, there was diversity in Aboriginal families. Some Native bands were **patrilineal** (determining kinship along the *male* line), some were **matrilineal** (determining kinship along the *female* line); some

lived in societies structured around family-based clans, others did not. The European development of primary industries brought other diverse and changing forms. Fur traders sometimes had European wives in Quebec and Aboriginal wives in the West. Loggers and fishers spent such long periods away from home that they were visitors when they returned. Age at marriage has varied in Canada, rising and falling with changes to economic prosperity of the country and the availability of jobs. Women, who in the late nineteenth century worked for pay only when they were unmarried, have become more and more immersed in the workforce throughout the twentieth century and into the twenty-first, and men, if statistics are to be believed, are taking on a greater share of responsibilities around the home.

It would be wrong to say that any one form or structure is consistently better or worse than any other for its members. And yet newspapers, other media, and even snippets of day-to-day conversation we might overhear on the street are filled with judgemental remarks about contemporary family forms. Even traditional sociology is not free from this bias. If you were presented with the terms **nuclear family** (which includes a parent or parents and children) and **extended family** (which might include, in addition, grandparents, aunts, uncles and cousins), you might be led to believe that the former is basic, 'normal', and the other some kind of modification of the regular model; you might even associate it with a particular ethnic or immigrant population. Such is not the case. For some cultures, historical and current, calling the nuclear family by the name 'family' would be as odd as referring to the arm as the body.

The Huron language of the seventeenth century had no terms for 'nuclear' or 'extended' family. Instead, the noun root -*ndat*-, meaning 'place', was used to refer to those people who lived in the same small section of a longhouse (a dwelling that might house up to 60 members of a band). This might be roughly equivalent to what we would today call a nuclear family, although a better modern translation is 'household'. The more common way for the Huron to refer to family was through the noun root -*hwat-sir*-, meaning 'matrilineage', or the verb root -*entio*-, meaning 'to belong to a matrilineal clan'. Matrilineage is the line of descendants that follows the mother's line. A woman, her sisters and brothers, and their mother would belong to the same matrilineage. A longhouse may be dominated by one matrilineage, with married sisters and their husbands and children being the base of the people living in one house. Thus the most common term for 'family' in the Huron language referred to a model we would probably brand with the term 'extended family', a variation of the model contemporary sociologists have deemed normal.

More useful, perhaps, than 'nuclear family' and 'extended family' are terms proposed by Frances Goldscheider and Regina Bures in their study of intergenerational living arrangements in White and Black households in the US: *simple households* and *complex households*. A **simple household** consists of unrelated adults with or without children. Conversely, a **complex household** includes 'two or more adults who are related but not married to each other and hence could reasonably be expected to live separately' (2003). Simple households tend to consist of a single adult or married adults living with or without children; the most common example of a complex household today is one in which adult children live at home with a parent or parents.

Using census data from 1940 to 1990, Goldscheider and Bures demonstrated that there was a 'crossover' in household patterns between Black and White families. From the 1940s to 1960s Black families were less likely to live in complex households than were White

Would you call this a typical Canadian family? How many families do you know that look like this? (© Photodisc)

families. By 1990, the pattern had reversed: White families were significantly more likely to live in simple households, Black families more likely to live in complex ones. (As we will see below, a similar change occurred in Quebec during the same period.) The study illustrates a very important principle about family. It is **dynamic**—that is, like other social institutions it changes, adapting to changing circumstances.

We should point out that when sociologists talk of 'diversity' in the Canadian family, they may be using either of two meanings of the term. Some mean it merely in the sense that there are different family structures: dual-earner, single-earner/two-parent, lone-parent. We use it here and throughout this text in a broader sense that includes not just differences in structure but also cultural diversity and different beliefs in

Canadian Sociology in Action
The Crestwood Heights Family

During the period from 1948–53, John Seeley, R. Alexander Sim, and E.W. Loosley studied an upper-middle-class White neighbourhood in northern Toronto, to which they gave the fictitious name 'Crestwood Heights'. The following is a brief introduction to their chapter on the family:

> The family of Crestwood Heights . . . consists of father, mother, and two (rarely more) children. The children are healthy, physically well developed, attractively dressed, and poised as to outward behavior. The mother, assured in manner, is as like an illustration from *Vogue* or *Harper's Bazaar* as financial means and physical appearance will allow. The father, well tailored, more or less successful in radiating an impression of prosperity and power, rounds out the family group.
>
> This small family unit is both lone and love-based. It is, more often than not, formed by the marriage of two persons from unrelated and often unacquainted families . . . who are assumed to have chosen each other because they are 'in love'. Other reasons for the choice (perpetuation of property within one family, the linking of business or professional interest, an unadorned urge to upward social mobility and so on), even if influential, could not reputably be admitted as grounds for marriage.
>
> This family unit is not embedded in any extended kinship system. The newly formed family is frequently isolated geographically and often socially from the parental families. It is expected that the bride and groom will maintain a separate dwelling removed by varying degrees of distance from that of each set of parents. . . . The isolation of each family acts to decrease the ability of the family to transmit traditional patterns of behavior, which might otherwise be absorbed from close contact with, for instance, grandparents. The absence of kinship bonds also tends to concentrate the emotional life of the family upon a few individuals. . . . (Seeley et al. 1956:159–60)

What do you think?

1. How many families do you know that conform to the Crestwood Heights model?

2. In what respects does your own family differ, if at all, from the description given here? In what respects does it resemble this model?

conjugal and gender roles. The discussion of the family in Quebec later in this chapter highlights this broader sense of diversity.

Changes in and Questions about the Canadian Family

There are a number of changes occurring in the makeup and behaviour of Canadian families today. It is interesting to note that in a number of these areas, families in Quebec score most highly. This is not to say that they are 'farther ahead' in some kind of modernist progressive model but that they offer the most evidence of certain general trends.

1. The marriage rate is decreasing while the cohabitation rate is rising.

A quick look at crude marriage rates will tell a sociologist if it's true that fewer people are getting married these days. The **crude marriage rate** is the number of marriages per 1,000 people in a population. Since the population keeps rising, looking at the crude marriage rate will give a better indication of trends than looking at the number of marriages alone. If the number of marriages was the same for 1991 and 2001, the actual rate would have to be decreasing, and our sociologist could conclude that fewer people indeed are getting married these days.

The crude marriage rate has fluctuated over the years in which it has been calculated. In 1920, it was relatively low at 6.1, probably because so many young men had died during World War I and the Spanish flu epidemic that followed it. When I think of that statistic I think of two of my great aunts who were young then, Aunt Nell the nurse, Aunt Margaret the teacher, both of whom I got to know very well. They were gifted, intelligent women adored by the children and grandchildren of their married brothers. Neither of them ever got married.

The number rose to a peak of 7.9 marriages per 1,000 people in 1950, representing a post-

Compare this photo with the one on page 150. Is this family any less typical of the families you know? What factors in our culture might lead us to view one family as more conventional than another? (Michael Newman/PhotoEdit Inc.)

World War II marriage boom that would precede (and contribute to) the post-war Baby Boom. My sister and I, and our many cousins, are all products of the Baby Boom. After dropping a little, the rate remained fairly high over the next three decades and peaked at 8.0 in 1980 (one year before my second marriage). That was just before the recession hit. Since then, the rate has dropped steadily, plummeting to 5.5 in 1995 and 4.7 in 2001.

Of course, fewer marriages does not mean fewer couples. The number of **common-law**, or **cohabiting**, unions has risen during that time. Precise figures are difficult to track, since society doesn't mark the beginning of such relationships the way it records marriages. Still, we do know that the percentage of all couples that are common-law or cohabiting has risen from 0.7 per cent in 1976 to 16.0 per cent in 2001. The cohabitation rate in the United States is always lower than that in Canada (the US rate for 2001 is 8.2 per cent of all couples). Can you think of why that is? Here's a hint: Quebec (with a cohabitation rate of about 30 per cent of all couples) skews the Canadian figures here. If we exclude Quebec from the statistics, the rate for the remaining provinces is 11.7 per cent. Now can you guess? Our discussion of Quebec later on may give some help.

There are a number of other good questions that can be addressed here. For instance, is cohabitation replacing marriage? Does cohabitation benefit men more than women? How does cohabitation versus marriage affect children? One of my favourite questions to address is the following, which seems to generate a considerable amount of spurious reasoning. People who cohabit prior to marriage are more likely to divorce than those who go straight from living apart to marriage. A survey done in 1990 found that after 10 years of marriage, the breakup rate was 26 per cent for those who had cohabited first and 16 per cent for those who had not (Le Bourdais and Marcil-Gratton 1996:428). When students are asked to propose reasons, they often come up with false causation: something happening during cohabitation, or the couples who cohabited became tired of each during marriage, and so on. A better answer that they seem to miss comes is that people with more liberal values are both more likely to cohabit and also more likely to leave a bad marriage. Another possibility: people who are afraid of commitment are more likely to cohabit and to leave a marriage.

2. *The age of first marriage is rising.*

The age of first marriage can be calculated in terms of median age (the middle value of a series of numbers) or average age, the latter being slightly higher. The following table features the average age for three years, with the median age for two years given for comparison:

Table 6.1 >> Average age of first marriage for brides and grooms, 1991, 1996, and 2001

YEAR	FIRST-TIME BRIDES		FIRST-TIME GROOMS	
	AVERAGE	MEDIAN	AVERAGE	MEDIAN
1991	25.7	25.1	27.7	27.0
1996	27.3	26.3	29.3	28.3
2001	28.2		30.2	

Before we look at the rise over this 10-year period, we must also look at the long term, for reasons that I hope become obvious. In 1921, the average age of first marriage for brides in Canada was 24.5, 28.0 for grooms. It is important to see that these figures are not very different from those of 1991, with 25.7 and 27.7 respectively. The figures rose slightly during the Depression of the 1930s, dropping slowly again in the 1940s. The drop became more dramatic in the 1950s and 1960s. In 1965, 30.8 per cent of first-time brides were under 20 years of age (Beaujot 2000:102). By 1971, the average ages of first-time brides and grooms were 22.6 and 25.0 respectively (median 21.3 and 23.5). My first marriage was in 1973: my wife was 22, I was 24.

The questions here are these: has this figure peaked, reaching levels that are only slightly higher than the 'strange times' of the 1950s and 1960s? Is this figure becoming increasingly meaningless as the cohabitation rate increases?

3. More women are having children in their thirties now than in earlier years. In 1976, 24 per cent of births were to women in their thirties. By 1996, that figure had jumped to 37 per cent. During the same 20-year period, the percentage of births to women younger than 24 dropped from 39 per cent to 28 per cent (Dumas and Belanger 1996:40).

What is important to consider here is the factor known as **fecundity**—that is, a woman's ability to conceive. This changes during a woman's fourth decade. It is estimated that 91 per cent of women at the age of 30 are physically able to become pregnant. This drops to 77 per cent of women at the age of 35 and just 53 per cent of women at 40 (Rajulton, Balakrisnhan, and Ravanera 1990). Do you hear the clock ticking? Do you think that this

Why do you think many North American women today are waiting until they are in their mid- to late-thirties before having their first child? (Photo © Macduff Everton/Corbis)

could have a significant effect in lowering the total fertility rate?

4. The number of children per family has dropped to below the 'replacement rate'.

The **total fertility rate** is an estimate of the average number of children that a woman between the ages of 15 and 49 will have in her lifetime if current age-specific fertility rates remain constant during her reproductive years. The replacement rate is the number of children born that is considered sufficient to replace the generation before them; the replacement rate is 2.1, meaning that for each woman aged 15–49, 2.1 children must be born in order for the population to hold constant.

You can see how things have changed by looking at the following contrasts. Of women born between 1927 and 1931, 31 per cent had five or more children. Compare that with women born between 1952 and 1956, of whom just 1.3 per cent had five or more children. Of the latter group, 38.3 per cent had just two children, and 33.7 per cent had one child or no children, meaning that a total of 72 per cent of women born 1952–6 had two children or fewer, compared with 42.7 per cent of women born 1927–31. The following table shows the total fertility rate for select years between 1941 and 1996.

In 2003 the total fertility rate was 1.61, so it seems to have bottomed out. The 100 most populous countries in the world during that year ranged from 3.86 to 6.98, the top 10 being in Africa. Those countries that were below Canada included the former communist countries in eastern Europe, ranging from the Czech Republic (1.18) to Georgia (1.51); some Mediterranean countries, including Italy (1.26), Greece (1.35), and Portugal (1.49); and several East Asian countries—Singapore (1.24), Hong Kong (1.32), Japan (1.38), South Korea (1.56), and Taiwan (1.57). In each of these countries, the population is expected to fall. Why do you think their fertility rates are so low? Is it just economics (at the country and family level), or is some pessimistic sense of the future involved as well?

Sociologists and politicians often argue that Canada makes up for a low fertility rate with high levels of immigration, this despite the fact that immigrants from countries with higher fertility rates soon begin to reproduce at a rate consistent with the fertility rate in this country. Are there other means by which the fertility rate can be raised? Would government incentives (such as those offered in Quebec) help to offset the cost of having and raising children? Would a system of universal daycare, similar to what exists in Quebec, change things significantly? Recent studies in the US suggest that women are willing to have more children when their husbands are willing to take a greater share of responsibility for childcare and general housework. Do you think that could be a significant factor?

5. There are more divorces.

Analyzing divorce statistics can be complicated. If you ask a group of people if the divorce rate is rising or falling (as I have often

Table 6.2 >> **Total fertility rate for select years, 1941–2007**										
1941	**1951**	**1961**	**1971**	**1976**	**1981**	**1986**	**1991**	**1996**	**2001**	**2007 (est.)**
2.8	3.5	3.8	2.2	1.8	1.7	1.7	1.8	1.6	1.5	1.6

Source: Adapted from Beaujot 2000:85–9.

done in class), they will typically say that it is going up. This is not the case. The rate has jumped on several occasions over brief periods of time, but we can account for these, in part, by looking at changes to the legislation surrounding divorce.

In 1961, there were 6,563 divorces in Canada, giving a divorce rate of 36.0 per 100,000 population. In 1968, the grounds for divorce were expanded in most of Canada: no longer was adultery the sole basis to sue for divorce. Between 1968 and 1971, the numbers shot up from 11,343 to 29,685, representing rates of 54.8 and 137.6 per 100,000 population. By 1982, the numbers had peaked (at 70,346, or a rate of 285.9); in fact, they were dropping slowly. Then in 1985, the Divorce Act was changed again, allowing marital breakdown as legitimate grounds for divorce. By 1987, the numbers had peaked again, this time at 90,985 (339.5 per 100,000 population). By 2002, the numbers were back down to 1982 levels: 70,155 divorces for a rate of 223.7, the lowest rate since the 1970s.

6. There are more lone-parent families than before.

There is a strong connection between lone-parent families, especially where the mother is the family head, and poverty. Beaujot uses an interesting statistic (2000:348) when he compares child poverty rates among lone-parent households for various countries before and after taxes have been deducted and transfer payments (social assistance) distributed. The countries include Canada, the US, Australia, Israel, and a number of European countries, all studied over a ten-year period from 1982 to 1992.

Before taxes and transfer payments, Canada has the sixth highest rate of child poverty in lone-parent households, with a 1991 pre-transfer payment rate of 68.2. What is more shocking is that Canada moves up to third on the list when the after-tax-and-transfer totals are considered. Canada, with a poverty rate in lone-parent households of 50.2 per cent, falls behind only the US (59.5 per cent) and Australia (56.2). This suggests that

Canada is not doing enough—less, certainly, than the other countries studied—to help children living in poverty in lone-parent families. What (if anything) do you think can be done to change this?

7. There are more people living alone than before.

In 1996, of the entire Canadian population aged 15 and over, 12 per cent were living alone. Contrary to what you might think, this rate is highest for those over 85 (48 per cent), and lowest for those younger than 55 (10 per cent or less; Beaujot 2000:117). Which do you think is the more significant cause of this statistic: the aging population or marriage delay among people under 30? What other figures might help you address this question?

What conditions do you think need to exist for a child to thrive in a lone-parent household? (Photo © Sophia Fortier)

8. Children are leaving home at a later age.

The term **cluttered nest** is sometimes used to describe the phenomenon in which adult children continue to live at home with their parents (the opposite, **empty nest**, describes a household in which children have moved out of the home). Statistically, we see that 'at age 20–24, 50.4 percent of women and 64.3 percent of men were living with parent(s) in 1996, compared to 33.6 and 51.4 percent respectively in 1981' (Boyd and Norris 1998, cited in Beaujot 2000:98). Causation is fairly easily to establish: it takes more time and education to establish a career. And with a higher cost of living, rising house prices, and a number of costs that earlier generations didn't have to face, it's more difficult to set oneself up on one's own. With couples marrying later and later in life, it takes that much longer to set up a dual-earner household, the only model that is financially viable for some people who want to move out of their parents' home.

Family in Quebec

By just about every statistical measure you can come up with, the family in Quebec is sociologically distinct from the family in other parts of Canada. In 1996, Quebec was the province with

- the highest cohabitation rate: 20.5 per cent of all families, almost twice the next highest rate in Canada (New Brunswick, at 10.9 per cent);
- the lowest marriage rate: 3.1 per 100,000, significantly lower than the next lowest rate, British Columbia's 5.2;
- the highest divorce rate: 45.7 per 100 marriages, a little ahead of BC's 45.0; and
- the highest number of divorces (per 100 marriages) among couples married less than thirty years, with 47.4 in the year 2000 (Alberta's rate of 41.5 is the next highest).

In 2001, Quebec led all provinces with an abortion rate of 19.6 per 1,000 women or 421.5 per 1,000 live births (trailing only the Northwest Territories in the latter statistic). In 2002, Quebec was the province with the greatest number of total births by single (never married) women; by percentage (55.3 per cent), they trailed only Nunavut. The province also had the greatest percentage of births to women who are divorced (2.1 per cent).

Another feature unique to Quebec is the province-wide support for same-sex marriage. In a poll conducted among 10,015 Canadian adults in August 2003, residents of Quebec showed the greatest support for changing the legal definition of marriage:

Table 6.3 >> Support for changing the definition of marriage to include same-sex unions, by region, 2003			
	AGREE SOMEWHAT	**AGREE STRONGLY**	**TOTAL**
Quebec	**36**	**25**	**61**
British Columbia	26	25	51
Atlantic Provinces	19	26	45
Ontario	19	23	42
Prairies	16	17	33

TNS Canadian Facts, http://www.tns-cf.com/news/03.09.05-samesex-charts.pdf, 2003. The study was conducted by TNS Canadian Facts (formerly NFO CFgroup), one of Canada's leading full-service marketing, opinion and social research organizations.

In the 1995 Bibby Report, Quebec was also shown to have the highest rate of approval for premarital and extramarital sex (Bibby 1995:76), with 88 per cent supporting the former (compared with 82 per cent, the next highest, in BC) and 24 per cent supporting the latter (compared with 14 per cent, the next highest, in the Prairies).

Quebec residents also show a difference when it comes to parenting, as indicated by a *Globe and Mail*/CTV poll of 648 Canadian parents conducted by Ipsos-Reid and published in the *Globe and Mail* on 10 April 2004. The poll noted the following results:

- The percentage of parents who said they spanked their children for disciplinary reasons:

Alberta	60%
British Columbia	52%
Saskatchewan/Manitoba	46%
Ontario	45%
Atlantic Provinces	42%
Quebec	**22%**

- The percentage of parents who agreed that using flashcards at an early age makes kids smarter:

British Columbia	71%
Saskatchewan/Manitoba	67%
Alberta	63%
Ontario	60%
Atlantic Provinces	57%
Quebec	**25%**

What should we make of all of this? First, it is important to note that a number of the statistical indicators discussed show a major change from the situation in Quebec prior to the Quiet Revolution of the 1960s. Take divorce, for example. Prior to 1968, if you were living in Quebec and you wanted a divorce, you had to seek it through Parliament (the situation was similar in Newfoundland). A growing separation from the Catholic Church has been cited (especially by religious officials) as a possible explanation for the rising divorce rate. Yet in the 2001 census, Quebec had the third-lowest number of residents declaring they had 'no religion' (a rate of 5.8 per cent, compared with the national average of 16.5 per cent). Of course, having an affiliation with the Church and being influenced by that affiliation can be two different matters. Suicide is considered a sin by the Catholic church, but Quebec, the most Catholic province, has the highest suicide rate in Canada, especially in the case of males: in 1999–2001 the suicide rate for Quebec males was 30.7 per 100,000, compared with 16.1 in the provinces of Ontario, Alberta, and British Columbia.

Can we say, as more right-wing or conservative interpreters would, that family life is falling apart in Quebec? One statistic we haven't presented might be seen as supporting that view. In 2002, Quebec had the highest rate of one-person households, about 30 per cent. But from our perspective, a more likely interpretation is that Quebec went through more rapid modernization and outright change during the last 40 years than any other province. The falling apart of old structures does not mean the falling apart of the institutions. Quebeckers are perhaps best seen as a people who are reinventing family as they are reinventing other institutions—political, religious, educational, and so on.

Conjugal Roles

Conjugal or **marital roles** are the distinctive roles of the husband and wife that result from the division of labour within the family. The first important sociological study done on this subject was British sociologist Elizabeth Bott's *Family and Social Networks* (1957), in which she differentiated these roles as being either **segregated**—in which tasks, interests, and activities are clearly different—or **joint**, in which many tasks, interests, and activities are shared. The study was set against a backdrop in which men were primarily responsible for the financial support of the family, while women were primarily responsible for the housework and childcare.

Earning and Caring: Changes in Conjugal Roles

In 2000, Canadian demographer Rod Beaujot published an important book on the Canadian family, entitled *Earning and Caring in Canadian Families* (2000). Winner of the 2000 Canadian Sociology and Anthropology Association's prestigious John Porter Award for outstanding scholarship, Beaujot aimed to discover 'how to better understand the changing links between earning and caring'. What did he mean by that? He wanted to study how conjugal roles were changing from a situation in which they were more or less complementary to one in which they were companionate. **Complementary**

In Other Words
Telling Your Family You're Gay

Growing up in the small town of Whitby, Ontario, I never felt the negative effects of discrimination. I am an English-speaking, Caucasian female and had never been a part of a minority group, in any sense of the word. At the age of 21, this changed and I became aware of how easily people are judged. I am a lesbian, and from the moment I became open about my sexual preferences, I felt first-hand what it feels like to be viewed based solely on one aspect of your life, and not as an entire person. When meeting someone new in my life it was as though I was wearing a sign on my forehead reading, 'I am gay', and it was perceived as 'I am gay . . . that is everything you need to know about me.' Once this information is divulged, almost instantly people form opinions on who I am as a person and who I should be. They develop expectations that quite often are illogical and unrealistic. By writing a paper such as this one, I am being given the opportunity to address a few of these numerous stereotypes and prejudiced beliefs. Hopefully, I can educate some to stop these beliefs from spreading.

From my experience, the original thought that people tend to have when finding out that I am gay is that it is simply a phase I am going through, a time of experimentation and rebellious behaviour. My brother's reaction was as such. He believed that it was just a phase and that it would pass. He continued to express this for an entire year after I had told him. He realizes otherwise now. . . . When telling my mother (who along with the rest of my family is extremely supportive of me), I was shocked to hear her initial reaction to what I had told her. After a moment or two of silence, she . . . said, 'But I thought you wanted to get married and have kids one day.' The thought of these dreams possibly fading away is what seemed to unsettle her the most. I found two things wrong and rather presumptuous about this statement. To begin with, the idea that a woman must want/need a husband and children to live a fulfilling life is old-fashioned and a step backward from the times we live in today. I figure, why can't a woman who is independent and who has a satisfying career be considered to lead a successful, happy life, despite the fact that she has no family to raise. Furthermore, my mother was correct in assuming that I did want a family, but it was not the family that she had in mind. Marriage and children are a large part of my future plans, and, with adoption, and artificial insemination, this is a very feasible option for lesbian couples. Simply because a woman falls in love with another woman, it does not mean that she didn't grow up with the same desire for nurturing children and caring for a home and family that a lot of heterosexual girls do.

roles (like Bott's model of *segregated roles*) cast men primarily as earners, breadwinners, doing paid work, with women involved primarily in the unpaid work of childcare and housework. In **companionate** relationships (like Bott's *joint relationship*) the roles overlap.

Beaujot notes that the shift is far from complete, which is not to say that complete overlap is possible or even desired. Genders roles are different to a significant extent because biologically men and women are different. But there is a point to which we may be able to say that a basic fairness or justice has been reached, and we are far from that point. As Beaujot—like others before him—several times documents, married women do more total work per day than married men do, even though married women are more likely to work part-time. Married women, especially those who are the mothers of small children, do much more unpaid work. And while women have entered new roles in the work world, men have not gone as far in entering new roles at home. This has created an imbalance in conjugal roles, leading some women to view their lives in terms such as 'double burden', 'double ghetto', or 'second shift'. The difficulty of correcting this imbalance in households with small children has led some women to conclude, pessimistically, that 'childlessness is the easiest route to equality' (Beaujot 2002:81).

In 1995, sociologist M. Reza Nakhaie published 'Housework in Canada: The National Picture', a summary of his study demonstrating that gender was the single most important factor—above relative income and time-availability—determining how much domestic labour or housework an individual did. The most striking point made by the author concerned the relationships between gender, hours of paid work, and share of the housework. Nakhaie discovered that there is an inverse relationship between the hours of paid work the man does and the size of his share of the housework: the more paid hours he has, the smaller his share of the housework. However, the same is not true for women. If fact, a direct rather than inverse relationships seems to exist over a particular number of hours of work: an increase

"*Gotta run, sweetheart. By the way, that was one fabulous job you did raising the children.*"

over 30 in the hours of paid work a week by a woman correlated to an increase in their contribution to housework.

The key to correcting the imbalance, as Beaujot and a number of other sociologists see it, is to recognize that gender roles are not carved in stone and handed down by society. Rather, they are products of what Arlie Hochschild terms a gender strategy, which is 'a plan of action through which a person tries to solve problems at hand, given the cultural notions of gender at play' (Hochschild 1989:15). These 'problems at hand' include the fact that small children have to be taken care of. From the studies that Beaujot cites, it is clear that the typical strategy for infant care is for the mother to take time off, then work part-time as the infant matures towards school age, and eventually try to go back to full-time work.

The responsibility for care of children is the main reason that married women are much more likely to work part-time than are married/ unmarried men or unmarried women. It is also the cause of what Beaujot calls the **occupational segregation** of men and women. Women choose occupations in fields such as education and healthcare, which have the greatest flexibility in terms of childcare-related **work interruptions** (which include staying home to care for a sick child or taking a longer-term leave to care for a newborn). Beaujot makes an interesting argument that this is something of a chicken-and-egg scenario: women seek out jobs in occupation areas that offer greater flexibility, but these jobs tend to offer greater flexibility, in part, because they are dominated by women. Is it possible, then, that if women were to enter other occupations in large numbers, a similar flexibility might develop?

The Ethnic Factor in Conjugal Roles

One weakness of Beaujot's work is that he completely ignores the ethnic factor, clearly a mistake. The classic study that looks at the division of conjugal roles among North American immigrant groups is S. Das Gupta's 'Conjugal roles and social network in Indian immigrant families:

In a situation often referred to as the 'double day' or 'double burden', women who are in the workforce end up doing the majority of housework. (© Photodisc)

Bott revisited' (1992). Although written about South Asian immigrants in the United States, this article has a general applicability in Canada. In her study of 25 couples, she found that segregated conjugal roles dominated. The men were invariably the primary breadwinners and made virtually all major decisions affecting the household, while the women, with few exceptions, were full-time homemakers and primary caretakers of the children. Interestingly, however, there were aspects of joint conjugal roles among the immigrant families that would not be nearly as well accepted back in India: joint discussion of the children's education and of the couple's social life (with joint leisure activities the norm).

Change will come, as immigrants to North America adopt more 'Western' approach to dividing conjugal roles, but the ethnic factor still must be considered in any study of gender roles in the Canadian family.

In Other Words
Italian Families and Conjugal Roles: Four Generations

When I think of the topic of gender in an Italian family, I laugh. The struggles between what it means to be male and what it means to be female arise so very often in my family, at every dinner and almost every conversation. The discussions are always split between the three generations because my grandmother lives with my parents and she never misses an opportunity to include her views. As you can probably guess it goes like this, the eldest generation undeniably believes that the female's role in life is to be a complement to her husband; everything she does is based on his needs and his demands. All domestic duties and child-rearing except for punishment are her responsibility. Working outside the home is secondary to household work. The husband makes all decisions, although she can make suggestions. It is the male's responsibility to take care of the family financially.

My parents (second generation) feel similarly, the main difference being the father should be very involved with the children, not solely in areas concerning punishment. Where my grandmother would discourage my father from helping around the house, my mother would welcome the help though not demand nor expect it. In this generation, family decisions are made together; however, household duties are still very divided, even with my mother working full time outside the home. For the female, post-secondary education and career are second to marriage and family. The main female role in life is keeping a clean house, cooking good homemade food, and keeping everyone happy and healthy. The main male role is to keep the food on the table by providing the family with its main source of income.

The third generation around the dinner table changed things a little. This generation in my family consists of my husband and I, the middle brother and his wife and the 'baby brother', though no longer a baby. Most of us are in agreement that gender roles in the new Italian family have changed. No longer is the female solely responsible for all household duties. Husbands cook, clean, and are physically able to change diapers, something my father had never done even with having thee children! The females have post-secondary education and careers and are not a complement to their husbands, but an equal.

I also grew up with a huge double standard that affected me immensely in all areas of my life. It goes something like this: 'This is what boys can do and this is what girls cannot do' (My father's infamous words). Boys can play all day and not help their mothers (girls can't), boys can

Endogamy and Ethnicity

Endogamy means 'marrying within'. It is the practice of marrying someone of the same ethnic, religious, or cultural group as oneself. My mother's mother wanted me to be religiously endogamous and marry a Protestant, not—God forbid—a Catholic. My cousin married a Jew, and I married a Protestant the same year; my stock rose, his fell. My mother, a woman of great understanding and respect for all people,

fight and play rough (girls can't), boys have to do well in school (girls don't have to), boys can go out whenever they want (girls can't), boys have to play sports (girls don't have to), boys can stay out late (girls have to come home early).

'This is what girls must do and this is what boys do not have to do.' Girls must cook and clean (boys do not), girls must learn the traditions (boys do not), girls must be good always (boys do not), girls must stay home to take care of the family (boys do not), girls must not be left alone with their boyfriends (boys can live with their girlfriends). I fought with my younger brothers fairly consistently growing up. The words, 'that is not fair' were spoken often. I actually disliked one of my brothers for years and it was not until he got a family of his own that we began to grow closer together. We even talked about the jealousy we felt for one another over different family issues and how the double standards we grew up with had a great deal to do with it.

Needless to say my family's views on gender have had a great impact on my life. It has carved me into the woman I am today. Much to my parents' chagrin, I cannot cook, I hate house cleaning, run away from tradition whenever I can, I am constantly in school working on a career, and even though I am married, I frequently go out with my friends and stay out late! Being married has been difficult at times also. I always have an intense instinct to run from the gender roles that surround me, and yet I realize that in many circumstances they are needed to preserve peace in a family. I now have many concerns for my daughter. I know she will not be faced with an obvious double standard, as I do not have any sons and I am fully aware that being completely opposite the Martha Stewart-like woman is not anything to be proud of. Something in the middle would be nice. Since little girls are greatly influenced by their mothers, I know I must be really careful to set a positive female role in our family. I truly hope the difference for my daughter will be the ability for her to choose the woman she wants to be instead of madly running away from what I demand her to become.

—Alina Mucci

What do you think?

1. Do you think the narrative writer's brothers would write a different story about conjugal roles?
2. Do you foresee any gender role conflict concerning the writer and her daughter?

once gave me a talk once about why I should not marry a Black woman. There is a strong tradition of endogamy in many cultures, where 'marrying in' is seen as the only way to preserved the purity of one's group.

Approval of its opposite, **exogamy** (marrying outside one's group), once quite low in Canada, is increasing. In Bibby's look at 'Approval of Intergroup Marriage: 1975 through 1995', he noted the following:

Table 6.4 >> Canadians' approval of intergroup marriage (%), 1975–1995

	1975	1980	1985	1990	1995
Whites and Natives	75	80	83	84	84
Whites and Asians (Orientals)	66	75	78	82	83
Whites and East Asians (Pakistanis)	58	66	72	77	80
Whites and Blacks	57	64	72	79	81
Protestants and Catholics	86	88	89	90	92
Protestants and Jews	80	94	84	86	90
Roman Catholics and Jews	78	81	82	85	89

Source: Bibby (1995).

I believe that this set of statistics gives a picture that is more positive than real. It seems more an expression of ideal culture than an indication of probable practice. Contrast it with the following series of comparable exogamy rates from the 1996.

In all of these groups, the vast majority of the people marry within their own group. Do you think that this will change significantly in the next decade or two? What about those examples in which there is a meaningful gender difference: with South East Asians (Thais,

Table 6.5 >> Rates of exogamy for men and for women, by ethnic group, 1996

	HUSBANDS	WIVES
Aboriginals	25.8	31.6
East Asian	7.5	5.8
Chinese	6.4	8.4
South East Asian	8.1	23.3
Filipino	6.7	28.6
Vietnamese	10.6	12.2
South Asian	7.4	5.8
African	25.3	15.1
Caribbean & Bermuda	23.3	18.7
Jewish	19.2	12.7

Under Canadian miscegenation laws, interracial marriages were illegal. However, intergroup marriage approval has been on a steady increase since 1975. Today, Vancouver has the highest rates of interracial marriage in Canada. (Photo © Eamon Mac Mahon, 2005)

Cambodians, Laotians, for example) and Filipinos? The difference among Filipinos may be attributed to the pattern of early immigration of women coming to Canada to obtain jobs in the health sciences. What do you think the reasoning might be for the South East Asians?

Family and Race

As we'll see in greater detail in Chapter 9, on race and ethnicity, there is a history in Canada of the federal government creating policies that denied family to immigrants. The prohibitive head tax levied on immigrants from China and South Asia made it impossible in many cases for married couples or their families to reunite in Canada. Canadian sociologists Nancy Mandell and Ann Duffy, in their text *Canadian Families: Diversity, Conflict and Change* (1995), noted a similar connection between government immigration policy and the denial of family for women of colour. They claim that 'it has been a policy of the government not to encourage the possibility of developing families among women of colour who came as domestic workers. Thus, their status as "single" and as "temporary" is deliberately organized by immigration policies' (1995:157). The policy they refer to was initiated in 1910–11, during one of the country's greatest periods of immigration. About a hundred Black women from Guadeloupe in the Caribbean came to Canada to work as domestic servants, but when authorities discovered that many of the women were not as 'unattached' as they had claimed to be—many had children they had been forced to leave behind—they were sent back.

Between 1955 and 1967, a number of women from the Caribbean—primarily Jamaica—were allowed to come to Canada to work as domestics. They had to be young, of 'good character', and single (in other words, not married or in a common-law relationship). They were given the status of landed immigrants, but they could not seek other work until they had served at least a year as a domestic. Roughly 300 Caribbean women came to Canada each year between 1955 and 1960, the number rising to about 1,000 a year during the 1960s (Bolaria and Li 1985:178). Many of them agreed to work as domestics, even though they were trained as teachers or secretaries; many, in order to be 'single', left family behind, all because it was the only way they could enter the country.

Naturally, those immigrants who left husbands and children in the Caribbean wanted to sponsor their families to join them in Canada, but their efforts were blocked by immigration officials. In 1976, seven Jamaican women applied to sponsor their children to come to Canada. They were ordered to be deported for having failed to report their children on their applications to come to Canada (Leah and Morgan 1979). Their cases were highly publicized, and after an intense struggle that involved community and labour groups, the seven women won their appeals and were allowed to stay in Canada.

Attacks on the Aboriginal Family

Immigrant families are not the only ones that have been touched by restrictive Canadian legislation. The Aboriginal family also has long been a target of federal policy and government agents. The following passage describes how an Indian Agent at the beginning of the twentieth century used the Blackfoot's need for food rations as a tool to ensure that the people remained monogamous:

It may be remembered that, in my last report, I expressed thankfulness that there had been no plural marriages during the preceding year. That report was barely out of my hand when I learned that three members of the band were dissatisfied with one wife each and had taken another. I immediately directed that the rations of these families be withheld until such time as they saw fit to obey the rules in this respect. One family missed one ration, and then decided that it was better to abide by the rules. The other two families held out for several rations, and then they succumbed and put away wife No. 2. (in Dosman 1972:52–3)

As outrageous as it sounds—withholding food rations to control marriage choices—this incident is not atypical of the kind of treatment Native families suffered at the hands of government agents. It's important to point out that actions like this are often products of well-meaning agencies and their representatives. With the benefit of modern perspective, we can see just how misguided—and, frankly, racist—these policies were. The following section looks closely at three policies aimed at controlling Native families. In some cases, as we will see, the same strategies have targeted other groups that governments have felt they needed to manage, including certain cultural and ethnic groups as well as people with physical or mental disabilities.

Residential Schools

Among institutionalized instruments of control to manage the lives of this country's Native populations, residential schools top the list for the devastating effects they have had on Aboriginal families. Officially started in 1910 but existing as 'industrial' and 'boarding' schools before then in the nineteenth century, residential schools were created with the almost explicit objective of keeping Aboriginal

Sociology in Action
Blaming the Victim: Daniel Moynihan and Black Families in the United States

In 1965, American sociologist Daniel Moynihan (1927–2003), acting in his capacity as assistant secretary of the US Department of Labor, compiled an ambitious document called *The Negro Family: The Call for National Action*. In it he presented a statistical profile of Black families in the United States and outlined a plan to address what, in his determination, was a growing problem in need of repair. Moynihan's plan was eventually scrapped as unworkable, but its influence persists. Every ten years, the conservative media celebrate the anniversary of the document's publication by arguing vociferously that Moynihan was right.

One of the strongest opponents of the approach and policy implications of what came to be called *The Moynihan Report* was William Ryan. His critique formed the basis for his most famous work, *Blaming the Victim* (1971). In a chapter facetiously titled 'Mammy Observed—Fixing the Negro Family', Ryan summarized what he felt were the five essential elements of Moynihan's work as follows:

First, the Negro family, as a major institution within the Negro subculture, is weak and unstable, tending toward a matriarchal form. Second, the present status of the Negro family is rooted in the experience of slavery. Third, the distortions in Negro family structure have been maintained by Negro unemployment that has continued at disastrously high levels for many decades. Fourth, the weakened Negro family produces children, particularly sons, who are so damaged by their family experience that they are unable to profit from educational and employment opportunities. Fifth, therefore efforts to achieve formal change in such social institutions as ghetto schools and discriminatory employment practices will have little effect on present patterns of inequality of status; the ending of inequality and poverty will not, and cannot, be achieved until something is done to strengthen and stabilize the Negro family. (Ryan 66–7)

What do you think?

1. Why would the conservative press support such a position?

2. Why can this be called 'blaming the victim'?

3. Can this position be reconciled with the growth of the complex household in Black families in the United States referred to earlier?

children away from the harmful influence of their parents and their home communities. Families were burst apart as parents reluctantly signed over legal guardianship of their children to school principals, then watched their children leave for the state- and church-run boarding schools, where they would live for most, if not all, of the year. Parents were discouraged from visiting, and those who did were closely monitored. Brothers and sisters were kept apart, sometimes not seeing each other for months on end. Many families were never reunited.

J.R. Miller, tells the story of a Cree woman who went to a residential school that was only 19 kilometres away from her reserve, though it might as well have been on another planet. For hours on end, she would stand at the corner of a fence that surrounded the school property:

> She would put her hand through the fence, because that meant she was closer to her home and family by the length of her arm and watch for her parents. She would say to herself, 'the next black horse that comes along' will be drawing her parents' wagon on a visit. Disappointment only led to repetitions of the childlike incantation, a wish and a prayer that never seemed to come true. (Miller 1996:338–9)

Physical, emotional, and sexual abuse by residential school employees demoralized the students. And as those who have been abused so often become abusers, many Aboriginal children grew up to bring the abuse they learned at school to their home community.

Sexual Sterilization

In its official definition of **genocide**, the United Nations includes attempts to destroy a people by imposing measures designed to prevent births within the group. This describes certain policies aimed at Canada's Native population. For instance, in 1928, the United Farmers party of Alberta passed the Sexual Sterilization Act, with the intent of sterilizing 'mental defectives' so that their 'bad genes' would not be passed on. The act reflects the early twentieth-century belief in **eugenics**, the flawed notion that a single gene responsible for intelligence was absent in 'stupid people', who would be capable of having only 'stupid children'—in other words, children inheriting their parents' defective intellect. We know now that there is a complex relationship between a number of yet-unidentified genes and the various aptitudes that make up the biological potential known as **intelligence**. It would be more be accurate to say that we have '**intelligences**' of various kinds and levels (for instance, I have a talent for writing, but I am inept in drawing). This complexity makes the degree to which intelligence is inherited uncertain; we just don't know.

Eugenics has rightly been called a kind of **scientific racism**, as it was used to justify prejudices based on the supposed genetic inferiority or 'feeble-mindedness' of certain groups of immigrants to North America—particularly those coming from eastern Europe (see Gould 1981 and 1983)—as well as of Black people and Native people. Since it was used to support prejudice against poor people, it could also be held up as an example of **scientific classism**. The traditional yardstick for measuring intelligence is the intelligence quotient test. We're all aware that a high IQ indicates a high degree of intelligence, but the test has been criticized for its bias against people representing certain language and culture groups. As well, the test perpetuates a myth that we all have a **general intelligence** to which a single number can be assigned.

During the history of Alberta's Sexual Sterilization Act, which lasted from 1928 to 1972, some 2,832 people were sterilized, most of them women. Sterilizations of Métis and First Nations people account for a disproportionately high number of the total, an estimated 25 per cent (roughly 10 times their percentage of the total population). Not surprisingly, eastern Europeans (e.g. Ukrainians, Russians) were also represented in high numbers in the sterilized group.

The province of British Columbia passed an act similar to Alberta's Sexual Sterilization Act in 1933, the same year that the notorious Law for the Prevention of Genetically Diseased Offspring was passed in Nazi Germany. Recently there have been accusations that, following both racial and religious prejudice, hundreds of non-Christian Aboriginal people were sterilized by a United Church missionary doctor in a church-run hospital in the BC coastal community of Bella Bella, and that a good number of young Aboriginal women made pregnant by residential school staff, clergy, and visiting officials were coerced into having abortions. While numbers are being contested in the courts, there seems little doubt that the practices did take place.

The Sixties Scoop

The UN's definition of genocide also includes attempts to destroy a people by forcibly transferring children of the group to another group. This characterizes what has been referred to as the **Sixties Scoop**, the removal beginning in the 1960s of large numbers of Aboriginal children from their families, their communities, and the Aboriginal world. Children were removed from their families by government by government-affiliated agencies for a variety of reasons: some were children of parents judged to be alcoholics, some were newborns needing hospital care taken to the nearest city (and in many cases never returned), some were living in crowded or 'sub-standard' homes. In 1964, the number of children of all backgrounds removed from their families was 4,228; 1,446 of these, roughly 34 per cent, were Aboriginal children.

Between 1971 and 1981 in Manitoba, where Aboriginal families were hardest hit, over 3,400 Aboriginal children were removed from their homes. Many were taken from the province, and more than 1,000 of them were sent to the United States, where American child welfare agencies could get as much as $4,000 for each child placed. The province later launched an investigation into the practice, led by Justice Edwin Kimelman. In his summary of the investigation, *No Quiet Place* (1985), he stated:

> [C]ultural genocide has been taking place in a systematic routine manner. One gets an image of children stacked in foster homes as used cars are stacked on corner lots, just waiting for the right 'buyer' to stroll by. (in Fournier and Crey 1997:88)

But statistics and judges' reports do not give a real sense of the suffering of those affected. The following statement comes from a research report on the emotional return of children to their families, communities, and people:

> I was sixteen years old when my daughter was taken from me. My partner at the time was drinking and at eighteen he went to prison. I had no way of looking after her and felt very alone. The social worker told me that my daughter would be better off with a 'nice, normal family'. I thought that I would at least be able to visit her sometimes, but she was placed in

Pennsylvania and we did not meet her again until she was 20 years old. I took a bus to Windsor and that is where we met. I was alone and scared. She looked just like me when I was twenty, but with a very different attitude. She had suffered sexual abuse in her adopted home and she blamed it on me. She had a little girl of her own, but she would not let me meet her. I wish there was someone who could help us get past this pain. (Budgell 1999:6)

Summary

As we said at the outset, good families exist in many forms in Canada, and always have. They differ in terms of ethnicity, structure, and sexual orientation, and the model continues to change. Perhaps it is better to say it is evolving, adapting to specific circumstances. From this standpoint, there is good reason to be optimistic about family in Canada.

Bob Daemmrich/Photo Edit Inc.

Questions for Critical Review and Discussion

1. Outline the diversity of the Canadian family, both culturally and historically.

2. Describe how family in Quebec is different from family in the rest of Canada.

3. Outline eight major changes taking place in the family.

4. Identify the different forms that conjugal roles can take.

5. Outline how Aboriginal families were 'under attack' during the twentieth century in Canada.

Suggested Readings

Duffy, Ann, Nancy Mandell & Norene Pupo (1989). *Few Choices: Women, Work and the Family*. Toronto: Garamond Press.

Giddens, Anthony (1992). *The Transformation of Intimacy: Sexuality, Love and Eroticism in Modern Societies*. Stanford: Stanford UP.

Hunter, Mark, ed. (1997). *The Family Experience: A Reader in Cultural Diversity*, 2nd ed. Boston: Allyn and Bacon.

Lasch, Christopher (1997). *Women and the Common Life: Love, Marriage, and Feminism*. E. Lasch-Quinn, ed. New York: W. W. Norton Co.

Luxton, Meg, ed. (1997). *Feminism and Families: Critical Policies and Changing Practices*. Halifax: Fernwood.

Risman, Barbara J. & Pepper Schwartz (1989). *Gender in Intimate Relationships: A Microstructural Approach*. Belmont, CA: Wadsworth Publishing.

Suggested Websites

Guide to the Sociology of the Family (Michael Kearl).
http://www.trinity.edu/~mkearl/family.html

PFLAG (Parents and Friends of Lesbians and Gays).
http://pflag.ca

Vanier Institute of the Family.
http://www.vifamily.ca/

Via-à-vis (National Newsletter on Family Violence).
http://www.ccsd.ca/viasvis.html

Health and Medicine

Contents

Key Terms

Aboriginal visions
absolutist
Arctic hysteria
biomedical hallucinations
biomedicine
brain drain
commodification
cultural syndromes
cultures of medicine
iatrogenesis
individual-centred
inverse care law
medicalization
racialized
radical monopoly
reductionist
sick role
social courses of disease
standpoints

Boxes and Tables

Canadian Sociology in Action The Social Course of Tuberculosis for the Inuit in the Mid-Twentieth Century

Quick Hits Hallucinations and Visions: Two 'Views'

Sociology in Action Illich Quotations Concerning Medicalization

In Other Words An Account of Systemic Racism from a Black First-Year Nursing Student

In Other Words SARS and Being Chinese

Learning Objectives

After reading this chapter, you should be able to

- discuss the significance of the social course of disease to medicine.
- outline the various aspects of biomedicine.
- contrast Aboriginal concepts of medicine with those of biomedicine.
- discuss how the process of medicalization takes place.
- articulate the different views surrounding the accreditation of immigrant doctors.
- outline Ivan Illich's critique of modern medicine.

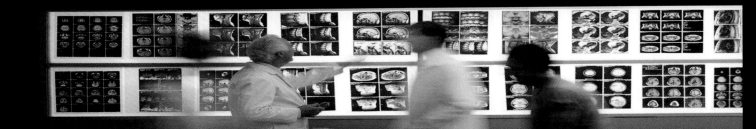

For Starters
Jean-Martin Charcot and the Social Cause of Hysteria

In the late 1870s, in a hospital in Paris, Dr Jean-Martin Charcot (1825–1893) treated a number of mostly middle-class women who exhibited 'wild' physical symptoms such as facial distortions and a peculiar twisting and turning of the body. Charcot would have a profound effect on the fields of neurology and psychoanalysis. Sigmund Freud was a student of his, and his 'hysteria lectures' at the University of Paris, which he gave with the dramatic flair of a showman, were very popular and intellectually influential in the Paris of his day.

Charcot diagnosed the women as suffering from 'hysteria' (a term that comes from the Greek word for 'uterus'). Within a short time, large numbers of women reported that they, too, suffered from this disorder. How might a sociologist explain this outbreak of hysteria? One interpretation might begin with the suppression of women's opportunities in middle-class France. It might also include the social learning process described as follows:

Charcot provided a socially-legitimated 'explanation' of their suffering, and under 'treatment' by Charcot, the women 'learnt' to display the syndrome he was looking for. The doctor and patient therefore met

Jean-Martin Charcot conducts 'A Clinical Lesson at the Salpetreire' in this painting by Pierre Andre Brouillet. What does the picture tell you about the relative power of men at the time to determine what was wrong—physically, mentally, emotionally—with women? (© Bettmann/Corbis)

each others' needs: the doctor for proof of his theory and the patient for recognition of her suffering. Women suffering from causes which they are unable to name, seeing or hearing about Dr Charcot's work, and sympathising with his patients, were either pressured into manifesting the symptoms of hysteria by their family, or acquired the syndrome themselves, as a relief from anxiety. The doctor's 'expert' description of the syndrome is in turn amplified and consolidated by artists and writers, who create fictitious characters suffering from the syndrome, journalists reporting 'outbreaks' and so on. As a result, people report to their own doctors that they are suffering from the same syndrome and demand to be diagnosed and treated accordingly. (www.marxist.org/glossary/terms/h/y.htm)

In other words, the women diagnosed learned to express their socially induced frustrations in socially approved ways. Charcot provided a medical explanation and remedy for a problem that in many cases was essentially a social one. Medical and social processes were inextricably linked.

Introduction

Medical sociology is based on the view that medical practices and beliefs are intensely social. A large part of it is policy sociology, involving health professionals such as doctors and professors of nursing, pharmacy, and medicine. Among the principal aims of medical sociology is to improve the delivery of health services through sociologically informed research. Critical sociology contributes significantly as well, especially when the practices of multinational pharmaceutical companies, medical schools (particularly when they raise their fees), and privately run, profit-making hospitals are objects of study.

Healing is achieved through social means, so it's natural that sociology has a lot to contribute to our understanding of the field of medicine. Race, gender, ethnicity, age, and class—all social factors—affect an individual's experience of the medical professions.

Sociological factors will affect the treatment you receive from your doctor. Let's say you are a middle-aged woman living outside the city, suffering from intensely sore feet. You go to your family doctor. She is of South Asian descent and was educated in Britain, having moved to Canada just five years ago. She can't find a cause for your ailment, so she recommends a number of specialists. Which specialists she recommends will depend on her social network, the circle of people she knows and trusts. This network depends on such social factors as the location of her practice (outside the city) and the level of status she has a doctor (itself possibly determined by how long she has been practising and the degree to which she has been politically active in medical associations). Religion can be a factor, since certain hospitals are governed by specific religious groups. Her gender alone might be a factor, as men are still more prominent in medicine than women.

For contrast, imagine that you are a very successful businessperson with a prominent white male doctor who has hospital privileges at one of the best hospitals in the city. Your doctor has been head of the provincial medical association and is often asked to present papers at medical conferences around the world. Imagine how his social network might differ from that of the doctor discussed in the preceding paragraph, and how your treatment might differ as a result.

Sick Role

American sociologist **Talcott Parsons** (1902–1979) came up with perhaps the first medical sociology term when, in his book *The Social System* (1951), he developed the concept of the **sick** (or **patient**) **role**. Like other sociological roles, he argued, being sick came with certain expectations—four, to be exact. In his thinking, two relate to what the sick person can expect from society, two to what society should expect of the sick person. The four expectations are outlined as follows:

The person engaged in the sick role
1) should expect to be granted 'exemption from normal social responsibilities'. In other words, the patient does not have to work, either at home or at his or her job, because of illness.
2) should expect to be 'taken care of' rather than having to take care of him- or herself.
3) is socially obligated to try to 'get well' rather than remain in the undesirable state of being ill.
4) is socially obligated to 'seek technically competent help' (in other words, the help of a qualified health professional).

The sick role, according to Parsons, gave the individual licence to be temporarily 'deviant' (Parsons' own choice of word) with regards to the first two expectations provided that he or she acts in accordance with the second two.

Parsons' work is considered to be the epitome of structural functionalism, both its strengths and (to a greater extent, in the view of many contemporary sociologists) its weaknesses. Structural functionalism presumes a social uniformity that conflict or critical sociologists would challenge. You have to ask yourself whether you think the sick role is the same for everybody.

The first challenge to the uniformity of the structural-functionalist model came quickly. In 1954, E.L. Koos published *The Health of Regionalville: What the People Thought and Did About It*. It was based research he carried out between 1946 and 1950 in order to look at differences in what people thought and did about their health depending on their class. What he found was that people in higher occupational groups were better able to afford to play the sick role, a privilege less available to those of lower occupational groups. Similar arguments against the uniformity of the sick role applied other standard sociological factors, such as gender, race, ethnicity, and age. Societies have different expectations for, as one commercial refers to her, 'Dr Mom' than they do for Dad. When children are sick, it is most often the mother who is expected to take time off work. Who is least likely to be able to play the sick role if the whole family gets sick? And what about people with chronic illnesses or disabilities? Are they to be considered permanently 'deviant' according to this model?

Not only is it hard to defend the uniformity of Parsons' original model of the sick role, but it is clear that the model changes over time. In his article 'Patients in the New Economy: The "Sick Role" in a Time of Economic Discipline' (2002), Ivan Emke proposes that in Canada at the turn of the twenty-first century there are five new expectations of the patient's role. Two of these are central. The first is that 'patients in the New Economy are responsible for their own illnesses.' Emke's point is that rather than looking at social causes of sickness (pollution, unsafe working and living conditions, stress through overworking, economic insecurity, and social disruption), we've become more inclined to blame individual and debatable 'choices' (smoking, drinking, not belonging to a health club, not making time for exercise, eating foods with transfats). Emke remarks on the fact that the bulk of cancer information now provided to people focuses on individual risk factors, rather than those presented by society. This expectation, by lowering society's sense that everyone is completely entitled to free health-care, is born at least in part of the search for ways to lower rising healthcare costs in Canada. You can see how those who buy into this expectation might use the underlying argument to justify charging 'user fees' for some medical services.

The second new expectation we'd like to highlight is really a conflation of two expectations Emke identified: 'the patient in the new economy is instructed to tread lightly on the system,' and 'patients in the new economy are not to be trusted.' We could call it 'patients are assumed to be abusing the system.' Emke raises it in connection with the increasing 'public education' campaign to encourage people to use as few medical services as they can. He cites as an example a 1994 pilot project by the Ontario government designed to encourage

residents of the city of London to stop going to their family doctor for relatively minor complaints. No research had been done before to see if people were 'abusing' the system, but the assumption underlying the project was clearly that escalating healthcare costs can be attributed to a large number of billable visits to family doctors, some—if not many—of which could be avoided. Perhaps, though, rising healthcare costs are actually the result of building huge technology-intensive hospitals that are less cost-effective than having a greater number of small-town and community medical centres. Perhaps lower-paid nurses should be given more responsibility for performing basic medical procedures (stitching wounds, for example) than the more highly paid doctors, so that the same work can be done at lower cost. The key here is that like the first expectation, this thrusts greater responsibility onto the person in the sick role.

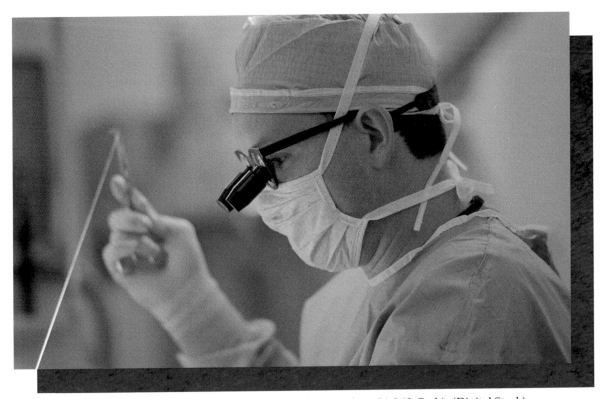

Should nurses be allowed to perform medical procedures such as this? (© Corbis/Digital Stock)

What do you think?

1. How might factors such as gender and ethnicity affect the universality of Parsons' sick role?
2. Do you believe that people who smoke are entitled to free healthcare? People who eat badly?
3. Do you agree with new trends Emke identified in Canadian healthcare?
4. Could you argue that the social nature of healthcare—how it reflects social factors such as economics and ethnicity—abuses the system more than its users do? In what way?

The Social Course of Disease

One of the medical breakthroughs of the nineteenth century was the realization that every disease has a natural, or biological, course it goes through, a lifespan during which you catch the disease, suffer through it, and gradually get well (or, in some cases, sicker). It depends on the virus or bacteria, and the way the human body reacts to it. Think of a cold virus: doctors can prescribe medicine to help alleviate the symptoms and speed up recovery, but they can't fundamentally change the natural course of the illness.

Likewise, we can speak of the **social course** that diseases and disorders go through, a course affected by sociological factors such as ethnic background, culture, class, age, and gender. Leading medical anthropologist Arthur Kleinman demonstrates this convincingly in his discussion of the social course of epilepsy in China:

> The social course of epilepsy indicates that epilepsy develops in a local context where economic, moral, and social institutional factors powerfully affect the lived experience of seizures, treatment, and their social consequences. The social course of epilepsy, furthermore, is plural, heterogeneous [i.e. there is more than one course that it can take], and changing. It is as distinctive as are different moral worlds, different social networks, different social histories. . . .

> Framing epilepsy in terms of its social course suggests that to improve the quality of life and reduce disability, it is essential that health and social policy address the context of social experience. Stigma, institution discrimination, the relatively high cost of care in a setting of chronic deprivation, and the other specific social consequences we have delineated, including the social resistance put up by sufferers, are as important for health and health policy as is basic medical services. Indeed, they are as salient for the content of medical care as are diagnosis and pharmacology. The social course of illness constitutes much of what is meant by prognosis. Health education, disability laws and services, community action projects, and work- and family-based rehabilitation programs are essential to this orientation. (Kleinman 1995:171–2)

The box on page 180–1 provides another example of factors that affect the social course of a disease. It is good to keep in mind that the social course of a disease, just like physical factors such as medicine, clean living conditions, rest, and so on, can help or hinder the healing process.

Biomedicine

Biomedicine involves the application of standard principles and practices of Western scientific disciplines, particularly biology, in the diagnosis and treatment of symptoms of illness and disease. It uses physical tests to find defined, purely physical entities (such as bacteria, viruses, and trauma) and the application of purely physical medicines and therapies. Sometimes described as 'conventional medicine', it is the dominant practice in Western society.

When, suffering from migraine headaches, you visit your family doctor and she prescribes medication to reduce the severity of your symptoms, you have experienced biomedicine. If you've grown up in Canada or the US, this is likely the approach you expected—even hoped for—when you booked your appointment. But there are other approaches to treatment that fall outside of mainstream medical practice. We refer to these approaches collectively as **alternative** or **complementary medicine**. Your doctor, for instance, might have recommended acupuncture for your migraines. Or she might have recommended massage therapy or yoga as means of reducing the stress that may have contributed to your headaches. She might have tried to discover any environmental causes—bright lights in the area where you read or study, for example—of your condition. These would all be considered alternative approaches.

Alternative approaches are used to treat the gamut of medical ailments. Recent research in **psychoneuroimmunology**—the study of the effect of the mind on health and resistance to disease—has shown links between a person's psychological state and his or her ability to fight diseases such as cancer. A study at the University of Texas monitored the spread of cancer in two groups of mice. One group was placed in small plastic chambers for several hours at a time, which caused a surge in their stress hormones. Tumours in these mice grew more quickly and in greater number than those in the mice that were not confined, suggesting a link between stress and the spread of the disease (Philip 2006). As the *Globe and Mail*'s Margaret Philip reports, this study is one of a number that have caused oncologists to consider more holistic approaches to treating cancer sufferers, using massage, meditation, music therapy, and support groups to help reduce tension (Philip 2006).

A good example of divergent biomedical and alternative approaches to health is childbirth. Most North American women choose to deliver their infants at a hospital under the care of a

When you see this picture, do you think that the woman is being treated by 'health professionals'? An illegal practice less than 20 years ago, midwives are now an integral part of the medical system. Why was midwifery illegal? (Photo by Guy Kirby Letts, 2006)

Canadian Sociology in Action
The Social Course of Tuberculosis for the Inuit in the Mid-Twentieth Century

Race can be a powerful factor affecting the social course of a disease. Witness, for example, the treatment of Inuit with tuberculosis. At the beginning of the twentieth century, tuberculosis was responsible for the deaths of tens of thousands of Canadians, especially immigrants living in squalid conditions that fostered the disease. In 1908, the annual rate of tuberculosis-related deaths was 165 per 100,000 population; since the country's population was about 6,625,000 in 1908, that meant that over 7,500 Canadians died from tuberculosis that year alone.

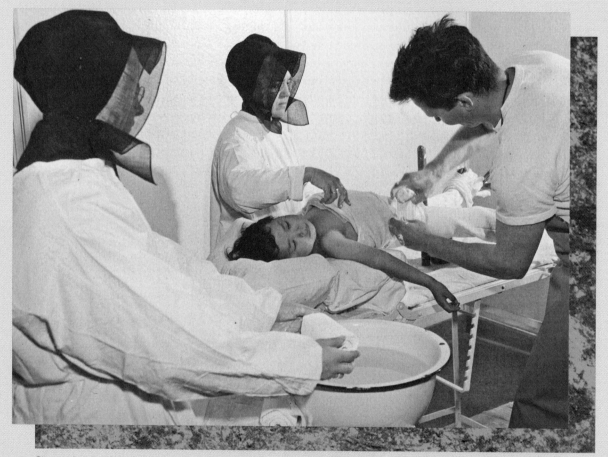

Sisters J. Marchand (left) and M. Lachambie assist Dr L.J. Mulvihill, superintendent of Indian Health Services, place a cast on an Aboriginal boy suffering from tuberculosis of the hip c. 1949. (© Library and Archives Canada 002414883)

By 1949, new antibiotics combined with improved sanitation, screening, and treatment helped reduce the rate in Canada to about 33 deaths per 100,000. But at the same time, the rate among Canada's Inuit population was rising dramatically, peaking at an alarming 569 per 100,000 (then the highest in the world) in 1952. To get a feel for how high that is, compare it with the high rate of TB found in prisons in post-Communist Russia: 484 per 100,000. In that year, 54 of the roughly 10,000 Canadian Inuit died.

There were a number of reasons for the high rate of TB among Canada's Inuit. First, the severe cold of the Arctic—not cold enough to kill the tuberculosis bacillus—made the Inuit especially susceptible to respiratory problems. The intimate closeness of the Inuit in their igloos facilitated the spread of tuberculosis from one family member to another. More significant were the causes related to the increasing contact with people from the rest of Canada. Pat Grygier, in *A Long Way from Home: The Tuberculosis Epidemic among the Inuit*, explains that

> as the Inuit adapted to accommodate the desires of the newcomers, trapping to exchange furs for store goods or working for the RCMP or on military construction sites for cash, their highly nutritious fresh-meat or fish diet and their warm caribou-skin clothing were gradually exchanged for a diet largely of white flour, lard, tea, jam, and canned goods, and for much less warm southern clothing. When the caribou declined or the pattern of migration changed (possibly as a result of the incursions of military and mining into the North), malnutrition occurred. (Grygier 1994:55)

Arguably as devastating as the disease, however, was the way in which Inuit TB sufferers were treated. At the time, the standard treatment for tuberculosis involved a period of confinement—from six months to two years—in a hospital or sanatorium. These were not to be built in the Arctic, so the Inuit with tuberculosis were brought (or, more accurately, taken, since many were most reluctant to leave their homes) to southern Canada. Grygier eloquently describes what would happen once health professionals, brought north by ship, had conducted their patient examinations:

> When the doctors had made their final decision on whether an individual should go to hospital for treatment or stay in the North, the evacuees were sent down to the Inuit quarters in the prow of the ship and the rest were sent ashore. The evacuees were not allowed to go ashore to collect belongings, to say goodbye, or to make arrangements for their families or goods. If a mother was judged sick but her children were not infected, the children (sometimes including unweaned babies) were given to an Inuk woman going ashore. Fathers had no chance to arrange for someone to hunt for food for their families or to look after their dogs and equipment. Mothers had no chance to arrange for someone to care for their children or to sew and process the skins needed to keep the family warm. . . . Those needing hospital treatment were kept on board, the rest sent ashore, and on sailed the ship to the next settlement. (Grygier 1994:96)

The tuberculosis rate among the Inuit dropped during the 1950s to a low of 53 per 100,000 (just 5 in number) in 1959, but the effects of the separation were to last. Many families were never reunited, often because a sick loved one died but in many cases even when the TB-suffering family member recovered.

team of medical professionals including an obstetrician, an anaesthesiologist, and several nurses. Increasingly, women are choosing to stay at home to give birth under the care of a midwife or doula. There are good reasons to recommend the latter approach. For one thing, many people find hospitals uncomfortable. Some women do not want to be separated from their families—especially if they have other young children—and knowing they will remain at home eliminates stressful contemplation of the hurried trip to the hospital once the contractions begin. Many new mothers-to-be find that a doula is more available to provide support and answer questions than is an obstetrician. And, it's important to point out, for thousands of years and in many parts of the world today, giving birth at home was and is the only option. On the other hand, there are many advantages to having a hospital birth, including ready access to doctors and medical equipment in the event that either the mother or the infant requires immediate care for life-threatening complications. It's worth noting that some women choose to combine these approaches by having a hospital birth attended by the midwife or doula who has guided them through their pregnancy. In cases such as this, the term 'complementary medicine' is really more apt: biomedicine and alternative medicine do not need to be mutually exclusive.

Biomedicine remains the norm in North American society, but it is increasingly called into question by those who endorse a more holistic approach to diagnosis and treatment. Biomedicine has been criticized for looking at health from a **reductionist** perspective that attributes medical conditions to single factors treatable with single remedies; it fails to take into account the broader set of circumstances surrounding a person's health or illness. Those involved in biomedicine are sometimes accused of being **absolutist**, of failing to recognize that just as there are cultures of business, policing, and clothing, there are **cultures of medicine**, each with a unique approach to interpreting medicine in ways that reflect and reinforce other aspects of the culture from

which it is derived. Every patient, critics argue, should be treated in the context of his or her culture; no single treatment should be applied universally across all cultures.

In Chapter 3 we touched on Anne Fadiman's study of the Hmong people living in the United States (Fadiman 1997). Originally from China, the Hmong people were forced to flee their homeland after resisting the Chinese government and encouraging the participation of the United States in the Southeast Asian wars of the 1960s and 1970s. Fadiman's study shows how Hmong refugees suffered because of narrow Western medical practices that did not respect their cultural beliefs. She cites, as just one example, the failure of North American doctors to take into account the fear—widespread among the Hmong people—of losing their soul. The Hmong wear (and put on their infants) neck-rings and cotton-string spirit bracelets to combat their fear of soul-loss, and they rely on their spirit doctors or shamans, the *tsiv neebs*, to address and help them overcome these fears. Problems occurred when Hmong patients arriving at a refugee camp in Ban Vinai, Thailand, had their spirit strings cut by American health workers, who claimed they were unsanitary. The neck-rings thought to hold the souls of babies intact were also removed, placing this especially vulnerable (in the eyes of the Hmong) group in graver danger of soul-loss.

Cultural Syndromes

Another way in which Western medicine has marginalized minority cultures is by inventing **cultural syndromes** (disorders supposed to afflict only people of certain ethnicities) in order to psychologize problems brought on by Western colonial control. Cultural syndromes are responsible for establishing or perpetuating stereotypes that can be difficult to stamp out. (Consider, as an example, the condition known as 'amok', a term used by the Portuguese to describe the homicidal frenzy supposedly typical of the Malayan people; the term survives in the English expression 'to run amok'.)

A classic example of this is 'Arctic hysteria', a syndrome first identified and described by the

>> Quick Hits
Hallucinations and Visions: Two 'Views'

As evidence that medicine has cultures, consider the following descriptions of hallucinations, from a biomedical perspective, and visions, from an Aboriginal perspective. Are they really different, or is it in only in how we look at them?

HALLUCINATIONS
- things that are seen but are not physically there
- associated with drug use, nervous disorders, stress
- sign of mental or emotional instability

VISIONS
- pictures, words, tunes, dances coming from a quest for visions
- associated with inspiration, intuition, 'sixth sense'
- sign of spiritual health, creativity

wife of Arctic explorer Robert Peary in 1892. In her journal, Josephine Peary described the 'crazy' acts of Inuit women who would suddenly scream, tear their clothes off, imitate the sound of some bird or animal, or run in circles—apparently for no reason—to the point of collapse. White visitors to the Arctic began to record this phenomenon as pibloktuq (or any one of a number of linguistically challenged variations of this).

The name first entered the historical record, then the psychiatric medical record, as a form of '**Arctic hysteria**' (Brill 1913). It still exists as a psychological disorder legitimated by a medical name, authenticated by case studies. It also became enshrined in anthropology textbooks (e.g. Harris 1987:328–9, and Barnouw 1987:207) as one of a number of culture-specific syndromes or psychoses.

In a 1995 article entitled '"Pibloktoq" (Arctic Hysteria): A Construction of European–Inuit Relations?', historian Lyle Dick challenged the existence of the phenomenon as a part of traditional Inuit culture. He offers his opinion (with which I agree) that it is more likely the creature of the White–Inuit power imbalance embodied in such contexts as the obsessively driven Robert Peary forcing the Inuit to take unwise risks in exploration that they would not normally take, and in sexual abuse by White men of Inuit women.

Medicalization

A product of the biomedical approach to medicine is the phenomenon known as **medicalization**. Chang and Christakis, sociologists at the University of Chicago, define medicalization in the following way:

Medicalisation refers to the process by which certain behaviours or conditions are defined as medical problems (rather than, for example, as moral or legal problems), and medical intervention becomes the focus of remedy and social control. (Chang and Christakis 2002:152)

The point of reference for Chang and Christakis's discussion of medicalization is obesity. The two authors were summarizing the results of a content analysis aimed at investigating how the discussion of obesity had changed between 1927 and 2000 in a widely consulted American medical textbook, the *Cecil Textbook of Medicine*. They found that, although the textbook was consistent over time in citing as the root cause of obesity the obvious factor of caloric intake exceeding energy expenditure, it had medicalized obesity through its successive editions. Early editions of the textbook identified 'aberrant individual activities such as habitual overeating' as being of great significance. It placed blame for the condition squarely on the individual. Later editions looked more to genetic and social environmental factors (for instance, the increased availability of fast food and the decreased amount of physical labour required in many jobs).

Critics of the health industry's tendency to medicalize conditions describe the practice as a form of reductionism that reduces medical conditions to biomedical causes without examining possible sociocultural or political factors. A second, and related, criticism is that Western health professionals are too quick to situate the problem exclusively or primarily in the individual human body, not, say, in an oppressive social or political system. Medicalization, by ascribing conditions like alcoholism to genetic factors, does benefit the sufferer by removing individual blame, but at the same time it portrays the sufferer as a genetic 'victim' who can be saved only by the medical profession; in this way, it takes away the individual's ability to make empowering choices that will affect the outcome of his or her condition. 'You can't stop overeating,' says the medicalizing health professional, 'it's in your genes. Your only recourse is a tummy tuck.' This leads to a fourth criticism, that medicalization contributes to the **commodification** of healthcare, by identifying certain conditions that might be considered normal (though slightly regrettable) as diseases that may be treated with 'commodity cures' (such as certain drugs or procedures). Part of this commodifying process involves turning conditions that might be, in medical terms, relatively normal into deviant disorders (to use sociological terms). Examples for the aging male include obesity, male pattern baldness, increasingly frequent nighttime trips to the bathroom, and erectile 'dysfunction'. These are not diseases; they are relatively normal aspects of the aging process and do not need to be medicalized. If it ain't broke (just a little bent), don't fix it.

Government agencies and health professionals are sometimes guilty of medicalizing disorders that can be traced to complicated social or environmental factors much more difficult to address than the purely medical factors. Medical journalist Lynn Payer offers an example in her eye-opening work *Disease-Mongers: How Doctors, Drug Companies, and Insurers Are Making You Feel Sick* (1992):

> When . . . a child died of lead poisoning in Michigan, there was a call for screening for lead poisoning. But when you read the circumstances, you found that the child was homeless, living in an abandoned building. Calling for blood testing was obviously easier than calling for a policy of providing safe and low-cost shelter for the poor, but who can doubt which policy would really benefit such children more? (Payer 1992:39)

Posttraumatic stress disorder is another condition that is often medicalized (see Kleinman 1995). Suffered by those who have experienced the extreme violence of warfare (as soldiers or civilians) or violent political oppression, PTSD was first diagnosed by Western psychiatrists who traced its origins to bleak, unstable environments in countries such as Cambodia, El Salvador, Tibet, and the former Republic of Yugoslavia. Gradually, though, the focus of treatment has shifted from the pathology of the environment to the pathology of the individual. Patients are treated as though their psychobiological reactions to these harrowing circumstances are not normal; they are labelled 'victims', deprived of social agency. To be clear, it is not wrong to help people by recognizing that they have suffered psychological trauma, but it is misleading to remove from an individual's story the sociopolitical situation in which that person fought and survived, won freedom, and maybe lost loved ones.

Ivan Illich: Pioneering Critic of Medicalization

Ivan Illich (1927–2002) introduced the notion of medicalization in his highly creative and popular work. Although he was trained as a medieval

A Canadian peacekeeper in Bosnia peers out from a tank. Canadian peacekeepers faced unstable and hostile conditions during their mission in the former Yugoslavia. In September 1993, they were ordered into the volatile 'Medak Pocket' of southern Croatia to enforce a ceasfire between Serbian and Croatian forces. After a prolonged firefight with Croatian forces opposed to the ceasefire, they moved into the local Serbian villages, whose civilian inhabitants had been massacred, their villages levelled by Croatian forces. It was the role of Canadians to search for survivors and record evidence of the 'ethnic cleansing' that had occurred. Would you consider symptoms of posttraumatic stress disorder among Canadian peacekeepers a natural consequence of their work? (Damir Sagolj/Reuters)

historian, theologian, and philosopher, sociologists stake claim to him as a public sociologist.

Illich developed the concept of medicalization as part of a general critique of what he called **radical monopolies** in industrial societies. He defined these as follows:

> A radical monopoly goes deeper than that of any one corporation or any one government. It can take many forms. . . . Ordinary monopolies corner the market; radical monopolies disable people from doing or making things on their own. . . . They impose a society-wide substitution of commodities for use-values by reshaping the milieu and by 'appropriating'

those of its general characteristics which have enabled people so far to cope on their own. Intensive education turns autodidacts [people who teach themselves] into unemployables, intensive agriculture destroys the subsistence farmer, and the deployment of police undermines the community's self control. The malignant spread of medicine has comparable results: it turns mutual care and self-medication into misdemeanors or felonies. (1995:42)

In *Medical Nemesis: The Limits of Medicine*, which opens with the claim, 'The medical establishment has become a major threat to

Sociology in Action
Illich Quotations Concerning Medicalization

What do you think Illich meant by each of the following statements? Do you agree with him?

The fact that the doctor population is higher where certain diseases have become rare has little to do with the doctors' ability to control or eliminate them. It simply means that doctors deploy themselves as they like, more so than other professionals, and that they tend to gather where the climate is healthy, where the water is clean, and where people are employed and can pay for their services. (1976:21–2)

In a complex technological hospital, negligence becomes 'random human error' or 'system breakdown', callousness becomes 'scientific detachment', and incompetence becomes 'a lack of specialized equipment'. The depersonalization of diagnosis and therapy has changed malpractice from an ethnical into a technical problem. (1976:30)

In every society, medicine, like law and religion, defines what is normal, proper, or desirable. Medicine has the authority to label one man's complaint a legitimate illness, to declare a second man sick though he himself does not complain, and to refuse a third social recognition of his pain, his disability, and even his death. It is medicine which stamps some pain as 'merely subjective', some impairment as malingering, and some deaths—though not others—as suicide.' (1976:45)

Medicine always creates illness as a social state. The recognized healer transmits to individuals the social possibilities for acting sick. Each culture has its own characteristic perception of disease and thus its unique hygienic mask. Disease takes its features from the physician who casts the actors into one of the available roles. To make people legitimately sick is as implicit in the physicians power as the poisonous potential of the remedy that works. (1995:44)

---

health' (1976:1), Illich identified a 'doctor-generated epidemic' that was harming the health of people in industrialized society by taking away people's freedom to heal themselves or prevent their illnesses, and their freedom to criticize industrial society for the ills of stress, pollution, and general danger he said was 'sickening' (i.e. making sick) the people. His term for this was **iatrogenesis**, and he distinguished three different kinds: clinical, social, and cultural. **Clinical iatrogenesis** refers to the various ways in which diagnosis and cure cause problems that are equal to or greater than the health problems they are meant to resolve. This occurs, for example, when a patient enters hospital for treatment of one ailment and becomes infected with a virus originating in the hospital. **Social iatrogenesis**, of greater interest to sociologists (unless they are in hospitals), is the deliberate obscuring of political conditions that 'render society unhealthy' (1995:9). **Cultural iatrogenesis** takes place when the knowledge and abilities of the medical community are extolled or mythologized to the point where the authority of the health profession 'tends to mystify and to expropriate the power of the individual to heal himself and to shape his or her environment.' (1995:9)

Ethnicity and Medical Sociology

Unemployed Immigrant Doctors: A Problem with Many Standpoints

The Canadian healthcare system is currently facing a shortage of doctors in some communities. At the same time, the country is welcoming immigrants with medical degrees and general credentials that are considered insufficient to qualify them to practise medicine in this country. It is a perplexing issue, one that must be considered from a number of **standpoints** (perspectives shaped by social location). The sections that follow outline four of these differing standpoints.

a) Immigrant Doctors

As an immigrant doctor, you have come to a country with greater financial opportunity for you and your family. You have scored highly in the 'point system', by which the worthiness of candidates for of immigration is judged. It seems as though the Canadian government is encouraging you to come.

As soon as you arrive in Canada, the problems hit you in the face. If you chosen to settle in Toronto—as many have—you are faced with a two-step problem. First, your skills and knowledge must be assessed through a training program. The Ontario International Medical Graduate Program takes 48 weeks—close to a year—and has limited entrance. Assuming you manage to gain entrance and do well in the program, you still face a second, even higher hurdle: you must go through a residency program of several years in which you essentially re-learn everything you needed to know to earn your medical qualifications in the first place. But like many others in your position, you accept this and are eager to get on with it. However—and this is the biggest problem you face—there are so very few residencies available. You are one of more than 1,100 immigrant doctors in Ontario competing for just 36 spots open in year in the residency program.

In the meantime, your family must eat. If you are fortunate, you may get a job in the medical field, possibly (with training) as a lab assistant. But it is more likely you will end up in telemarketing, driving a taxi, delivering pizza, or doing manual labour in factories. Your dream of practising your profession in this country supposedly rich in opportunity has proven elusive.

b) Rural Communities

You live in a community that is home to fewer and fewer doctors. The older ones retire, the young graduates opt to take up medical work in the big city. Your family doctor has retired and closed her practice, and you, like her other patients, are scrambling to find another doctor

Photo © Ingram

to take you on. But most family doctors are already seeing more patients than they can handle. You once laughed at the joke that the best way to find a family doctor with an opening was to check the obituaries, but you're desperate enough you might resort to this tactic in earnest. But you're older, and, face it, older people have more complicated and time-consuming medical problems, so you're not the most attractive candidate even if you managed to find a doctor taking new patients. So you put up with minor complaints, knowing that anything more serious will require a trip down to the big city, where the bigger research hospitals and more lucrative practices are.

Occasionally you wonder whether there's something your town should be doing to attract doctors. You don't very much care where they come from. In Ontario, 136 communities have been designated as 'underserved' by the provincial ministry of health. Saskatchewan and Newfoundland and Labrador have higher percentages of foreign-trained doctors than other provinces. The reason: not as many obstacles for immigrant doctors.

c) Countries of Origin of Internationally Trained Doctors

You think *you're* underserved. In developing countries, especially in rural areas, there are fewer doctors per population than there are in Canada's rural communities. The cost of educating medical professionals is prohibitively high. It is much more likely that your country will lose trained doctors to emigration than benefit from an influx of health professionals. In post-apartheid South Africa, the government decided to block doctors immigrating from other African nations to halt the **brain drain**— the exodus of educated professionals—eroding the healthcare systems of those countries. Canada experiences a bit of that brain drain when some of its medical specialists go to the US—but it's nothing compared to the brain drain of doctors leaving developing countries for North America.

d) Doctors' Associations

Placing restrictions on internationally trained medical graduates gives Canadian-trained doctors more power as a sociopolitical body of professionals. As Linda McQuaig explains in her commentary on a doctors' strike in New Brunswick in 2004,

> Doctors have managed to maintain enormous bargaining power in Canada by threatening, from time to time, to abandon us for more prosperous climes. But these threats only have teeth because doctors can rely on the fact that there is no one here to replace them if they go—even when potential replacements are already here and desperate to get to work. (McQuaig 2004)

On the other side, in their 4 April 2002 'Position Paper on Physician Workforce Policy and Planning', a document addressing concerns of the Ontario Medical Association (OMA) about 'the problem of inadequate physician human resources, and the related consequences for public access to medical treatment', one of their 18 recommendations was to 'Temporarily increase the number of fully qualified international medical graduate (IMG) positions'. In a 20 April 2004 speech by Dr Larry Erlick, President of the OMA, addressing the same problems, he noted that

> We . . . need more foreign-trained physicians to practice in Ontario. The fact that we have relied on foreign trained physicians in the past should come as a surprise, as 25% of physicians practicing today in this province are in fact international medical graduates! Some of the red tape has to be cut.

Still, in both documents, helping foreign-trained physicians was clearly seen as of secondary importance. The words 'temporarily' and 'fully qualified' in the first statement leaves holes in that support, and the recommendation by the OMA president was among the 'short-term recommendations', given decidedly less priority than bringing back Ontario medical graduates practising elsewhere.

What do you think?

1. Are there any other sides or 'stakeholders' in this issue that should be covered?

2. What do you think the position of Canadian universities with medical schools would be?

3. Why do you think the word 'temporarily' was put into the recommendation?

4. What is your position in this matter?

Quebec

As we have seen elsewhere, Quebec, from a sociological point of view, is quite different from other provinces in Canada. Here are four areas in the sociology of health and medicine in which this statement is true:

- the relative number of male nurses
- the number of female medical students
- the number of people without regular doctors
- the cost of tuition fees for medical students

In 2002, there were 219,161 women registered nurses (RNs) in Canada, compared with just 11,796 male registered nurses (about 5.4 per cent of the total). In Quebec, the 5,272 male RNs make up roughly 9.8 per cent of the total (59,193). A more striking statistic is that approximately 45 per cent of the male nurses in Canada were in working in Quebec.

It should not be surprising, then, that there is also a difference in non-traditional gender with Quebec medical students. The number of female medical students is consistently higher in Quebec than elsewhere in Canada. In 1997, 59 per cent of the students at Quebec's four medical schools were women, compared with 46 per cent in the 12 schools throughout the rest of the country. That year, the University of Sherbrooke had the highest proportion of women starting medical school—71 per cent—compared with just 30 per cent, the lowest

Do you think the use of this photo, featuring two male students, on a McGill University School of Nursing webpage has any bearing on male enrolment at the school? (© McGill University; design: dubreuilmedia)

figure, at the University of Manitoba. In the 2003–4 academic year, the Université de Laval had the highest percentage of female first-year medical students, with 74 per cent; the University of Saskatchewan had the lowest, with 43 per cent. Overall, 68 per cent of all medical students in Quebec in 2003–4 were women.

The third factor, relating to people without regular doctors, is borne out by a 1994–5 study of Canadians over the age of 20. About 14 per cent of the people studied were without regular doctors, but the figure for Quebec residents without regular doctors was 25.6 per cent in Quebec, by far the highest of any province (with the exception of Newfoundland and Labrador, which ranked a fairly close second).

The fourth factor is the cost of a medical degree, which is much lower at universities in Quebec than in medical schools elsewhere in Canada. Compare the following figures for 2003–4, presented in order of most to least expensive:

Table 7.1 >> Average annual cost of attending medical school, by province, 2003–4	
Ontario	$14,878
Nova Scotia	$10,460
Saskatchewan	$9,774
British Columbia	$8,876
Alberta	$7,493
Manitoba	$6,693
Newfoundland and Labrador	$6,250
Quebec	**$2,781**

It should also be noted that with the exception of Newfoundland and Labrador, whose medical school tuition fees have not risen for four years, and Manitoba, where fees dropped in 2000–1 and then held constant for the next three years, Quebec has the slowest growth rate in medical school fees, rising by just $200 over the last four years (compare that with the $6,216 rise in Ontario, where medical school fees are the highest in Canada).

The Intersection of Race and Medicine

From a sociological perspective, one of the most interesting points of intersection between race and the medical professions in Canada is the issue of nurses who are not White. The following two sections take a closer look at this issue.

The Filipino Nurses

Filipinos were later than other Asian immigrant groups—Chinese, Japanese, Koreans, and South Asians—to come to Canada. It was only after some of the more overt forms of discrimination in Canada's immigration policy were abolished in 1962 and the points system, rewarding candidates with desirable skills and education, was established in 1967 that Filipino immigration to this country became significant.

In 1967, the demand for nurses in Canada outstripped the field of qualified nursing professionals. That year, 4,262 nurses were allowed to immigrate to Canada. Filipino nurses made up 1,140, or 26.7 per cent, of that figure, and 43.3 per cent of the 2,632 immigrants from the Philippines. Over the next three years, 2,002 of the 8,897 immigrant nurses—22.5 per cent—were Filipinos. While the numbers dropped slightly in the following years, a total of more than a thousand Filipino nurses entered the country over the next five years.

During the same period the United States also accepted a large number of Filipino nurses, but the American approach to immigration was different from the Canadian in one crucial regard: whereas Canada limited the immigration of Filipinos to those with nursing experience or training, the US welcomed all manner of Filipino health professionals, including physicians, surgeons, and dentists. In 1970, for example, 968 Filipino physicians, surgeons, and dentists entered the US, compared with 954 nurses; that same year, all but 53 of the 571 Filipino health professionals to enter Canada were nurses.

Given that most of the Filipino nurses coming to Canada were young women in their twenties, Canada's immigration policy resulted in a huge gender imbalance among the Canadian Filipino population during the early years of Filipino immigration. The sex ratio of males to females among immigrants from the Philippines between 1967 and 1969 was about 1 to 2.75, with 2,293 men and 6,380 women coming to Canada during that time. While this rate would even out over the next two decades, with the percentage of male Filipino immigrants rising to 74 per cent of the total in 1971, 90 per cent in 1975, and 86 in 1979, a second wave of large-scale immigration would lower it again, so that by 1992 it was back down to 50 per cent.

Sociological studies suggest that because they were fluent English speakers and Christians, coming from a capitalist country where they were very familiar with Western culture, the Filipino immigrants adapted more easily than other Asian groups. Even so, Winn (1988), in a study of 15 ethnic groups in Canada, demonstrated that while the Filipinos ranked the highest in college or university education, their ranking dropped when it came to income return on university education. Imagine, as well, the effect on women coming from a culture where family is an extremely strong social element to one where they would often have to delay marriage until eligible Filipino immigrants arrived. Others, married in their home country, had to leave their husbands behind until, years later, they could sponsor them.

The Racialization of Disease

We describe an illness or disease as having been **racialized** when it has become strongly associated with people of a particular ethnic background. The result is that we may treat all people sharing this ethnicity, whether or not they have the ailment, differently because of their supposed connection to it. Here we're not thinking of illnesses such as German measles or the Spanish flu—most of us don't avoid people of Spanish or German background for fear of catching these viruses. A better example is SARS, a respiratory ailment that, during a 2003 outbreak, afflicted Canadians of all ethnic backgrounds but became primarily associated with two.

SARS: *The Racialization of Disease*

Canadians first began hearing about SARS (Severe Acute Respiratory Syndrome) in March 2003, and throughout the spring and early summer it became the focus of widespread media attention. Over the course of this period, the disease became racialized. Because it originated in China, and because a Filipino Catholic charismatic community (Bukas-Loob Sa Diyos) had members who contracted it, the disease took on a racial identity. Chinese and Filipino-Canadians became targets of discrimination.

In a web-published report released in June 2004, researchers Carrianne Leung and Jian

In Other Words
An Account of Systemic Racism from a Black First-Year Nursing Student

Unfortunately, I regret to say that I have had my first clinical experience in the nursing profession and I feel I have already been subjected to systemic racism. Examples of this include disciplinary actions that are different from other student nurses such as when myself and a non-Black student returned late from break. I was pulled aside and it was stated that the teacher felt sorry for the other student. When I asked 'why', it was implied that I coerced her into returning late against her will. Also, vague work appraisals are given and no specific areas of improvement are suggested. Comments such as, 'You seem like a very angry person', and 'I have a hard time approaching you and can only imagine how the residents feel' or 'Any monkey can be trained to take a blood pressure' are an every day occurrence. There are many cases where my mistakes are far more noted and exaggerated than those of other students. When defending myself (as I feel I am performing equally well to everyone else), I am labelled as not being 'self-aware' and not accepting feedback. Yet, when feedback is taken and changes are made, I am told I take things too literally. As a result, I can do no right.

It is sad to say that events like these are commonplace. As a result, promotions as well as workload may not be fairly distributed.

—Nadine Smith

Guan noted, among other things, how the mainstream media racialized SARS by portraying Asians as carriers of disease in a way that spread fear among non-Asian Canadians. Table 7.2 summarizes Leung and Guan's findings about the content of pictures featured with SARS articles in four national newspapers and periodicals (Leung and Guan 2004:9, 10).

Leung and Guan found that photographs accompanying stories about SARS tended to feature Asians, particularly Asians wearing masks to reduce the spread of the disease. The researchers noted that the exaggerated use of frightening words and unreasonable parallels drawn between SARS and the Spanish influenza pandemic of 1918–19 (in which at least 20 million people died over an 18-month period) were also part of media fear mongering. SARS had a devastating economic impact on parts of Canada where the outbreak was prevalent, notably Toronto and, in particular, its various Chinatowns. Commentators were quick to note that many of the patrons suddenly avoiding Chinese business communities and restaurants were themselves Chinese, as though this fact somehow justified similar acts of discrimination on the part of non-Asian Canadians. But whether the economic losses can be attributed more to a drop in Chinese Canadian patronage or to decreased patronage by non-Chinese Canadians has no bearing on the fact that the loss of business occurred, and it did so because the disease was racialized to the point where many Canadians, of all ethnic backgrounds, temporarily changed their purchasing habits as a precaution against contracting the virus in communities where it was thought to be prevalent.

Throughout their report, Leung and Guan note the effect of acts of discrimination, large and small, on individuals of Asian ancestry. In the narrative on page 194, one student tells her story.

Table 7.2 >> Photographic treatment of SARS in the national media, 2003

NEWSPAPER/ MAGAZINE	NUMBER OF PICTURES	SHOWING PEOPLE	SHOWING ASIANS	SHOWING ASIANS WITH MASKS
National Post	120	95 (82.0%)	65 (54.2%)	60 (50.0%)
Globe and Mail	119	68 (57.1%)	52 (43.9%)	41 (34.45%)
Maclean's	27	17 (63.0%)	8 (29.6%)	6 (22.2%)
Time (Canada)	17	15 (88.2%)	8 (47.0%)	6 (35.3%)

Source: Leung and Guan (2004).

THURSDAY, APRIL 3, 2003 ★ **TORONTO STAR** ★ B3

SARS Outbreak

China admits wider spread of SARS

12 more deaths reported among inland provinces

First cases found in Latin America and Israel

ANN PERRY
STAFF REPORTER

The global death toll from Severe Acute Respiratory Syndrome jumped yesterday as China broke its silence and admitted it had more cases in more provinces than it had previously revealed.

The South China Morning Post reported today that the first victims of the deadly illness were people in China's southern province of Guangdong who ate or handled wild game, confirming earlier reports linking the disease to ducks.

China said it had 1,190 suspected cases through the end of March, and 46 deaths instead of the 34 it had admitted. Cases were reported in Guangxi, Hunan and Sichuan provinces as well as Guangdong for the first time.

In total, the World Health Organization estimated that SARS has infected more than 2,200 people worldwide and killed an estimated 78.

Brazil reported its first suspected case, which, if confirmed, would be the first in Latin America. Israel also reported its first suspected case.

China agreed yesterday to let a team of WHO investigators visit the southern province of Guangdong, where the disease is believed to have started.

The four-member international team, which will leave Beijing today, will take samples from suspected patients to help identify a culprit virus and assess how infectious and virulent it is.

And, for the first time in its 55-year-history, WHO recommended that travellers avoid part of the world because of an infectious disease: Hong Kong and adjoining Guangdong province.

In the first public statement by a senior leader, Chinese Health Minister Zhang Wenkang said the outbreak was "under effective control."

He said 80 per cent of those diagnosed with SARS have recovered.

For weeks, U.N. agency officials have appealed for more cooperation from China.

"Because the mainland is not sharing information . . . the outbreak has been lengthened," Taiwan's Mainland Affairs Council said in a recent report.

Laboratories around the world are racing to come up with a test for SARS.

The U.S. Centers for Disease Control has issued two tests that health officials can give to patients with suspected SARS. Dr. Julie Gerberding, the director of the Atlanta-based centre, said until a large number of people are tested, no one can say whether the disease is caused by the main suspect — a coronavirus.

But she said so far 400 healthy people had been tested for the virus, a previously unknown relative of one of the common cold viruses, and all had tested negative.

Several patients with SARS have tested positive.

"It is not yet proof. There are other viruses still under investigation," she said. In Toronto, Dr. Raymond Tellier of the Hospital for Sick Children, has developed a test that detects this new species of coronavirus. It is currently being used here.

A top health expert in China told a newspaper the earliest SARS patients in Guangdong had close and continuous contact with chickens, ducks, pigeons and owls.

"We will explore further if the disease was passed to human beings from wild animals. You know, Guangdong people like eating exotic animals and I don't find it a healthy practice," said Bi Shengli, a vice-director at the Chinese Centre for Disease Control and Prevention.

The earliest cases of the disease were traced to either chefs or bird vendors, Bi said.

In Thailand yesterday, the government said it would turn back foreigners suspected of having SARS and would force those allowed in from affected countries to wear masks in public.

In the Philippines, which has no confirmed cases, President Gloria Macapagal Arroyo put in place a contingency plan — including air and seaport checks — to prevent an outbreak. Health officials in New Zealand urged indigenous Maori tribesmen to forgo their traditional "hongi" nose-rubbing greeting for visiting Chinese at a convention.

In Hong Kong, the Roman Catholic Church ordered priests to wear masks during Communion and put wafers in the hands of the faithful rather than on the tongue.

FROM STAR WIRE SERVICES

REUTERS

With Hong Kong being the global centre of the SARS outbreak, face masks are common on the city's streets. Some residents strive for their own style amid the crisis. Chinese officials are reporting there are more cases and more deaths than they previously admitted.

Courtesy Toronto Star Archives

In Other Words
SARS and Being Chinese

Around the time of the SARS crisis, being Chinese made people look at me in a different way, whether it was at school, work, or in public places such as the subway and buses. It did not bother me at first, but as more and more individuals died due to SARS, the more I kept my eyes open for tainted looks darting in my direction.

Around that time in school, it wasn't so much the looks, but comments made in class about the situation. What I have learned and understood in this game we call life is that everyone is entitled to his or her opinion. I have also learned and understood that not all opinions are necessarily right or wrong. Unfortunately, not all people feel that their opinions are wrong, hurtful, disrespectful, condescending, and rude.

One incident happened in my math class at college. Our class got off topic, and our focus was turned from present and future value to SARS. Our teacher was reminding us that proper hand washing helps in preventing the spread of infection. One obnoxious fellow who felt he was the class clown replied to our teacher's comment and stated that to prevent the spread of infection, we need to stay away from all those darn Chinese people. His language use and vocabulary was a little cruder. Being the only Asian person in the class, everyone turned and looked in my direction as if they were expecting me to curse at him. I was beside myself and decided to let the one and only authority figure take care of his biased opinion. However, our teacher said absolutely nothing, except to get on with the lesson. His comments offended me and our teacher not correcting him hurt my feelings. It made me pay more attention to the things that were being said in all the rest of my classes. The impact it had on my school life made me more defensive towards what my peers had to say about those of Asian descent. . . .

Ethnicity is a sociological factor that made an impact on my life within the last year. Because I have been on the end of a biased opinion at school and indirect discrimination at work, I have further learned another aspect of the game of life; the value and meaning of equality and fairness and that even though there are different ethnicities and races, we are all part of one race called the human race.

—Karin Koo

What do you think?

1. Can we assign blame for the racialization of a disease like SARS? If so, where?

2. Does blame lie with the media, for exaggerating the facts surrounding the outbreak and feeding public fears? Or is it the media's responsibility to make people aware of the gravest possible outcomes of an event?

3. Does blame lie with individuals, for succumbing to fear mongering? Can regular patrons of Chinatown businesses be blamed for altering their purchasing habits if there's any chance at all that not doing so will increase their odds of contracting the virus? Should people be expected to weigh decisions about their personal health against the greater economic and social impact of their decisions?

Whose Diseases are Important? An Exercise in Medical Ethnocentrism

The most devastating disease in history was the bubonic or black plague that occurred in the fourteenth century (see Weatherford 2004: 242–50). During the period of its most powerful effect, it may have reduced the world's population from about 450 million to somewhere between 350 and 375 million. It affected Africa, Asia, and Europe equally. China, where it began, may have suffered a population loss of close to 60 million, reducing the overall population from 123 to 65 million. The population of Europe, where the plague spread next, fell from about 75 million to perhaps as low as 50 million. Africa, the next continent to be hit, lost 12 million of its approximately 80 million inhabitants.

Ethnocentrism is an excessive focus on one culture as a model or standard. Eurocentrism occurs when this focus is placed on the European situation or standpoint as if it were the only important one. Now, if you were to do an Internet search using the words 'Black Plague', what you would find are stories of what happened in Europe, nowhere else. The only mention of places outside of Europe are brief and occasional references to China or Asia as the point of origin.

What do you think?

1. Do you own Internet search on 'Black Death' or 'Bubonic Plague' and briefly summarize the results. Can you account for the ethnocentric perspective of these reports?

2. What effect do you think this presentation of knowledge would have on students of history in secondary or post-secondary schools?

3. Can you think of any contemporary diseases that might receive a similarly ethnocentric treatment?

Gender and Medical Sociology

Physicians and Gender

Both the number and the percentage of women in and graduating from medical schools in Canada is increasing. In 1959, women accounted for just 6 per cent of medical school graduates; forty years later, they made up 44 per cent of the graduating class. According to Burton and Wong, authors of a paper called 'A Force to Contend With: The Gender Gap Closes in Canadian Medical Schools' (2004), Canadian medical school classes today 'have a range of 43%–74% women (mean 58%), compared with a range of 26%–57% men (mean 42%)'. The percentage of women graduating from medical school and entering the health profession will only increase in the coming years, as the majority of doctors approaching retirement are men. Male doctors in Canada make up 74 per cent of physicians aged between 45 and 65, and 90 per cent of those over 65.

How might this trend affect the profession? How are female physicians different from their male counterparts? A number of features have been regularly noted in the literature. Female doctors are more likely to

- screen their patients for preventable illnesses,
- spend time counselling about psychosocial issues,
- enter primary care (i.e. become family physicians),
- work fewer hours and see fewer patients, and
- leave the profession sooner.

Women doctors are less likely to

- become surgeons,
- be sued for malpractice, and
- join professional organizations.

What do you think?

1. How much do you think this changing gender dynamic will affect the practice of medicine in Canada?

2. Do you think that this could lead to a reduction in the power differential between doctors and nurses in Canadian hospitals?

Pharmacy Professors in Canada and Gender

In an article detailing the practices of departments of pharmaceutical sciences at Canadian colleges and universities during the 1990s, sociologist Linda Muzzin noted several gender-based patterns. To gain a proper perspective of these patterns, it is important to know that there is an almost class-like distinction between the two kinds of jobs held by pharmacy professors. The first position involves basic science teaching and some molecular biology research. This position offers a lighter teaching load and tends to be a 'tenure-stream' position, making it the more highly valued than the second class of jobs, which Muzzin describes as the 'professional caring' or clinical and social-administrative jobs. The distinction between the two kinds of position within the department falls along gender lines. Consider the following points, noted by Muzzin:

- In 1996, a substantially higher proportion of the professional caring jobs were held by women, except in smaller universities, where a higher percentage the professional caring jobs are tenured or tenure-stream positions—in these cases, the jobs are more likely to be held by men.
- The majority (86 per cent) of the basic science jobs are tenured or tenure-stream positions, while only 37 per cent of the professional caring jobs were.
- Only 15 of the 112 (13 per cent) tenured or tenure-stream basic science jobs were held by women.
- A majority (65 per cent) of the contract or part-time staff of the professional caring jobs were held by women.

What do you think?

1. How could you argue that these findings prove that women pharmacology professors are being discriminated against?

2. How might university presidents or department heads explain the distribution of jobs in a way that sounds reasonable?

Class and Medical Sociology

The Inverse Care Law

Dr Julian Tudor Hart's parents were doctors. He studied medicine at Cambridge and interned at the equally prestigious St George's Hospital. A natural career move for a British doctor on that path would have been to serve the needs of the middle class or the rich in London or some other big city.

Instead, he moved to Glyncorrwg, to dedicate his life to helping the citizens of a working-class mining village in south Wales. Dr Hart became famous among medical sociologists for the introductory paragraph to an article he wrote in 1971 and published in the famous British medical journal *The Lancet*. In it he introduced the idea of the **inverse care law**:

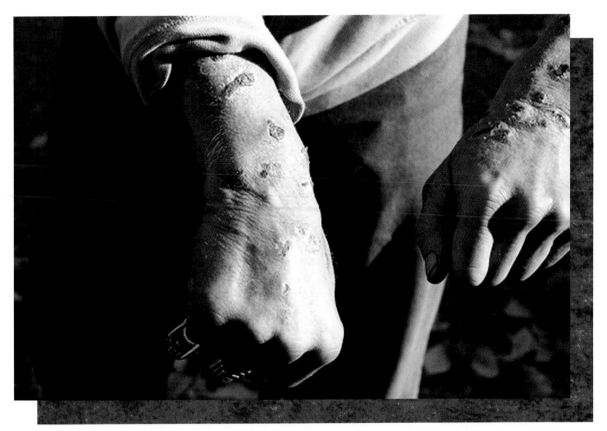

Journalists at a homeless protest are called over by a man revealing festering sores on his hands and arms, which he says doctors refuse to treat because he's on methadone. Why is this man being refused medical treatment? Does our healthcare system discriminate against different segments of society? (Photo © M-J Milloy, 2006)

The availability of good medical care tends to vary inversely with the need for it in the population served. This inverse care law operates more completely where medical care is most exposed to market forces, and less so where such exposure is reduced. The market distribution of medical care is a primitive and historically outdated social form, and any return to it would further exaggerate the maldistribution of medical resources. (Hart 1971:405)

He was describing a system that had, for almost 20 years, experienced socialized health care similar to that in Canada, a system markedly different from the private or market-force system in the United States. What the inverse care law meant in terms of the Britain he was describing can be seen in a series of statistics concerning infant mortality from the years 1949–53. From his perspective, they

showed combined social classes I and II (wholly non-manual) with a standardised mortality form all causes 18% below the mean, and combined social classes IV and V (wholly manual) 5% about it. Infant mortality was 37% below the mean for social class I (professional) and 38% about it for social class V (unskilled manual). (Hart 1971:405)

Medical students protest government cuts to student grants in front of the Quebec legislature, 23 March 2005. (Jacques Boissinot/CP Photo)

In other words, the lower classes experienced a greater likelihood of infant mortality (i.e. death of an infant during the first year of life). This, of course, would tend to reflect both the working and living conditions of the different classes, as well as differences in medical care in areas where the various classes live, work and see doctors. Regarding doctors, which were the main focus of his article, he observed the following trends:

> In areas with most sickness and death, general practitioners have more work, larger lists [of patients], less hospital support, and inherit more clinically ineffective traditions of consultation [e.g. short visits with little listening to patients' problems] than in the healthiest areas; and hospital doctors shoulder heavier case-loads with less staff and equipment, more obsolete buildings, and suffer recurrent crises in the availability of beds and replacement staff. (Hart 1971:412)

What do you think?

1. Do you think that the inverse care law holds in Canada?

2. How would you as a sociologist go about trying to prove or disprove whether the inverse care law holds in Canada?

3. How does class affect the social course of disease?

Rising Tuition Fees and Medical Students

Most students can relate to the effects of rising tuition fees. How does that affect medical students? A study conducted by Kwong et al. in early 2001 compared tuition costs in Ontario with costs in the rest of Canada (except for Quebec, which, as is so often the case, was excluded). The reason for highlighting Ontario tuition costs is that medical students in that province had the greatest hike in tuition fees in Canada from 1997–8 to 2000–1. The cost of tuition at the University of Toronto, for example, nearly tripled over that period, from $4,844 per year to $14,000.

The researchers contrasted people in their fourth year with those in their first, because they represented the two extremes. They found that there were three differences between the two academic cohorts that were unique to Ontario. First, the proportion of respondents with a family income of less than $40,000 declined significantly, from 22.6 per cent to 15.0 per cent. The same figure among non-Ontario schools stayed just about the same (decreasing slightly from 16.0 per cent to 15.8 per cent). The figure of $40,000 was chosen to represent 'low income', as it was beneath the median family income of $46,951 in Canada in 1996. Another difference between the groups was that the median debt level anticipated upon graduation by first-year medical students in Ontario was $80,000; the debt anticipated by the graduating class was a lower, but still nasty, $57,000. No such contrast existed in the other provinces. The problem here for the sociologist is that there are no earlier studies with which these findings can be compared. What if first-year medical students often project a higher figure than their more experience graduating colleagues? Is the control group sufficient here for comparative purposes? What do you think?

Finally, first-year medical students in Ontario were more likely than fourth-year students to report that their financial situation was 'very' or 'extremely' stressful (20.5 per cent vs 17.5 per cent—the reverse was true in other provinces, 11.9 per cent vs 15.8 per cent) and to cite financial considerations as having a major influence on their choice of speciality or practice location (25.4 per cent vs 13.3 per cent, compared with a reverse ratio of 21.4 per cent to 26.0 per cent in the other provinces). Again, is this a cohort problem or a stage problem somehow conditioned by being in Ontario?

Twelve Sociological Tips for Better Health

In 1999, British sociologist David Gordon made up the following 'Alternative 10 Tips for Better Health'; it was an alternative to British Medical Officer's 10 health tips, which included the usual things about smoking, eating right, drinking in moderation, driving safely, etc:

1. Don't be poor. If you can, stop. If you can't, try not to be poor for long.
2. Don' have poor parents.
3. Own a car.
4. Don't work in a stressful, low paid manual job.
5. Don't live in damp, low quality housing.
6. Be able to afford to go on a foreign holiday and sunbathe.
7. Practice not losing your job and don't become unemployed.
8. Take up all benefits you are entitled to, if you are unemployed, retired or sick or disabled.
9. Don't live next to a busy major road or near a polluting factory.
10. Learn how to fill in the complex housing benefit/asylum application forms before you become homeless or destitute. (Lisa Pohlmann, 'Inequality is Bad for Your Health', 2002, www.mecep.or/MEChoices02/ch_029.htm)

This tongue-in-cheek but accurate appraisal has been adapted a number of times. In a speech he delivered on 8 May 2003, Roy Romanow, author of the Romanow Report on Canada's healthcare, adapted this list to also include two additional items:

11. Graduate from high school and then go on to college or university. Health status improves with your level of education.
12. Be sure to live in a community where you trust your neighbours and feel that you belong. A civil and trusting community promotes health and life expectancy.

What do you think?

How do these 'health tips' reflect William Ryan's idea of 'blaming the victim?'

Questions for Critical Review and Discussion

1. Take a particular disease or injury that you have experienced and discuss the social course that you went through to get cured or healed. Where did you go? Who treated you? How were you socially processed?

2. Identify what biomedicine is and talk about its weaknesses and strengths. In terms of its weaknesses, think of what happens when a Western practitioner of medicine encounters non-Western people or Aboriginal people who have different medical traditions and explanations.

3. How and why does medicalization take place during the treatment of a particular physical condition? When is medicalization more harmful than helpful?

4. How do you think the question of immigrant doctors should be handled?

5. How does Ivan Illich critique modern medicine? Do you agree or disagree with his views? Why?

Suggested Readings

Foucault, Michel (1973). *The Birth of the Clinic: An Archaeology of Medical Perception*. A.M.S. Smith trans. New York: Vintage Books.

Goffman, Erving (1961). *Asylums: Essays on the Social Situation of Mental Patients and Other Inmates*. New York: Doubleday.

Lorde, Audre (1980). *The Cancer Journals*. San Francisco: aunt lute books.

Turner, Bryan (1984). *The Body and Society: Explorations in Social Theory*. London: Sage.

Wertz, Richard W. & Dorthy C. Wertz (1989). *Lying-In: A History of Childbirth in America*. Yale UP.

Yalom, Marilyn (1997). *A History of the Breast*. New York: Harper Collins.

Suggested Websites

Children's Environmental Health Project.
http://www.cape.ca/children/index.html

National Aboriginal Health Organization.
http://www.naho.ca/english/

The Canadian Women's Health Network.
http://www.cwhn.ca/indexeng.html

World Health Organization.
http://www.who.int/en/

Social Inequality: Stratification

Contents

Key Terms

American Dream
aristocrats
blaming the victim
capital
capitalists (bourgeoisie)
caste (varna)
class
class consciousness
class reductionism
corporate (or organic)
   identity
Dalits (Untouchables)
deciles
dominant ideology
false consciousness
food bank
hegemony
Highland Clearances
ideology
Indo-European
jati
liberal ideology
lumpenproletariat
means of production
mobility sports
peasants
petty bourgeoisie
professionalization
quintiles
relational
social gospel
social inequality
social mobility
strata
trickle down
workers (proletariat)

PART FOUR
SOCIAL DIFFERENCE

Boxes and Tables

Canadian Sociology in Action Early Studies in Canadian Social Stratification
Sociology in Action Sport and Class

Learning Objectives

After reading this chapter you should be able to

- differentiate between class and strata.
- discuss liberal ideology critically.
- distinguish between a Marxist notion of class and one that includes a middle class.
- critically discuss the history of caste with respect to Hinduism.
- contrast the use of quintiles and deciles.
- describe the paths taken to becoming billionaires in Canada.

For Starters
A Picture of Poverty

In his biography of Tommy Douglas, the late Canadian writer Walter Stewart wrote the following about Glasgow, Scotland's largest city, in 1914, when Douglas was living there:

> Most Glaswegians lived in tenements, filthy hovels with no indoor plumbing, cesspools of squalor and despair. These were the 'ticketed class', so called because outside the door of each of the tiny apartments that made up the beehive of a tenement, a ticket was attached to indicate how many people were allowed to live inside. A typical ticket read, '2000 Cubic Feet* 5 Adults.' It was illegal to cram more than five adults, with however many children survived the diseases that decimated the population from time to time, into this tiny space.
>
> Most of these little caves were 'single end' apartments, with one door opening into a space split into a kitchen and one other room, with shelves for sleeping. There would be a bathroom a couple of floors away, shared by several dozen families. . . . (Stewart 2003:31)

*Imagine a room measuring about 3 by 8 metres, with 2.5 metre-high ceilings.

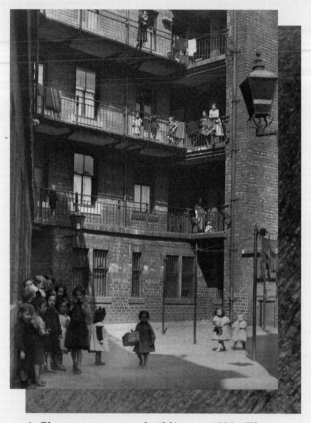

A Glasgow tenement building, *c.* 1920. (Photo courtesy Glasgow City Council Mitchell Library)

Introduction to Class and Social Stratification

The study of social inequality has long been a part of the sociological tradition, both generally and, as we will see, particularly in Canada. Social inequality is a function of several different elements, only some of which will be discussed in this chapter. The elements of 'race', 'ethnicity', and gender are discussed in their own chapters. Here we will focus mainly on class and stratification.

Few areas are more contentious in the sociological, economic, or political study of societies than the study of **social inequality**, the long-term existence of significant differences in access to goods and services among social groups. The main term used to talk about social inequality is **class**, the definition of which has been the subject of great debate since the term was popularized by the political philosopher and economist **Karl Marx** (1818–1883). Near the beginning of *The Communist Manifesto* (1888), which Marx co-wrote with Friedrich Engels (1820–1895), the authors write:

> The history of all hitherto existing society is the history of class struggles. Freeman and slave, patrician and plebian, lord and serf, guild-master and journeyman, in a word, oppressor and oppressed, stood in constant opposition to one another, carried on an uninterrupted, now hidden, now open fight, a fight that each time ended, either in a revolutionary reconstitution of society at large, or in the common ruin of the contending classes. . . .
>
> The modern bourgeois society that has sprouted from the ruins of feudal society has not done away with class antagonisms. It has but established new classes, new conditions of oppression, new forms of struggle in place of the old ones.
>
> Our epoch, the epoch of the bourgeoisie, possesses, however, this distinct feature: it has simplified class antagonisms. Society as a whole is more and more splitting up into two great hostile camps, into two great classes directly facing each other—bourgeoisie and proletariat.

There is a special language to interpreting Marx, and we apologize now for the large number of bold terms you will find bearing down on you as you read the following sentences.

Class as Marx described it was **relational**, in that it reflects a relationship to what he called the **means of production**—the main means or resources needed to produce goods (and, hence, wealth). In Europe before the Industrial Revolution, the means of production was land. Wealth was produced by growing food crops and raising livestock. Once Europe started to become industrialized during the eighteenth century—the time in which Marx lived—the means of production became **capital**, the money needed to build factories, purchase raw materials, and pay labourers to turn raw mate-rials into manufactured products. In spite of the fact he devoted an entire book to the topic (*Das Kapital*), the precise meaning Marx gave to the term *capital* has been contested, but we can refer to it here as meaning the funds and properties necessary for typically large-scale manufacturing and trading.

For Marx, there were only two possible relationships to the means of production. Either you owned it or you worked for those who did. In pre-industrial Europe, the owners were called **aristocrats** and the workers **peasants**. Marx referred to the owners of capital in industrial-era Europe as **capitalists**; he referred to the members of this class collectively as the **bourgeoisie**. Marx called the class of **workers**, which succeeded the peasant class in the industrial era, the **proletariat**.

Though Marx himself said he was not a Marxist, he retains the title as the most influential philosopher in contemporary history. His work has influenced all of the social sciences, contributed to the emergence of social programs, and significantly affected global geopolitics.

Marx identified various sub-classes—the **petite** or **petty bourgeoisie**, made up of small-time owners with little capital, and the **lumpenproletariat**, the small-time criminals, beggars, and unemployed—but these terms do not have the significance of his two primary classes.

Marx's Historical Context

If you wonder at Marx's black-and-white view of things, remember the conditions he saw, and the context in which he himself lived. It was a time of laissez-faire capitalism in Britain, in which business was supposed to take care of itself without any 'interference' by government. The Factory Act of 1833, which targeted primarily the booming textile mills of Britain, was considered radical at the time as it 'interfered' with the 'natural course' of business by 'severely' limiting the hours that people worked. Factory owners complained that the Act would ruin them financially, even drive them out of business. It proposed that the working day was to start at 5:30 a.m. and end at 8:30 p.m. It included the following additional provisions:

> [N]o person under eighteen years of age shall [work] between half-past eight in the evening and half-past five in the morning, in any cotton, woollen, worsted, hemp, flax, tow, linen or silk mill. . . .
>
> [N]o person under the age of eighteen shall be employed in any such mill . . . more than twelve hours in . . . one day, nor more than sixty-nine hours in . . . one week. . . .
>
> It shall not be lawful . . . to employ in any factory . . . as aforesaid, except in mills for the manufacture of silk, any child who shall not have completed his or her ninth year.
>
> It shall not be lawful for any person to employ . . . in any factory . . . for longer than forty-eight hours in one week, nor for longer than nine hours in one day, any child who shall not have completed his or her eleventh year. . . .
>
> Every child restricted to the performance of forty-eight hours of labour in any one week shall attend some school. (*Statutes of the Realm*, 3 & 4 William IV, c. 103)

Of course, such 'liberal' rules would not apply to adults.

Class as a Social Identity

Another characteristic of class in Marx's view is that it has a **corporate** or **organic identity** as a real social group. There is a shared sense of common membership and common purpose. Part of this can include **class consciousness**, which is an awareness of what is in the best interests of one's class. Marx believed that the owner class had always possessed class consciousness, had always known what was in its best interests, and had attempted to set up society following those interests. Good evidence of this is seen in the **Highland clearances** that occurred in Scotland in the late eighteenth and early nineteenth centuries. Land-owning aristocrats, recognizing the increasing value of wool to the rapidly industrializing textile industry, began evicting tenant farmers from their estates to make room for sheep. The clearances caused extreme hardship among the evicted 'crofters', and many were forced to emigrate, notably to North America.

The worker class, on the other hand, had not always had such an awareness. Indeed, it often has **false consciousness**, the idea that something is in its best interests when it is not. False consciousness sometimes occurs in societies that are divided by ethnicity or race. A good example is Rwanda, where, during its colonial period, the Tutsi were able to obtain the greater share of power and wealth that did not go to the imperial power. But it was only a handful of the Tutsi that held such positions. The rest, the majority, were exploited by this Tutsi elite, whom they could not challenge because the elite would play the 'common ethnicity' card to demand their loyalty. The exploited Tutsi had class interests in common with the Hutu, who had become the most exploited group in the country with the Tutsi rise to power; however the two groups did not share class consciousness: they did not recognize the class interests they had in common. We can argue, then, that false consciousness prevented the two exploited groups from forming a mutually beneficial alliance capable of grabbing a share of power and wealth from the Tutsi elite. The situation would later repeat itself in the reverse following the overthrow of the Tutsi monarchy by the Hutu people in 1962. The majority of the Hutu, impoverished and under the thumb of the ruling Hutu elite, could not help but think of all Tutsi as former feudal exploiters, even though many had never been any richer than the Hutu were at the time. We'll examine Rwanda's ethnic conflict further in Chapter 9.

Marx himself saw false consciousness operating most clearly in organized religion. 'Religion is the opiate of the masses,' he famously wrote, meaning that religion deludes the workers about what is in the best interests of their class. By encouraging the working poor to look ahead to the next life, in heaven or hell, religion distracted workers from scrutinizing and revolting against the terrible conditions in which they lived. Why are the peasants poor and the aristocrats rich, Marx might have asked? Because God (or organized religion, as controlled by the wealthy class) ensured it. Look at the following verse from the popular hymn 'All Things Bright and Beautiful'. From a Marxist perspective, the last line in particular teaches that God assigned you your station in life, and you should not try to change it:

> The rich man in his castle
> The poor man at his gate
> God made them, high or lowly
> And ordered their estate

Further, those involved in the upper levels of organized religion tended to be drawn from the educated elite, so when it came to matters of class interests and the possibility of social revolution, the religious leaders would naturally side with their class. Nevertheless, the idea that religion always forms a false consciousness can be contested. At various times in the history of all major religions, there have been movements within the faith to better serve the poor at the expense of the rich. In Marx's own time, Methodist ministers were typically drawn from among the workers themselves. Not only did they work in the tin and coal mines and textile factories, they also were important leaders of the union movement in Britain. The social gospel movement, as noted later on in the chapter, sprouted directly from the Methodist church and in Canada was involved with the union movement. The New Democratic Party, the party traditionally most allied with workers' groups in Canada, can trace its history through the Commonwealth of Canadian Farmers to the social gospel movement, which was championed by trained ministers such as J.S. Woodsworth and Tommy Douglas.

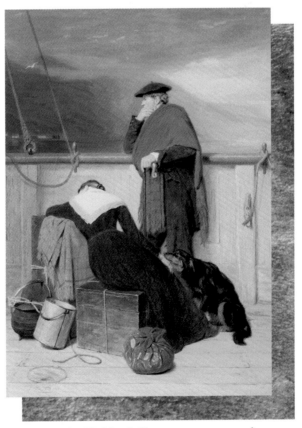

During the Highland Clearances, many crofters left Scotland for North America. (*Lochaber No More*, 1883, by John Watson Nicol © The Fleming-Wyfold Art Foundation/The Bridgeman Art Library)

Problems with Marx's Perspective

There are several problems with applying a classical Marxist class paradigm to societies in countries such as Canada. One is that there are people who, as employees of large corporations (bank presidents, corporate lawyers, hospital administrators, high ranking government bureaucrats, professional hockey players), are termed 'workers', even though their incomes put them on a par with some owners. Likewise, there are farmers, owners of small retail stories, and other small businesses operators who have incomes and levels of control that are more like those of workers. And we can argue for the existence of a middle class with a strong sense of itself as a class.

Class in Canada

We can apply Marx's class paradigm within a Canadian context by arguing that there are essentially three different classes in this country. Following Curtis, Grabb, and Guppy (1999), we would define them as follows:

1. a **dominant capitalist class**: 'composed mainly of those who own or control large-scale production' (Curtis, Grabb, and Guppy 1999:ix)
2. a **middle class**: 'a mixed . . . middle category of small-scale business people, educated professional-technical or administrative personnel, and various salaried employees or wage earners possessing some certifiable credentials, training, or skills' (Curtis, Grabb, and Guppy 1999:xiii)
3. a **working class** or **proletariat**: 'made up of people who lack resources or capacities apart from their own labour power' (Curtis, Grabb, and Guppy 1999:ix)

Marx's analysis of class probably has greatest applicability today if you add other factors to class: ethnicity and nation state. When companies based in the West have non-unionized, low-wage, factories with unsafe working and environmental conditions in poor countries such as Mexico, Haiti, Thailand, and a number of African countries, employing people of particular ethnicities who are being exploited within their own country, then Marx's capitalist–worker class structure exists in a true sense.

Ideology

Ideology is a relatively coherent set of interrelated beliefs about society and the people in it. There are various types. The **dominant ideology** is that set of beliefs put forward by and supportive of the dominant culture and/or classes within a society. In Marxist terms, it relates to the class consciousness of the ruling class. A **counter ideology** is one that offers a critique of this ideology, that challenges its justice and its applicability to society. Here's a somewhat facetious example: many people subscribe to the **trickle down** theory, which states that if you allow the rich the freedom to accumulate wealth and make investments, the wealth will trickle down to the average worker and eventually to the poor; this is an example of a dominant ideology. Others mock such a theory by referring to it as the 'horse and sparrow' theory: give the horse ready access to lots of oats, and the sparrow will benefit from what the horse produces by way of digestion—but, of course, it will have to eat shit. This is a counter ideology.

Liberal ideology focuses on the individual as a more or less independent player on the sociological scene. It reflects a belief in **social mobility**—that is, the ability of individuals to move (generally upward) from one class or strata to another—and minimizes criticism of social inequality. If an individual is successful, it is because he or she has earned that success, not because he or she has benefited from the social privileges of ethnic background, class, or gender. The **American dream**—the belief that anyone who works hard and applies him- or herself can 'make it', be successful—reflects liberal ideology. Its opposite, failure (or the 'American nightmare' of poverty), is likewise

Canadian Sociology in Action
Early Studies in Canadian Social Stratification

Sociology in Canada began as the study of social stratification. We get an excellent survey of stratification by examining the work of three Canadian sociology pioneers: Herbert Brown Ames, Colin McKay, and James S. Woodsworth.

Herbert Brown Ames: A Businessman's Sociology

During the last half of the nineteenth century, the population of Montreal grew fourfold to over 270,000. With growth came social problems. This led **Herbert Brown Ames** (1863–1954) to engage in Canada's first comprehensive urban sociological study, designed to promote the construction of affordable housing for the working-class people of Montreal's west end.

Montreal-born, Ames had inherited a prosperous business that would guarantee him a lifetime of financial stability. But he wanted more than to earn easy money: he wanted to improve the city of his birth. He became involved in politics at the municipal and federal levels, and he engaged in ambitious sociological research. In 1896, he and members of his research team went door-to-door to canvass the inhabitants of an area he called 'the city below the hill'. The study was very detailed for its time. His fascination for statistics sometimes overwhelms even the modern reader, and at the time of the study his approach was unique. He was possibly the first person in Canada to speak of family size not in round numbers but with decimals, saying the average size of families he studied was '4.90 people', 1.41 in each family working for wages and 1.64 being children under 16. He was keenly aware that this level of precision was key to achieving the most suitable remedy for the housing problem:

> Should the time come when capital shall be ready to be invested in the erection of improved industrial dwellings, it is evident that for its intelligent expenditure, in this or that locality, definite knowledge must be in hand as to the personnel and composition of the average family of the section selected. The number and size of the rooms to be provided, in the improved dwelling for the average family, will depend not only upon the size of the family, but also upon its composition, since the larger the proportion of the adult or school-child element the more the amount of space and air that will need to be allowed.
>
> To make a success of this work of improvement we can afford to allow no facts to be overlooked. (Ames 1972:30)

His plan was to have old, inadequate housing torn down, and then have business leaders finance construction of new housing. Ames led by example, bankrolling the construction of model apartments for 39 families. Unfortunately, but predictably, others were reluctant to follow his lead.

With hindsight, we can argue that Ames was naive. We can be amused by the powerful rhetoric he invoked to declare his determination to get rid of the 5,800 outhouses he reckoned there were in the city ('That the privy pit is a danger to public health and morals needs no demonstration, and yet in "the city below the hill" *more than half the households* are dependent entirely upon such accommodation [Ames 1972:45]). But we must admire Ames for his concern for the lives of the working class and for his passion, shared by many Canadian sociologists to follow him.

Colin McKay: A Worker's Sociology

Nova Scotian **Colin McKay** (1876–1939) was described by Ian McKay (an unrelated namesake) as 'a working-class intellectual who exemplified a widespread enthusiasm for radical sociology in turn-of-the-century Canada', and who, 'drawing upon theories of Karl Marx and Herbert Spencer, . . . developed [his] own critical understanding of capitalist development' (McKay 1998:390). McKay was a self-educated man who worked as a merchant seaman, soldier, labour organizer, and journalist. At 24, he spent a short time in jail for 'defaming the reputation of a cigar factory proprietor notorious for mistreating children [workers] and discriminating against trade unionists' (McKay 1998:401).

He was a prodigious writer, contributing at least 952 articles and letters-to-the-editor to union publications such as the *Canadian Railway Employees Monthly*, the *Canadian Unionist*, *Eastern Labor News*, *Butler's Journal*, *Cotton's Weekly*, *Le Monde Ouvrier*, *Citizen and Country*, and *Western Clarion*. The scope of his work is revealed in a few selected titles—'Duty of the rich to the poverty-stricken: The philosophy of charity, showing it to be to the interest of the rich and strong to help the weak' (*Montreal Herald*, 21 Jan. 1899); 'The small business man. How the capitalist system annihilates self-earned private property and reduced the small business man to the economic category of the worker' (*Eastern Labor News*, 8 June 1912); 'The crime of low wages' (*Labor World / Le Monde Ouvrier*, 18 April 1925). As part of a vigorous working-class press with considerable influence, Colin McKay

> was widely acknowledged as one of Canadian labour's leading intellectuals. It seems very likely that McKay's writings, which in the 1930s were reaching thousands of working-class readers in at least four major journals, probably reached far more people than ever read the works of the contemporary academic sociologists in Canada. (McKay 1998:415)

Most Canadian sociologists today would be envious of such a large audience for their work. Ian McKay suggests that with the death of Colin McKay and the greater institutionalization (or departmentalization) of sociology, there was loss as well as gain. The drive of the well-read working-class radicals such as McKay and his peers is sorely missed in the efforts of sociologists to make a difference in the social inequality of their country.

James S. Woodsworth: A Minister's Sociology

Canadian churches produced some of the first people engaged in sociological work in the name of the **social gospel**. The movement, which lasted in Canada from about the 1890s to the 1930s, developed as an attempt to apply the human welfare principles of Christianity to address the social, medical, and psychological ills brought on by the industrialization and uncontrolled capitalism in North America and Europe in the late nineteenth century. One of its great achievements in this country was the Social Service Council of Canada (1912), which, through churches, conducted the earliest sociological surveys of Canadian cities and, in 1914, sponsored the first national meeting in Canada to address social problems.

One of the most influential figures to come out of this tradition in Canada was **James S. Woodsworth** (1874–1942), a Methodist minister by training. His work among the impoverished immigrant communities of Winnipeg and Toronto inspired him to embrace the social gospel. In 1913 he conducted a church-sponsored survey on social conditions in Regina. After becoming disenchanted with the church, which he felt never went far enough in advocating for the poor, he resigned his position as minister and became a writer, and later a politician, dedicated to the welfare of farmers, immigrants, and labourers. He was elected as a Labour Member of Parliament for Winnipeg North Centre in 1921, a seat he held until his death. In 1932, he was one of the founding members of the Canadian Commonwealth Federation or CCF, a precursor to the New Democratic Party.

James Woodsworth addresses a crowd in 1935, in the middle of the Depression. Can you imagine the context for his speech. Here's a hint: one of the placards reads 'Work and Wages NOT Relief'. (Library and Archives Canada, C-055451)

placed solely on the back of the individual. American psychologist William Ryan referred to this as **blaming the victim**, assigning individuals more or less complete responsibility for events or circumstances that have broader social causes. The American Dream, he might argue, fails to account for the notion that schools may privilege White middle-class culture over children from non-White or poorer socioeconomic families. We can see the liberal ideology of blaming the victim in any of the following arguments:

- People are alcoholics because they have little will power; no biological factors of genetic predisposition or sociological factors of racial or ethnic stereotypes (e.g., 'the drunk Indian') or systematic oppression need be seriously considered.
- People are on welfare because they lack a strong work ethic, not because they come from a poor family with the odds of success stacked against them.
- Criminals commit crimes because they have a 'criminal mind', not because 'the

street' offered the greatest chance they saw for success.

C. Wright Mills, introduced in Chapter 1, critiqued American liberal ideology during the 1950s in two influential studies of the middle and upper classes, *White Collar: The American Middle Classes* (1951) and *The Power Elite* (1956). The excerpt below, from the former book, contains some of his criticism of the liberal ideology of the American Dream, as he discusses how the upper class perpetuates its own power:

> The recent social history of American capitalism does not reveal any distinct break in the continuity of the higher capitalist class. . . . [I]n the economy as in the political order, there has been a remarkable continuity of interests, vested in the types of higher economic men who guard and advance them. The main drift of the upper classes, composed of several consistent trends, points unambiguously to the continuation of a world that is quite congenial to the continuation the corporate rich. . . .
>
> The propertied class, in the age of corporate property, has become a corporate rich, and in becoming corporate has consolidated its power. . . . Its members have become self-conscious in terms of the corporate world they represent. As men of status they have secured their privileges and prerogatives in the most stable private institutions of American society. They are a corporate rich because they depend directly, as well as indirectly, for their money, their privileges, their securities, their advantages, their powers on the world of the big corporations. (Horowitz 1971:82–3)

What do you think?

1. Do you think that what Mills said is just as true today?

2. How would you find out?

Hegemony

Another critic of dominant ideology was Antonio Gramsci (1891–1937). The Italian-born political theorist and activist was a co-founder and leader of the Italian Communist party and opponent of Fascist dictator Benito Mussolini. He was jailed in November 1926 and remained a political prisoner for nearly ten years until just before his death. During that time he wrote some 500 letters, a selection of which were collected and published in the two-volume series *Prison Notebooks* (1994). Among the concepts he developed was **hegemony**, which nevertheless manages to elude clear definition in his writing. Gramsci tended to use hegemony to mean a non-coercive method of maintaining power used by the dominant class, but it is perhaps best defined by Kate Crehan in her study of Gramsci. She uses it to refer to all means through which 'the power relations underpinning various forms of inequality are produced and reproduced' (Crehan 2002:104).

Hegemonic means of maintaining the power of the dominant class can include the way textbooks are written to support the status quo of society. That would happen if a sociologist wrote as if there were no destructive social splits in Canadian society based on race, ethnicity, and class. They include the way the media present computers as creating equality among the world's people while failing to note that technology does more to manufacture a digital divide between rich and poor. Hegemony can be expressed in the reproduction of the American Dream discussed above.

A failed application of hegemony occurred during the 1960 provincial election in Saskatchewan, when the Canadian Medical Association, using its influence as a respected professional body and raising money to back up this influence, attempted to block the passage of the law introducing medicare to that province. In an article apparently supporting the CMA's movement, the *Leader Post*, a conservative Regina daily, reported the results of a survey showing that 60 per cent of Saskatchewan doctors would leave the province if the NDP government did not withdraw the plan. The survey, it turned out, was based on interviews with just seven doctors, who claimed to represent additional groups of doctors totalling only 63 (Stewart 2003:228–9). In this case, attempts on the part of the dominant class to preserve the status quo were unsuccessful.

Class Reductionism

Class reductionism occurs when a sociologist studying a situation attributes all forms of oppression to class, ignoring or downplaying the impact of such factors as colonialism, race, ethnicity, gender, age, and sexual orientation. Social scientists in the former USSR were often guilty of class reductionism when they justified the Russian oppression of the indigenous peoples of Siberia in the name of class revolution against the indigenous bourgeoisie, when in fact in the pre-industrial world in which these peoples lived, there was no bourgeoisie. There were usually just herders who had more or fewer animals (yaks, camels, horses, etc). Calling those with more animals the 'bourgeoisie' and using that as a justification for trying to get rid of private ownership of animals was a serious distortion of Marx' analysis, and a good example of class reductionism.

Albert Memmi, who, along with Franz Fanon, was one of the founders of anti-colonialism theory, argued against class reductionism in colonial studies in his classic work *The Colonizer and the Colonized*:

To observe the life of the colonizer and the colonized is to discover rapidly that the daily humiliations of the colonized, his objective subjugation, are not merely economic. Even the poorest colonizer thought himself to be—and actually was—superior to the colonized. This too was part of colonial privilege. The Marxist discovery of the importance of the economy in all oppressive relationships is not to the point. This relationship has other characteristics which I believe I have discovered in the colonial relationship. (Memmi 1965:xii)

The failings of class reductionism are, of course, shared by anyone who reduces oppression to a single factor or fails to examine all relevant factors. This includes paying insufficient attention to the words or voice of the people affected. Edgar Dosman, in a study of Native people in Saskatoon carried out in 1968–9, rarely included Aboriginal voices at all. When he did, it was usually to criticize a comment or the individual quoted. He stressed the significance of class over the unifying experience of race among urban Aboriginal people, referring to groups with the somewhat patronizing and misleading labels of 'aristocracy', 'bourgeoisie', and 'welfare and anomic'. In so doing, he disqualified the leaders in the urban Aboriginal community from legitimately articulating a position worthy of sociological consideration.

He also directly attacked two important Aboriginal leaders of the time: Métis academic Howard Adams and Cree politician Harold Cardinal, both of whom were authors of influential works published around the time of Dosman's study (Adams in 1975 and Cardinal in 1969 and 1977). Dosman criticized Adams's work for being 'too flowery and intellectual for the native people; it is geared to the young students who crowd his meetings' (Dosman 1972:162). He formed this purely speculative opinion without asking Aboriginal people of all 'classes' what they thought of Adams (a well-respected figure in Aboriginal circles). He later dismisses a comment of Cardinal's with the terse remark, 'What, however, does that mean in the real world' (Dosman 1972:183). Clearly, he was not prepared to respect the standpoint Cardinal brought to the discussion.

The Caste System

A different kind of social stratification is the caste system that is in place in the Hindu areas of south Asia. **Castes**, or **varnas**, are groups of people born into the unequal possession of specific occupations, dharma (duty in life), rights to foods, colours of clothing (varna means 'colour'), religious practices, and imputed personal qualities. The system can be divided into five ranked categories:

- **Brahmins**: priests, political leaders, teachers
- **Kshatriyas**: military leaders, landowners
- **Vaishyas**: merchants, craftspeople
- **Shudras**: manual labourers
- **Dalits ('Untouchables')**: butchers, leather-workers, streetcleaners

The first three are the highest-ranking castes. Members of these are known as 'twice-born', referring to physical birth and later religious rebirth (similar to confirmation in the Christian tradition). From a historical standpoint, they are associated with Indo-European conquerors who came to the north of India/Pakistan from somewhere in the Steppes or plains area of Eastern Europe and Central Asia in migrations between 1500 and 1300 BC (Keay 2000:27). (**Indo-European** refers to speakers of a family of languages that includes almost all European languages, the main languages of Iran and Afghanistan, and northern Indian languages such as Hindi, Urdu, Bengali, and Punjabi.) The division of the three twice-born castes might be based on the class-like system of the early Celtic people, whose Druids have much in common with the Brahmins.

Hinduism and Hindu thinkers have sometimes been criticized, especially by people of Western background, for supporting the social inequality created by the caste system. This is often the result of a lack of exposure to the history of the faith and its believers. Hinduism has at various times in its history been interpreted in egalitarian, social reformist ways. When Hinduism was first developing (around 1500 BC), its earliest religious texts, the four Vedas and the later Brahamas, strongly supported the social authority of the higher castes, especially that of the Brahmin priests. Later religious texts (c. 800–300 BC), however, offered what can be called a more democratic view of spirituality. During this period two high-caste spiritual leaders rejected their privileged positions to form more democratic religious/philosophical movements rooted in Hinduism. Siddhartha Gautauma (540–480 BC) was a Brahmin who founded Buddhism. Mahavira (599–27 BC) was a Kshatriya ('warrior caste') who initiated Jainism.

In the ninth century, Shankara (c. 788–820), a Tamil Brahmin, went through a similar process, though he kept closer to the orthodoxy of the Hindu faith. He rejected his upper-caste life to become a travelling monk and scholar, and developed teachings based on the undifferentiated oneness of God with every individual soul. Shankara did not support the ranked division of society based on caste, as he saw no spiritual distinction between people. A famous story tells of how once, as he walked with students, a man of low caste approached from the opposite direction. One of Shankara's students told the man to get out of the way. The man, in turn, asked Shankara whether his egalitarian beliefs were just theories and not practices, given the discriminatory behaviour of his follower. Shankara felt that the man was the god Shiva, appearing in this way to teach him an important lesson about the spiritual equality of all people.

Mahatma Mohandes Gandhi (1869–1948), who led India to independence from British colonialism, is a figure from the India's more recent history of social reform. He strongly opposed the social restrictions and oppression of the caste system, and worked with and fought for the rights of the low-caste Untouchables (so-named because their very touch was considered by many upper-caste people to be spiritually polluting).

What do you think?

What would be misleading about thinking of the Hindu caste system merely as a form of social inequality?

Sociology in Action
Sport and Class

There is a strong connection between sport and class. The traditional association of sports like golf and tennis with the wealthy classes has been reinforced through the prohibitive cost of—and prestige surrounding—membership at golf and tennis clubs. Compare that with membership at a curling club, where players enjoy a sport generally seen as having more of a working-class appeal. Marketers and advertisers involved in professional sports will often exploit these associations to attract a particular fan base to their sport, in spite of the fact that most professional athletes earn lucrative salaries that put them squarely in upper class.

Sports that offer people from poorer socio-economic backgrounds the chance to reap large financial rewards as professional athletes can be called **mobility sports**. Generally, any sport that is cheap to play (with low costs for equipment and enrolment in organized competition), in which opportunities to play and 'be discovered' are readily available to people of all classes and that provides middle- to upper-class incomes for the relatively few that 'make it' can be considered a mobility sport. Historically and currently, boxing does that. It provides young, violent men raised in poverty an alternative to 'the streets'. Professional boxers rarely come from the middle class. During the last 20 years, basketball has been a mobility sport for young Black men in North America. Across the world, particularly in developing countries, soccer also provides mobility for the poor, especially the racialized poor.

Is hockey a mobility sport in Canada? Canadian hockey lore is replete with stories of poor young men from farming communities in the West or mining towns in the East rising from poverty and obscurity to celebrity. Gordie Howe was one of nine children raised on a failing farm in Depression-era Floral, Saskatchewan; he became one of the greatest stars of the game.

Johnny Bucyk, who grew up in the tough north part of Edmonton, the son of parents who were Ukrainian (a group then often minoritized), recalls learning to play hockey with 'road apples', without sticks, pads, or skates:

> I can remember playing street hockey when I was a kid, maybe seven or eight years old. In those days you couldn't afford

French critic Roland Barthes called wrestling the 'spectacle of excess', where 'wrestlers remain gods because they are, for a few moments, the key which opens Nature, the pure gesture which separates Good from Evil, and unveils the form of a Justice which is at last intelligible' (26). Do you agree? What kinds of people go to wrestling matches? Why would there be a need for such a justice? (Photo © M.J. Milloy)

to buy hockey sticks, nobody in our group could. I was from a poor family and I really didn't know what it was to own a hockey stick, so I didn't care. I played a lot of street hockey and we used brooms for sticks. We couldn't afford pucks either, so we'd follow the milk wagon which was pulled by a couple of horses, waiting until the horses did their job, dropping a good hunk of manure. Usually it would be a cold day, anytime between the start of October through the end of April, and we'd let it freeze up solid. We'd use it as a hockey puck.... I didn't get my first pair of skates until I was about 10 years old. It was a pair of my older brother Bill's, which he outgrew. (in Lowe, Fischler, and Fischler 1988:43–4)

Bucyk played in the NHL from 1956 to 1978, was the fifth NHLer to score 50 goals in a season, and was inducted into the Hockey Hall of Fame in 1981.

Players like Howe and Bucyk earned decent livings playing hockey, though they came nowhere near the earnings of star players today. They also grew up a time when the costs associated with playing organized hockey were relative low compared to now. Over the last 20 years, the cost of supporting a potential professional hockey player has shot up. Beyond the cost of equipment and league fees, a player who shows skill enough to play for a rep or select team will incur travel costs and increased rink fees (both for practices and for games). Players in the elite Greater Toronto Hockey League pay between $500 and $1,599 just in annual fees. The rise in costs is a feature of the **professionalization** of elite minor hockey, which now depends more on professional coaches and trainers rather than volunteers. The trend is evident also in other sports, as well as in activities like music, drama, and dance, and it reflects changing middle- and upper-class expectations concerning supposed recreational activities. The result is that many lower-class families cannot provide the same experience for their children, giving middle- and upper-class families a distinct advantage and making various sports—hockey in this case—much less of a mobility sport.

Contemporary Caste

When India's constitution was drafted in 1950, caste was officially abolished, and some former Untouchables, now typically termed **Dalits** ('Broken People'), have benefited from India's policy of quotas in education and government jobs. However, the situation is far from resolved. Middle- and upper-caste groups have mobilized politically to fight policies and legislation that are designed to support the 'scheduled castes' (a term not unlike 'designated groups', the Canadian equity term referring to women, Aboriginal peoples, visible minorities, and the disabled).

There are roughly 160 million Dalits in India, making up about one-sixth of the country's population. Most of them suffer from incredible poverty and discrimination. Caste is used as an excuse to oppress them. In 1989, the Scheduled Castes and Tribes (Prevention of Atrocities Act) was passed to try to prevent the harshest of caste abuses and abusers. According to Human Rights Watch (1999), caste-related offences include

forcing members of a scheduled caste or scheduled tribe [e.g., an indigenous group] to drink or eat any inedible or obnoxious substance; dumping excreta, waste manner, carcasses or any other obnoxious substance in their premises or neighborhood; forcibly removing their clothes and parading them naked or with painted face or body; interfering with their rights to land; compelling a member of a scheduled caste or scheduled tribe into forms of forced or bonded labor; corrupting or fouling the water of any spring, reservoir or any other source ordinarily used by scheduled castes or scheduled tribes; denying right of passage to a place of public resort; and using a position of dominance to exploit a scheduled caste or scheduled tribe woman sexually. (Human Rights Watch 1999)

Between 1994 and 1996, a total of 98,349 crimes against scheduled castes were registered with the police. Of this number, 38,483 were registered under the Prevention of Atrocities Act. The actual number of offences would certainly be much higher were it not for reluctance on the part of many Dalits to report offences and lack of co-operation on the part of police. The plight of Dalits has opened up a new area of sociological research in India.

Strata

When we talk about social stratification, we're borrowing a geological term to describe society as though it were divided into a series of layers. In geology, a stratum is a single level or layer of rock made up of tiny particles deposited together; if you look at a cross-section of sedimentary rock, you will be able to see the different strata and note the differences.

In sociology, a stratum is a level or class to which people are assigned according to their social status, education, or income. It's usually each of a number of equal groups into which a population has been divided for comparison. Strata are used as units of analysis in stratified sampling, an approach to statistical research in which a sample is drawn from each stratum or level of the population rather than drawn at random from the whole population. This produces a more representative sample for analysis. The following discussion will focus on two kinds of stratum used in sociological research: the quintile and the decile.

Quintiles

Perhaps the most common method of using strata in sociology in Canada is through **quintiles**. A quintile is each of five equal groups into which a population is divided according to the distribution of values of a particular variable; each one represents 20 per cent of the

Though the caste system was officially banned in India after independence, caste still exists informally and acts as a barrier to social equality. What is the difference between a caste and class? (Photo courtesy of Nishant Lalwani/Asian Foundation for Philanthropy)

population. Let's say, for example, that we wanted to divide the population into quintiles according to household (family) income. Grattan (2003) offers a good explanation of how we arrive at our quintiles:

Imagine that all families are placed in a line, a family's place being determined by its income level. The poorest family is placed at the front of the line, followed by the next poorest, and so on, until the last family, with the highest income, is placed at the end. Next, the line is split into five equal groups. The first group, or quintile, is composed of the first 20 percent of the population. The first 20 percent of the line. Obviously, this group will consist of the poorest people. The next group consists of the next 20 percent. A similar process occurs in selecting the third, fourth, and fifth groups. The fifth group, of course, comprises those families with the highest incomes.' (Grattan 2003:64–5)

Quintiles are useful for comparative purposes, both across time periods and across countries. Look at the following table. Keep in mind that if the total income for all families were distributed equally, each of the five quintiles would earn 20 per cent; however, this is not the case, as the table shows.

Table 8.1 >> Percentage of total before-tax income going to families and unattached individuals, by quintile, 1951–1996							
INCOME QUINTILES	**1951**	**1961**	**1971**	**1981**	**1991**	**1995**	**1996**
Lowest	4.4	4.2	3.6	4.6	4.7	4.7	4.6
Second	11.2	11.9	10.6	10.9	10.3	10.2	10.0
Middle	18.3	18.3	17.6	17.6	16.6	16.4	16.3
Fourth	23.3	24.3	24.9	25.1	24.7	24.5	24.7
Fifth	42.8	41.4	43.4	41.7	43.8	44.1	44.5

Source: Urmetzer and Guppy (1999:59).

We can see that over a 45-year period, the share of the total income in Canada earned by the top 20 per cent of earners increased by almost 2 per cent, increasing by nearly 3 per cent between 1981 and 1996. As Urmetzer and Guppy note, this last figure 'may appear to be a trivial amount, but given that the total income generated in Canada surpasses half a trillion dollars a year, this increase translates into more than 14 billion dollars—enough to eliminate poverty in Canada' (1999:59). During the same period (1981–96), the percentage earned by the three middle-income groups dropped.

The federal government helps to even off some of these differences between the groups with transfer payments to the less wealthy provinces. The following table shows the income figures for 1995 only; two additional columns show percentages of total income per quintile before federal transfer payments are made and after taxes have been deducted from family incomes:

Table 8.2 >> Percentage of total 1995 income going to families before transfers and after taxes, by quintile

QUINTILE	INCOME BEFORE TRANSFERS	TOTAL INCOME	INCOME AFTER TAXES
Lowest	0.8	4.7	5.7
Second	7.5	10.2	11.5
Middle	16.1	16.4	17.2
Fourth	26.2	24.5	24.5
Fifth	49.5	44.1	41.1

Source: Urmetzer and Guppy (1999:60).

Note here just 20 per cent of families earned almost half of all income earned by Canadians before taxes and transfer payments.

After drawing our conclusions about these figures, we can gain some added perspective by comparing the Canadian results with those of other countries. This is exactly what Urmetzer and Guppy did when they compared the Canadian results with those of 16 other countries for the years 1995–7. The following is a shorter version; in each column, the highest and lowest two extremes are indicated in bold and in italics, respectively.

Table 8.3 >> Percentage of total after-tax income going to families, by quintile, 1995

	LOWEST	SECOND	MIDDLE	FOURTH	HIGHEST
Canada	5.7	11.8	*17.7*	24.6	40.2
U.S.	4.7	11.0	17.4	*25.0*	41.9
Australia	4.4	10.0	*17.5*	24.8	42.2
Sweden	8.0	*13.2*	17.4	24.5	**36.9**
Japan	*8.7*	*13.2*	17.5	23.1	**37.5**
Brazil	**2.1**	**4.9**	**8.9**	**16.8**	*67.5*
South Africa	**3.3**	**5.8**	**9.8**	**17.7**	*63.3*

Source: Urmetzer and Guppy (1999:62).

From these figures we can make several tentative conclusions. First, we can see that the greatest amount of equality exists in Sweden and Japan, as they score highly in the percentage of the first three quintiles and low on the last two quintiles. Conversely, Brazil and South Africa have the greatest inequality, having low scores in all but the highest quintile. Canada compares favourably with the United States (our constant comparison companion), slightly less favourably with Australia. It is interesting to see in these cases that ethnicity would appear to play a role here, as the countries with the greatest social inequality are those that have a White minority and a Black (in South Africa) or a Black/Native (in Brazil) majority. The two least ethnically diverse countries have the greatest equality.

Deciles

Deciles are created with a similar methodology, but the population of census families is divided into ten, rather than five. This makes finer distinctions, and has a greater capacity to detect and show inequality. There is greater distinction between the very rich that are in the tenth or highest decile and the very poor that are in the first or lowest decile; the more we lump families into fewer strata, the less apparent the discrepancies between extremes become. If you were a sociologist working for a provincial gov-

	1973	1996	QUINTILE RATIO (1ST : 5TH, 1995)
Table 8.4 >> Total family income, 1st and 10th deciles compared, 1973, 1996			
A. Average market income (includes earnings from all sources and returns on investments)			
1st decile	$5,204	$435	—
10th decile	$107,253	$136,736	—
Ratio	20.61	314.34	61.875
B. Average total income (includes transfers from government income support programs)			
1st decile	$12,913	$13,522	—
10th decile	$109,260	$138,157	—
Ratio	8.46	10.22	5.21
C. Average after-tax income (includes federal and provincial tax systems)			
1st decile	$12,732	$13,353	—
10th decile	$86,196	$97,372	—
Ratio	6.77	7.24	7.21

Source: Yalnizyan (1998:128).

What do you think?

How does the 1995 quintile ratio differ from the 1996 decile ratio in each case? In what situation might it be better to use the quintile ratios for the data?

ernment that wants to show that 'things are getting better' for the poor, you would be more likely to use quintiles because they will show a narrower gap between poor and rich. If you were a working for a research institute that wanted to talk about the extremes of inequality, data tabulated in deciles would more effectively illustrate your message.

A good example of the use of deciles in Canadian sociological research comes from Armine Yalnizyan's *The Growing Gap: A Report on Growing Inequality Between the Rich and Poor in Canada* (1998). Yalnizyan (see Table 8.4) demonstrated how in the mid-1990s CEOs of large companies were receiving huge increases in salary and stock benefits at a time when 'the average worker' was experiencing minimal pay increases and fear of being 'downsized' or laid off. In a series of tables comparing total family income for 1973 and 1996, tabulated in deciles, Yalnizyan drew a compelling picture of social inequality in Canada. For each of the three parts we have added, with figures for

1995, the ratio of the first and fifth quintiles to show how tabulating the data in quintiles rather than deciles would give a different impression of the results.

Social Inequality and Education

Post-secondary education is a major avenue of social mobility, offering people from lower-class families the opportunity to secure jobs paying middle- or upper-class salaries. But if post-secondary education becomes too expensive for low-income students, then this avenue for mobility is blocked. In Canada, college tuition costs less and is therefore more accessible than university education. Look at the figures in the following table. Do you think the figures point to something of a 'class system' of post-secondary education? (Note that the data is tabulated in *quartiles*—four levels—rather than quintiles or deciles.)

Table 8.5 >>   Participation in post-secondary education and family income, 1998

	FAMILY INCOME AT AGE 16			
HIGHEST LEVEL OF EDUCATION	**LOWEST QUARTILE**	**MIDDLE HALF**	**HIGHEST**	**AVERAGE QUARTILE**
All post-secondary	56.1	62.2	69.7	62.7
University	18.8	27.5	38.7	28.4
College	28.8	28.8	28.3	28.7

What quartile are the families of these university students most likely to be in? How would that change if this were a college library instead of a university library? (© Photodisc)

Tuition Fees and University Education

Tuition fees for university education rose significantly during the 1990s, and have continued to rise, albeit not as dramatically, in the years since 2000. The average undergraduate tuition fee in Canada rose climbed from $1,464 in the 1990–1 academic year to $4,172 in 2004–5. A key factor here is government funding of post-secondary education: from 1990 to 1999, university operating revenues from government sources declined by 25 per cent.

There is regional disparity in this area. The highest average fees—$5,984 and $4,960 respectively—were in Nova Scotia and Ontario, where tuitions nearly tripled over the 15-year period. This contrasts sharply with the lowest average fees—$1,890 in Quebec and $2,606 in Newfoundland and Labrador (where tuition at one time was free)—both of which roughly doubled during the study period.

Of course, what you pay depends on not just where you're studying but what you're studying. The so-called 'professional schools' of dentistry, medicine, and law have the highest average fees across the country, scoring $12,331, $9,977, and $6,471 respectively in 2004–5; the last two of these had the two highest single-year increases—9.2 per cent for medicine and 7.9 per cent for law. This has affected who goes to the professional schools. A study undertaken in 2004 by the five law schools in Ontario (where the tuition is highest) found their schools were attended by 'more students from affluent homes headed by parents with a university education: two-thirds of law students come from the top 40 per cent of the family income distribution and about 10 per cent from the bottom 40 per cent of the distribution' (Social Program Evaluation Group, Queen's University 2004). (And think of how much greater the disparity would look if deciles or even quintiles had been reported.)

The situation at professional schools changed dramatically after 1997, when tuition fees were de-regulated (meaning that there were no governmental controls on what the universities could charge). The law school study reported that since 1997 there had been 'an increase of 4.7 per cent in the proportion of law students' parents who earn incomes in the top 40 per cent of the average family income distribution for Canada and a decrease in the proportion of students whose parents earn incomes in the middle 20 per cent of the distribution' (Social Program Evaluation Group, Queen's University 2004).

As with post-secondary tuition fees generally, there is a regional disparity in what it costs to attend a professional school. The following figures for 2003–4 show the average cost of attending medical school for eight provinces, presented in order of most expensive to least expensive:

Table 8.6 >> Selected average provincial costs of medical school tuition, 2003–4			
Ontario	**$14,878**	Alberta	$7,493
Nova Scotia	$10,460	Manitoba	$6,693
Saskatchewan	$9,774	Nfld & Labrador	$6,250
British Columbia	$8,876	**Quebec**	**$2,781**

What do you think?

Universities charging relatively high fees for professional schools usually justify their higher fees as a way of generating the revenue needed to attract 'star professors' and (for medical school) to purchase better equipment. Do you think this justifies the lack of social mobility this creates? Is it reasonable to say there's nothing wrong with students from poorer families attending cheaper universities?

Extremes

As we've seen throughout this chapter, studying social inequality is often about looking at the extremes that exist in issues such as family income and cost of post-secondary education. In this section we'll take a broader look at extremes of social inequality by looking first at food bank use and then at Canada's ten wealthiest people.

Food Banks

One indicator of the social inequality that exists in Canada comes from the food banks used in this country. A **food bank**, as defined by the Canadian Association of Food Banks (2004), is a 'central warehouse or clearing house, registered as a non-profit organization for the purpose of collecting, storing and distributing food, free of charge, directly or through front line agencies which may also provide meals to the hungry.' Every year the Canadian Association of Food Banks issues a statement called *HungerCount*, which offers statistics on food bank use. These statistics are generated from an 18-item survey distributed annually in March to food banks across the country. The 2004 figures are based on responses from 517 organizations (a 94 per cent participation rate). They indicate increases in food bank use of 8.5 per cent (amounting to 65,714 people) over 2003 figures, 26.6 per cent since 1997, and 122.7 per cent since 1989, when statistics were first taken.

HungerCount also shows the regional distribution of food bank use, calculated as a percentage of the total provincial population. Newfoundland and Labrador had the highest rate: 5.67 per cent of the province's population had used a food bank in 2004. The next highest percentages were in Manitoba (3.64 per cent), Quebec (3.6 per cent), and Ontario 2.64 (per cent).

The family composition of food recipients was recorded in 483 of the surveys. Theses figures showed that the two largest groups of food bank users are single people (making up 35.5 per cent of all food bank users) and single-parent families (31.0 per cent). That these two groups make up the majority of food bank users is perhaps not surprising. What is surprising, however, is how many of those who used a food

Lifestyles of the rich and famous from a 1937 edition of the *Boston Sunday Post*. How would readers of the time have reacted to the juxtaposition of these images? Are there still these kinds of disparities in society today? (Prints & Photographs Division, Library of Congress)

Though more economic wealth and millionaires were created in the 1990s than in any other decade in Canadian history, there were significant increases in poverty and food bank use during the same period. Why would poverty increase at the same time that overall wealth increased? (T. Myers/Ivy Images)

bank were from two-parent families (23.5 per cent) or were couples without children (10.0 per cent). This means that most of the recipients (64.5 per cent) were families, and most were families with children (54.5 per cent), the latter figure supported by the fact that approximately 40 per cent of the food recipients were children.

The primary income source of food recipients was indicated in 385 of the surveys received. A total of 54.4 per cent of the food bank users listed social assistance as their primary income. The next-highest figure is startling: 13.3 per cent of food bank users listed a job or employment as their main source of income.

What do you think?

1. Which of the following social policies do you think would best stop and possibly reverse the growth of food bank dependency? For each policy, indicate which of Canada's three major political parties would be most likely to propose it.
   a) issue welfare cheques as food coupons;
   b) increase the minimum wage;
   c) increase family allowance cheques;
   d) increase the availability of low-cost housing.

2. Do you think that food banks are a permanent feature of Canadian life?

Canada's Ten Wealthiest People

Now we'll take a look at how the other half lives, with a focus on what it takes to be extremely wealthy. Having the right idea at the right time and pursuing your goals with great determination certainly help, but in many cases it's more a matter of having extremely wealthy parents. The following is a short discussion of the ten wealthiest people or families in Canada and how they obtained their wealth.

Kenneth Thomson (estimated as being worth roughly 22 billion dollars)

Born in Toronto in 1923, Ken Thomson is the only son of media mogul Roy Thomson, himself the son of a barber, who got involved in the radio business just as it was starting out. After settling in Scotland, Roy Thomson began acquiring newspapers, later expanding his assets to include television and radio stations in Britain and around the world. In 1964, he was knighted 'Baron Thomson of Fleet'. Kenneth Thomson inherited both the media empire and the title, and expanded the holdings.

Galen Weston ($8.67 billion)

Garfield Weston (1889–1978) took a small chain of bakeries inherited from his father (George Weston) and turned it into an empire of grocery stores and food processing companies, including Neilson's dairy, Nabob coffee, and the grocery giant Loblaw's. Garfield's son Galen expanded the holdings of George Weston Foods to include the President's Choice label and a fisheries department that farms salmon in North America and Chile. Another generation is poised to take over, with Australian-born George Weston, named CEO in 2003, at the helm.

Jeff Skoll ($6.66 billion)

Like Roy Thomson, who was an early player in the radio and television industries, Jeff Skoll was in the right business to capitalize on the expansion of an industry. The 40-year-old billionaire is the co-founder of eBay Inc. Born and raised in Montreal, he received a degree in electrical engineering from the University of Toronto before earning an MBA at Stanford University, about the same time he founded two small computer businesses in California's 'Silicon Valley'. It was there he met with Pierre Omidyar, who invited Skoll to draw up a business plan to turn his not-for-profit Internet auction house into a profit-making venture.

James, Arthur, and John Irving ($4.99 billion)

You know you're in the Maritimes when you see the signs for Irving Oil. Kenneth Colin Irving (1899–1992) was a two-time university dropout who trained as a pilot in World War I but never flew in combat. After dabbling at a few jobs following the war he opened a Ford dealership in his hometown of Buctouche, New Brunswick, convinced that the automobile was the way of the future. Recognizing that people would need gas to fuel their cars, he became Imperial Oil's local dealer and later established his own K.C. Irving Gas and Oil Company, which he gradually expanded throughout the Maritimes and New England. Within 20 years he had his first oil refinery. When his father died he inherited the family lumber business, and he went on to diversify his holdings with interests in pulp and paper, mining, shipyards and shipping, steel, newspapers, and even french fries. His sons James, Arthur, and John inherited the Irving empire on the death of K.C. Irving in 1992.

James Pattison ($4.17 billion)

The history of James Pattison combines several elements of the biographies above. Like K.C. Irving, he got his start selling cars after dropping out of university, and would later acquire vast newspaper holdings. Like Roy Thomson, he became involved with radio and television, owning 20 radio stations and 3 TV stations. Like the Westons, he expanded into the food industry, investing in packaging (Gen Pak for example), fish (Gold Seal salmon), and a chain of grocery stores in Alberta and British Columbia. Unique is his large illuminated signs industry (you'll see his name on billboards and other forms of outdoor advertising). He now owns 13 car dealerships in his home province of British Columbia and is the second largest supplier of periodicals in North America, and his Jim Pattison Group is the third-largest privately held company in Canada.

Paul Desmarais Sr ($3.94 billion)

Paul Desmarais came from a fairly well-to-do family. He was born in Sudbury, where, after he received a BA in Commerce from the University of Ottawa, he took control of a bus company. Expanding his transportation company during the 1950s, he acquired the capital to invest in life insurance. Today, his Power Corporation owns Great-West Life Assurance Company and London Life Assurance Company, as well has some European holdings. Another of his successful ventures, one that should not be surprising by now, is newspaper ownership. In 1967, he bought the influential Montreal daily *La Presse*; since then others have been added to the holdings of his Gesca Ltée.

Saputo Family ($2.78 billion)

Giuseppe Saputo embodies the archetype of the poor immigrant from Europe who achieved phenomenal wealth and success in North America. A cheese maker from Sicily, he emigrated to Montreal in 1950 with his eldest son Frank, followed two years later by the rest of his family, including his mother, two sons, and four daughters. The family business, which began as a cheese shop in the Italian community of Montreal, is now the leading producer of mozzarella for food services, having capitalized on the rise in popularity in North America of Italian cuisine during the 1960s and 1970s. The company also managed to increase its market share by building their own factories. In 1999, the company grabbed a big piece of Quebec culture when it acquired a share of Culinar Inc, which manufacturers the popular Vachon snack cakes.

Dr Bernard Sherman ($2.5 billion)

Certainly the most educated of Canada's top ten billionaires, Bernard Sherman graduated with his degree in engineering physics from the University of Toronto before heading to the prestigious Massachusetts Institute of Technology (MIT), where he received both a masters in aeronautics and astronautics and a PhD in systems engineering. But although he had opportunities to work in the American space program, he returned in 1967 to Canada, where he and a friend bought his uncle Lou Winter's small generic drug company, Empire Laboratories Ltd, for $250,000. He would use the profits from the sale of this company six years later to set up his own generic drug company, Apotex, in 1974. It started small, with three employees, but took off in 1980 with the introduction of a generic alternative to a popular—and more expensive—brand of medication for high blood pressure. Sherman had to battle the drug giants with often successful legal challenges to their patents, and by the time the federal government put greater protection on these patents, Apotex had its own patents and was taking larger and larger pieces of the pharmaceutical pie.

David Azriel ($2.26 billion)

Born in Poland in 1922, David Azriel came to Canada from Israel in 1954, the same year the Sicilian Saputo family established its business in Montreal. Having studied in Israel to become an architect, he was able to get a job working for an architectural firm. By 1958, he had established Canpro Investments, which had constructed four duplexes in Montreal's east end. Azriel became a commercial developer involved in the construction of office buildings and malls. Canpro Investments later expanded its operations to Ontario and New England,

and eventually to Israel. At 75, he completed his MA in architecture at Carleton University, after which he made a substantial donation to that institution.

Edward (Ted) Rogers ($2.21 billion)

Ted Rogers followed his father in getting involved in the radio industry. Edward Rogers, Sr, at 24, invented the first alternating current (AC) radio tube, technology that enabled radios to be used in homes, powered by the small household electrical current. Seven years later, he was awarded an experimental TV licence. He died at 38, still working on new electronic technology.

Ted Rogers, while articling as a student at Osgoode Hall Law School, started Roger Radio Broadcasting Limited and in 1962 CHFI-FM, Canada's first FM station, which pioneered stereo broadcasting and became the most profitable FM station in the country. He was also involved in the early days of cable television, and by the 1970s, Rogers Cable TV offered the largest selection of channels in Canada. In the 1980s, he got involved with the fledgling cellular phone business, and by 1992 his company was competing with Bell for long-distance calling. Rogers Communications Inc. continues to be one of the country's telecommunications leaders.

Summary of Canada's Wealthiest

So how do you become one of the wealthiest people in Canada? It helps to come from money, as Ken Thomson, Galen Weston, and the Irving brothers did. Catching in on a 'way of the future' is another key—oil and gas in the case of K.C. Irving, online bidding in the case of Jeff Skoll, telecommunications in the case of Ted Rogers.

But the sociologist is quick to note that these types of opportunities are rare. The social structure allows for very few people to gain in this way. The path to success for these individuals is littered with the corpses of dead companies and failed competitors who might have 'made it' but for fortune and the limits of the social structure. Only one can be the biggest and most powerful in any area, and in some areas, there isn't a lot of money in being number two or three.

'Asphyxiating Wealth' by Lydia Reid, 2007. A student began this sketch during a lecture on extremes of social inequality. How would you interpret it?

Questions for Critical Review and Discussion

1. Distinguish between a Marxist notion of class and a system that includes a middle class.

2. Differentiate between *class* and *strata*.

3. Identify what deciles and quintiles are and demonstrate how they are used.

4. Identify what caste is and outline how it may sometimes be misunderstood.

5. Identify what liberal ideology is and outline potential weaknesses.

Suggested Readings

Bauman, Zygmunt (1998). *Work, Consumerism and the New Poor*. Philadelphia: Open UP.

Bottomore, Tom, & Robert J. Brym, eds. (1989). *The Capitalist Class: An International Study*. New York: New York UP.

Burstyn, Varda, & Dorothy E. Smith (1983). *Women, Class, Family and the State*. Toronto: Garamond Press.

Das Gupta, Tania (1996). *Racism and Paid Work*. Toronto: Garamond Press.

Leidner, Robin (1993). *Fast Food, Fast Talk: Service Work and the Routinization of Everyday Life*. Berkeley: U of California P.

Rudner, David West (1994). *Caste and Capitalism in Colonial India: The Nattukottai Chettiars*. Berkeley: U of California P.

Suggested Websites

Canadian Council on Social Development.
http:www.ccsd.ca/home.htm

Forbes' Listing of World's Billionaires.
http://www.forbes.com/tool/toolbox/billnew/1998.asp

International Social Inequality and Classes (Albert Benschop, Social & Behavioral Sciences/Media Studies, University of Amsterdam).
http://www2.fmg.uva.nl/sociosite/topics/inequality.html

National Anti-Poverty Organization.
http://www.napo-onap.ca

CHAPTER 9

'Race' and Ethnicity: Sites of Inequality

Contents

Key Terms

anti-colonialism
colonialism
cultural mosaic
discrimination
dual colonialism
epiphenomenal
ethnic class
ethnic entrepreneurs
indirect rule
institutional or systematic
   racism
instrumentalism
internal colonialism
Inuit
melting pot
Métis
minoritized
multiculturalism
Pan-African
Powley test
prejudice
primordialism
Quiet Revolution
racialization
racial time
registered Indian
relational accountability
scrip
smiling racism
social construct
token
urban reserve
vertical mosaic

Boxes and Tables

Quick Hits Blacks in Canada: Four Mind Traps
In Our View Racialized Views of a Canadian Institution
In Other Words Ethnicity and Class in Sept-Îles During the 1960s and 1970s
Canadian Sociology in Action A Minoritizing Episode
Quick Hits Who Has the Right to Vote?

Table 9.1 Salmon gill net licences issued 1922–1925
Table 9.2 French and British in the professional and financial occupation

Learning Objectives

After reading this chapter, you should be able to

- discuss the extent to which race, ethnicity, and gender are social constructs.
- distinguish between forms of racism.
- outline four 'mind traps' of studying Blacks in Canada.
- demonstrate how, historically, Canadian laws can be said to be racist.
- contrast the social inequality in Quebec before and after the Quiet Revolution.

>>> # For Starters
The Invisibility of Being White

Most White people living in North America are for all intents and purposes invisible. That invisibility affords a safety that is easily taken for granted.

In the 1960s, I—a White male—became visible for a time because of my long hair. With this status I took a few baby steps down the long path of unmasked prejudice. Police, folks from small towns, and denizens of Toronto's 'greaser' neighbourhoods all made me highly aware of my visibility, causing me to feel vulnerable to the emotions of others. Once, waiting for a bus in Northern Ontario, dark from a summer's work in forestry, straight hair hanging well below my shoulders, one of the people working at the bus depot thought I was Native. I got a brief glimpse of the gaze of racial disdain.

Age and a respectable career made me invisible again. That is, unlike a young Black male, I am not watched carefully in convenience stores, nor stopped for no apparent reason while driving. White people, even when they are visible, do not lose status; on the contrary, in many cases, with greater visibility comes a rise in status. When I went to Taiwan, I had visibility with prestige. Children watched me with respect. They would practise English with 'the expert'. Among school children on a trip to the museum, I became a walking exhibit of the West. They passed me defer-

Peterborough fans at a Memorial Cup game in Moncton, NB, represent 'the invisibility of Whiteness', which speaks both to a homogeneous demographic and to a society that is constructed around White beliefs, values, and ideals—anything other than White becomes 'visible'. (CP Photo/Andrew Vaughan)

ence, 'Hi how are you' spoken to their face-covering hands.

When I took the train south to the mid-sized city of Hualien, a small boy played repeated rounds of English peek-a-boo with me, with his 'Hi, how are you?' met by my 'Fine. How are you?'. My visibility helped me at the Hualien train station, when the person who was supposed to meet me failed to turn up. Taxi drivers helped me use the phone (I was unsure of which coins to use), even when I told them I wouldn't be needing a ride. Would a Taiwanese person in a mid-sized, racially homogeneous city in Canada have been served that well?

For the first time in my life, I didn't see a White person for an entire day. Far from disappearing anonymously into crowds, I parted crowds like Moses through the Red Sea (the beard might have helped). I felt as though I was always on stage, but with a friendly audience.

Coming back, I needed to get a taxi from the station to the airport. I knew the name of the airport, but that didn't help me as I passed from taxi to taxi trying to communicate what I needed, each time to baffled looks. Knowing that fluency in English and administrative status often went hand in hand in Taiwan, I went to the office of the station manager, who wrote down what I wanted so that I could show it to one of the taxi drivers. Can you imagine a non-English speaker, non-White person doing that in Canada? Imagine the response.

It was a good lesson for me to be visible, even if the visibility was not a negative one. It helped me imagine what it would be like if the roles were reversed.

Introduction to 'Race'

The term 'race' was first applied to humans in the context of Spanish and English colonial expansion during the sixteenth and seventeenth centuries. Use of the term reflected—and still does reflect—beliefs about 'natural' or 'biological' superiority and inferiority in the context of colonial power. It does not boil down to the formula 'lighter skin = good, pure / darker skin = bad, corrupt': witness, for example, Russian racism directed at Siberian peoples speaking languages related to Finnish and Hungarian, and Japanese racism towards their indigenous people (the Ainu and the Okinawans), and the racism of the Chinese concerning Tibetans. However, White supremacy—which amounts to discrimination against anyone not of western European ethnic background—has been the prevailing pattern since people began discussing humans in terms of different races, each with its own set of qualities and characteristics.

It is important to understand that as biological entities, races do not exist among humans.

When early scientists tried to divide humans into three 'races'—Caucasian (named after the mountains in which 'pure' whites were supposed to live), Mongoloid, and Negroid—there were always peoples left over. Where do you file the Ainu of Japan, the Aborigines of Australia, the peoples of various physical differences living in the South Asian subcontinent? Differences *within* supposed races often outnumbered those *between* races. 'Negroid' people included both the tallest and shortest people in the world, and people of greatly varying skin colour. English-born anthropologist Ashley Montagu published a landmark argument against the existence of separate human races in *Man's Most Dangerous Myth: The Fallacy of Race*, first printed in 1942. Since then, science has shown that there is but one human species, albeit one that displays variation among its members. More damning is recent evidence from genetics researchers

But **racialization** does exist. It is a social process in which people are viewed and judged as essentially different in terms of their intellect, their morality, their values, and their innate worth because of differences of physical type or cultural heritage.

A Sociological Profile of Canada's Native People

Racialization occurs in Canada, as elsewhere. It is perhaps most evident in the way Native people have been and still are treated. Native racialization in Europe began with a discussion in the sixteenth century of whether or not Aboriginal people were even human and had souls. They were an 'Other' that needed to be explained, and racialization was part of that explanation. A few facts from the sociological profile of Canada's Native People shows how this racialization has occurred.

First, Native people have been living in what is now Canada for a very long time: a conservative estimate is 12,000 years. If you figure that the first Europeans (the Norse explorers, or Vikings) visited Canada's eastern shores about 1,000 years ago (and left shortly afterwards), that means that roughly 92 per cent of Canadian history is Aboriginal history alone. The first non-Native settlements in Canada were founded just 400 years ago. That means that non-Aboriginal people have lived continuously in this country for only 3.3 per cent of its history.

Second, from a sociological perspective, Aboriginal people have been studied primarily as social problems. Aboriginal writers have been loud in their criticism of this preoccupation and have called for a more balanced approach. Métis writer Emma LaRoque expresses her own criticism as follows:

> Several years ago in a sociology class on social problems, I recall wondering if anyone else was poor, because the professor repeatedly referred to Native people as statistical examples of poverty. . . . Not for one moment would I make light of the ugly effects of poverty. But if classroom groups must talk about Indians and poverty, then they must also point out the ways in which Native people are operating on this cancer. To be sure, the operations are always struggles and sometimes failures, but each new

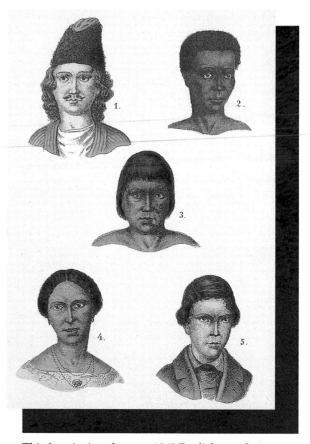

This frontispiece from an 1862 English translation of *Martin's Natural History* shows three of five supposed principal 'races' together with two mixed races: 1. the White or Caucasian race; 2. the Black or Negro race; 3. the American or Red Race; 4. the Mulatto mixed race; 5. the Mestizza mixed race. The other two principal races identified in the book are the Yellow or Mongolian race and the Brown or Malayan race. (From S.A. Myers, trans., *Martin's Natural History*, First Series, New York: Blackeman & Mason, 1862:frontispiece.)

operation is faced with more experience, more skill, more confidence and more success. (LaRoque 1993:212)

LaRoque here calls for a perspective that attempts to balance how people are seen, a perspective based on what Wilson and Wilson refer to as **relational accountability**. This is an approach that balances the social portrayal of a people so that both strengths and weaknesses, problems and successes can be seen. Third, Aboriginal voices have barely been heard in the sociological study of their people in Canada

(Steckley 2003). Unfortunately, as Aboriginal people have only recently been able to take advantage of graduate-level work in Canadian universities, and as sociology has been tainted, like anthropology, as an outsider-privileged research area, it will be a while yet before these voices speak loudly in sociology in Canada.

Fourth, Aboriginal people are defined by a complex system of legal status that separates them in a number of ways from non-Aboriginal people, and from each other. The main designations are:

- registered Indian
- Bill C-31 Indian
- band member
- reserve resident
- treaty Indian
- Métis
- Eskimo

The legal differences come from the Indian Act, which is administered by the federal Department of Indian Affairs. Passed in 1876, the Indian Act enshrined a sexist definition of 'Indian' as any man of 'Indian blood' reputed to belong to a particular band, any child of such a man, or any woman married to such a man. A man kept his status, no matter whom he married, but a woman, if she married someone not legally an Indian, lost her status, and her children would share that fate. Ironically, a non-Native woman could gain Indian status by marrying an Indian man. This discriminatory law was in force until 1985, when Bill C-31 was passed, enabling people who had lost their Indian status through marriage or through the marriage of their mother to apply to be reinstated.

Inuit (from a word meaning 'people') differ from Indians, having been in being in Canada for a shorter time, somewhere between 5,000 and 10,000 years. It was not until 1939, when the federal government wanted to assert territorial claims in the Arctic, that Canada officially took responsibility for the Inuit. Each Inuk was given a metal disk with a number that was used as a token of their status. Today, about 60 per cent of Inuit have disk numbers. The lives of Canada's Northern Aboriginal population changed on 1 April 1999, when the territory of Nunavut (meaning 'Our Land') came into being. More than 80 per cent of Nunavut's 25,000 residents are Inuit. They own 18 per cent of the land, have subsurface rights to oil, gas, and other minerals for about 2 per cent of Nunavut, and will receive royalties from the extraction of those minerals from the rest of the territory. They do not require a licence to hunt or fish to meet their basic needs.

The term **Métis** is used in two ways. It is commonly used, often with a lowercase *m*, to refer to anyone of mixed Native and non-Native heritage. With an uppercase *M* it usually refers to the descendants of French fur traders and Cree women. Starting in the late eighteenth century, the Métis developed a culture that brought together European and Native features. Over time, they came to regard themselves as a nation, having achieved a sense of solidarity from their shared legal struggles with the Hudson's Bay Company (HBC) over the HBC's trade monopoly. The HBC owned most of the prairies and about half of present-day Canada thanks to a 1670 charter granted by the English King Charles II, who little knew what he was signing away. In 1867, the HBC negotiated the sale of most of its charter lands to the Government of Canada, which, with no regard for Métis land rights, moved to set up a colony in Manitoba. In 1869, led by 25-year-old, college-educated Louis Riel, the Métis achieved a military takeover in the colony and set up an independent government to negotiate with Ottawa. The *Manitoba Act* of 1870 established the province and recognized the rights of the Métis. The Métis were given **scrips**, certificates declaring that the bearer could receive payment in land, cash, or goods. But government officials and land speculators swindled the Métis out of their land by buying up the scrips. Most Métis simply moved west. In 1885, with western expansion again threatening their rights to the land, the Métis, led still by Louis Riel, set up an independent government in Saskatchewan. Federal Canadian forces attacked and defeated them, and this time Riel was hanged for treason.

The Métis settled in a patchwork of rural prairie communities and nearly disappeared altogether. But during the 1930s, Alberta Métis pushed for the creation of communal settlements similar to reserves. In 1938, eleven Métis 'colonies' were formed (eight remain today). These colonies carry some political rights, making them more like rural municipalities; however, the Métis do not have rights to the royalties for oil and gas extracted from the land. Beyond the colonies, the Métis are represented by the Métis National Council and provincial organizations in Ontario and the Western provinces. These organizations suffer from difficulties of legal definition and lack of recognition.

Two Recent Changes in Aboriginal Canada

In 1993, Steve Powley and his son, both Métis, were charged with unlawfully hunting and possessing a moose. They fought the case on the grounds of their rights as Aboriginal people to hunt for food. On 23 September 2003, the Supreme Court of Canada upheld Powley's right to hunt for food out of season and without a provincial licence. The case helped established what has been called the **Powley test**, used to determine whether Native and Métis people can lawfully hunt without a licence. According to the test, one must be able to show that he or she has been identified as Métis for a long time and is accepted as a member in a community that was historically and currently is Métis. Powley's community of 900, just outside of Sault Ste Marie in northwestern Ontario, qualified. The Powley case has been used by the Métis to obtain hunting rights in parts of British Columbia, Alberta, and Saskatchewan.

What do you think?

1. Who would oppose the successful invocation of the Powley test?

2. How could this opposition be overcome?

Recently, **urban reserves** have been created in Saskatchewan. Unlike reserves in other provinces that became urban as cities grew around them, these are lands located within a municipality or Northern Administrative District that have been given official reserve status to compensate Native peoples who were promised land more than 100 years ago. The main function of these urban reserves is to provide central urban locations for Aboriginal businesses. More than 1,350 people work in the businesses set up in Saskatchewan's 28 urban reserves.

Muskeg Lake Cree Nation was the first band to develop an urban reserve. It has about 1,200 members, most living off reserve. They were granted 33 acres of land in Saskatoon. In 1993, they signed a services agreement with the city, under which the band makes an annual payment for municipal services such as snow and garbage removal; electricity and water charges are billed directly to individual customers on the reserve. Businesses operating there are almost all owned by Aboriginal people, and nearly all of the 300 employees are Native.

Blacks in Canada

Black communities have existed in Nova Scotia since the British Proclamation of 1779 offered freedom to slaves who left their American masters to fight on the British side in the American Revolution. Over 3,000 African Americans moved north, followed twenty years later by 2,000 more, who came to the Maritime colonies when they were offered their freedom by the British government during the War of 1812, in which Britons and Canadians fought Americans (Conrad and Hiller 2001:103, 111). They were offered significantly less land and fewer opportunities than White immigrants (see Whitfield 2004), and they endured incredible hardship and prejudice.

The Black population of Canada has declined several times. In 1792, nearly 1,200 Black Loyalists left the Atlantic colonies for the new colony of Sierra Leone (Conrad and Hiller 2001:103), and many more returned to the United States following the Civil War. Between 1871 and 1911 there was a slow decline in the population of Black people in Canada from 21,500 to 16,900, and a further drop, from 22,200

>>> **Quick Hits**
Blacks in Canada: Four Mind Traps

Four mind traps in studying Blacks in Canada are that:

• the Black population is recent;
• most Blacks are immigrants to Canada;
• the vast majority of Blacks coming to Toronto are from Jamaica;
• when Blacks receive post-secondary education they will do as well as non-Blacks.

What do you think?

Native people have made up a disproportionately high percentage of the poor in Canadian cities. Will urban reserves change this significantly?

This engraving, from a sketch by William Carlisle and bearing the caption 'HALIFAX, N.S. – NEGRESSES SELLING MAYFLOWERS ON THE MARKET PLACE', appeared in the *Canadian Illustrated News* on 25 May 1872. What does it tell you about the social differences between Halifax's Black and White citizens at the time? (Courtesy of the Charles deVolpi Collection, Special Collections, Dalhousie University Libraries)

A young woman walks along the tracks in Africville, which was demolished, its residents relocated, between 1964 and 1967. (CP Photo/Halifax Chronicle Herald)

to 18,000, between 1941 and 1951. The Black population began to increase consistently only during the 1970s, when it climbed from 34,400 in 1971 to 239,500 at the end of the decade (Milan and Tran 2004:3). In 2001 there were 662,200 Blacks living in Canada, making them the country's third highest visible minority, behind Chinese and South Asians.

While there is a tendency to think of Black Canadians as immigrants, almost half the Black population was born in Canada. The tendency of Torontonians (whose city is home to nearly half of Canada's Black population) to think of all Black immigrants as 'Jamaicans' is also flawed, as there is a growing number coming from African countries. Of the roughly 139,800 Black immigrants who came to Canada between 1991 and 2001, only 20 per cent came from Jamaica; 12 per cent came from French-speaking island of Haiti (settling mostly in Montreal), while 23 per cent came from three African countries, Somalia (10 per cent), Ghana (8 per cent), and Ethiopia (5 per cent).

Education does not seem to benefit Black people as much as it does others. In 2001, Canadian-born Blacks between the ages of 25 and 54 were just as likely as other Canadian-born citizens to be university graduates (21 per cent) and slightly more likely to have a college diploma (23 per cent compared with the national average of 20 per cent). Still, the average income of Canadian-born Blacks was substantially lower than the average for all Canadian-born people ($29,700 versus $37,200). Some analysts have tried to 'explain away' this discrepancy by citing the fact that the majority of working Black citizens are relatively young, earning the lower incomes typical of younger workers. Yet, when the income of Canadian-born Blacks is age-standardized to overcome the statistical bias, the result is an annual income of $32,000, which is still significantly lower than the national average.

Racism

Four Elements of Racism

Racism can be understood as the product of four linked elements. The first is the construction of certain groups of people as biologically superior or inferior. This fosters ideas of relative worth and quality, which leads to the second element, **prejudice**, the 'pre-judgement' of others on the basis of their group membership. The third element is **discrimination**, which includes acts by which individuals are treated differently—rewarded or punished—based on their group membership. Finally, there is power, which is manifested when institutionalized advantages are regularly handed to one or more groups over others. Tatum, addressing the question *Can non-White people be racist?*, touches on the importance of power in this equation when she writes:

> People of color are not racist because they do not systematically benefit from racism. And equally important, there is no systematic cultural and institutional support or sanction for the racial bigotry of people of color. In my view, reserving the term 'racist' only for behaviors committed by whites in the context of a white-dominated society is a way of acknowledging the ever-present power differential afforded whites by the culture and institutions that make up the system of advantage and continue to reinforce notions of white superiority. (in Codjoe 2001:287)

Those who take this position believe that without power, non-White people in Canada cannot, strictly speaking, be racist. They can be prejudiced. They can perform discriminatory acts. But they cannot be racist without institutional, structural, ideological, and historical support. Certainly this is true of systemic racism, which by definition involves power. But this view does not adequately account for situations in which one racialized group that lacks power puts down another. In such an instance, both groups are sharing in the racism of the dominant 'race'. Cree leader David Ahenakew's public—and much publicized—anti-Jewish sentiments in 2002 are a case in point. Both Aboriginal and Jewish people have been and continue to be victims of racism in Canada. But although it would

be mistaken to call Aboriginal people in Canada racists, Ahenakew contributed to anti-Jewish racism with his prejudiced remarks.

There are different kinds of racism. **Racial bigotry** is the open, conscious expression of racist views by an individual. When racist practices, rules, and laws become institutionalized, 'part of the system'—no matter how aware or unaware people are of their discriminatory nature—then we have **systematic** or **institutional racism**. Sometimes, racism can be subtle, hidden in a way behind a smile or words that seem friendly to the perpetrator. This is called **polite, smiling**, or **friendly racism**. Henry Martey Codjoe provides an example:

> Canada's 'smiling racism' was with me until the very day I left the country. The realtor who showed our house to prospective buyers quietly hinted that if I wanted my house to sell quickly, I would have to remove all traces of anything that indicated that Blacks had lived in the house: no family pictures, no African art or crafts, everything Black or African must go, and we must be out of the house before he showed the house to prospective buyers. He would call and let us know. No matter what we were doing, we must leave. One time we were late in getting out and we ended up hiding in our minivan in the garage. When he showed the garage, we ducked. It was a shameful and degrading experience. The house sold, but my wife and I never did meet the family that bought it. (Codjoe 2001:286)

Master Narratives and Buried Knowledge

In the **master narratives** that countries construct about themselves, which get repeated in school textbooks and in the stories people (especially politicians) tell about their country, racism is often downplayed or altogether concealed. Stories about the mistreatment of minorities, stories that make the people or their ancestors look bad, are often excluded. For example, the master

>>> In Our View
Racialized Views of a Canadian Institution

According to CBC hockey analyst Don Cherry, he had told us all along that Russians were 'quitters'. He was referring to an apparent threat by the Russian team to pull out of the 2002 Winter Olympics in Salt Lake City over alleged bias in drug testing. 'I've been trying to tell you people for so long about the Russians, what kind of people they are,' Cherry told viewers, 'and you just love them in Canada with your multiculturalism.'

Cherry's comments sparked an angry reaction among many Canadians. Nevertheless, he stood by his comments, although he issued a statement a week later to 'clarify' his remarks. According to Cherry, he was referring not to the Russian people as a whole but to the Russian delegation 'who threatened to pull out of the Olympics because they got caught with drugs and were losing'. Anyone who heard the statement, however, knows that Cherry had been addressing what he considered an essential and long-held character trait of the Russian people.

Among those in Canada stunned by Cherry's comments was Maia Master, publisher of the *Russian Express*, a Toronto-based newspaper serving the needs of the city's 160,000 Russian Canadians, who was flooded with calls com-plaining about the remarks. During an interview shortly afterwards on *CBC NewsWorld*, Master was informed by a smirking Dennis Trudeau that Cherry was still popular enough to remain on the air despite having insulted other groups before (including Quebecers, whom he described on air in 1998 as 'whiners'). Trudeau's suggestion that Don Cherry was simply being himself and that his comments should not be taken personally was nearly as disturbing as Cherry's original views. Russian Canadians, he seemed to suggest, should simply put up with such slights, like all immigrants and minorities in Canada.

Canadian corporate mass media continues to be an active agent in perpetuating a cohesive social order based on affluence, while simultaneously telling us that 'good' people tolerate prejudice, discrimination, racism, and other forms of repression. Yet we must be intolerant of intolerance. Russian Canadians, like all immigrants and minorities, have a right to complain and to speak out as Canadian citizens about those things that are unacceptable in what is supposed to be a multicultural society. To capitulate to the tyranny of silence is to capitulate to one's own repression.

—G.L.

narrative of early Canadian history describes how Native people co-operated with Europeans to make the fur trade successful, by obtaining the furs, teaching Europeans how to use canoes and snowshoes, and providing the Europeans with new foods (such as pemmican and corn). This 'official' version of the story often appears in elementary and middle-school textbooks; it overlooks the exploitation and social destruction that occurred when Europeans introduced alcohol into the fur trade. To use Michel Foucault's terminology, that story is buried knowledge.

Canada's master narrative depicts a country that is more multicultural than the United States. There is some evidence to support this, but the master narrative does not include some buried knowledge about the history of certain racial groups in Canada. The following three stories are part of that buried knowledge.

1) An Act to Prevent the Employment of Female Labour in Certain Capacities

The head tax of $500 on Chinese immigrants imposed in 1903 had a dramatic effect on immigration. For the overwhelmingly male population of Chinese immigrants who had already settled in Canada, it meant the chances of marrying a Chinese woman were greatly reduced. Many Chinese-Canadian men were forced to lead a bachelor's life, and this made them a threat to White women in the eyes of some European Canadians. This prejudice brought about Saskatchewan's *Act to Prevent the Employment of Female Labour in Certain Capacities* on 5 March 1912. It declared that

> No person shall employ in any capacity any white woman or girl or permit any white woman or girl to reside or lodge in or to work in or, save as a *bona fide* customer in a public apartment thereof only, to frequent any restaurant, laundry or other place of business or amusement owned, kept or managed by any Japanese, Chinaman or other Oriental person. (Backhouse 1999:136)

In May 1912, Quong Wing was convicted and fined for employing two White women in his restaurant. His appeals to the Supreme Court of Saskatchewan and of Canada failed.

In 1924 in Regina, Yee Clun, owner of the Exchange Grill and Rooming House, challenged the law. He had strong personal support in the city from members of both the Chinese and non-Chinese community. Two White women who ran the Chinese mission spoke of his upstanding moral character. But local newspapers were spreading poorly researched stories of Chinese men bringing opium into Saskatchewan and turning White women into 'drug fiends'. Clun won the case in court but found his efforts foiled by the Saskatchewan Legislature, which simply passed another statute authorizing any municipal council to revoke the court ruling. The Act wasn't repealed until 1969.

2) Punished for Success: Japanese-Canadian Fishers

What happens when a group that considers itself superior begins losing a competition with one it deems inferior? In the competition for fish in early twentieth-century British Columbia, the answer was that the rules were changed to favour the 'superior race'.

In 1919, the Federal Department of Marine and Fisheries responded to growing concern that Japanese-Canadian gill net salmon fishers were 'taking over' at the expense of White Canadian fishers. In the ironic words of Major R.J. Burde, MP for Port Alberni, reported in the Victoria *Colonist* on 22 May 1920, 'they have become so arrogant in their feeling of security that many white settlers are reaching the limit of tolerance' (Adachi 1977:105). The government reacted by drastically reducing the number of licences that Japanese-Canadian fishers could obtain (see Table 9.1).

In just three years, White fishers gained 493 licences, an increase of 33.5 per cent; Aboriginal fishers gained 215 (up 20.8 per cent). Japanese

Table 9.1 >> Salmon gill net licences issued 1922–1925				
	TO WHITES	**TO INDIANS**	**TO JAPANESE**	**TOTAL**
1922	1,470	1,032	1,989	4,491
1923	1,642	1,122	1,193	3,957
1925	1,963	1,247	1,015	4,225

Source: Adachi 1977:383.

fishers, by contrast, lost 974 licences, a drop of 48.9 per cent. Japanese-Canadian fishers in the north Skeena area were even prohibited from using power boats between 1925 and 1930. The rules had been changed, and the playing field was no longer level.

3) *The Komagata Maru*

Most of the first South Asians to come to Canada, in the late nineteenth century, were Sikhs, who had been given special status by the British as soldiers and police serving imperial purposes throughout the world. In 1904 they began to arrive in small numbers, many of them settling in Port Moody, east of Vancouver. By 1906, those small numbers had increased considerably, with as many as 5,000 Sikhs entering the country between 1905 and 1908 (Johnston 1989:5; Burnet with Palmer 1988:31). They were young men, most of them single,

though a good number had wives back in India, and they arrived at a time when there was a shortage of labourers in British Columbia willing to work in the sawmills, on the roads, and in the bush cutting wood and clearing land. They were greeted with a measure of respect, as many were British army veterans, and they soon earned a reputation for working hard for low wages. A report in the Vancouver *Daily Province* in October 1906 quoted an employer as saying, 'I would have White labourers of course if I can get them. . . . But I would rather give employment to these old soldiers who have helped fight for the British Empire than entire aliens.'

BC's natural resources-based economy has long fluctuated between being wildly successful, with employers happy to hire anyone willing to work hard, and short periods of unemployment in which newcomers are seen

Sikh passengers aboard the *Komagata Maru*. The treatment of what was called 'the Hindu problem' has left a dark legacy in Canada's history. Despite that fact that Sikhs have been in Canada since 1904, their 'visibility' still prompts the question: *Where are you from?* (Vancouver Public Library, Special Collections, VPL 6231)

as taking jobs from Whites. It wasn't long before the initial acceptance of the hard-working Sikh immigrants was undermined by a growing unease with their rise in numbers. The local press fuelled the simmering discord with stories about the unfamiliar cultural practices of these 'Hindus' (as South Asians collectively were called, regardless of their actual religion). 'Hindus Cover Dead Bodies with Butter' announced a headline in the 20 October 1906 edition of Vancouver *Daily Province* (Johnston 1989:3).

Vancouver police began taking Sikh immigrants directly from the immigration shed to the BC interior to keep them out of the city. In spite of the mounting effects of racism and the deplorable accommodations in which they were placed—some were housed in an abandoned cannery with no running water and little electricity—the Sikhs showed tremendous resilience, as Johnston explains:

> Two thousand had arrived during the latter half of 1906. By the end of December, with the exception of some 300 who had taken steamers for Seattle and San Francisco, all but fifty or sixty had found employment in British Columbia, most of them in saw mills. The authorities would gladly have deported any convicted of vagrancy, but there were few such cases; those who were out of work were looked after by their companions, and, . . . none became a public charge. (Johnston 1989:3)

Facing pressure both from White British Columbians disconcerted by the influx of Sikh immigrants and from British government officials in India, who wanted to curtail emigration, the Canadian government responded with clever discrimination. They passed a law requiring that all Asian immigrants entering Canada possess at least $200—a large sum for people who typically earned about 10 to 20 cents a day. They also prohibited the landing of any immigrant arriving directly from any point outside of India—significant because most Sikhs were making the journey from Punjab province by way of Hong Kong—while pressuring steamship companies not to provide India-to-Canada service or to sell tickets to Canada from Indian ports. These measures brought Sikh immigration to a halt. Unable to bring their wives and families over, denied the right to vote or hold public office, and facing open discrimination from local leaders, Canada's Sikh population became discouraged. Dr Sundar Singh, in an address at the Empire Club in Toronto on 25 January 1912, articulated the frustration many Sikhs were feeling:

> Just at present there are two Sikh women confined on board a boat at Vancouver. . . . One is the wife of a merchant, the other is the wife of a missionary. These men have been settled in this country for five years, and are well spoken of. They went back some time ago to bring out their wives and children. . . They came to Hong Kong, and the steamship company refused to sell them tickets; they waited there since last March and last month the CPR sold them tickets. On the 22nd, they arrived here, and the men were allowed to land, but the ladies are still confined as if they were criminals.
>
> We have the promise of Queen Victoria that all British subjects, no matter what race or creed they belong to, shall be treated alike. . . . The Indian people are loyal British subjects. They are as loyal as anybody else. Why should there be such a difference in the treatment of these loyal people?
>
> We appeal to you, gentlemen, to say that in any country, under any conditions, the treatment of the Sikhs are receiving is not fair. . . . You may well imagine the feeling of these two men, who are suffering as I have described, for no fault at all, except that they are Sikhs. (www.empireclubfoundatiohn.com/details.asp?SpeechID=2519&FT=yes)

But opposition to Sikh immigration continued to grow. On 1 December 1913, the

In Other Words
Ethnicity and Class in Sept-Îles During the 1960s and 1970s

Sept-Îles is located on the north shore of the Gulf of St Lawrence, in Quebec. During the 1960s and early 1970s it was often described in superlatives, thanks to a couple of American-owned mining companies. Iron ore had been discovered in the 1950s in the Quebec–Labrador peninsula. Consequently, the Iron Ore Company of Canada and Wabush Mines set up shop. The Quebec North Shore and Labrador Railway delivered the ore to Sept-Îles from the mines nearly 600 kilometres north of town. Sept-Îles was for a while the richest city in Canada in per capita income and the biggest port in terms of sheer tonnage shipped.

Originally a fishing village with a few hundred people, it grew rapidly. At its peak, it had a population of about 35,000, about 85–90 per cent French-speaking, and about 10 per cent English-speaking. A small minority were Innu. They had a reserve in town and another about 15–20 kilometres east of town.

Many of the English-speaking population came from Atlantic Canada. Many were Newfoundlanders and those who were known as 'Coasters', people who came from further along the coast as it stretched toward Labrador. They sought employment outside their traditionally impoverished areas. There were also many Europeans and Americans. The former brought skilled trades and professional training with them. Many of the French-speaking population were from Gaspé and the south shore of the St Lawrence.

Even as a young boy, I could discern disparities within the community. There were two better neighbourhoods in town, known locally as 'Executive Point' and 'the Wabush Ghetto'. These areas were where the executives of the two companies lived. Although small—only a dozen or so houses in each—they were the most desirable areas of town. They were where power and money resided in the community. The residents were almost entirely English-speaking.

Within the companies, it seemed that there were unwritten rules. Unilingual French speakers could not aspire to a position above foreman

Vancouver *Province* claimed that the 'Hindu problem' had assumed 'a most serious and menacing aspect' (Johnston 1989:22), even though only 39 Sikhs had entered the area that year.

The following spring, on 3 May 1914, the Japanese steamship *Komagata Maru* left Yokohama headed for Canada. Rented by a 55-year-old Sikh, Bhai Gurdit Singh, the ship contained 376 passengers: 340 Sikhs, 24 Muslims, and 12 Hindus. News of the ship's approach was announced in headlines such as 'Boat Loads of Hindus on Way to Vancouver' and 'Hindu Invasion of Canada' in British Columbia dailies. When the ship reached Vancouver on 23 May 1914, the local South Asian community was ready with lawyers, funds, and food to assist the passengers. Local immigration officials, politicians, and vigilante groups were also ready. For about two months, the ship's passengers were forced to endure legal battles, severe shortages of food and water, and a confrontation with the *H.M.C.S. Rainbow*. Finally, on 23 July 1914, the *Komagata Maru* was forced to leave. Only 24 passengers were permitted to enter Canada.

On 26 September, as the ship approached Calcutta, the remaining passengers were told that they would have to be put on a special train taking them to the Punjab area. Amidst confusion and frustration, a riot ensued.

within the companies and they would be very lucky indeed to reach assistant foreman-level speaking only French. The opposite was true with unilingual English speakers: the sky was the limit. The top executives, more often than not, were brought in from the parent companies, i.e. from the United States.

I spent two summers working on the railroad and got to see these disparities firsthand. Most of the foremen were English-speaking, some were bilingual, and some were not. The French-speaking foremen inevitably spoke English as well as their native tongue. Unfortunately, there were many people who simply did not think they had to learn French. They believed it was up to French-speaking Quebecois to learn English. I knew far too many such people.

There were a number of French-speaking schools and two English-speaking school systems: public and Catholic. The Protestant schools, which I attended, were Fleming Elementary and Queen Elizabeth High School ('Queenie' to her students). When I graduated, Fleming and Queenie had a total student population of fewer than 300. When I was a teenager, there was not a lot of dating among the groups. A few people dated students from the English Catholic school, fewer still who dated French-speaking students. However, it did exist. My sister married a French Canadian. Her children are all fluently bilingual. Two are with French Canadian girls.

There was a movement, initiated by my dear old mother, to have a school uniform. The daughters of Executive Point made monthly trips on the company plane to Montreal, 1,000 kilometres away, to buy clothes. Keeping up with the daughters of the executives was a costly prospect, so a school uniform was adopted. There were blue blazers, white shirts and ties and grey flannel pants for boys, and kilts and white blouses for girls.

The uniform had a number of unintended consequences. It enhanced school pride. There was a levelling effect, with less competition over fashionable clothing. But, I cannot help but think that the school uniform, so visible as we walked home and to the shopping centre after school each day, contributed to a sense of divisiveness within the community. It was clear that the ASPs held the best jobs and, in some cases, lived in the best neighbourhoods. Here was the symbolic marker, paraded by their youths.

—Bryan Cummins

Twenty of the passengers were killed; others were imprisoned or became fugitives. Gurdit Singh was a fugitive for more than seven years before being captured and imprisoned for five years. In his early seventies he was elected to the All-India Congress.

Little changed afterwards. After 1918, a few of the men were able to bring over to Canada their long absent wives and children, but most could not afford such an expense. By 1941, there were no more than 1,500 South Asians in Canada. Most were male, many aged between 50 and 65. Only when India was granted its independence from British imperial control in 1947 were South Asians given the vote and full citizenship status.

Ethnicity

Just as everyone speaks with an accent, so everyone belongs to at least one ethnic group. But understanding ethnicity is not just a matter of collecting ethnic traits—language, clothing, religion, foods, and so on—and applying the appropriate ethnic label. This would not help us understand conflict between closely related ethnic groups, nor would it help us understand why 'ethnic pride' surfaces in certain times and situations, and not during others.

There are various ways of theorizing ethnicity. We will confine our discussion here to five approaches. Political sociologists and political scientists often divide theoretical approaches to ethnicity into three categories: **social constructivism**, **instrumentalism**, and **primordialism**. Wsevolod W. Isajiw, in *Understanding Diversity: Ethnicity and Race in the Canadian Context*, discusses primordialism in relation to the **epiphenomenal** approach, which will be helpful to consider here. To this list we will add one more approach, **anti-colonialism**, because it is essential to understanding ethnicity in the context of the case study we are about to present.

One of the most savage and destructive ethnic conflicts of the twentieth century involved rival Hutu and Tutsi tribes in Rwanda (as well as neighbouring Burundi). The history of the country since it gained independence in 1962 has been punctuated by uprisings of the disenfranchised Hutu majority against the ruling Tutsi elite, which have brought about the deaths of hundreds of thousands of civilians in both groups. The violence reached a bloody peak during the spring and summer of 1994, when Hutu military forces massacred between 500,000 and 1,000,000 of the Tutsi minority, sending more than a million destitute Hutu civilians, fearing reprisals from the surviving Tutsi population, fleeing to refugee camps in neighbouring Zaire and Tanzania. It is easy for a sociology student in Canada to dismiss this as 'just another explosion of "tribal violence" in Africa', but this is far from the truth. What happened presents a challenge of interpretation that can be facilitated by looking at it through the lens of various theories of ethnicity.

Primordialism

Primordialism (sometimes referred to as **essentialism**) is the view that every ethnic group is made up of a 'laundry list' of traits that have been carried down from the past to the present with little or no change. A danger of adopting this view uncritically is that it leads to believing that the tribal conflicts in Africa have a deep history that existed long before colonialism, and are reignited only once the 'stabilizing influence' of the colonial power has left. It does not allow for conflicts to arise during colonization, and so it absolves colonial powers of any blame for regional conflicts.

Primordialism presents a static, as opposed to a dynamic, view of culture. In this view, culture does not seem to change from the inside; change is ascribed primarily or entirely to outside forces. 'Modernization', for example, is credited solely to colonial outsiders. Primordialism therefore is a kind of functionalist theory, displaying what may be called the weakest aspects of functionalism: that it poorly explains the development of internally generated conflict and change generally.

Anti-Colonialism

Colonialism is the economic and political exploitation of a weaker country or people by a stronger one. Typically—historically—it involves the domination by a European state of an African, Asian, or American people; however, it is not limited to this. The Chinese have exercised and continue to wield colonial control over the people of Tibet. **Internal colonialism** is colonialism of one people by another within a single country. The history of Canada involves the internal colonialism of Aboriginal peoples by European settlers and their governments.

Anti-colonialism, or **post-colonialism**, is a theoretical framework that analyzes the destructive impact colonialism has on both the colonizer and the colonized. It was first developed by writers such as **Franz Fanon** (1925–1961) and **Albert Memmi** (b. 1920) to examine French colonies in North Africa and their fight for independence from France. Fanon, born in the French colony of Martinique in the West Indies, was radicalized by his experience as a Black intellectual in France and by his work as a doctor and psychiatrist in Algeria during the fight for independence there. His influential works *Black Skin, White Masks* (1952) and *The Wretched of the Earth* (1961) deal with the psychological effects of colonization and have inspired considerable sociological study.

A refugee camp in Goma, Zaire, July 1994, where thousands of Rwandans sought refuge from the fighting in Rwanda. Many became sick and died of cholera. (© Peter Turnley/Corbis)

Albert Memmi was a Jew born in the predominately Muslim country of Tunisia, which gained its independence in 1956 (six years before neighbouring Algeria). His major work, *The Colonizer and the Colonized* (1957), demonstrated how the two groups negatively conditioned each other, and how no party could be 'neutral' in the relationship between the two.

Anti-colonialism theory as it applies to ethnicity involves identifying colonialism as a factor in the development or escalation of conflict between ethnic groups. In Canada, for example, anti-colonialism theory could be used to explain the increasing conflict between the Huron and Iroquois during the 1640s in terms of the former group's connections with the French and the latter's ties with the English. In the African context, it is usefully applied to study situations involving the concept of **indirect rule**, the policy in which a European nation uses the members of a particular ethnic group as its intermediaries in ruling an area of Africa.

(Here we prefer the term *area* to *nation* because the territorial boundaries were often defined or altered by colonizing European powers.)

One problem with anti-colonialism as a theory is that it can attribute every negative change in a colonized area to outside forces. It does not leave much room for agency of one or more of the colonized groups. A corrective for this is **dual colonialism**, the idea that under a colonial regime, the most oppressed groups suffer both at the hands of the colonizing outsider group and at the hands of a local group that is given privilege and power by the outsider group. Political scientist Catharine Newbury applies this idea well in her discussion of Rwanda in *Cohesion of Oppression* (1988), which we will discuss in the following section.

Primordialism, Anti-Colonialism, and Rwanda

As you read the following description of ethnic conflict in Rwanda, consider how well the theories of primordialism and anti-colonialism apply to the situation there.

In Rwanda three main ethnic groups are currently recognized: Hutu, Tutsi and Twa. Numerically, the Hutu are by far the dominant group. The 1956 census, lists 83 per cent of the population as Hutu, with 16 per cent Tutsi and 1 per cent Twa (Newbury 1988:3). Yet from at least the eighteenth century onwards, the Tutsi have been the group with the most power. If we consider a list of typical 'ethnic traits'—including physical attributes, language, religion, kinship structure, occupation, and economic circumstances—we gain some interesting findings about Rwanda prior to colonization.

PHYSICAL APPEARANCE

Beginning with the biggest differences, Tutsi and Hutu tended to differ in their physical appearance, with the former being taller and thinner than the latter, with longer and thinner faces. One study (Chrétien 1967) found that the Tutsi averaged 1.75 metres in height, the Hutu 1.66 metres. We must note that before the colonial period, it was not uncommon for people to pass from one group to the other for largely economic reasons. The physical differences combined with the fact that the Tutsi appear to have come later to Rwanda than the Hutu led colonial administrators and social scientists to draw otherwise unfounded conclusions about the Tutsi being a 'superior, conquering race'. This helped justify European colonial support of the Tutsi elite at the cost of the Hutu and of poorer Tutsi.

OCCUPATION

Concerning occupation, the Tutsi were, in the pre-colonial period, primarily *pastoralists*—that is, they herded cattle. The Hutu, on the other hand, were primarily agriculturalists, growing crops. The division was not absolute: some Hutu, particularly those heading up the richer lineages, herded cattle, and some Tutsi were agriculturalists. But during the colonial period, the more powerful Tutsi took advantage of their enhanced privileges to gain a greater share of the cattle.

LANGUAGE

The people of Rwanda—Hutu, Tutsi, and Twa—all speak the same language, with regional dialect variants. The language, belonging to the local Bantu group of languages, was likely spoken in Rwanda before the Tutsi moved into the area (probably from Ethiopia), a fact that diminishes somewhat the sense that the Tutsi were a powerful conquering people.

RELIGION

In terms of religion, the three ethnic groups did not differ historically, and in the colonial period most were converted to Christianity through Catholic missionaries. However, religion would, through the education system, come to have a powerful effect on the development of a strong sense of ethnicity in Rwanda by entrenching the ethnic-based class system that placed the Tutsi at the top and the Hutu at the bottom. Established in 1932 and recognized as the best school in Rwanda, the Groupe Scolaire played a part in promoting class and ethnic divisions, as Newbury explains. One of the goals of this school was to create a 'new social class',

> and in accordance with this goal . . . very few Hutu were admitted; indeed, after World War II the school even had a minimum height requirement for admission. Graduates of the Groupe Scolaire considered themselves superior to other educated Rwandans . . . , and their diplomas were accorded greater value by the Belgian [colonial] administration. Thus, in theory because of their professional qualifications but in reality because they were overwhelmingly drawn from among the families of Tutsi chiefs, the graduates of the Groupe Scolaire enjoyed the benefits of both the 'traditional' economic structures, and of the higher status jobs and

better pay available in the 'modern' sector. (Newbury 1988:116)

In recent years, Islam has spread among both the Tutsi and the Hutu population. By making people Muslims first, Tutsi or Hutu second, it has had the effect of taking people 'outside ethnicity', diminishing the importance of ethnic differences.

IDENTITY

Identity is difficult to characterize historically. It seems that prior to the colonial period, sense of identity was derived mainly from lineage, clan, chiefdom, or kingdom, and from a general sense of being Rwandan. Of the kin groups, the two that were of the greatest significance (and remain important today) are lineage and clan. Lineage heads were important figures, and a person's primary identity came from lineage. Clan was less important, but, interestingly, a single clan could include members of all three Rwandan ethnic groups.

Under colonialism lineage heads lost power, being replaced by centrally appointed chiefs who were overwhelmingly Tutsi. The distinction between Tutsi and Hutu, which was of less significance in the time before the colonial period, became much more of a factor, its importance reinforced by the fact that Rwandan citizens now had to carry identification cards with 'Hutu', 'Tutsi', or 'Twa' written on them.

The growing central authority of the king during the colonial period also helped to enhance the status of the Rwandan Tutsi. During the reign of Kigeri Rwabugiri (c.1860–1895), the king's central authority grew to encompass chiefdoms and kingdoms, some of them Hutu, that until then had been relatively independent. The colonial administration and the Tutsi elite collaborated to take away the more diverse traditional government forms through which the Hutu in particular could play one authority against another into a more simplified and powerful system. A system of taxes payable either in money or with labour was developed and exploited, with colonial support, by unscrupulous Tutsi chiefs who took advantage of free labour from Hutu civilians.

Altogether we see a situation that is not well explained by primordialism, but which fits well with dual colonialism theory. How do other theories fit into this situation?

Ethnicity as Epiphenomenal

The word **epiphenomenal** is used to describe a secondary effect or phenomenon that arises from but does not causally influence a separate phenomenon. Marx was the first to apply it in a sociological context. He believed that economic structure was the main causal factor in society, and everything else was epiphenomenal or insignificant.

When applied to ethnicity, the epiphenomenal theory suggests that any ethnic conflict is really just a by-product of the struggle between economic classes. Thus, the strife in Rwanda stems from a situation in which the country's rich and powerful (the Tutsi elite) were exploiting its poor (the Hutu and the poorer Tutsi). Ethnicity was just a smokescreen, a kind of false consciousness that made it impossible for poorer Hutu and Tutsi with shared class interests to overcome oppression by the Tutsi elite. This lasted through the 1950s, when Hutu of all classes shared what Newbury termed a 'cohesion of oppression', until 1962, when the country became independent and witnessed a social revolution that replaced the Tutsi elite with a Hutu one. The Hutu elite used the pretense of democracy to gain broader Hutu support. There is a measure of truth in the epiphenomenal explanation, yet it fails to fully account for why the poor would identify with the rich.

Instrumentalism

Traditionally presented in direct opposition to primordialism and compatible with the epiphenomenal approach is **instrumentalism**. Instrumentalism focuses on emerging ethnicity rather than on long-established ethnic characteristics. It acknowledges that elites can and do mobilize others who identify with them ethnically, rather than attributing modernization to outside forces. Ethnic identification and action come from a competition for scarce resources for and by the elite. In Newbury's words, ethnic groups are created or transformed when

> groups gain self-awareness (become 'self-conscious communities') largely as the result of the activities of leaders who mobilize ethnic followings in order to compete more effectively. Improved communications and the spread of writing are important in this process; so is 'ethnic learning', where groups develop ethnic awareness as a result of seeing others using ethnic solidarities to compete. The state is important, instrumentalists suggest, as an arena in which competition between these groups occurs (the state controls many of the scarce resources over which elites are competing), and also because government policies can significantly affect the strategies chosen by ethnic leaders. (Newbury 1988:15)

Elite members who mobilize ethnicity in order to gain personal wealth and power are sometimes known as **ethnic entrepreneurs**. Textbook examples of ethnic entrepreneurship include Adolph Hitler's construction and manipulation of the German 'Aryan race' and Slobodan Milosovic's use of Serb ethnic symbols to achieve and maintain dictatorial power in the former Yugoslavia. An instrumentalist approach better explains how a frustrated Hutu leadership could invoke the injustice of Tutsi elite oppression to draw poorer Hutu into their political parties and their acts of revolution.

Social Constructivism

Social constructivism is the view that ethnicity is constructed by individuals for varying social purposes. Instrumentalism can be considered a partly formed social constructivism in that it shows how ethnicity is constructed by the elite; however, it suffers as a theory of ethnicity and ethnic action by overstating the influence and impact of the elite. It generally fails to attribute the non-elite members any agency, any power to choose and act without being manipulated. A social constructivist theory of ethnicity would look to the motivations of the broader group.

The social constructivist approach makes sense in the case of Rwanda, where it helps to explain why the general rural population of Hutu became so thoroughly engaged in driving off and killing local Tutsi (often neighbours). Rwanda was, for most of the twentieth century, a very crowded land, with many people, particularly Hutu, being regularly malnourished because their working farms were insufficient for their needs. Unlike in the nineteenth century, when there was considerably more space and people could move to new land in difficult situations, during the twentieth century people suffered through various famines and cattle diseases while the country's rise in population shrunk farm size. Drive your neighbours out and you and your family have an improved chance of survival.

Summary

So what can our five approaches to studying ethnicity tell us about the Hutu and Tutsi in Rwanda? We can say that by the middle of the nineteenth century, some people in the area were taller and were more likely to herd cattle, but being a member of an ethnic group was not a major part of the day-to-day lives of most Rwandans—not like lineage, region, and sometimes individual chiefdom or kingdom. First with the growth in power and widespread influence of the king (who was a Tutsi) and his court working toward the development of a modern state, and then more tellingly from the effects of colonialism (first German, then

Belgian), a dual colonialism developed in which Europeans and elite Tutsi collaborated to put social, economic, and political substance to an increasingly rigid 'ethnic' divide between Hutu and Tutsi. And when, in the 1950s, European colonialism began to fade in Rwanda, the common experience of oppression experienced by Hutu of all classes, particularly the peasant class, led to a social revolution in which the majority Hutu overthrew their oppressors, only to set up an ethnic dictatorship of their own. Ethnic violence was a not surprising effect, and an easily fanned racial hatred combined with a powerful need for land led in 1994 to the massacre of the Tutsi.

Ethnicity in Canada: Classic Studies

Ethnic Class: English and French in Quebec

When **Everett C. Hughes** (1897–1983) entered the sociology department at McGill in 1927, the focus of his research became what he termed the 'ethnic division of labour' between the English, who held positions of power, and the French, who seemed to occupy the lowest rung of the employment ladder. This was a wrong that he wished to right.

In *French Canada in Transition*, Hughes studied the small industrial city of Drummondville in the mid- to late-1930s. He noted that there were two types of industries there. First, there were small, local, French-Canadian–run industries, which 'do not make the town grow but proliferate and grow with it' (Hughes 1963:47). Second, and more important, there were '*nos grandes industries*'. The top nine of these eleven 'big industries' had headquarters in Montreal, England, and the United States. Their managers were Americans, English Canadians, and Britons. In 1937, the largest of these industries, a textile company, employed 389 'English and Others' and 2,337 French workers. The former

occupied 24 of the 25 positions above the foreman level and 57 of the 82 foreman's jobs. The vast majority of the French employees (1,882) were on the 'factory floor', involved directly in textile production (Hughes 1963:55).

In a 1954 study of intergenerational (father to son) occupational mobility, Yves de Jocas and Guy Rocher (1957) found that Anglophones in Quebec cities scored much higher than Francophones (11.8 per cent versus 3.2 per cent) in the occupational category they called 'professional, proprietor, manager', and that the discrepancy among their sons was even greater (17.3 per cent versus 6.8 per cent; in Langlois 1999:73). This suggested that the ethnic division of labour was increasing. John Porter, in *The Vertical Mosaic*, observed a similar growing separation (see Table 9.2). French-Canadian sociologists Jacques Dofny and Marcel Rioux (1962) described this separation as the phenomenon of **ethnic class**, in which people of a particular ethnicity belong predominantly to one class.

During the 1960s the balance shifted somewhat with the Quiet Revolution, which represented an attempt by a growing educated, skilled, and urban middle class to overthrow three social bodies that combined to restrict the people: the English-dominated large businesses; the Union Nationale, a provincial political party that exerted great conservative control through the rurally supported premier Maurice Duplessis (1936–9 and 1944–59); and the Catholic Church (which had a firm grip on education, the press, and the unions). In large measure, the decrease in inequality between French and English was brought about by provincial policies and practices, designed in part by sociologists, enacted as part of a concerted effort to make French-Canadians 'maîtres chez nous' ('masters in our own house').

John Porter and the Vertical Mosaic

Generally recognized as the best-known book of Canadian sociology is the classic *The Vertical*

>>> **Canadian Sociology in Action**
A Minoritizing Episode

On 21 August 1914, shortly after the start of World War I, a group of Canadians was minoritized through the War Measures Act, which would be used as a weapon of discrimination against Japanese Canadians nearly 30 years later and then, almost another 30 years after that, against French Canadians. As with South Asians ethnic groups—Sikhs, Hindus, and Muslims—that were lumped together as 'Hindoos' and, decades later, as 'Pakis', the chosen identity of this minoritized group was ignored for another, 'alien' one. Like Aboriginal people in both World Wars, they would sometimes have to pass as Canadian to be able to join up to fight, lying about their identity and changing their names. Like the Chinese, South Asians, Native people, and women of their time, many would be denied the federal vote. During the next war they were put into concentration camps, like the Japanese. Surprisingly, the members of this group were White.

Britain and her allies, including Canada, were fighting Germany and the decrepit Austro-Hungarian empire. The latter was home to a people who thought of themselves as Ukrainians by nationality, even though their official citizenship was 'Austrian'. The War Measures Act led to the internment of 8,579 people labelled 'enemy aliens' in 24 camps spread across Canada. More than 5,000 of them were Ukrainians, though they were called Ruthenians, Galicians, and Bukovynans. Another 80,000—again, most of them Ukrainians—had to register as 'enemy aliens'. More than 10,000 Ukrainians enlisted in the Canadian army, some by faking their names and identity to conceal their true ethnicity. Among them was Filip Konoval, who was one of only 83 Canadians to be awarded the prestigious Victoria Cross. Still, the War Elections Act denied most Ukrainians the right to vote.

Those who spent time in internment camps worked hard, developing Banff National Park, logging, working in mines and in steel mills. One hundred and seven internees died. Tuberculosis killed twenty-six, pneumonia, twenty-two. Six were shot to death trying to escape camp, three committed suicide. An undetermined number died due to unsafe working conditions. One hundred and six were sent to mental institutions, all but three eventually deported. There was a riot in Kapuskasing, Ontario. In Sydney, Nova Scotia, there was a hunger strike. Running the camps cost Canadian taxpayers $3.2 million.

The effects of the discrimination did not end with the war. Some of the land, valuables, and money possessed by Ukrainian Canadians and confiscated by the Canadian government 'disappeared'. Internment and suspicion killed the spirit of many who had been keen to contribute to the growth of Canada, who had nurtured high hopes for their new home.

Mosaic: An Analysis of Social Class and Power in Canada (1965) by **John Porter** (1921–1979). Porter's title derives from the often-stated notion that Canadian society is a **cultural mosaic** rather than a **melting pot**. The term 'cultural mosaic' applies to societies in which individual ethnic, cultural, and religious groups are able to maintain separate identities; the word 'mosaic' refers to artwork made up of many tiles that lend different colours to the picture. The opposite model is the 'melting pot', where immigrating ethnic, cultural, and religious groups are encouraged to assimilate into their new society; it is the term typically used to describe American society.

Table 9.2 >>	French and British in the professional and financial occupation		
YEAR	**FRENCH**	**BRITISH**	**DIFFERENCE**
1931	6.2%	7.1%	0.9%
1951	6.0%	7.2%	1.2%
1961	7.8%	9.3%	1.5%

Source: Porter 1965:94.

The **vertical mosaic**, as coined by Porter, refers to a situation in which there is a hierarchy, or ranking, of higher and lower ethnic, cultural, and religious groups. To keep with the metaphor of the mosaic, Porter found that the different tiles were stacked, not placed evenly, so that the White-Anglo-Saxon-Protestant tiles are on top.

Sociologists of Colour

As we have seen earlier, standpoint theory suggests that sociological researchers bring a different perspective to their work based on their 'social location'—their gender, age, ethnicity, and sexual orientation. This does not mean that only women sociologists can study women, only White male sociologists can study White men. What it means is that the pioneers in in the sociological study of specific groups—women, for instance, or Black people—are often those who belong to the group themselves, and that they have unique and valuable insights that everyone can learn from.

W.E.B. DuBois: First Black Sociologist
W.E.B. DuBois (1868–1963) was the first African-American sociologist. He researched and wrote about the major problems and concerns of Africans, both those living in the United States and those living in the rest of the world. In this sense he can be called a pan-Africanist, one who sees the connection between the oppression and success of Africans and that of their descendants around the world. His sociology had a definite applied perspective to it. He was one of the founders of the NAACP (National Association for the Advancement of Colored People), and he used his position as editor-in-chief of their magazine, *Crisis*, to push for such varied causes as opening up Black officer training schools and initiating legal action against White people who lynched African Americans. Throughout his long life he was a prolific writer; his master works include his doctoral thesis, The Suppression of the African Slave Trade in America (1896); his comprehensive study for the University of Pennsylvania of Philadelphia's black slums, *The Philadelphia Negro* (1896); *The Souls of Black Folks* (1903); *Black Reconstruction* (1935); and *Dusk of Dawn* (1940). The following captures the oratorical power and sense of fairness of his writing:

[I]t is the duty of black men to judge the South discriminatingly. The present gen-

>>> Quick Hits
Who Has the Right to Vote?

- 1867   Canadian federal and provincial vote given only to White men with property
- 1875   Chinese denied the provincial vote in British Columbia
- 1885   'Indians' west of Ontario are denied the vote; eastern 'Indian' males are given the vote only if they own land separate from the reserve and have made at least $150 of improvements
  Chinese denied the federal vote
- 1895   Japanese denied the provincial vote in BC
- 1898   'Indian' males east of Manitoba denied the federal vote regardless of property
  White males without property given the vote federally and provincially
- 1907   South Asians denied the federal vote
- 1908   Chinese denied the provincial vote in Saskatchewan
- 1917   People born in 'enemy countries' (i.e. Ukrainians) are denied the vote
  Japanese-Canadian war veterans are promised the federal vote
- 1931   Japanese-Canadian war veterans actually receive the federal vote
- 1947   Chinese and South Asians get the federal vote and the provincial vote in British Columbia
- 1948   Japanese-Canadians get the federal vote
- 1949   'Indians' get the provincial vote in British Columbia and Newfoundland
  Japanese-Canadians get the provincial vote in British Columbia
- 1951   Chinese get the provincial vote in Saskatchewan
- 1952   'Indians' get the provincial vote in Manitoba
- 1954   'Indians' get the provincial vote in Ontario
- 1960   'Indians' get the provincial vote in Yukon and Saskatchewan
- 1963   'Indians' get the provincial vote in New Brunswick and Nova Scotia
- 1965   'Indians' get the provincial vote in Alberta
- 1969   'Indians' get the provincial vote in Quebec

eration of Southerners are not responsible for the past, and they should not be blindly hated or blamed for it. . . . The South is not 'solid'; it is a land in the ferment of social change, wherein forces of all kinds are fighting for supremacy; and to praise the ill the South is today perpetrating is just as wrong as to condemn the good. Discriminating and broad-minded criticism is what the South needs,—needs it for the sake of her own white sons and daughters, and for the insurance of robust, healthy mental and moral development.

Today even the attitude of the Southern whites toward the blacks is not, as so many assume, in all cases the same; the ignorant Southerner hates the Negro, the working-men fear his competition, the money-makers wish to use him as a laborer, some of the educated see a menace in his upward development, while others . . . wish to help him to rise. National opinion has enabled this last class to maintain the Negro common schools, and to protect the Negro partially in property, life, and limb. Through the pressure of the money-makers, the Negro is in danger of being reduced to semi-slavery . . . ; the working-men, and those of the educated who fear the Negro, have united to disfranchise him . . . while the passions of the ignorant are easily aroused to lynch and abuse any black man. To praise this intricate whirl of thought and prejudice is nonsense; to inveigh indiscriminately against 'the South' is unjust. . . . (DuBois 1903)

W.E.B. DuBois, after receiving an honorary degree from the University of Ghana, Accra, on the afternoon of his ninety-fifth birthday, 23 February 1963. (Special Collections Department, W.E.B. Du Bois Library, University of Massachusetts Amherst)

Daniel G. Hill:
First Black Canadian Sociologist

The face of sociology in Canada has been almost exclusively a White face. Finding a South Asian, Black, East Asian, or Aboriginal sociologist who has had an impact is not easy. Daniel G. Hill (1923–2003) is an exception. Although he was not born in Canada, he is considered the first Black Canadian sociologist. He studied sociology at the University of Toronto, receiving his MA in 1951 and his PhD in 1960. His primary writings include his doctoral dissertation, Negroes in Toronto: A Sociological Study of a Minority Group (1960), and *The Freedom Seekers: Blacks in Early Canada* (1981). But it is mainly in applied work that Hill's sociology is expressed. He was a researcher for the Social Planning Council of Metropolitan Toronto (1955–8), executive secretary of the North York Social Planning Council (1958–60), and assistant director of the Alcoholism and Drug Addiction Research Foundation (1960). In 1962, Hill became the first full-time director of the Ontario Human Rights Commission, and ten years later, he became Ontario Human Rights Commissioner. He formed his own human rights consulting firm in 1973, working at various times for the Metropolitan Police Service, the Canadian Labour Congress, and the government of British Columbia. From 1984 to 1989, he served as Ontario Ombudsman,

fielding complaints from people concerning their treatment by provincial government agencies. In 1999 he was made a Member of the Order of Canada.

Daniel G. Hill, O.C., O.Ont., Ph.D., LL.D., receives the Order of Canada from Governor General Adrienne Clarkson, 5 February 2000 (Photo by Sgt Joanne Stoeckl)

What do you think?

1. Why is it more likely that a Black Canadian sociologist would get involved in human rights work than a White Canadian sociologist would?

2. How could you determine whether Hill served as a token (i.e. as a Black person hired merely so that the committees he was involved with could point to him as proof of their commitment to addressing the concerns of the Black community) or as a meaningfully employed member of the social committees he was on?

Questions for Critical Review and Discussion

1. Discuss the extent to which race, ethnicity, and gender are social constructs.

2. Explain what is meant by a White person being 'invisible' in Canada.

3. How is institutional, or systemic, racism different from other forms of discrimination?

4. What groups have been discriminated against by voting laws in Canada?

5. How did the Quiet Revolution change the social position of Francophones in Quebec?

6. How were Ukrainians minoritized during World War I? What effect do you think that had on their participation in Canadian society for the period that immediately followed?

Suggested Readings

Anderson, Kay J. (1991). *Vancouver's Chinatown: Racial Discourse in Canada, 1875–1980*. Montreal: McGill-Queens UP.

Bannerji, Himani, ed. (1993). *Returning the Gaze: Essays on Racism, Feminism and Politics*. Toronto: Sister Vision Press.

Calliste, Anges & George J. Sefa Dei, eds. (2000). *Anti-Racist Feminism: Critical Race and Gender Studies*. Halifax: Fernwood.

Goldberg, David Theo (1993). *Racist Culture: Philosophy and the Politics of Meaning*. Cambridge: Blackwell.

hooks, bell (1992). *Black Looks: Race and Representation*. Toronto: Between the Lines.

Paul, Daniel N. (2000). *We Were Not the Savages: A Mi'kmaq Perspective on the Collision between European and Native American Civilizations*. Halifax: Fernwood.

Suggested Websites

Canadian Race Relations Foundation.
http://www.crr.ca

The Metropolis Project.
http://www.canada.metropolis.net

Canadian Alliance in Solidarity with the Native Peoples.
http://www.users.cyberglobe.net/casnp

Department of Heritage and Multiculturalism.
http://www.pch.gc.ca/multi/html/English.html

Gender

Contents

Key Terms

age-standardized
complicit masculinity
dragon lady
feminist essentialism
feminist liberalism
feminist postmodernists
feminist socialists
feminization of poverty
geisha
gender
gender roles
hegemonic masculinity
ideology of fag
Indian Princess
lotus blossom baby
marginalized masculinity
pay equity
queer theory
sex
squaw
subordinate masculinity
tabula rasa

Boxes and Tables

Canadian Sociology in Action David Reimer: Assigning Gender
Quick Hits Selected Articles by Annie Marion MacLean
Sociology in Action Gender and the Bible
Quick Hits The Ninauposkitzipxpe, or 'Manly-Hearted Women', of the Peigan
In Other Words Gender Roles and Being Lesbian
Canadian Sociology in Action The Famous Five and the 'Persons' Case
Quick Hits Granting the Provincial and Federal Vote to Women
Sociology in Action Indian Princesses and Cowgirls: Stereotypes from the Frontier

Learning Objectives

After reading this chapter, you should be able to

- outline the feminist work done by early female sociologists.
- compare and contrast the four different categories of feminism outlined in this chapter.
- contrast the roles of biological and sociological influences on the gender of David Reimer.
- discuss what 'gendering' and the 'feminization' of a job means.
- compare and contrast the four masculinities outlined in the section on male daycare workers.
- discuss the stereotyping involved in the intersection of female gender and minoritized ethnicity/race.

For Starters
What it Means to Be a Man

How flexible are we concerning gender roles?

Most of us like to think we're very flexible, both in the way we act and in the way we perceive others, but I have to be honest: although I feel 'secure in my masculinity', as they say, there are a number of things I—a Toronto-bred White man in my fifties—will not do because they're inconsistent with my own sense of being male, and with the sense of maleness I wish to project for others. For instance, I will not

- carry or use an umbrella (in part from having lived in Newfoundland, where a 'real man' is not afraid of getting wet).
- use a hair dryer (despite having rather long hair—it seems effeminate to me to blow your hair around like you're in a shampoo commercial).
- use one of those convenient book and file carriers on wheels, the ones that remind me of a flight attendant's suitcase (a man should carry a briefcase).
- cry at the microphone during a press release (all right, I don't do a lot of press releases, but when I was growing up, athletes didn't cry when they announced their retirement).
- wear clothes that are yellow, orange, or pink (high school classmates of mine wearing those colours were given a hard time).

A portrait of the author as he sees himself.   A portrait of the author as he is.

- use a snow blower instead of a shovel (real men aren't afraid of getting wet *or* heaving snow).
- spend longer than five minutes getting dressed or fifteen minutes in any one clothing store (maybe this reflects my male body image hangup).
- clip favourite recipes from a magazine (man's food is that which may be fried, barbecued, or boiled in a bag).
- shake hands in a 'wimpy way' (a man is still judged by how strong his handshake is; I don't make a contest of it—as some do—but I try to meet a minimum standard).
- wear a cologne or 'body spray' (women should smell good; men should just try not to smell bad).
- dye my hair (or my beard).
- use the word 'lovely' without being sarcastic.
- have a manicure.

And of course, real men don't eat quiche or ask directions, so I don't do those things either. And when I first became a stepfather and my very shy eight-year-old stepson wanted to hold my hand in public, I felt *extremely* uncomfortable (but I still did it). It's important to point out that this list reflects my own assumptions, as a White middle-aged man, of what my gender role is.

I'd like male readers to think about this list. Do you share my inflexibility on these issues? What other things will you not do out of male pride. Women readers can set us straight: would you be bothered if you knew the male student next to you has weekly manicures? Now comes the critical question: why do we feel the way we do, and how flexible are we really when it comes to gender? Here are two other scenarios to consider:

- *How would you feel if your son took an interest in figure skating rather than hockey?* One of my nephews, when he first learned to skate, became really interested in figure skating and adopted Elvis Stojko as a hero. He took lessons for two years before he eventually quit, in large part, I suspect, because his father (my brother-in-law) didn't encourage him in this interest. To give him credit, he never made fun of the sport, but I don't think he gave his budding figure skater the kind of support he might have given a budding hockey player.
- *What is your reaction to a man who wants to become a nurse?* Nursing programs are dominated by women; men are few and far between. Male students get asked questions like 'Why don't you want to be a doctor?', a question less often asked of female nursing students.

Compare notes on the topics above with your classmates, and you're likely to find a fair bit of disagreement. That's because as inflexible as we might be when it comes to how we see gender, we all—men and women, homosexuals and heterosexuals, Blacks and Whites and Jews and Asians, and so on and so on—see gender differently.

Introduction to Gender

Gender is a highly contested area within sociology today. Sociologists theorizing about gender and gender roles differ sharply, particularly on the degree to which gender is determined by either culture or biology. Even the absolute duality (male–female) of gender is contested. Not surprisingly, the greatest part of the critical work on gender has been carried out by feminist scholars, reflecting the (now) obvious fact before the 'Women's Movement' of the 1960s and 1970s, male sociologists had done an inadequate job on the subject.

Gender is different from **sex**. British sociologist Ann Oakley formally stated the distinction between sex and gender when she argued that the former refers 'to the biological division into male and female' while the latter refers to 'the parallel and socially unequal division into femininity and masculinity' (Oakley 1972 in Marshall 1998:250). *Gender*, in other words, is a sociological term that refers to the roles and characteristics society assigns to women and men, and has built within in it the inequality of women and men; *sex* refers merely to anatomical or biological characteristics of women and men.

Another key term to establish here is gender role. A gender role is a set of expectations concerning behaviour and attitudes that relates to being male or female. It may be useful here to think of a gender role as being similar to a movie role: it is a part we're assigned at birth, and how we play it reflects what we understand about what it means to act as either a girl/woman or a boy/man. Gender roles differ across cultures, both in content—in the specific expectations society holds for each sex—and in the severity or permissiveness with which society treats those whose behaviour contravenes the expectations for their gender.

The 'Founding Mother of Sociology' and the Sociology of Gender

British writer **Harriet Martineau** (1802–1876) can be called the founding mother of sociology. She wrote over 6,000 articles, many of them on the social condition of women in her time. In 1834 she began a two-year study of the United States, published as *Society in America* (1837) and *Retrospect of Western Travel* (1838). Her feminist thinking can be seen in her comparison of women to slaves in a chapter revealingly called 'The Political Non-Existence of Women'. That

"Sex brought us together, but gender drove us apart."

feminism, and her opposition to slavery, made her unpopular in the United States. After travelling to the Middle East, she published *Eastern Life Past and Present* (1848), in which she struggled between her intended sociological spirit of impartiality, and her moral condemnation of polygyny (one husband with more than one wife).

Three Early Women Sociologists and the Writing of Gender in Canada

Annie Marion MacLean

Annie Marion MacLean (*c*. 1870–1934) was the first Canadian to obtain a PhD in sociology. Born in Prince Edward Island, she received her first two degrees form Acadia University before earning the PhD at the University of Chicago. She went on to teach at the University of Chicago, although, despite her excellent qualifications, in a very subordinate position.

MacLean pioneered the sociological study of women, especially in her study of *Wage-Earning Women*, which was based on a survey of some

Canadian Sociology in Action
David Reimer: Assigning Gender

In May 2004, 38-year-old David Reimer of Winnipeg committed suicide. His decision to take his life was likely influenced by his separation from his wife, the loss of his job, and the suicide death of his twin brother two years earlier. But there is a deeper, older cause that must be cited, too. He was the victim of a medical accident compounded by an unsuccessful social experiment.

During his first year of life, he and his brother were both circumcised electronically using an experimental method. During David's circumcision, too much electricity was applied, and his penis was badly burned; there was no chance it could be even surgically repaired.

Desperate for a solution, David's parents consulted numerous doctors and specialists. At the time, a psychological school of thought known as behaviourism, which emphasized the power of socialization (nurture) over biology (nature), was popular. It had a certain popularity among feminist psychologists (both male and female), as it supported the notion that gender and gender roles were taught, not 'natural'. In its extreme version, behaviourism advanced the notion that each one of us is a **tabula rasa**, or blank slate, on which our social environment writes our lives. A proponent of this school, the psychologist Dr John Money of Johns Hopkins University in Baltimore, was one of the specialists contacted by David's parents. He persuaded them to have David castrated and given female hormones, and to rename their child 'Brenda', to be raised as a girl.

Money's articles made the 'John/Joan' case study famous. The doctor claimed that that Reimer was adapting successfully to his new gender, socially taught and hormonally enhanced. But this view of the situation was, as it turns out, based more on wishes than facts. In a journalistic biography, *As Nature Made Him*, writer John Colapinto showed that David's childhood was highly conflicted. He felt he was male, not female, and preferred to play with boys than with girls. He wasn't told he had been born male until he was 13, when his parents, under pressure from Dr Money, approached him about allowing surgeons to create a vagina. David rebelled, attempting suicide a number of times. He abandoned his female identity and sought out surgery, which he eventually received, to have his male sex restored. He later married and had stepchildren, but the effects of both the accident and the social experiment never left him.

David Reimer's tragic case illustrates that while gender is a social construct, it also involves biology. It also shows, as recent research confirms (Kruijver et al. 2000), that gender has a neurological component in addition to the biological features of genitals and hormones: the brain helps to shape our gender. It also clearly demonstrates the dangers of allowing social theory to impose itself into unthinking social practice.

What do you think?

1. In what way(s) can we say that David Reimer's brain was male?
2. How can we argue that he was not a gender tabula rasa?

13,500 women. She conducted her research while working in department stores, in 'sweat shop' factories, in Oregon, picking hops, and she sent out a team of women to discover more about the unfair and unsafe conditions in which women were forced to work. The titles of her articles tell you a lot about her research. She was never hired by a Canadian university.

Aileen Ross

The first woman hired as a sociologist at a university in Canada was **Aileen Ross** (1902–1995), a native of Montreal who taught sociology at the University of Toronto for three years, from 1942 to 1945, before joining the faculty at McGill University. She took her first degree at the London School of Economics, and got her MA (1941) and PhD (1950) from the University of Chicago. A founding member of the Canadian Human Rights Foundation, she devoted her books to two main concerns: women and India. Her last book was *The Lost and the Lonely: Homeless Women in Montreal* (1982). Upon retirement, she had helped to organize a shelter for homeless women in her hometown, and wrote the book to enable them to tell their stories. Her second book, *The Hindu Family in an Urban Setting* (1962), was the product of several years' research in India. She also wrote a series of articles about Indian business-women (1976, 1977, and 1979).

Helen Abell

Helen Abell (b. 1917) was born in Medicine Hat, Alberta, and grew up in Toronto. She has been called the founder of rural sociology in Canada. After receiving a degree in Human Nutrition at the University of Toronto (1941), she worked as a nutritionist for the Ontario Department of Agriculture, then as an officer in the Canadian Women's Army Corps during World War II. She received her PhD in rural sociology (the first Canadian to do so) in 1951. She then established a rural sociology research unit in the Federal Department of Agriculture. Her role as a sociologist is summarized by Jenny Kendrick as follows:

> Helen Abell's research played an important role in identifying systematically the roles women played on the farm. This was an invaluable contribution to the policy arena, virtually forcing society and policymakers to lay aside their stereotypes of the marginal contributions of farm women to agriculture.' (Eichler 2001:382)

What do you think?

Why do you think that these early women sociologists wrote primarily about women? Does that say something about the gender role of a female sociologist?

>>> Quick Hits
Selected Articles by Annie Marion MacLean

- 1897–8   'Factory Legislation for Women in the United States'. *American Journal of Sociology*, 3 183–205.
- 1898   'Two Weeks in a Department Store'. *American Journal of Sociology*, 4, 721–41.
- 1899–1900   'Faculty Legislation for Women in Canada'. *American Journal of Sociology*, 5, 172–81.
- 1903–4   'The Sweat Shop Summer'. *American Journal of Sociology*, 9, 289–309.
- 1908-09   'Life in the Pennsylvania Coal Fields'. *American Journal of Sociology*, 14, 329–51.
- 1909–10   'With the Oregon Hop Pickers'. *American Journal of Sociology*, 15, 83–95.
- 1923   'Four Months in a Model Factory'. *Century* 106 (July), 436–44.

Feminism and Gender Theory: Four Categories

In 'Feminist Social Theories: Theme and Variations' (2003, orig. 1995), Beatrice Kachuck usefully divides feminist theories into four broad categories, each having variations: *feminist liberalism*, *feminist essentialism*, *feminist socialism*, and *feminist postmodernism*. We'll examine each of these in turn.

Feminist Liberalism

Feminist liberalism, Kachuck explains, 'identifies women as a class entitled to rights as women' (Kachuck 2003:81). In terms of gender roles, this approach values the contributions of women in the public realm of the workplace and examines whether women receive fair pay for the work they do. In this sense, it is associated with the fight for **pay equity**, the guarantee that women in traditionally female-dominated industries (such as nursing, childcare, and library science) receive compensation similar to the salaries of those working in comparable (in terms of educational qualifications required, hours worked, and social value) professions that are typically dominated by men. Think of it this way: if we value our children so much, why do we pay so little to those in primary and early childhood education, who play such an important role in the social and educational development of our children? Liberal feminism is credited with securing benefits for women on maternity leave, including the rights to claim employment insurance and to return to the same or an equivalent job in the same company after a fixed period of time (up to a year in Canada).

Criticism of liberal feminism and its view of gender roles centres around the idea that it universalizes the position of White, middle-class, heterosexual Western women. It does not recognize that the social location of this category of women enables them to benefits not available to other women. White, middle-class women in Europe and North America are the main beneficiaries of the gains that liberal feminism has obtained; considerably less

How do you measure the social value of the work done by an early childhood educator versus that of an investment banker, or a professional athlete, or a sociology professor? (© Photodisc)

Sociology in Action
Gender and the Bible

The holy books of the largest established religious traditions were developed in the context of specific cultures. The Judeo-Christian and Islamic sacred texts were developed in cultures that valued pastoralism (the herding of animals such as sheep, goats, camels, or cows as the primary means of obtaining food). Pastoral cultures are most often patriarchal in ideology, with males significantly dominant over females, and some theorists attribute a perceived patriarchal bias concerning gender roles in the holy books to the patriarchal ideology prevalent at the time the books were written.

The Words of Paul the Apostle
- 'A man . . . is the image and glory of God; but woman is the glory of man. For man was not made from woman, but woman from man. Neither man created from woman, but woman for man.' (1 Cor. 11:7–9)
- 'As in all the churches of the saints, the women should keep silence in the churches. For they are not permitted to speak, but should be subordinate, as even the law says. If there is anything they desire to know, let them ask their husbands at home. For it is shameful for a woman to speak in church.'(1 Cor. 14:33–5)
- 'Wives, be subject to your husbands, as to the Lord. For the husband is the head of the wife as Christ is the head of the church. . . . As the church is subject to Christ, so let wives also be subject in everything to their husbands.' (Eph. 5:22–4)
- 'Let a woman learn in silence with all submissiveness. I permit no woman to teach or to have authority over men; she is to keep silent. For Adam was formed first, then Eve; and Adam was not deceived, but the woman was deceived and became a transgressor. Yet woman will be saved through bearing children, if she continues in faith and love and holiness, with modesty.' (1 Tim. 2:11–15)

What do you think?

1. What do these statements say about the culture that Paul was part of?
2. Do you think that statements such as these have influenced the fact that the Catholic church does not allow women to hold mass or have any position of power?

successful with feminist liberal gains are women who differ in terms of class, ethnicity, sexual orientation, and country.

Feminist Essentialism
While feminist liberalism concentrates essentially on making women equal to men in terms of employment opportunities and salary, **feminist essentialism** looks at differences between the way women and men think, and argues for the equality—and even female superiority—in that difference. Women's morality (Gilligan 1982) and their 'maternal thinking' (Ruddick 1989) involve social norms that are more or less 'natural' to them. Added to this is the idea that this morality is negatively valued in a patriarchal society. For

Kachuck, feminist essentialism is useful in that it 'generates profound questions. Should we understand women in terms of patriarchal constructions or value their models of human ideals? How is women's sexuality to be comprehended outside of patriarchal visions? How do women resist control?' (Kachuk 2003:66–7).

Kachuk presents the criticisms of the feminist essentialist approach to gender thinking in terms of what other Western feminists think and also in terms of what feminists in India have to say. In the eyes of the first, she writes, feminist essentialism has the following flaws:

- It universalizes women, assuming erroneously that all experience gender alike.
- It confuses natural phenomena with women's strategies for coping with patriarchal demands.
- It invites continued perceptions of women as social housekeepers in worlds that men build. (Kachuk 2003:66)

She adds that feminists in India have separate concerns about feminist essentialism:

Indian feminists deplore assumptions of women's inherent caring function as an ideology that impedes their full human development. Thus, essays on education critique practices that socialize girls for dedication to family service. . . . This puts them [Indian feminists] in opposition to calls for women's devotion to families as their national identity. (Kachuk 2003:66)

In sum, then, while feminist essentialism speaks constructively about the potential for women's differences from men to be positively valued, it can fall into the trap of generalizing from the Western model, a trap that Western social scientists have often fallen into.

Feminist Socialism

Feminist socialists, according to Kachuk, have to 'revise their Marxism so as to account for gender, something that Marx ignored. They want sexuality and gender relations included in analyses of society' (Kachuk 2003:67). There is insight to be gained from looking at the intersections of oppression between class and gender. The struggles faced by and resources available to lower-class women can be different from those of middle- and upper-class women, and feminist socialism is useful in identifying these. Still, there is the danger that factors such as race, ethnicity, and sexual orientation get overlooked in the focus on class. Black women in North America face some of the same difficulties of prejudice and stereotyping regardless of whether they come from the upper or lower classes.

Feminist Postmodernism

Feminist postmodernism takes the strongest social constructionist position, a position almost diametrically opposed to that of feminist essentialism. Some postmodernists even contest the widely held view that all women are biologically all female, all men are all male. Feminist postmodernism refers to women more as subjects than as objects of sociological study, allowing the perspective of the women studied to guide the research. Standpoint theory is an important aspect of this category of feminism.

Another methodology that fits within the broad-ranging perspective of feminist postmodernism is **queer theory**, first articulated in the book *Gender Trouble* (1990) by Judith Butler, professor of comparative literature and rhetoric at the University of California, Berkeley. Queer theory rejects the idea that male and female gender are natural binary opposites. It disputes the idea that gender identity is connected to some biological 'essence', arguing instead that gender identity is related to the dramatic effect of a gender performance. Gender is seen not as each of two categories—male and female—but as a continuum with male and female at the extremes; individuals act, or perform, more one way or another along the continuum at different times and in different situations.

Quick Hits
The Ninauposkitzipxpe, or 'Manly-Hearted Women', of the Peigan

About a third of elderly (sixty years or older) North Piegan women in 1939, and a few younger women, were considered manly-hearted. . . . Such women owned property, were good managers and usually effective workers, were forthright and assertive in public, in their homes, and as sexual partners, and were active in religious rituals. They were called 'manly-hearted' because boldness, aggressiveness, and a drive to amass property and social power are held to be ideal traits for men. . . . [T]he manly-hearted woman is admired as well as feared by both men and women. (Kehoe 1995:115)

What do you think?

How do we in Canadian society tend to characterize women who are bold, aggressive, and career-oriented? Can we say that we think of them as positively as the traditional Blackfoot did?

Cultural configurations and norms of gender keep us from playing out a broader variety of gender performances. In this sense, gender performances are restricted by sanctions. Consider the gender performance of a male athlete crying in public, as he announces that he is retiring or apologizes for having failed a drug test or having ended the playing career of an opponent he sucker-punched. Comic routines on the situation by late-night talk-show hosts or comments by former coaches turned pundits appearing during the first period intermission of the Saturday night broadcast can be seen as negative sanctions of that kind of gender performance.

Professional sport—and sport in general—because it is a prominent theatre for gender performance, is a breeding ground for negative sanctions. In hockey, refusing to drop the gloves against a taunting opponent and donning a protective visor are just two actions that could incur the negative sanction known as the **ideology of fag**, which is used throughout society to keep people in line. If you violate gender roles then you are accused of being gay or lesbian. It is a very powerful sanction.

Kachuk's main criticism of feminist postmodernism (criticism that could just as easily be applied to many forms of postmodernism) is that it leads to no conclusions. It merely problematizes other people's conclusions and generates no solid criteria for judging better or worse positions, but satisfies itself with 'constructing a "feminine" space where intellectuals aggressively play out tentative ideas' (Kachuk 2003:81).

Gendered Occupation and Education

Certain jobs, and the college and university programs preparing people to work in those jobs, are **gendered**. That means two things. First, one gender will be prevalent among job holders or students in a program. When we talk about gender prevalence or gender dominance, we mean that as many as 85 per cent of students or employees may be of one gender. Second, as Sargent puts it, 'the work itself is typically imbued with gendered meanings and defined in gendered terms' (Sargent 2005). What this

Monica Seles returns the ball during a Canadian Open tennis match, August 1999. Women tennis players are frequently subject to negative sanction by fans and media alike for grunting and other on-court behaviour deemed 'unladylike'. What does this tell you about female gender performance in a sport like tennis? (CP Photo/Kevin Frayer)

means is that, for example, the gendered profession of nursing is associated with words like 'caring' and 'nurturing' that are typically associated with women; nursing is thus characterized as a natural offshoot of the mother role. By contrast, the job of police officer (still often called 'policeman') is described in terms of 'toughness' and the 'brotherhood' of officers.

In 2001, men outnumbered women by a ratio of at least 3:1 in the following occupations categorized by Statistics Canada:

- the primary industries of forestry, fishing, mining, and oil and gas
- the utilities
- construction
- transportation and warehousing

In the prestigious occupational fields of 'professional, scientific and technical services', men outnumbered women by 14 per cent (567,800 to 431,700); in the administrator category of 'business, building, and other support services', men outnumbered women by 10 per cent (352,200 to 287,000).

By comparison, women outnumbered men in the following categories:

- finance, insurance, real estate, and leasing
- educational services
- accommodation and food services
- health care and social assistance

In the last of these categories the dominance was more than 4:1.

In Other Words
Gender Roles and Being Lesbian

People in my life in the past have tended to believe that because I am a lesbian, I automatically have more male-specific interests, and that I do not enjoy typical girl-oriented activities. Shortly after I told my brother, he invited me to a football game, stating, 'you like football now don't you?' Although he was joking at the time, this is an example of a very typical comment often made to me. Although I may enjoy fixing things around the house, my partner is a sports fanatic, and while I like to sew and knit, she enjoys cooking and romantic comedies. The gender stereotyping, which is exactly what this comes down to, even goes so far as to include the style of clothes I wear. I remember one time that I went into work wearing a baseball cap, although I usually do not wear a hat to work, as I find it unprofessional. This particular day I was coming from school and in a rush. Immediately after entering work I began to hear comments and mutters from my co-workers. It seemed that in their eyes because I was wearing a hat, I was portraying a male characteristic and they assumed that being a lesbian is the next closest thing to being a male.

There is a significant difference between sexual orientation and gender identity. All of the gay people that I know, including myself, are very happy with their sex. They just happen to be attracted to the same sex as well. I am proud to be a woman and I enjoy it and would not want to change that. This leads me to my next point. For one reason or another people with little understanding of the gay population seem to need a definite clarification of 'who's the man and who's the woman', which is a question that I have been asked on too many occasions to count. The truth is that in many gay relationships there are no specific roles, and each individual's identity is not masculine or feminine, but it slides on a continuum. It is almost ridiculous to assume that there is a male and female figure in the relationship, after all, if I wanted a male–female partnership, I wouldn't be gay.

Another opinion that I have found many people have is that gay people, male or female, are involved in a sexual scene full of promiscuity, voyeurism, and ménages à trois. This is evidenced by the number of people that have made suggestive comments to me about non-committed casual sexual encounters. Although these beliefs are positive in one aspect as they break down the very untrue opinion that women cannot have the high sex drive that men are more known for, it also reflects a larger belief that being in a gay relationship is all about the sex. This leads people to believe that gay people do not commit and take part in stable, settled relationships. I remember talking with my father once about the relationship I was in and he responded, 'It's alright if that's what you want, but it's unfortunate because those relationships don't last, they just don't settle.' Ironically, I must say that gay relationships in fact have very little to do with sex. As a heterosexual relationship has many dimensions, so does the homosexual one, encompassing all one's needs such as emotional support, companionship, the sharing of values and spirituality, and of course, physical attraction does play its role as well. I once saw an advertisement that mocked this expectation of such extravagant sex lives. The poster was in a bookstore located in a gay community. The caption read: 'What do lesbians do in bed?' and the picture had two women in bed wearing flannel pajamas, one watching television and the other reading a book. I saw this as an accurate portrayal and a clever way to challenge this opinion.

Sociology students need to look at what might cause these gender specializations to occur. A place to start would be post-secondary education, where men and women typically take different routes. In both community college and university, men greatly outnumber women as graduates in the engineering and applied sciences programs. For instance, in 1998–9, almost four times as many men as women received diplomas in the area, and the difference grew by slightly more than 3,000 students from 1994 to 1995. In 1999–2000, men received slightly more than three times as many university degrees in the area than women did, the difference dropping slightly from 1995–6. Similarly, more than twice as many men as women received degrees in mathematics and physical sciences in 1999–2000.

On the other hand, women greatly outnumber men in college diplomas and university degrees in health professions and related occupations. This is true especially of college diplomas (where the difference is growing), which typically qualify students for less prestigious and more poorly paid occupations, such as pharmacy assistants and nursing assistants. Similarly, women dominate in fields such as social sciences and services at the community college level, and education at the university level.

In sum, there appear to be separate spheres of post-secondary education for men and women, with no sign that the trend is changing. On the contrary, in several areas—engineering and applied sciences, health sciences, and social sciences and services in community

While the number of women attending university in Canada has increased from 10 per cent of the total in 1970 to over 50 per cent in 2005, women are still underrepresented in disciplines such as engineering, math, and physics. What are some of the barriers preventing women from entering those fields? (© Najlah Feanny/Corbis)

colleges—the disparity seems to have grown since the early 1990s.

In Chapter 4 we looked at some of the factors that lead men and women into different programs. As Table 10.1 shows, the effect of different routes through education is that men and women are presented with different employment opportunities once they graduate. In all age groups, there are more men than women working at full-time jobs, and more women than men working at part-time jobs. For the age groups 15–24, and 45+, the difference between the two age groups is growing, especially in the latter group; only in the group aged 24–44 is the gap between the two genders narrowing.

When looking at gender difference in occupations it is important, too, to consider relative earnings. In this area, the overall ratio does not appear to be changing. From 1992 to 2001 the earnings ratio for women relative to men has varied slightly from a low of 62.0 per cent in 1994 (when women earned 62 per cent of what men earned) to a high of 64.8 per cent in 1995. The ratio in 2001 was 64.2, slightly below the high.

The disparity in relative earnings decreases when education is taken into account. For instance, in 1993, women aged 25–34 with a university degree earned 84 per cent of what male degree-holders in the same age bracket earned. However, women aged 45–54 with university degrees earned less, just 72 per cent of what

Table 10.1 >> Full- and part-time gender employment in 2007 (×1,000)

AGE	FULL-TIME EMPLOYMENT			PART-TIME EMPLOYMENT		
15–24	**1999**	**2007**	**CHANGE**	**1999**	**2007**	**CHANGE**
Males	712.5	828.5	116.0	428.5	484.8	56.3
Females	510.5	606.6	96.1	554.9	669.5	114.6
Difference	202.0	221.9	−19.9	126.4	184.7	+58.3
25–44	**1999**	**2007**	**CHANGE**	**1999**	**2007**	**CHANGE**
Males	3,908.0	3,840.2	−67.8	184.3	192.5	8.2
Females	2,751.6	2,934.2	182.6	790.8	692.0	−98.8
Difference	1,156.4	906.0	+250.4	606.5	499.5	−90.6
45+	**1999**	**2007**	**CHANGE**	**1999**	**2007**	**CHANGE**
Males	2,431.7	3,241.3	803.6	200.9	301.7	100.8
Females	1,534.9	2,352.4	817.5	522.6	722.8	200.2
Differences	896.8	888.9	+13.9	321.7	421.1	99.4

±The plus or minus refers to a gain or loss by women in this category.

Source: Adapted from www.statcan.ca/english/Pgdb/labor (2 Feb. 2004), www40.statcan.ca/101/cst01/labor12.htm.

their male counterparts earned. It is interesting to note that relative earnings do not vary with age to the same degree among people holding community college diplomas rather than university degrees: women diploma-holders aged 25–34 earned 75 per cent of what men earned, while those aged 45–54 earned 73 per cent.

Feminization of Occupations

The **feminization** of an occupational sphere occurs when a particular job, profession, or industry comes to be dominated by or predominantly associated with women. Since the start of the First World War, when women began to work outside the home in greater numbers, many occupations have become feminized, including bank teller and secretary (or, now, administrative assistant), but there are instances of job feminization occurring well before that, as the first of the two examples below describes. Typically, the feminization of an industry works to the disadvantage of those involved in it, who earn lower salaries with fewer protections and benefits than those enjoyed by workers outside the feminized occupational sphere.

Women's Work During the London 'Gin Craze' of the Eighteenth Century

Beginning around 1720 there was a a sudden rise in the selling and drinking of gin in London, England. During the so-called 'gin craze', which lasted until the middle of the

English artist William Hogarth became famous for engravings that satirized the vices of high and low society in mid-eighteenth-century London. What does this one, *Gin Lane* (1851), tell you about his impressions of the London gin trade? Would he have been sympathetic to or critical of the London gin sellers? (© Burstein Collection/Corbis)

century, the liquor was sold not just in bars, but in the streets from wheelbarrows and baskets, in alleyway stalls, in shady one-room gin shops, and from boats floating in the Thames.

Anyone selling without a licence was operating illegally. This was the case for the majority of the thousands of women involved in the gin trade, who couldn't afford the expensive licence. They operated at great risk, and were primary targets of the Gin Acts, which were passed chiefly to restrict the selling of gin to bars owned predominantly by middle-class men. Women were more likely than men to be arrested, and also were more likely to be put in prison if convicted.

Why take the chance? At the time, thousands of young women were immigrating to London from Scotland, Ireland, and rural England, looking for jobs and for husbands. The quality and availability of both turned out to be greatly lacking. So why turn to hawking gin? Historian Jessica Warner gives three reasons:

> [I]t required little or no capital; it did not require membership in a professional organization; and it was one of the few occupations from which women were not effectively or explicitly excluded. It was, in other words, a means of economic survival. (Warner 2002:51)

The Gin Acts often pitted women against women. Enforcement depended heavily on the presence of paid informers, half of whom were women. The harsh economics that drove these women to rat out illegal gin sellers is well described by Warner:

> Consider the options of a young woman newly arrived in London in 1737 or 1738. She could work for a year as a maid and earn £5 in addition to receiving room and board, or she could inform against one gin-seller, and upon securing a conviction collect a reward of £5. There were two ways to make money, one hard, the other easy, and many people naturally chose

the latter. Most did so only once, collecting their reward and then attempting to hide as best they could. (Warner 2002:137)

This could be called danger pay, as informers were not well liked.

Women's Clerical Work in Canada, 1891–1971

The early twentieth century saw spectacular growth of clerical workers in the Canadian labour force. It also saw the feminization of the position, along with the degradation of the position, measured in terms of wages, skill level, and opportunity for promotion. How all three trends—growth, feminization, and degradation—mesh together is a story that gives insight on both the past and the present.

Clerical work had traditionally been done by men: the male bookkeeper. His work involved what we would call now multitasking. As companies grew in size, there was much more clerical work that needed to be done, and businesses moved towards a system of 'scientific management', which was seen as a more rationalized and efficient approach to task management. It involved the rapid performance of repeated simple tasks, and it created a kind of assembly-line office work, with few opportunities to move up in the company. The growing belief, based on assumptions about women's limited capabilities, that this was ideal work for women, who were supposed to be wives and mothers first and workers second, were reinforced by discrimination that allowed them few alternatives. The thinking of the time is illustrated in William Leffingwell's *Office Management, Principles and Practice*, published in 1925:

> A woman is to be preferred for the secretarial position for she is not averse to doing minor tasks, work involving the handling of petty details, which would irk and irritate ambitious young men, who usually feel that the work they are doing is of no importance if it can be performed by some person with a lower salary. Most

Secretaries and assistants at a publishing house, 1964, work in an open-concept environment. Across the hall, out of view, are the individual offices of their managers. What does this tell you about the division of men's and women's office work at the time? (Photo © Oxford University Press)

such men are also anxious to get ahead and to be promoted from position to position, and consequently if there is much work of a detail character to be done, and they are expected to perform it, they will not remain satisfied and will probably seek a position elsewhere. (1925:116)

This job transformation got a big push during World War I (1914–18), when women seized the opportunity to enter the workforce to replace men who had gone overseas to serve in Europe. The number of clerical workers jumped by 113,148, around half of them women. The percentage of women clerks working for the Bank of Nova Scotia's Ontario region jumped from 8.5 per cent in 1911 to 40.7 per cent in 1916. Although it fell somewhat when the men returned from the war, the number of women clerical workers remained high and steadily grew (see Table 10.2).

What do you think?

1. How do the gin business in the eighteenth century and the rise of clerical work in the early twentieth century demonstrate what is meant by the 'feminization of occupation'.

2. To what extent is feminization of occupation occurring in Canada today? Where, if at all, can we find evidence of it?

3. Could we say that the reverse happens, that an occupation 'masculinizes', acquiring greater prestige and, of course, greater pay? (Think, perhaps, of the teaching profession.)

Table 10.2 >> Feminization of clerical workers

YEAR	CLERICAL WORKERS	WOMEN CLERICAL WORKERS	
		NUMBER	PERCENTAGE
1891	133,017	4,710	14.3
1901	57,231	12,660	22.1
1911	103,543	33,723	32.6
1921	216,691	90,577	41.8
1931	260,674	117,637	45.1
1941	303,655	152,216	50.1
1951	563,083	319,183	56.7
1961	818,912	503,660	61.5
1971	1,310,910	903,395	68.9

Being a Gender Minority in a Gendered Occupation

When individuals find themselves in gendered jobs and they are of the minority, or 'wrong', gender, it can have a profound effect on their gender performance on the job. Paul Sargent discusses the phenomenon with great clarity in his look at men in early childhood education (which, for Sargent's purposes, includes the lower grades of primary school as well as the daycare profession, where most ECE teaching jobs are found). Sargent incorporates R. Connell's (1995) four performances of masculinity, four ways in which men act out gender roles. These are **hegemonic**, **subordinate**, **marginalized**, and **complicit**:

> Hegemonic masculine practices are those that serve to normalize and naturalize men's dominance and women's subordination. Subordinate masculinities are those behaviors and presentations of self that could threaten the legitimacy of hege-

monic masculinity. Gay men, effeminate men, and men who eschew competition or traditional definitions of success are examples frequently cited. . . . These men are vulnerable to being abused and ridiculed by others. Marginalized masculinities represent the adaptation of masculinities to such issues as race and class. For example, a Black man may enjoy certain privileges that stem from success as a small business owner, yet still find himself unable to hail a cab. . . . Finally, complicit masculinities are those that do not embody hegemonic processes *per se*, but benefit from the ways in which hegemonic masculinities construct the gender order and local gender regimes. (Sargent 2005)

Using these terms, Sargent argues that men working in early childhood education are caught up in a conflict between performing a *subordinate masculinity* (for example, by being 'nurturing'), which would make them good

Canadian Sociology in Action
The Famous Five and the 'Persons' Case

'The famous five' is the name given to five Canadian women who fought for equal rights during the first half of the twentieth century. They are Henrietta Muir Edwards (1849–1931), Nellie McClung (1873–1951), Louise McKinney (1868–1931), Emily Murphy (1868–1933), and Irene Parlby (1868–1965). Among their distinguished achievements is their successful campaign to have women declared 'persons' under British and Canadian law.

When Emily Murphy was appointed in 1916 as the first woman police magistrate in Alberta, her appointment was challenged on the grounds that women were not 'persons' under the British North America (BNA) Act, which had officially created the Dominion of Canada in 1867. It was understood, when the BNA Act was written, that 'persons' meant 'men', for women were not allowed to vote or hold public office. In 1917, the Supreme Court of Alberta ruled that women were, in fact, 'persons' in that province, and Emily Murphy was officially the first woman magistrate in the British Empire. In order to advance the cause of women aspiring to hold public office at the federal level, she then had her name put forward as a candidate for the Canadian Senate, but the Conservative prime minister Robert Borden, invoking the BNA Act and its reference to 'persons', rejected her bid.

In her popular writing, Nellie McClung often drew her readers' attention to the hard-working reality of farm women. During the early 1920s, she was a Member of the Legislative Assembly in Alberta (NAC, PA030212).

In the years that followed the fight to have women in the Senate was taken up by numerous women's groups across the country. In 1927, Murphy and the other four members of the famous five, all of them prominent women's rights activists in Alberta, petitioned the Supreme Court of Canada with the question *'Does the word "persons" in Section 24, of The British North America Act, 1867, include female persons?'*. The Court answered that it did not. At that time there were no women in the House of Lords in Britain, so the notion that there might be female members in the Canadian Senate was easily dismissed. But the famous five were undeterred and took their case to a higher court of appeal: the Judicial Committee of the Privy Council in Britain. On 18 October 1929, the Lord Chancellor of the Privy Council announcing the judicial committee's decision, ruled that 'women are persons . . . and eligible to be summoned and may become Members of the Senate of Canada'. In their decision, the committee stated 'that the exclusion of women from all public offices is a relic of days more barbarous than ours. And to those who would ask why the word "persons" should include females, the obvious answer is, why should it not?'

The following year, 1930, Montreal-born Cairine Reay Wilson became the first woman appointed to the Senate of Canada.

Quick Hits
Granting the Provincial and Federal Vote to Women

- 1867   Canadian federal and provincial vote given only to White men with property.
- 1916   Women in Manitoba, Saskatchewan, and Alberta get the provincial vote.
- 1917   World War I nurses and the female relatives of soldiers get the federal vote.
          Women in British Columbia and Ontario get the provincial vote.
- 1918   Women in Canada get the federal vote.
          Women in Nova Scotia get the provincial vote.
- 1918   First woman provincial cabinet minister (Mary Ellen Smith, BC)
- 1919   Women in New Brunswick get the provincial vote.
- 1921   First woman federal cabinet minister (Mary Ellen Smith)
- 1922   Women in Prince Edward Island get the provincial vote.
- 1925   Women in the British colony of Newfoundland get the vote.
- 1930   First woman senator in Canada (Cairine Wilson)
- 1936   First ordained woman United Church minister (18 years after formation of
          United Church)
- 1940   Women in Quebec get the provincial vote
- 1951   First woman mayor in Canada (Charlotte Whitten, Ottawa)
- 1976   First ordained woman Anglican priest
- 1991   First woman provincial premier (Rita Johnson, B.C.)
- 1993   First woman prime minister (Kim Campbell)

teachers, and more stereotypical masculinity performances, which are imposed on them by the gendered nature of the job. The male gen-

der images involved here are 'homosexual-pedophile' and 'man as disciplinarian'. Male ECE teachers are not allowed the caring physical contact that female teachers are encouraged to have. As one male teacher's narrative explains, 'Women's laps are places of love. Men's are places of danger.' This stems from the popularly reproduced image of the homosexual-pedophile, which mistakenly conflates, or links, two different sexualities. As a result, male teachers are reduced to less threatening and safe complicit male masculinity performances, which include 'high fives' and handshakes rather than hugs and rewarding children with prizes and names written on the board rather than physical contact. This can be demoralizing for the male early childhood educator. As one male teacher wrote in a narrative, 'I sometimes feel really inadequate when I watch the kids draped all over the women and all I'm doing is keeping them busy, handing out trinkets, or slapping high fives.'

The 'man as disciplinarian' gender image also restricts the performance of male gender roles in the ECE environment. Because it is assumed that men more naturally perform discipline, they are assigned greater responsibility for monitoring the behaviour of 'problem kids'. Classrooms occupied by male teachers then become seen as sites of discipline. No matter what the particular male's natural inclinations or teaching styles are—whether or not they are more nurturant or 'female defined'— these teachers are forced to conform to a masculinity performance that reinforces male authoritarian stereotypes.

Men in early childhood education are expected to want to move into occupational positions more in keeping or complicit with male hegemony: administrative positions in ECE organizations and higher grades in elementary schools. Sargent's study did not verify this trend, but we could argue that a longitudinal approach, looking at male teachers' careers over time, would yield evidence of men 'moving up' in the system. We might find, too, that this kind of trend is as much or more the product of the gendered nature of the organizations as of the individuals' actual intent.

What do you think?

In some ways it's easier to examine the impact on men of working in a female-gendered occupation because it is much less common than the reverse: women working in male-dominated occupations. Think of three jobs defined as male. What would restrict female performance of gender in these jobs?

Race and Gender: Intersecting Oppression

Race and gender can intersect as forms of oppression. Racial prejudice and discrimination can often reinforce gender bias, and vice versa. In some cases, opposing gender/race stereotypes can affect an oppressed group, as in the case of Asian women, described below.

Opposing Gender/Race Stereotypes

There is a tendency to stereotype visible minority women into two extremes. So, for example, Renee Tajima (1989) writes about how an East Asian woman may be stereotyped either as the 'Lotus Blossom Baby' or as the 'Dragon Lady'. In Tania Das Gupta's words, the former stereotype 'encompasses the images of the China doll, the geisha girl and shy Polynesian beauty. The latter includes prostitutes and "devious madams"' (Das Gupta 1996:27). Any fan of the TV series MASH would recognize both stereotypes. Popular during the 1970s and 1980s, the show, which revolved around a unit of American doctors and nurses stationed near Seoul during the Korean War of the early 1950s, featured numerous sly allusions to geisha girls and occasional appearances by Asian women who periodically became involved with the leading male characters. It also featured characters who fit the 'Dragon Lady' stereotype, including the sharp businesswoman Rosie, of Rosie's Bar and Grill, and a woman who threatens the male character

Klinger with a pitchfork when she believes he is fooling around with her daughter.

The stereotype of the Lotus Blossom Baby, which gained popularity during the American occupation of Japan after World War II, has contributed to the image, prevalent in the West, of a geisha as an expensive prostitute. This is a narrow view, as Mineko Iwasaki makes clear in *Geisha, A Life* (2002). Born in 1949, Iwasaki was Japan's foremost geisha, having begun her training at the age of four and retired wealthy at 29. She entertained such prominent Western figures as the British royal family and the American General Douglas MacArthur. In her book she describes her strict training in calligraphy, dance, music, serving tea, and the other hostess functions of a geisha. She dispels the stereotype of 'geisha as prostitute', explaining that there were occasionally 'romantic entanglements' between rich patrons and geisha artists, leading to marriage, affairs, or 'heartache', but that 'in the same way that a patron of the opera does not expect sexual favors from the diva', a rich and powerful man would more often support a prominent geisha 'solely because of the artistic perfection that she embodied and the luster that she lent to his reputation' (Iwasaki 2002:51–2).

Black women also face discrimination on the basis of opposing race/gender stereotypes. Das Gupta describes the double image as follows:

On the one hand there was the slow, de-sexed, 'cow-like' mammy, evolved into

'A Bust Portrait of a Young Woman Leaning on a Balcony' by Goyo (© Christie's Images/Corbis) and 'A Modern Housewife' by Yoshitoshi (© Asian Art & Archaeology, Inc./Corbis). These images were created in 1920 and 1878 respectively. Where can we find evidence of the gender/race stereotypes of the 'Lotus Blossom Baby' and the 'Dragon Lady' today?

the 'Aunt Jemima figure'—familiar to many from older boxes of pancake mix—a servile and contented image which brings together gender and race ideologies. On the other hand, there was the sexual objectification of Black women's bodies, or body parts to be more exact. (Das Gupta 1996:27)

The sexually objectified Black woman is a familiar figure in music videos, but the brief and supposedly inadvertent exposure of Black singer Janet Jackson's breast during the broadcast of 2004 Super Bowl halftime show sparked outrage among American viewers (as well as among many people who had merely heard about the incident). Why the big fuss? The sudden appearance in prime time of the sexually objectified Black woman in the midst of a 'wardrobe malfunction' seemed to have caught a largely White middle-class audience by surprise. Were these viewers right to object? Or is the North American viewing public guilty of a double standard, finding it okay for the sexually objectified woman to appear in videos on MTV, but not on 'family entertainment' on ABC?

The Indian Princess and the Squaw

Aboriginal women have long been subject to the opposing gender/race stereotypes of the 'Indian Princess' and the 'Squaw'. In the United States, the Indian Princess is a heroine that forms an integral part of the American story of how their country was built. She is the beautiful Pocahontas of Disney's worldview, saving the handsome John Smith from certain death, in the process abandoning her people to serve the interests of the incoming colonial power. She is Sacajawea, the Shoshone woman who aided the Lewis and Clark Expedition from 1804 to 1806, helping to open the West to 'civilization' and the eventual reservation entrapment of her people and their Plains neighbours.

The Indian Princess is not part of the founding mythology, or master narrative, of Canada. Still, she is found here and there across the country. Emily Pauline Johnson, popular Mohawk poet and novelist at the turn of the twentieth century, was frequently billed as 'The Mohawk Princess' to audiences in North America and Britain, for whom she performed her poetry. Catharine Sutton, a heroic Ojibwa woman of the nineteenth century, is known in Owen Sound, Ontario, as 'the Indian Princess' (see Steckley 1999).

While the stereotype of the Indian Princess has been used as a metaphor for the supposed open-armed acceptance by North American Native people of European colonizers, the Squaw is a figure that has been used by White writers (including American presidents Thomas Jefferson and Theodore Roosevelt) to characterize Aboriginal people as savages, providing ample justification for White colonial

The daughter of an English mother and a Mohawk father, E. Pauline Johnson played up her mixed heritage in her popular performances, often appearing for the first part of a show in traditional Native costume before changing into a formal evening dress for the remainder of the performance. (Library and Archives Canada, C-14141)

dominance (Smits 1982). The image summarizes the impressions of Aboriginal culture as brutal and barbaric, with lazy, abusive Native men overworking and generally mistreating their wives, sisters, mothers, and daughters.

The squaw figure is a familiar one in the Canadian literature on Aboriginal women (see McLean 1970:148–9 and Jenness 1932:403). The way the distorted depiction of the lives of Aboriginal women was used to justify White colonialism is clearly seen in the following passage written by a nineteenth-century missionary, Egerton R. Young:

> Marvelous were the charges wrought among these Indians when they became Christians. And in no way was the change greater or more visible than in the improved conditions of women. In paganism she has not the life of a dog. She is kicked and cuffed and maltreated continually. She is the beast of burden and has to do all the heavy work. . . . Very quickly after they become Christians does all this change. Then happy homes begin. Mother and wife and sister and daughter are loved and kindly cared for. (Young 1970:148–9)

In contemporary society, the Squaw image is often blended with the stereotype of the 'drunk Indian', with tragic consequences. Consider the case of Minnie Sutherland, a 40-year-old Cree woman who was struck by a car in downtown Hull, Quebec, while walking with her cousin on New Year's Eve, 1989. The car was driven by two White nurses, who quickly stopped and got out of their car, and were soon joined by two White police officers and three university students who were witnesses to the incident. The students explained that Minnie had been hit by a car, but according to John Nihmey, who had access to the transcript of the hearing that would follow, the officers 'were perplexed by what seemed to be an overreaction to a drunk woman who had either slipped on an ice patch and fallen, or walked into a car that couldn't have been going very fast given all the traffic'

(Nihmey 1998:82–3). In communication with police headquarters, the officers referred to Minnie as 'the squaw' (Nihmey 1998:84).

With Minnie barely conscious, the police and students left. An attending paramedic arriving with another police officer concluded that Minnie was drunk and suggested that she be taken to a detoxification centre. However, when the officer brought her to a detox centre, she was turned away on the grounds that the facility would not admit non-ambulatory people. The officer eventually drove Minnie to a nearby hospital, where she died 11 days later as the result of a blood clot in the back of her brain caused by her accident. The doctors, unaware of the blood clot, hadn't considered her case serious enough to warrant an MRI. On 17 January, a doctor from the hospital sent the following letter to the Hull police:

> There is no doubt that the lack of information about the traumatic event was of great significance in making the initial diagnosis of the abnormality and in following this up to a logical conclusion which may have been able to prevent her demise. . . . In particular, if the allegations of the conduct of the Hull Police are correct, then a serious error in judgment has been made by the officers concerned and this should be investigated. (Nihmey 1998:163)

A coroner's jury ruled that the Hull police should offer compulsory courses to sensitize officers to the needs of visible minorities. At the same time, four out of five jurors felt that racism was not a factor in the case. The Quebec Police Commission cleared its officers of racism charges.

Gender and Immigration

There have been several instances in Canadian history when only the men or the women of a particular ethnic group were permitted or encouraged to immigrate. We have seen, in Chapter 9 on race and ethnicity, that Chinese and South Asian women were effectively

Sociology in Action
Indian Princesses and Cowgirls: Stereotypes from the Frontier

Pocahontas, Calamity Jane, and Annie Oakley. When we think of women in the Wild West, these are the images that come to mind. The Indian princess is a serene, noble savage, while the cowgirl is a smart-talking, gun-slinging dynamo. These stereotypes are so deeply ingrained in our popular culture that we scarcely give them a second thought.

A recent exhibit of popular-culture images of Indian and western women from the nineteenth and twentieth centuries unveiled and challenged these representational stereotypes. *Indian Princess and Cowgirls: Stereotypes from the Frontier*, shown across Canada between 1997 and 2000, featured over 200 photographs, postcards, calendars, and other historical images of 'Indian princesses' and 'cowgirls' that graphically depict the historical representation of women, race, and the colonial west. Together, the images demonstrated how European notions of femininity and wild savagery were grafted onto First Nations and frontier women, bringing civilization to the wild and the wild to civilization in a more palatable form. In essence, Native women were made more 'feminine' and White, while White frontier women were made wilder and more Native.

According to Gail Valaskakis, one of two curators of the exhibit, 'The discourse of the Indian as noble and savage, the villain and the victim . . . is threaded through the narratives of the dominant culture and its shifting perceptions of the western frontier as a land of savagery and a land of promise.' Like the cultural narratives of the western frontier which sustained them, textual representations of real First Nations peoples reveal stories of conquest and its legacies. For Valaskakis, this ambiguous representation of Native women 'has been with us since the earliest colonization of the Americas'. As representations changed, the images of First Nations' women as Indian princesses who embodied mystery and exoticism began to emerge. During the post-World War I era, the Indian princess was repeatedly portrayed alone in the pristine wilderness, scantily clad in a buckskin or tunic dress, sporting a jaunty feather over two long braids. Most striking, the models in the images are notably white-skinned.

Meanwhile, the masculine transgression of cowgirls in Wild West fiction depicted the romanticism of their underlying 'Indian nature'. Pictures of cowgirls, adventure heroines, and outlaw women were first produced for rodeo and vaudeville shows, dime novels, and monograms as a means to promote sales. But in actual frontier society, many women deliberately took on this fictional role by 'playing Indian'. Playing Indian gave White women the opportunity to escape the conventional and often restrictive boundaries of society. Rodeo shows frequently featured women in pants performing death-defying stunts on horseback, performances that mimicked the fantasy of the Native huntress and warrior as imagined by nineteenth-century onlookers.

blocked from entering Canada for significant parts of the twentieth century. In what follows, we will see the difficulties Filipino women faced when they made up the majority of those allowed to immigrate to Canada from the Philippines.

Filipino Immigrants:
A Second Wave of Pioneering Women
Filipino immigration to Canada is unique in that women have been the 'pioneers'—arriving first before their husbands and other male family members, sending most of their money together

with care packages of bargain-hunted goods back home to their families, sponsoring relatives and providing them with a place to stay. There have been two waves of Filipino immigration. The first wave, discussed in Chapter 8, brought nurses, mostly women, while the second wave brought nannies, who suffer more from the inequalities of gender and race than did the earlier generation of Filipino immigrants.

In 1981, the Canadian government instituted its Foreign Domestic Movement Program (FDMP) to address the growing need for in-house childcare created as more and more women began working outside the home. In 1992, the FDMP was replaced by the more restrictive Live-In Caregiver Program, which required selected immigrants to commit to 24 months of domestic work within a three-year period, during which time they were also required to 'live in' with the family. Nannies came mainly from three countries: the Philippines, Jamaica, and the United Kingdom. Filipino nannies dominated the figures, the percentage of domestics coming from the Philippines rising between 1982 and 1990 from 10.60 per cent to 50.52 per cent. This trend occurred not just in Canada but in Hong Kong, Singapore, Saudi Arabia, Britain, and the United States. The political and economic unrest that surrounded the fall of the corrupt Marcos government made the Philippines a place many wanted to leave if they could.

The women of the second wave of Filipino immigration were older than their compatriots who had migrated earlier: those aged 30–34 predominated, with those aged 25–29 and 35–39 forming smaller but roughly equal groups, and those aged 20–24 and 50–54 sharing about the same low percentage. It was more difficult for this generation of Filipino immigrants. They were better educated than immigrating British and Jamaican nannies: among those receiving temporary employment authorization as nannies between 1982 and 1990, 8 per cent held Bachelor's degrees, 7 per cent had at least some

university education, 17 per cent had some trade and technology training, and 12 per cent had other non-university training. Working as nannies made these women grossly underemployed, as sociologist Anita Beltran Chen argues (Chen 1998). Yet domestic work was the only kind of work that could bring them to Canada, so they took their chances.

As women, as visible minorities, and as temporary and poorly paid employees subject to few industrial controls, they were vulnerable to exploitation and physical, emotional, and sexual abuse. Those who had been trained in a specific field such as nursing also had to fight losing their skills through disuse. Between 15 and 20 per cent were married and had to endure separation from their husbands and, in many cases, children. Those who were single returned a large portion (estimates vary around 75 per cent) of their income to their family back home, holding onto little money to look after themselves. In short, they are restricted by the stereotypes of race and gender that treat Asian women as caregivers, overlooking skills that might make them productive in other areas of Western society.

Summary and Conclusions

You need be neither a woman nor a feminist to recognize that feminization of an occupation—in the sense of making it unrewarding in terms of pay, power, and social status—helps to create inequality between men and women. This inequality, reflected in pay ratio and in the greater likelihood of women working part-time, is changing very little. As sociologists, we need to investigate why this is so, and look for ways to address the inequity. We also must ask ourselves whether the separate paths that men and women take in post-secondary education lead to social inequality or just difference, an issue we raised in Chapter 4, on socialization.

Questions for Critical Review and Discussion

1. Outline the feminist work done by early women sociologists in Canada.

2. Compare and contrast the four different categories of feminism outlined in the chapter.

3. Outline the roles that biological and social influences had on determining David Reimer's gender.

4. Compare and contrast the four masculinities outlined in the section on male daycare workers.

5. Describe how gender and ethnicity intersect in creating female stereotypes.

Suggested Readings

Chodrow, Nancy J. (1994). *Femininities, Masculinities, Sexualities: Freud and Beyond*. Lexington, Kentucky: The UP of Kentucky.

Fausto-Sterling, Anne (1985). *Myths of Gender: Biological Theories about Women and Men*. New York: Basic Books.

Foucault, Michel (1978). The *History of Sexuality: An Introduction*, vol. 1. R. Hurley, trans. New York: Vintage.

Medovarski, Andrea, & Brenda Cranney, eds. (2006). *Canadian Women Studies: An Introductory Reader*, 2nd edn. Toronto: INANNA.

Seidman, Steven, ed. (1996). *Queer Theory / Sociology*. Cambridge: Blackwell.

Silman, Janet; As Told To (1987). *Enough is Enough: Aboriginal Women Speak Out*. Toronto: Women's Press.

Suggested Websites

Canadian Women's Internet Association.
http://wwwherplace.org

Gender Watch.
http://www.genderwatch.com/products/pt-product-genderwatch.shtml

International Gay and Lesbian Human Rights Commission.
http://www.iglhrc.org/

Andrea Dworkin Online Library.
http://www.igc.org/Womennet/dworkin/index.html

CHAPTER 11

Globalization

Contents

Key Terms

anti-corporate globalization
   movement
biodiversity
crusade
cultural globalization
economic globalization
embedded journalist
First World
globalism/globalists
globality
globalization
globalization from above
globalization from below
glocalization
government terrorism
hyperglobalizers
Islamists
jihad
jihad-i-akbar
jihad-i-asghar
Khudai Khidmatgar
liberalism
neoconservativism
neoliberalism
(The) North
oligarchy
particularist protectionist
polyarchy
preventative war
skeptical globalizers
Second World
sociological imagination
(The) South
terrorism
Third World
transnational corporation
tribalism
ummaic jihad
universalist protectionist

Boxes

Learning Objectives

After reading this chapter, you should be able to

- outline the various forms of globalization.
- distinguish between hyperglobalizers and skeptical globalizers.
- discuss the social effects of neoliberalism on 'developing nations'.
- recognize the problematic nature of defining and attaching the labels of 'democracy' and 'terrorism'.
- distinguish between universalist and particularist protectionism.

>>> For Starters
Pioneer Global Village

I was asked to help guide Indonesian science teachers on a bus trip to a few of the educational sites near my college in northwestern Toronto. We went to Crawford Lake Conservation Area, where they have reconstructed fourteenth-century Iroquois longhouses. These were easy to explain to my visitors, who knew of cultures in their own country that had lived in similar dwellings. I was aware of this connection, and it made my explanations that much simpler.

The next sight we were going to visit would, I thought, be more difficult to contextualize. We were going to Black Creek Pioneer Village, a reconstructed nineteenth-century settler community where historical interpreters dressed in period costume demonstrate various aspects of pioneer life to school groups and tourists. As we approached the site, I was frantically searching my mind for points of connection that would make this part of the trip understandable.

I need not have bothered. For as I entered the park with my Indonesian teachers, and they all looked out in interest, one loud voice was heard to say, 'Heh, it's just like *Little House on the Prairie*'. That television show, based on the novels of Laura Ingalls and depicting life in the American West during the 1870s, had been shown from 1975 to 1982 in North America, but had lived on in reruns around the world—including Indonesia.

My visitor's ready reference to a classic American television show caught me by surprise, but then the American Midwest of the nineteenth century has no less to do with Indonesia than turn-of-the-twentieth-century Prince Edward Island has to do with Japan, where Lucy Maud Montgomery's heroine

Anne of Green Gables flourishes as a cultural icon. Should we feel proud, as Canadians, that one of our great literary figures has been embraced halfway around the globe or unnerved that a piece of cultural property has been bought and transformed to serve the global marketplace?

© Nippon Animation Co, Ltd 1979

Introduction

Globalization as a social process is not unlike the **sociological imagination**, which we discussed in the opening chapter. Both are about making connections between the small and the large. For the sociological imagination, that connection is one that is made in the mind between the individual and the greater society. For globalization, the connection is any of the various processes that link the local community with the global one.

The study of globalization is part of many disciplines—political science, economics, anthropology, and cultural studies, to name a few in the vanguard of globalization research. Sociology can generally be said to be lagging behind these other disciplines in the study, though sociologists have a great deal to add, particularly in the area of social inequality. One sociologist who has already made important contributions in this area is Roland Robertson. Currently serving as chair of the Department of Sociology at the University of Aberdeen, Scotland, and director of its Centre for the Study of Globalization, he has also taught in the US, Sweden, Japan, Hong Kong, the Czech Republic, and Brazil (four continents!). His work has been translated into German, Spanish, Danish, Japanese, Mandarin, Turkish, Italian, Portuguese, and Polish. Later on in this chapter we will discuss some of his influential work in the study of globalization.

Globalization is also a very contested area of study, owing to the fact that globalization has its champions and its opponents. Those who support and promote the process view globalization as a dream, a modernist heaven-on-earth. Manfred Steger, who will be quoted at some length in this chapter, refers to such people as **hyperglobalizers**. A hint of the fervour of their belief can be glimpsed in the following quotation that the American investment firm Merrill Lynch ran in major newspapers in 1998. It was a response to the global economic mini-crisis of the time, brought on by the collapse of several Asian economies. It is remarkable as a statement of blind faith coming from otherwise well-educated and experienced people:

The World is 10 Years Old
It was born when the [Berlin] Wall fell in 1989. It's no surprise that the world's youngest economy—the global econ-

Quick Hits
Confessions of a Globalizer: American General Smedley D. Butler

I spent thirty years and four months as a member of . . . the Marine Corps. And during that period, I spent most of my time being a high-class muscleman for Big Business, for Wall Street, and for the bankers. . . . Thus, I helped make Mexico . . . safe for American oil interests in 1914. I helped make Haiti and Cuba a decent place for the National City Bank to collect revenues. . . . I helped purify Nicaragua for the international banking house of Brown Brothers in 1909–1912. I brought light to the Dominican Republic for American sugar interests in 1916. I helped make Honduras 'right' for American fruit companies in 1903. (quoted in Bellegarde-Smith 2004:93)

omy—is still finding its bearings. The intricate checks and balances that stabilize economies are only incorporated with time. Many world markets are only recently freed, governed for the first time by the emotions of the people rather than the fists of the state. From where we sit [i.e. on top of an economic hierarchy] none of this diminishes the promise offered a decade ago by the demise of the walled-off world. . . . The spread of free markets and democracy around the world is permitting more people everywhere to turn their aspirations into achievements. And technology, properly harnessed and liberally distributed, has the power to erase not just geographical borders but also human ones. It seems to us that, for a 10-year-old, the world continues to hold great promise. In the meantime, no one ever said growing up was easy. (Friedman: 2000:xvi)

Outside of the naive nature of this statement, which testifies to the ignorance of social inequality held by people who stand on the top rung of the ladder, the writers show a lack of knowledge of history. Global economies have existed before, and will be mentioned in scattered references throughout this chapter, and we would do well to learn their lessons. The last one crashed with the Great Depression of the 1930s.

At the opposite end of the spectrum and looking upon globalization as very dangerous to the world's environment and to the economies and social welfare of the 'have-not' countries are those Steger refers to as **skeptical globalizers**. The position we take in this chapter is essentially an optimistic one, but one that definitely leans towards the stance of the latter group. This is one of those areas where a sociologist cannot pretend to be neutral 'in the interests of science'.

There is a great need for definition of terms in the study of globalization, as it is a relatively new field of academic interest. We will be relying heavily on Manfred Steger's excellent *Globalization: A Very Short Introduction* (2003) for terms and much of the perspective taken here. First of all, it is important to think of **globalization** as a social *process*, not as a set of social *conditions*. Steger uses the term **globality** (2003:7) to refer to the set of globalized social conditions that exist at any one time. These conditions include the amount of global interdependence (social, economic, cultural, and political) and the rate of exchange (or, if in one direction, flow) of social, economic, and political information and materials between global markets. Globality, like globalization itself, is contested. If you believed everything you saw in computer and cell phone commercials (generally not a good thing to do from a sociological standpoint), you would think that the state of globality is higher than it actually is. We in North America tend to have a grossly exaggerated understanding of how 'connected' the world is. The vast majority of the people in the world have never even seen a cell phone, and most have never used a computer. One of many shocks for people of Indonesia and the smaller Pacific islands in the aftermath of the December 2004 tsunami was their sudden exposure to strange people and strange technology coming to their aid.

Globalization involves those processes that lead the world towards a state of globality, of connectedness and interdependence. Steger explains it in the following way:

Globalization refers to a multidimensional set of social processes that create, multiply, stretch and intensify worldwide social interdependencies and exchanges while at the same time fostering in people a growing awareness of deepening connections between the local and the distant. (Steger 2003:13)

The key point here is that globalization exists in several dimensions: social, economic, political, cultural, and ideological. It falls not just within the domain of sociologists but is relevant to a number of different disciplines: political science, economics, history, anthropology, and the newly developing cultural studies. For this reason, it will be useful to look at globalization in the context of each of these dimensions. But before we get to that, we need to go over who the main 'players' are in any examination of globalization.

There are rich countries and there are poor countries. Both have been given various names over the years. For a long time they were known as **First World** countries and **Third World** countries. The latter term was coined by French social scientist **Alfred Sauvy** (1898–1990) in 1952. The First World was seen as including the rich capitalist countries, while the Third World comprised those countries without social or economic power. The USSR and the Eastern European countries under its power (sometimes called Soviet Bloc or Eastern Bloc) were identified as the **Second World**.

Somewhat more recent terminology avoids the First World–Third World designation and distinguishes instead between **developed nations** and **developing nations**. One problem with this is that not all of the so-called developing nations are necessarily developing. According to the skeptical globalization position, they should really be called 'underdeveloped nations', or perhaps more accurately 'underdevelop*ing* nations', since they are under a constant process of being exploited and running up huge debts incurred as a result of globalization.

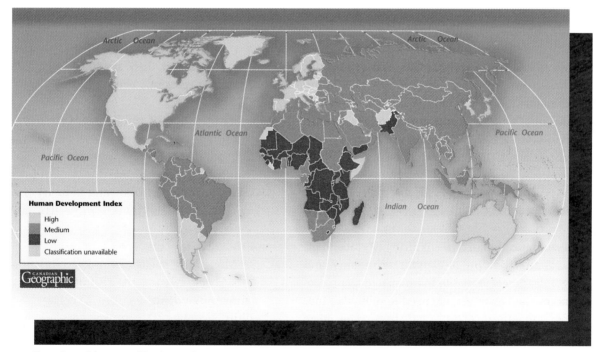

Based on this map of high, medium, and low development, does it make sense to you to divide the world conceptually into North and South? East and West? (www.canadiangeographic.ca/worldmap)

More recently, theorists have divided the world conceptually into **the North** and **the South**, based on the plain fact that almost all of the powerful and rich nations are in the northern hemisphere, while the less powerful and poor nations are typically found in the southern hemisphere. Of course, this has some flaws, too: Australia and New Zealand, squarely in the southern hemisphere, are not among the worlds poorest nations, and a number of the northern hemisphere's central Asian countries are considerably poorer than their immediate neighbours. Nevertheless, we will use that term in the discussion that follows.

This introduction ends with a disclaimer. Despite appearances to the contrary, this chapter is not meant to be an anti-American diatribe. The country that produced C. Wright Mills, Martin Luther King, baseball, the blues, jazz, rock 'n' roll, and the writer John Steinbeck deserves a great deal of respect for its continuous capacity to produce beautiful minds. It is, to use Mills's term, the **power elite**—those wielding significant financial and political power—that we will be taking issue with here. Further, globalization is not, like baseball or jazz, an American-grown phenomenon. The more dynamic economies in Asia and Europe (those of Japan and Germany in particular) are also major agents of globalization, especially economic globalization. Even Canada plays a role.

Economic Globalization

Economic globalization is all about global markets and the flow of capital, technology, and goods (Steger 2003:37). In order to explain economic globalization, we need to define a number of other terms need first. The term **neoliberalism** can be confusing for students, as it is essentially identical to the seemingly opposite term **neoconservativism** (rather like the way *flammable* and *inflammable* mean the same

thing). It helps to think of liberalism as an old idea, born and raised in the eighteenth and nineteenth centuries. It also helps to think of the root of the word—*liberate*, meaning 'to free'—especially as it applies to the marketplace.

Liberalism, as conceived by early economists such as **Adam Smith** (1723–1790), was the idea that the market was like a living thing that needed to be free to expand and grow in a healthy way. It is related to laissez-faire capitalism, a policy of not interfering with market processes. The market, in this view, is seen as a self-regulating organism, responding to the dictates of supply and demand. Restricting forces, such as the stifling 'chains' of taxes, tariffs, customs duties, and the like, created by government and state bureaucracies, were considered detrimental to the growth and overall health of this organism.

Neoliberalism, an offshoot of traditional liberalism, came to the fore in the United States, Canada, and Britain during the political regimes of Ronald Reagan, Brian Mulroney, and Margaret Thatcher during the 1980s. It gained strength with the fall of communism in 1989–91. As Steger neatly summarizes it, there are 10 key elements in the political economic agenda of neoliberals:

1. Privatization of public enterprises [i.e. utilities like water, gas, and electricity]
2. Deregulation of the economy [i.e. not imposing caps on things like tuition costs]
3. Liberalization of trade and industry [i.e. reducing or eliminating protective tariffs; free trade]
4. Massive tax cuts
5. 'Monetarist' measures to keep inflation in check, even at the risk of increasing unemployment
6. Strict control on organized labour
7. The reduction of public expenditures, particularly social spending [on things like education and healthcare]
8. The down-sizing of government

Maintaining production facilities abroad exempts transnational corporations from having to pay to maintain pollution standards of their home country. What kind of impact do you think shipping has on the environment? (© Digital Vision)

9. The expansion of international markets
10. The removal of controls on global financial flows (Steger 2003:41)

Almost all of these measures were brought into effect in Ontario during the reign of the provincial Conservative Party (1995–2003) under Premier Mike Harris, who was neoliberal but definitely not Liberal.

Steger introduces another important term, **globalism**, to refer to 'an ideology that endows the concept of globalization with neoliberal values and meanings' (Steger 2003:94). Globalists are those who think that the only way for globalization to occur is through the implementation of neoliberalist policies. As we will see later, there are those who believe that globalization can take other paths.

An integral element of economic globalization is the **transnational corporation** (formerly known as the multinational corporation or, simply, a multinational). Transnational corporations are companies that are typically based in countries in the North (over two-thirds have their head offices in the United States, Japan, or Germany) but with branches all over the world. Examples are numerous, but they include car manufacturers, such as General Motors, Honda, and Volkswagen; oil companies, such as Exxon-Mobil and Royal Dutch/Shell; computer firms, such as Microsoft—whose owner and CEO is by far the richest man in the world—and IBM; high-tech companies, such as Sony, Hitachi, and Nokia; clothing manufacturers, such as Nike; and retailers, such as Walmart. The economic power of these companies can be seen in the sta-

The student reader by now will be slightly reeling with the number of terms that begin with *global-*. Here they are all together, so the distinction can be clear:

NAME	NATURE
globalization	an ongoing social process
globality	a set of social conditions (at a particular time)
globalism	an ideology connecting neoliberalism with globalization
globalist	a proponent of globalism

tistic noted by Steger that of the world's 100 largest economies, only 49 are actual countries; the majority—51—are transnational corporations (Steger 2003:48).

Transnational corporations are often condemned by unionists, environmentalists, and nationalists from the developed nations in which they are based for having a high percentage, if not all, of their manufacturing or production carried out in developing countries, where labour costs are much lower than they are in the North. Maintaining production facilities abroad also exempts these corporations from having to pay to maintain the pollution and safety standards of their base country.

A good example of how certain forms of economic globalization can yield unequal gains comes from statistics reported in several sources late in 2002 (see, for example, Bezlova 2002). According to these statistics, if you were to buy a Barbie Doll at a Walmart store in the United States, you would pay about $10. However, the import price at the US customs would be only about $2. Of that $2, half would be for transportation (which, of course, would include American carriers) and management fees (part of that would go back to Walmart), and 65 cents would be for raw materials (which would not have come from China). The manu-

facturing costs would be 35 cents a doll. You can imagine what that would leave to pay the workers who manufactured the doll.

As Steger notes, hyperglobalizers claim, among other things, that globalization benefits everyone more or less equally (Steger 2003:103). Economically, this seems a rather spurious claim, as the beneficiaries would appear to be the rich countries of the North. In Steger's words,

> Data published in the 1999 and 2000 editions of the *UN Human Development Report* show that, before the onset of globalization in 1973, the income ratio between the richest and poorest countries was at about 44 to 1. Twenty-five years later it had climbed to 74 to 1. (Steger 2003:105)

One major cause of this apparently growing gap is the existence of instruments of globalization such as the World Bank, the World Trade Organization (WTO), and the International Monetary Fund (IMF), which grant loans to the developing countries. In exchange, the borrowing countries must agree to adopt certain neoliberal policies. And as Steger explains,

> Unfortunately, however, large portions of the 'development loans' granted by these

institutions have either been pocketed by authoritarian political leaders or have enriched local businesses and the Northern corporations they usually serve. . . . Most importantly, however, structural adjustment programmes rarely produce the desired result of 'developing' debtor societies, because mandated cuts in public spending translate into fewer social programmes, reduced educational opportunities, more environmental pollution, and greater poverty for the vast majority of people. Typically, the largest share of the national budget is spent on servicing outstanding debts. For example, in 1997, developing countries paid a combined $292 billion in debt service, while receiving only $269 billion in new loans. (Steger 2003:53–4)

In total, then, according to this 1997 statistic, the countries receiving the loans and paying the debts are losing $23 billion. How can they develop that way? This particular globalization process would seem to lead to underdevelopment.

In *Globalization and its Discontents* (2003), Joseph E. Stiglitz, a winner of the Nobel Prize in economics criticized IMF programs and ideology for reducing or eliminating trade protections on local industry in countries of the South. He contrasts the neoliberal theory of trade liberalization, designed to enhance a country's income by forcing resources from less to more productive uses, with the reality of the situation in many of these countries, where, under IMF programs, those human and capital resources are altogether lost through diminished productivity and job loss:

It is easy to destroy jobs, and this is often the immediate impact of trade liberalization, as inefficient industries close down under pressure from international competition. IMF ideology holds that new, more productive jobs will be created as the old,

inefficient jobs that have been created behind protectionist walls are eliminated. But that is simply not the case. . . . It takes capital and entrepreneurship to create new firms and jobs, and in developing countries there is often a shortage of the latter, due to lack of education, and of the former, due to lack of bank financing. The IMF in many countries has made matters worse, because its austerity programs often also entailed such high interest rates . . . that job and enterprise creation would have been an impossibility even in a good economic environment such as the United States. The necessary capital for growth is simply too costly. (Stiglitz 2003:59–60)

Haiti, often referred to as the poorest nation in the world, provides an excellent but depressing example of how economic globalization can harm a country in the South. Haitian scholar Patrick Bellegarde-Smith discusses this as follows:

High unemployment, low wages, political repression, and high productivity— the very same factors that render the country politically unstable—make Haiti a manufacturer's paradise. Corporations 'can count on a profit margin of at least 30 percent, and sometimes as much as 100 percent, from their Haitian operations'. The low investment rates; the absence of restriction on profit 'repatriation' [returning to the country of investment origin], a primary feature of the Haitian model; and low labor costs make these high profit margins possible. Government policy has led to foreign business opportunism and a domestic lack of opportunity. Haiti has, in a sense, become the 'land of opportunism'. (Bellegarde-Smith 2004:153)

In 2004, a bill with the self-congratulatory name HERO (Haiti Economic Recovery Opportunity) was proposed in the United

A supervisor takes notes behind a woman who sews clothing in a factory of Port au Prince, Haiti. (Photo © Owen Franken/Corbis)

States, designed to expand certain preferential trade treatment for Haiti. While this was hailed by its supporters as being long overdue aid for long suffering Haitians, it just meant, in essence, that foreign-run companies in Haiti would get better trade agreements, with the lion's share of the benefit going to the foreigners, not the Haitians.

Political Globalization

Steger defines **political globalization** as 'the intensification and expansion of political inter-relations across the globe' (Steger 2003:56). These interrelations tend to range across whole groups of countries. They include the United Nations and its affiliated organizations as well as regional coalitions such as the European Community and NATO (the North Atlantic Treaty Organization); they also include NGOs (non-government organizations) such as Amnesty International and Greenpeace.

Among the concerns posed by the spread of political globalization are questions about **democracy**. According to Steger, champions of globalization argue that it furthers the spread of democracy around the world (Steger 2003:110). The validity of this claim depends on how you define democracy. At the foundation of a democracy is a government elected by its citizens. But this is a rather thin definition; merely holding a vote for a leader does not guarantee true democracy. Even in the former USSR people used to vote for the one person on a ballot. And how many people must be allowed to vote in order for there to be a true democracy? A broader definition of democracy might include such features as the following:

- a broad-based electorate in terms of gender, class, ethnicity, and race

In Our View
The New Realities of Slavery and Consumerism

Wipe the sleep of slavery from your eyes.
—Tecumseh

It is estimated that some 27 million people today are currently 'enslaved', even though slavery is illegal in practically every country around the globe. From indentured brickmakers in Pakistan to child prostitutes right here in Canada, they are people who have become enslaved as a result of an expanding global economy. Those who live in violence and servitude, despair and bondage are the people who make it possible for us to fulfill our insatiable appetite to consume. A can of Coke, a pair of Nikes, or the latest fashions at the GAP—so many of our wants and 'needs' are made abundant and affordable through the misery of others.

The chain of events goes something like this: Transnational corporations and their shareholders, always looking to increase profits, together with the national governments of 'overdeveloped' countries, which want to encourage economic growth, rely on increases in the consumption of goods to fulfill their objectives. In order for companies to maximize increases in consumption, their goods must be desirable, readily available, and inexpensive. The mass production of inexpensive goods and services requires the use of cheap labour—the cheaper the labour, the cheaper the good produced—which is gained by exploiting the poor, the desperate, and the vulnerable. Thus, the increased demand for profits demands an increase in cheap labour, which encourages the global practice of slave labour.

It is important to recognize that while cheap labour is a necessary component in maintaining this cycle of greed, so too is the practice of consumption. Though it is less obvious and operates covertly, consumerism itself acts to enslave our minds, bodies, and identities on a daily basis. Reproducing the practices of consumption requires the corporate reformulation of desire, whereby our natural desires are redirected to conform to market commodities. Sexuality, for instance, takes the form of a shampoo, loneliness gets transfigured into dating services, and the freedom of mobility can be found in a new car or cell phone. Advertising is a key element in the decoding and recoding of our desires. The business of advertising works to destabilize our identities, our perceptions, and our ability to reason. We are bombarded with reminders that we aren't skinny enough, pretty enough, smart enough, popular enough, or rich enough, but products *X*, *Y*, and *Z* will magically transform ourselves and our lives. These attacks on our personhood are not only demeaning but create deep insecurities which lead to and reinforce low self-esteem, loneliness, depression, anxiety, and eating disorders, to name just a few symptoms.

One of the pillars of our capitalist society is the belief that consumerism is a democratic practice through which freedom, liberty, and equality are realized. But how much freedom do we have when we are manipulated into buying products we don't need. Where is the liberty for the commuter stuck in rush-hour traffic in a new car. And what do we mean by *equality* if it comes at the expense of someone else's freedom?

The politics of consumerism acts to enslave both producers and consumers. Until we become conscious of our own slave mentality the number of enslaved labourers and consumers will continue to increase and with it, the continued decrease of our own humanity.

—G.L.

- freedom of the press and freedom of speech
- freedom of association and of travel (within and between countries)
- the presence of a viable opposition (and one that does not literally fear for its life)
- a system of education in which people can teach and take courses that can be critical of society's institutions
- protection of the rights of minorities
- relative equality of men and women

Thin democracy might be spreading, but broad democracy really is not.

The American government has a consistent record of supporting the 'stable' governments of democracy-crushing dictators—Ferdinand Marcos in the Philippines (in power 1965–86); Raden Suharto in Indonesia (in power 1965–1998); Nicolae Ceauşescu in Romania (in power 1967–89 and once referred to by American Secretary of State George Shultz as among the 'good communists'); Jean-Claude

Sociology in Action
When Do We Have Democracy?

Around the time of the US-led invasion of Iraq in 2003, there was a joke going around that George W. Bush was trying to bring democracy to Iraq—and if it worked there, he was going to try to bring it to Florida (Florida, where his brother Jeb Bush is governor, was the deciding state in the 2000 presidential election and became the focus of allegations of voter fraud).

This joke raises an interesting question: When do we have democracy? A typical definition of democracy involves some notion of government by citizens—note the Greek root of the word *demos-*, meaning 'the people'. But the ancient Greeks, who coined the term, can hardly be said to have had democracy themselves. After all, women and the large class of slaves were excluded from having a voice.

What are the analytical alternatives to 'democracy' when describing a society? In *A*

Preface to Democratic Theory (1956), American political scientist and sociologist **Robert A. Dahl** (b. 1915) suggested that modern industrial states were governed by **polyarchies,** shifting coalitions of powerful interest groups. But in *Power Elite*, published that same year, C. Wright Mills disagreed, arguing that the power elite, who ran the big companies and had the most significant say in government, was governing, and that its governance was relatively stable. In essence, he claimed that there was an **oligarchy**, rule by a few powerful individuals or groups.

It has been argued by Kirkpatrick Sale (1980) that democracy cannot exist in a population over 10,000, so that we can only have relative degrees of democracy in state-level societies. While the actual number might be somewhat higher, the basic premise seems sound.

What do you think?

1. What features would have to be in place in a society that can be considered relatively 'democratic'?

2. In what ways would you consider Canada 'democratic' and 'undemocratic'?

'Baby Doc' Duvalier, like his father 'President for Life' in Haiti (1971–86); Muhammad Reza Pahlavi, the Shah of Iran (a title inherited from his fellow-dictator father; 1941–79, except for a brief period in 1953 before being returned to power following a CIA-supported coup). Some, such as Saddam Hussain of Iraq and Manuel Noriega of Panama were supported by Washington until they were 'suddenly discovered' to be dictators, upon ceasing to be useful to Washington or opposing policies of the American power elite.

The opposition of the American government to democracy in foreign countries when it countered their neoliberal agenda was never more in evidence than during their involvement in Haiti. The United States 'temporarily' took control of the country in the name of its economic interests between 1915 and 1934 (during which time Hollywood contributed Haiti's poor image in the US by vilifying Voodoo, the island country's main religion). They then had the nerve, as a public relations gesture, to hold a plebiscite to legalize the occupation. Only 5 per cent of eligible voters took part in the poll to rubber-stamp a policy they knew they couldn't change. After supporting dictator after dictator—particularly the Duvaliers, father and son, who ruled Haiti with ruthless but stable government—the US tried to set up another election in 1990 and failed. Haitian sociologist Alex Dupuy captures the political sense of the moment well:

[T]here was the United States, which after the fall of communism, sought to change its ugly image as the defender of dictatorship by promoting an 'ersatz [cheap substitute] of democracy' in the poor countries. In Haiti, the problem for Washington was how to compel its traditional allies—the bourgeoisie and the military establishment—to accept a minimal democracy . . . while at the same time preserving Haiti as a source of cheap labor for the assembly industries and the multinational agribusinesses. The solution lay in electing a candidate who accepted the new game plan and who was supported by the local oligarchies and the United States. Unfortunately, the Haitian masses . . . spoiled it by voting for their own unexpected and unpredictable candidate [37-year-old priest Father Jean-Bertrand Aristide, who won 67.7 per cent of the vote]. (Dupuy 1997:133)

Noam Chomsky's Skeptical Political Globalization Challenge

Noam Chomsky, although not a sociologist, has taken the place of C. Wright Mills as America's foremost public intellectual critic (a more educated and better dressed version of subversive documentary filmmaker Michael Moore of *Fahrenheit 911* fame). He began his career as a linguist and revolutionized his discipline. He now teaches primarily as a philosopher of modern society and writes prolifically. In his recent *Hegemony or Survival: America's Quest for Global Dominance* (2004), he discussed the Bush government's policy of attacking countries in the name of **preventive war** (i.e. attacking another country before that country attacks yours). He claimed that the target of such a preventive war must meet three conditions:

1. It must be virtually defenseless.
2. It must be important enough to be worth the trouble [i.e. by having desirable natural resources such as oil or a strategic military position].
3. There must be a way to portray it as the ultimate evil and an imminent threat to our survival. (Chomsky 2004:14)

What do you think?

To what extent is this an accurate portrayal of the political globalization tactics of the American governments? Potential examples to try this out on include Afghanistan, Haiti, Iraq, Libya, and Nicaragua (see below).

Terrorism: A Slippery Term

No discussion of political globalization would be complete without a discussion of **terrorism**. The fact that the term is used so frequently in the media does not mean that we can easily define it sociologically. Who should be labelled a terrorist and who should not? Can terrorism ever be considered a legitimate form of political protest? Does terrorism act only against globalization?

A rough working definition of terrorism is the intentional use or threat of violence against civilians (people who are not soldiers, political leaders, or police) in order to attain political objectives (freeing 'political' prisoners, establishing an independent nation, destabilizing a political regime, and so on). But it is important that there not just be one way of viewing terrorism. Colonial powers (including the US, Britain, China, and Russia, as well as Canada, Australia, and New Zealand in their relationship to their indigenous people) have the upper hand in defining their position and presenting it to other members of the global community. In a war between equals—either of the two World Wars, for example—each side, although defaming the other, grants its opponent formal equality of status. Colonial powers downgrade the status of their subject populations with names that 'outlaw' them in order to delegitimize their cause. Indian anthropologist Mukulika Banerjee make this important point as follows:

> [V]iolent acts by such groups were categorized by colonial states as revolt, rebellion, insurrection, sedition, terrorism, banditry, brigandage, mutiny, piracy, faction fighting or murder—as anything other than legitimate wars of independence. Classified as domestic troubles requiring police action, the acts of violence by the indigenes were thereby denied any political status. Thus when the Waziris [a people living on the Northwest Frontier of the colony of India]

Venezuelan president Hugo Chavez holds a translation of Noam Chomsky's *Hegemony or Survival* during a press conference at the United Nations Headquarters in New York City, September 2006. What message do you think he was sending to American political leaders? (Photo © Justin Lane/epa/Corbis)

launched a guerrilla campaign against the British in the 1930s they were simultaneously denied the dignity of war's status, being condemned by the authorities as mere insurrectionists and bandits, but given full 'benefit' of modern air raids and bombardment. (Banerjee 2000:102)

In the Canadian 'master narrative' we read of victories by Aboriginal peoples resisting the encroachment of European settlers described as 'massacres', which delegitimizes the victors. And when the Métis, a people that developed a unique culture and sense of identity from their mixed Aboriginal and European roots, opposed the Canadian government's attempts to deny their rights and identity on two occasions (1869–70 and 1885), they had these two moments of resistance branded 'rebellions' (they remain known as the 'Riel Rebellions', named for the Métis leader Louis Riel, who was executed for his efforts).

Who do we think of when we hear the word 'terrorist'? In the Western media, the label 'terrorist' is normally reserved for Middle Eastern Muslim fundamentalists. In fact, terrorism includes people of many religions and locations: the Muslim Chechens in Russia, the Catholic Irish Republican Army in the United Kingdom of Britain and Northern Ireland, and the Hindu Tamil Tigers in Sri Lanka. The Basques, a people who speak a language unrelated to any in the world, and who live on both sides of the Spanish–French border, have within their number an extremist group that wants to separate from Spain; these separatists have been identified as terrorists. If you believe the Chinese government (you shouldn't), Tibetans (Buddhists) are terrorists, and have been since the Chinese took over their country in 1950. To complete the religious ecumenicalism of terrorism, in 1947, the Jewish terrorist group known as Lehi (from Lohamei Herut Israel, Fighters for the Freedom of Israel) assassinated UN peacekeeper Count Folke Bernadette of Sweden because they felt he would favour Arabs in the creation of the Jewish state of Israel.

Government Terrorism

But are we missing any major groups in our list of terrorists? Should we include the CIA, for undermining regimes the American government did not like in Latin America and in the Middle East? A good case study here is the CIA involvement in Chile.

The CIA and Chile in the 1970s

In September 1970, the Chilean people elected Salvator Allende, leader of the Popular Unity party and a Marxist, the country's new president, much to the chagrin of Washington. In response, American President Richard Nixon ordered the CIA to do all it could to prevent Allende's inauguration. National security adviser to the president Henry Kissinger supervised the allocation of US$10 million to oust Allende through such means as attempting to bribe Chilean politicians and funding a coup attempt by military officers.

In 1971, Allende socialized the economy, taking it out of private hands and placing it in government control by nationalizing US-controlled copper mines and other foreign-controlled businesses and industries. He turned management of many factories over to the workers and the state, while raising salaries and stabilizing prices for basic goods.

In 1972, the Chilean economy went into decline, owing in part to some of the government's own mistakes but also to American boycots and their withdrawal of financial assistance and loans (except to the Chilean military). At the same time, the CIA received $7 million dollars to fund Chilean opposition groups, and to exploit the economic weaknesses of the country. Paralyzed by economic problems, external opposition, and internal division, all influenced by the CIA, the government was forced to call another election. However, the election of March 1973 was inconclusive. This development was met with protests and strikes, some of them sparked by CIA-financed unions, others merely a reflection of the country's dissatisfaction with the political stalemate.

In September 1973, with US Navy ships on alert offshore, with 32 US observation and fighter planes landing in Argentina near the Chilean border, and beneath a US-piloted airborne communications control system, US-trained extremists in the Chilean military led by General Augusto Pinochet overthrew the government and assassinated Allende and

In Our View

The Day I Learned that Libyans Were Human Beings: Lessons in Globalization

It was early 1983, and I was teaching English as a Second Language at a private school in Toronto, a job I had held for about a year. So far, most of the students had been Venezuelans. Then a group of Libyan students arrived. I imagine they came to us because they weren't allowed into the US. Libyans were portrayed in the media as the great enemy of the West during the 1980s. 'Libyan' became a kind of shorthand for 'terrorist'. Even the 1985 movie *Back to the Future* featured Libyan terrorists with automatic weapons to play the role of evil gunmen whose motives did not have to be explained. Libyan terrorists; story told. Libyan leader Mu'ammar Gaddafi was the Saddam Hussein of his day (Saddam at that time was seen as harmless, despite his oppression of the Kurds and other Iraqis, and a trusty ally against Iran).

Despite my sociological training, I was suspicious of the new students. Growing up in Toronto in the 1950s and 1960s, I had only encountered a few Arabs: a geography teacher and two schoolmates—a brother and sister—in high school. In my first few classes with the Libyans, I found them quieter than the students I was used to, and I did not know how to read that quiet. I half wondered whether some of them were involved in or somehow connected to terrorism. I was different too. Humour is a teaching tool I fall back on regularly, but I was hesitant to use it. I didn't want to offend.

Our school was right beside a subway stop. One morning, as I began the long climb out of the station, I met one of my Libyan students. We greeted each other politely and walked together with few words. Then we faced the long double escalator, flanked on either side by a set of stairs that is so seldom used it seems reserved for emergencies. He turned to me and said, 'Come on, we are both still young men.' We took the stairs at a run, together. At that moment, our common age and gender (and male pride) were all that mattered. It was a lesson for me.

I grew fond of my Libyan students. They reminded me of conservative Christians I had met: they didn't drink and were very polite. My humour re-entered the classroom ('Is that your father?' I asked when someone showed me a picture of Qaddafi). I learned about the beauty and creativity of Arab poetry, and how it could be chanted (the kind of chanting I had heard before only on TV when Arab 'terrorists' were being portrayed). I missed them when they left.

—J.S.

several cabinet members. Opposition parties were banned, and thousands of Chileans—many of them identified as 'radicals' on CIA lists—were tortured and killed. The US government officially recognized the Pinochet government and restored financial aid to the country.

From 1973 to 1990, Pinochet ruled Chile as dictator. US President Bill Clinton later apologized to the people of Chile for American intervention in the country. In 2000, Pinochet was arrested for crimes against humanity. He died in December 2006.

The CIA and Nicaragua in the 1980s

From the late 1930s to the 1970s, one family held enormous power in Nicaragua: the Somozas. Anastasio Somoza took over political control in 1966, at a time when Nicaragua was globalizing its economy by moving from subsistence farming to agriculture for export. But while aspects of the economy grew, the number of poor Nicaraguans increased. Somoza held onto political power by accepting money from the US for development and for fighting revolutionaries who opposed his dictatorship. His National Guard was an oppressive force that crushed revolutionaries and bullied those who came to the support of the guerrilla fighters of the Sandinista Front for National Liberation. During the early 1970s, Nicaragua was hit by an earthquake, and Somoza siphoned off much of the foreign aid money given to help rebuild Managua, the capital, which had been hardest hit by the earthquake.

Increasing opposition from the Sandinistas brought on further oppression of the people by the National Guard. The situation grew so grave that US President Jimmy Carter in 1978 cut American aid to the country because of human rights violations. The Sandinistas soon came into power, and within a few years, they made socio-economic improvements that the conservative World Bank deemed 'remarkable' (Chomsky 2004:98). In terms of healthcare, Nicaragua witnessed 'one of the most dramatic improvements in child survival in the developing world', according to a UNICEF document.

But the conservative American government took no pleasure in watching a politically independent Nicaragua, whose resources were not flowing freely into the US. In the 1980s,

In the three months following the September 1973 coup, an estimated 200–300 unidentified bodies of Pinochet's opponets were secretly buried in various sections of Santiago's General Cemetery, Patio 29. Thousands of people are still missing. Patio 29, is now a National Monument. (Photo © Ian Salas/EFE/Corbis)

during the White House administrations of Ronald Reagan and George H.W. Bush, Nicaragua was plagued by a CIA-backed terrorist group known as the Contras, many of them former members of Somoza's National Guard, who made a regular practice of terrorizing the people of the countryside. In 1985, the US Congress voted to cut off aid to the Contras, but the CIA continued to fund them through secret arms sales to Iran (then officially an enemy of the US). In 1986, the International Court of Justice at The Hague ruled that the US was guilty of 'unlawful use of force' (Chomsky 2004:99) in Nicaragua. The UN Security Council endorsed the world court's ruling, only to have their resolution vetoed by Washington's UN representatives.

In 1990, knowing that they had American guns literally pointed at their heads, the people of Nicaragua voted to turn the leadership of their country over to a US-endorsed candidate. One-sided economic globalization and wide-scale political corruption ensued. Nicaragua has become the second poorest nation in the Americas.

Episodes like the ones described here have happened both earlier (for example, the overthrow of the Iranian prime minister in favour of the Shah) and since (notably in Guatemala). This kind of involvement in foreign affairs by official government agencies can be called **government terrorism**. What is significant about government terrorism is that, contrary to the usual portrayal of terrorism as a narrow or particularlist (see below) *resistance* to globalism, government terrorism is often used to *promote* globalism (albeit a narrow-visioned imperialist form of it) with one or several countries only at the controls. When political commentator Benjamin Barber famously characterized opposition to globalization as 'Jihad vs McWorld' (in *The Atlantic Monthly* 1992), he meant that globalism (McWorld) was being opposed by a new **tribalism** (promoting the cause of smaller cultures rather than whole countries). Acknowledging that government terrorism is a major force in certain processes of

globalization, we would perhaps do better to characterize opposition to globalization as Jihad vs McJihad, or small tribalism vs big tribalism, both of them fighting against a more equitable globalization.

What do you think?

1. Is it possible for sociologists to define and discuss 'terrorism' in a textbook without showing their political biases?

2. Can terrorism be called 'legitimate' when it is in the name of freeing a people from oppression by the government of their own country or by an outside government (say for Tibetans against Chinese control)?

3. Would it be legitimate to call the political and economic violence of the dictatorial leaders of an undemocratic state a form of terrorism?

Jihad: A Misunderstood Term

A term often connected with terrorism is the Arabic word **jihad**. Movies, blogs, TV news shows and dramas, front-page newspaper headlines, radio phone-in shows, and even dictionaries and encyclopedias all typically lead us to believe that *jihad* means 'holy war'. But is that what it really means? Where should you go to find the meaning? If you look in English copies of the Koran, the Muslim holy book, you will find the Arabic word translated as 'struggle, striving, endeavour'. The following is an example taken from the Koran:

> Those who believe, and emigrate
> And **strive** with might
> And main, in Allah's cause
> With their goods and their persons,
> Have the highest rank
> In the sight of Allah:
> They are the people
> Who will achieve (salvation) (9:20)

There are three types of jihad: personal, community, and martial. In his insightful book *Global Islamic Politics*, Mir Zohair Husain explains these different types in the following way:

The personal jihad or **jihad-i-akbar**, is the greatest jihad. It represents the perpetual struggle required of all Muslims to purge their baser instincts. Greed, racism, hedonism, jealousy, revenge, hypocrisy, lying, cheating, and calumny [false and malicious accusation] must each be driven from the soul by waging jihad-i-akbar, warring against one's lower nature and leading a virtuous life. . . .

Likewise, **ummaic jihad** addresses wrongs within the community of Muslims, whether by the written word or by the spoken word. Ummaic jihad represents the nonviolent struggle for freedom, justice and truth within the dar-al-Islam [Muslim world]. . . .

Marital or violent jihad is referred to in Islam as **jihad-i-asghar** (lit., the smaller, lower, or lesser jihad). Martial jihad ideally represents a struggle against aggressors who are not practicing Muslims. . . . Martial jihad should be used to protect and to promote the integrity of Islam and to defend the umma [community] against hostile unbelievers, whether they are invading armies or un-Islamic internal despots. (Husain 1995:37–8)

Muslim college students asked for examples of jihad in their lives have given answers as varied as the following:

- donating money to a charity rather than spending it on yourself
- studying for an exam rather than watching television
- working hard at a job you don't like because your family needs the money
- avoiding temptation in all forms (similar to the Christian avoidance of the seven deadly sins)

A good example of how the Islamic principles surrounding jihad can be articulated in peaceful means is in the **Khudai Khidmatgar** ('Servants of God') movement of the Northwest Frontier of the Indian subcontinent, now part of Pakistan, from 1930 to 1947 (Banerjee 2000). It was led by Badshah Khan. He was Pathan, a member of a people who live on both sides of the border between Pakistan and Afghanistan border. The movement that Khan led unified a perpetually divided people against the oppression of the British and their locally powerful feudal lord. He did so by leading down the path of non-violent civil disobedience a people not unfairly labelled before as 'warlike' and subject to feuds of revenge. Their non-violent disobedience involved boycotting colonially controlled and corrupt courts, tax offices, schools, and police services, and setting up parallel institutions that served the Pathan people rather than their oppressors. They nearly succeeded in establishing an independent state before larger powers prevailed.

While the movement was developed more or less in tandem with the better known civil disobedience movement of Gandhi, Khan was no mere Pathan 'lieutenant' of Gandhi's. He and his followers built from Islamic principles (plus Pathan custom; see chapter six, Banerjee 2000), just as Gandhi constructed from Hinduism, an ideology of non-violence that created significant change in his land. The two men brought about similar results by similar means, beginning from different religious bases.

What do you think?

1. How do the three types of jihad differ?
2. Why do you think non-martial forms of jihad are not well known outside the Muslim world?

Crusade: A Parallel Term

Just as the term jihad has taken on a distorted meaning for Christians and Jews, the word **cru-**

sade, as it is understood by Muslims, is imbued with connotations of hatred and conflict. During the eleventh, twelfth, and thirteenth centuries, European Christians launched a series of military expeditions in an attempt to claim holy land from Muslims and Jews. These lands were no less sacred to Muslims and Jews, yet the Christians crusaders waged a bloody campaign to capture the territory. Consider the following:

- In 1096, the year after Pope Urban II called for the first Crusade, Crusaders killed French and German Jews on the way to the Holy Land.
- In 1099 Crusaders captured Jerusalem and killed some 40,000 Muslim prisoners in just two days.
- In 1187, the Muslim leader Saladin captured Jerusalem, killed no Christian prisoners, let Jews back into the city, set ransom of prisoners at a low rate, and granted his brother the right to release

1,000 prisoners outright. Saladin afterwards declared, 'Christians everywhere will remember the kindness we have done them'

Why, then, does the mostly Christian West consider holy war a uniquely Muslim campaign? Partly, of course, the fault lies with long-term ignorance, on the part of the West, about the Middle East in general and Islam in particular, something well documented by Edward Said. Part of the blame lies, too, with those extremists within Islam who have (literally) hijacked the term, have narrowed the term from a broader context and rubbed the noses of the West in that meaning.

Cultural Globalization

Steger defines **cultural globalization** as 'the intensification and expansion of cultural flows across the globe' (Steger 2003:69). The concern

What do you think?

1. What kind of definition do you predict you would find if you were to look up 'jihad' in an English dictionary? What about if you were to look up 'holy war'?

2. How free of bias would you expect an American encyclopedia to be in its discussion of the history of Islam?

3. How would you teach about the Crusades if you were an elementary school teacher in a multicultural school?

4. Compare the following pairs of entries from the same dictionaries:

   a) 'crusade . . . any of the expeditions in the 11th, 12th, and 13th centuries undertaken by Christian countries to take the Holy Land from the Muslims . . . a reforming enterprise undertaken with zeal'.
   'jihad . . . a Muslim holy war . . . Crusade' (Woolf 1974:385).

   b) 'crusade . . . a zealous campaign to defend a cause . . . -crusader, n. one engaged in a crusade, esp. (cap) in the "holy wars" of the Middle Ages'.
   'jihad . . . a Mohammedan religious war against unbelievers . . . any war or crusade in support of doctrine' (Morehead and Morehead 1981:292).

5. How would you differentiate between jihad and crusade?

here is with what some have called the 'Americanization' of the world, or with what can more broadly be termed the danger of a one-directional flow of culture. Think of the factors. First of all, English has emerged as by far the most prominent language of science, of the Internet, and of other powerful media. Second, American movies and television are seen in almost every country in the world. But to label this 'American' culture is perhaps giving it too broad a scope, when you consider that it is just a small number of transnational companies—AT&T, AOL/Time Warner, Universal, VIACOM, General Electric, and Walt Disney in the US, as well as the European companies Bertelsmann and Vivendi and SONY in Japan—that control most of the media. Not only do these companies reap enormous dividends by exporting their respective brands of Western culture to consumers across the globe, but as Steger points out, they draw audiences abroad away from the cul-ture of their own countries into a global 'gossip market' that revolves around the 'vacuous details off the private lives of American celebrities like Britney Spears, Jennifer Lopez, Leonardo DiCaprio, and Kobe Bryant' (Steger 2003:77).

During the US-led invasion of Iraq, news reports introduced the term **embedded journalist**, a term that described reporters stationed with American and British troops. Military leaders argued that this was a way of protecting journalists so that they could do their jobs without fear of being kidnapped by Iraqis or shot at by allies. Critics, however, argued that this was another example of a one-directional flow of information, which greatly diminished the independence and neutrality of reporters, who were presenting only what the military allowed them to see. Al-Jazeera, a Qatar-based television station, emerged as an Arab alternative to army-controlled American journalism.

An Indonesian boy sleeps on a piece of cardboard in a Jakarta slum. Global capitalism contributes not only to global poverty but also to cultural imperialism and the loss of cultural identity in favour of a homogeneous culture based on Western icons and values. (AP Photo/Ed Wray)

Another focus of studies of cultural globalization, because it deals with patterns of consumption, is resource use and its effect on the environment. The countries of the North consume much more than those of the South, both overall and on a per capita basis. Agricultural producers in the South, eager to supply the North with its most coveted crops (corn, coffee, and chocolate, for example), abandon their cultivation of less lucrative plants; the resulting decrease in **biodiversity** leaves some crops susceptible to extinction.

Opposing Globalization

Particularist Protectionism

There are fundamentally two kinds of opposition to globalization: **particularist protectionism** and **universalist protectionism**. Particularist protectionist opponents of globalization focus on the economic, political, and cultural problems caused in their home territory by increasing processes of globalization. In Steger's words,

> Fearing the loss of national self-determination and the destruction of their cultures, they pledge to protect their traditional ways of life from those 'foreign elements' they consider responsible for unleashing the forces of globalization. (Steger 2003:114)

This is a mixed group. It includes **Islamists**—people like Osama bin Laden and his Al-Qaeda network, who oppose globalization with narrow-minded and distorted fundamentalist notions of Islam. It also includes European ethnic entrepreneurs, who use the arguments of

Logs lie beside a river in Balikpapan, Indonesia. Illegal logging for the export market has had a devastating effect on Indonesia's rainforests. (© Photo disc)

particularist protectionism as a shield against the attacks of narrow-focused political parties campaigning for 'racial/national purity' (such as Jean-Marie Le Pen's French National Front, which strongly opposes any manifestation of Islam in France, and Gerhard Frey's German People's Union, a neo-Nazi party). The group of particular protectionists even includes Americans who argue that skilled and unskilled tradeworkers are losing their jobs to citizens of the South, and are not benefiting from economic globalization like the power elite are. While they sometimes identify 'big business' as the culprit, it is often easier to blame Japanese-owned firms. Sociologist Roland Robertson, who teaches in the United States, wrote the following for a Japanese publication in 1997:

> I can assure you that the *anti*-global sentiment is very, very strong in the United

Sociology in Action
Observing Cultural Globalization in Taiwan in 1997

As a product, and critic, of Western culture, I am always shocked when, travelling outside of the West, I see signs of Western popular culture.

On a recent trip to Taiwan, I was struck by evidence of cultural globalization all around me, particularly two instances. The first occurred as I was walking on the outskirts of an orange grove in what was, for all intents and purposes, a reserve of the local indigenous people (the Amis, an Austronesian people). In the distance I saw an old woman by herself, picking oranges. She was wearing one of those broad, conical 'coolie' hats made of straw, the kind that is so identifiable as a 'Chinese hat'. It made me feel, as I did more than once on that trip, that I was culturally a long way from home. Yet I felt much closer to home as I neared her and saw that she was wearing a T-shirt emblazoned with the Nike swoosh and the caption 'Just Do It'.

The second time cultural globalization struck me in Taiwan was in the Taipei night market. As I was looking for clothes, in a somewhat distracted way, I turned a corner and was jolted by the sudden appearance of a tall Black man. As my mind and eyes adjusted, I realized first that he looked familiar, second that it was none other than Michael Jordan, decked out in his

Basketball's popularity in China got a boost when the NBA's Houston Rockets drafted Chinese centre Yao Ming. But why are sports such as soccer, cricket, rugby, and lacrosse still not very popular in North America? (Photo by Rocky Widner/NBAE via Getty Images; Copyright 2006 NBAE)

familiar Chicago Bulls outfit. It was merely a life-sized cardboard cutout, used for promotional purposes, but it was a shock nevertheless.

A few days later, talking to a high school class, I asked what their favourite sport was. I was expecting 'baseball', given Taiwan's enviable international record in that sport. I was surprised to hear most of them reply, 'basketball'.

While writing up this narrative, I checked on some statistics (one of a sociologist's favourite activities), and I noticed something interesting, which may be significant. Look at the following statistics:

Taiwan Winners in International Baseball

LITTLE LEAGUE (9–12)	1969, 1971–4, 1977–81, 1986–8, 1990–1, 1995–6
SENIOR LEAGUE (14–16)	1973–80, 1983, 1985–6, 1988–92
BIG LEAGUE (16–18)	1974–8, 1981, 1983–4, 1987–91, 1993–6

1996 was the last year any Taiwanese baseball team won. The seven-year drought of 1997–2004 is the longest in all three leagues. Could Taiwan's baseball program be a victim of 1990s cultural globalization, with basketball being promoted more than baseball?

States of America. It is playing a key part in the current campaign to decide which candidate should run for president from the Republican Party; the phrase 'anti-globalism' is a significant one in American politics; there are numerous movements which are directed in opposition to the teaching of the subject of globalization, to-so-called 'international education'; there have been people protesting at school boards all over America about American children learning about other countries; they fear that if they learn about ancient Greek philosophy or about Japanese religion or French philosophy, that their minds will be destroyed, in other words, that their views will be relativized. (Robertson 1997)

But from a Canadian perspective, a certain amount of particularist protection would seem necessary. Only about 2 per cent of the movies we watch are Canadian, despite the fact that there is a relatively booming movie production business in Toronto and Vancouver. Think of how many times you have seen someone play the part of an American president in a movie. Can you ever remember seeing a movie with someone cast as the Canadian prime minister? Our stories are simply not being told on film, except in Quebec, where French-language films are being produced for the domestic market. Canadian content rules and specially funded programs have helped many of our musicians begin careers in the face of the competition from the loud voices to the south.

Glocalization

A useful, but contested, term to use in looking at resistance to globalization is **glocalization**. According to Roland Robertson (1997), this term first appeared in the 1980s in Japanese business literature, where it was used to describe the way Japanese transnational companies were tailoring their commodities to fit neatly into a local culture (in our view, rather like diseases that disguise themselves so that the immune system doesn't know they're invaders). More recently, the term—or the concept it describes—has come to be viewed more positively as a strategy worth adopting. One advocate of this strategy is Pulitzer Prize-winning American author Thomas Friedman. In his book *The Lexus and the Olive Tree* (2000), Friedman argues that economically weaker nations of the South must develop multiple filters when they receive the flow of cultural, political, and economic commodities from the North. In his words,

> I believe the most important filter is the ability to 'glocalize'. I define healthy glocalization as the ability of a culture, when it encounters other strong cultures, to absorb influences that naturally fit into and can enrich that culture, to resist those things that are truly alien and to compartmentalize those things that, while different, can nevertheless be enjoyed and celebrated as different. The whole purpose of glocalizing is to be able to assimilate aspects of globalization intro your country and culture in a way that adds to your growth and diversity, without overwhelming it. (Friedman 2000:295)

In support of his argument, he offers the example of Jewish scholars in the fourth century BC, who learned about Greek philosophical logic and incorporated it into their thinking. They succeeded in building on Greek scholarship without becoming overwhelmed by Greek culture, and without becoming heavily influenced by Greek polytheism and eroticism.

Modern examples are abundant. When, in the early 1990s, North American DJs of South Asian descent started splicing traditional Punjabi bhangra music in with electronic music, the resulting mix made its way through the urban dance clubs, and bhangra glocalization had arrived. Japanese animé is popular among young people in Canada. If a Canadian version were to develop (we could call it 'Canimé') featuring characters with big eyes and toques, then it could be seen as a glocalization.

Of course, there are different degrees of glocalization. McDonald's India serves dishes like Chicken Maharaja and Chicken McCurry Pan while proudly declaring that they serve no beef and no pork products, since many Hindus (who make up 80 per cent of India's population) will eat neither beef nor pork. But does this really represent resistance to globalization, the people of India accepting McDonald's on their terms? Or does it represent a clever marketing strategy by a multinational corporation that is willing to tailor its product to the market it hopes to dominate? What do *you* think?

Universalist Protectionism

At the outset of this discussion we noted that there are two kinds of opposition to globalization. Particularist protectionists argue that globalization causes political, cultural, and economic problems in their own countries. The second category is **universalist protectionism**. As Steger describes them, universalist protectionists promote a **globalization from below**, which represents the interests of the poor and other marginalized groups while advocating greater social, economic, environmental, political, and cultural equality worldwide (Steger 2003:115). Globalization from below operates in opposition to what Steger calls **globalization from above**, those processes controlled by the power elite of the North. Thus, while particularist protectionists are mostly concerned with how globalization operates in their own countries, universalist protectionists take up the cause of those hurt by globalization worldwide. Amnesty International, Doctors Without Borders, World Wildlife Federation, and similar organizations can be seen as universalist protectionist in this way.

The Anti-Corporate Globalization Movement

It is not just academics and transnational NGOs that have actively opposed globalization. There have also been large citizens' protests directed against meetings of pro-globalization organizations, including the World Trade Organization (WTO), the IMF, the World Bank, the Summit of the Americas, the European Economic Summit, the G8 (referring to the eight most powerful country economies in the world), and the World Economic Forum. Beginning with the 'Battle of Seattle' in 1999, tens of thousands of protestors have staged their opposition to globalization outside of meetings held in the US, Canada, Switzerland, Britain, Sweden, and Italy.

The global social movement behind these protests is generally referred to as the **anti-corporate globalization movement**, a term on which both insiders and social scientists agree. In an insightful article published in 2004, sociologists Frederick Buttel and Kenneth Gould identify some key factors in the social structure of these protests, while plotting the future trajectory of the anti-corporate globalization movement.

First, they note that most of the protests have taken place not in the North but in the global South (in Argentina, Bolivia, Brazil, Ecuador, Indonesia, and Thailand), where they have garnered less international media attention though they have been 'generally more radical and confrontational than their counterparts in the North' (Buttel and Gould 2004:42–3). Second, they point to the influence of NGO supporters and affiliates, which have provided some of the more prominent intellectual leaders, the best known of whom is Canadian social activist and writer Naomi Klein (*No Logo*, 2000, and *Fences and Windows: Dispatches from the Frontlines of the Globalization Debate*, 2002). Third, they remark on the fact that the movement is 'largely and consciously and intentionally acephalous' (Buttel and Gould 2004:44), meaning that is without a single head or leader outside of the local organizers of particular protests. Fourth, they note that young educated people make up the lion's share of the participants of the protests. Finally, they observe that the anti-corporate globalization movement has both benefited from and been hurt by coverage in the mainstream media, which has generated attention for the movement but has largely condemned the protests.

As for what lies ahead for the anti-corporate globalization movement, Buttel and Gould argue point out that since 11 September 2001, protests in the United States have been severely restricted by the curtailment of civil liberties through such newly passed bills as the USA Patriot Act. In addition, the non-governmental organizations that were very much involved in the protests could lose some of the government and corporate funding on which they depend as a result of their role in the protests. Finally, the authors believe that the future success of the movement hinges on preserving a strong link between environmental issues and issues of poverty in the South.

Questions for Critical Review and Discussion

1. Distinguish between the attitudes of hyperglobalizers and skeptical globalizers.

2. Outline what neoliberalism is and discuss the social effects that it has on 'developing nations'.

3. Describe the political difficulties of defining and identifying what democracy is.

4. Describe the political difficulties of defining and identifying what terrorism is.

5. Distinguish between universalist and particularist protectionism.

Suggested Readings

Ashcroft, Bill, Gareth Griffiths, & Helen Tiffin, eds (1995). *The Postcolonial Studies Reader*. London: Routledge.

Bales, Kevin (1999). *Disposable People: New Slavery in the Global Economy*. Berkeley: U of California P.

Brohman, John (1996). *Popular Development: Rethinking the Theory and Practice of Development*. Oxford: Blackwell.

Hardt, Michael, & Antonio Negri (2000). *Empire*. Cambridge: Harvard UP.

Robertson, Roland, & William R. Garrett, eds (1991). *Religion and Global Order: Religion and the Political Order, vol. 4*. New York: Paragon House.

Sassen, Saskia (1998). *Globalization and Its Discontents: Essays on the New Mobility of People and Money*. New York: The New York Press.

Suggested Websites

Global Slavery Resource Centre.
http://www.antislavery.org

Introduction to Anti-Globalization (Definitions and Resources).
http://www.anti-marketing.com/anti-globalization.html

Oxfam (International Development NGO).
http://www.oxfam.org.uk/

Themes in Theories of Colonialism and Postcolonialism.
http://www.postcolonialweb.org/poldiscourse/themes/themes.html

CHAPTER 12

Social Change and the Future

Contents

Key Terms

barbarism
civilization
conservatism
crusade
cultural norms
cycle of civilization
digital divide
headmen
hijab
jihad
Luddites
matrilineal
matrilocal
modernism
narrow vision
savagery
slippery slope
social change
social darwinism
statistical norms
survival of the fittest
ummaic jihad

PART FIVE
GLOBAL PERSPECTIVES

Boxes and Tables

Sociology in Action The Impending Collapse of the American Empire?
In Our View The F-Word and Social Change
In Other Words Irshad Manji on the Gender Challenge for Canadian Muslim Women

Table 12.1 Urban household possession of durable consumer goods (per 100 households)

Learning Objectives

Once you have read this chapter, you should be able to

• outline and contrast five different models of social change.
• discuss the application of the cycle of civilization to the United States.
• outline the social changes to which the Luddites were reacting.
• outline and discuss the applicability of Kroker's idea of the virtual class.
• distinguish between cultural and statistical norms.

For Starters
Raging Against the Machine

The following are the words of an English cropper (an independent producer of woollen cloth) from the county of Yorkshire in 1802, describing the desperate straits of people in his position, and what he wanted to do to the machines that were, in part, the cause of their difficulty:

> The burning of Factorys or setting fire to the property of People we know is not right but Starvation forces Nature to do that which he would not, nor would it reach his Thoughts had he sufficient Employ. We have tried every Effort to live by Pawning our Cloaths and Chattles so we are now on the brink for the last struggle. (Sale 1995:71)

People sharing this view would later be known as Luddites. Compare his attitude with the one expressed in the song lyrics below by the American band Rage Against the Machine, from their self-titled album released in 1992.

Take the Power Back
The present curriculum
I put my fist in 'em
Eurocentric every last one of 'em
See right through the red, white
  and blue disguise
With lecture I puncture the structure of lies
Installed in our minds and attempting
To hold us back
We've got to take it back

Protesters outside the security fence at the Summit of the Americas in Quebec City, April 2001. Can it be reasonably argued that 'Capitalism is Organized Crime'? (CP Photo/Jonathan Hayward)

'Cause holes in our spirit causin' tears
  and fears
One-sided stories for years and years
  and years
I'm inferior?
Who's inferior?

Yeah, we need to check the interior
Of the system that cares about only
  one culture
And that is why
We gotta take the power back

Introduction

What do we mean by **social change**? We mean that a group of people has experienced dramatic change in one part of their lives, and must make adjustments in other areas of their lives in order to adapt. The central fact about society today is that it is changing. Things are not what they used to be, even just a few short years ago. In terms of advancements in personal technology alone we need only to think back a few years to remember 'the first time I ever used' for a number of items: cellphones, iPods, digital cameras, and so on. Some of us can even remember life before touching a computer keyboard.

A cautionary note concerning any discussion of change: it is important to recognize that

Do you think the gentleman in the photo looks as cool as he must have thought he did when this mobile phone was the model of convenience and technological sophistication? (Photo © Photodisc)

as rapid as change is today, with advances in technology in particular enabling us to chart new territory in our social world, it would be wrong to say that earlier society was primarily static, sitting still. Think, for instance, of the Austronesian-speaking people who perhaps as far back as 2,000 years ago travelled from mainland Asia to the far-flung islands of Taiwan, Malaysia, Indonesia, Hawaii, Easter Island, New Zealand, and even Madagascar, hundreds of years before the era of modern travel—all in relatively small outrigger canoes. Think, too, of fourteenth-century China, Africa, and Europe, whose populations, recovering from the devastating effects of the Black Plague, saw their cultures change on a large scale. In Europe, traditional religious views were challenged, and surviving labourers of the plague-ravished workforce, in accordance with the principle of supply and demand, were able to charge more for their work. We can also cite those cultures of South and Central America, Africa, Asia, and Europe that, thousands of years ago, began to practise agriculture, changing the landscape forever. Dramatic social change, certainly a defining feature of our present age, is nevertheless not unique to it.

We can look at social change as affecting three areas of life: the material, the social, and the intellectual. This is clear when we take a look at the changes experienced by the person starting college or university. The student may have to move to another area to be closer to the school, or she may have to travel farther, by a different means of transportation. The cost of just about every aspect of life will go up. Books surround her life. These are all material changes.

In the social sphere, the student will encounter new groups of classmates, leaving behind some or all of the people she grew up with. If the college is located in the city and if the student is coming from a rural background, she may experience different ethnicities for the first time. Some of the students she shares classes with might be significantly older, and her relationships with instructors will be different from those she had with teachers in high school.

The student's intellectual sphere, her world of ideas, will change dramatically as well, and not just with the knowledge and new ideas she is exposed to in class. As just one example, the student learns to think of time in a different way. She may have more free time or spares outside of the classroom, but has to learn to budget that time to deal with a greater workload.

Thus, it's easy to see how one major change—starting college—necessitates changes in all areas of the student's life—material, social, and intellectual.

Five Interpretations of Social Change

Any one instance of social change may be interpreted in a number of different ways. No single model of interpretation is the 'right' one all the time. The five we are considering here have varying degrees of applicability at different times. They are

- *modernism,*
- *conservatism,*
- *postmodernism,*
- *evolution,* and
- *fashion.*

As we present each one, we will point out situations where it is and is not likely to apply. First, though, we offer a disclaimer concerning sociological models based on analogy. It comes from American sociologist Robert A. Nisbet in his classic study *Social Change and History: Aspects of the Western Theory of Development*:

No one has ever seen a civilization die, and it is unimaginable, short of cosmic disaster or thermonuclear holocaust, that anyone ever will. Nor has anyone ever seen a civilization—or culture or institution—in literal process of decay and degeneration, though there is a rich profusion of these words and their synonyms in Western thought from [the Greek writer]

Hesiod to [the early twentieth-century historian] Spengler. Nor, finally, has anyone ever seen—actually, empirically seen, as we see these things in the world of plants and animals—growth and development in civilizations and societies and cultures, with all that is clearly implied by these words: change proceeding gradually, cumulatively, and irreversibly, through a kind of unfolding of internal potentiality, the whole moving toward some end that is presumably contained in the process from the start. We see none of these in culture: death, degeneration, development, birth. (Nisbet 1969:3)

Modernism

Modernism and the discipline of sociology have long been connected. **Modernism** holds that change equals progress, that what is modern or new will automatically be better than the older thing it is replacing. It views society as advancing along some straight line from primitive to more sophisticated, from out-of-date to up-to-date, from worse to better. This change is usually portrayed as a single line, not being very open to different paths of development. Seen in its best light, the modernist view is the view of the future long envisioned by Gene Roddenberry, creator of *Star Trek*. Seen in a more sinister light, it reduces progress to a formula that equates 'new' with 'better' and simultaneously 'more expensive'. Education technology has co-opted the term *advanced learning* without even having to demonstrate that it is in any way more 'advanced' or 'better' than traditional methods of instruction. Teachers using older methods are portrayed as educational dinosaurs, even though they may be more effective educators than their pyrotechnically inclined colleagues.

The German philosopher **Georg Wilhelm Friedrich Hegel** (1770–1831), who strongly influenced Marx and many other early sociological thinkers, adopted a modernist view that history represented a steady progress in the freeing of the spirit, from freedom for the few to freedom for all, and that this reflected a geo-graphical movement, over time, from East (i.e. China and India) to West (from Greece and Rome to Germany):

> The History of the World travels from East to West, for Europe is absolutely the end of History, Asia the beginning. . . . The History of the World is the discipline of the uncontrolled natural will, bringing it into obedience to a Universal principle and conferring subjective freedom. The East knew and the present day knows only that *One* is Free; the Greek and Roman world, that *some* are free; the German World knows that *All* are free. The first political form therefore which we observe in History, is *Despotism*, the second *Democracy* and *Aristocracy*, the third *Monarchy*. (Hegel 1956:103–4)

French thinker, **August Comte** (1798–1857), often identified as the father of sociology, was also a cheerleader for modernism, as we can see in the following quotation:

> The true general spirit of social dynamics [i.e., sociology] then consists of each . . . social [state] as the necessary result of the preceding, and the indispensable mover of the following, according to the axiom of Leibniz,—the present is big [i.e., pregnant] with the future. In this view the object of science is to discover the laws which govern that continuity. (Comte 1853, in Nisbet 1969:159)

Positivism, which characterized Comte's view and dominated much of the early history of sociology, is an aspect of modernism. Positivism, as we defined it in the introductory chapter, involves a belief that the rules, methods, and presumed objectivity of the natural sciences can be applied to the social sciences with no accommodation made for the biases, or subjectivity, or personality of the social scientist.

Along with Charles Darwin's idea of evolution came the idea, often referred to as **social**

darwinism or social evolution, that societies naturally proceed from simple (and inferior) to complex (and superior), and that only the strongest societies triumph. This notion of progress was articulated by **Herbert Spencer** (1820–1903), who coined the expression **survival of the fittest** (in his *Social Statics*, 1851), later borrowed by Darwin—in a solely biological sense—to refer to societies. The idea that society progresses through stages was developed and put forward by anthropologist **Lewis Henry Morgan** (1818–1881), who identified the three stages of **savagery**, **barbarism**, and **civilization**. These, he felt, could be established by looking at seven different aspects of any society: subsistence, government, language, the family, religion, house life, and architecture and property (Morgan 1964:12). In the following passage, from the opening chapter of the aptly named *Ancient Society or Researches in the Lines of Human Progress from Savagery through Barbarism to Civilization*, Morgan sets out his aim of tracing human development through the three stages:

> The latest investigations respecting the early condition of the human race are tending to the conclusion that mankind commenced their career at the bottom of the scale and slowly worked their way up from savagery to civilization through the slow accumulations of experimental knowledge.
>
> As it is undeniable that portions of the human family have existed in a state of savagery, other portions in a state of barbarism, and still other portions in a state of civilization, it seems equally so that these three distinct conditions are connected with each other in a natural as well as necessary sequence of progress. Moreover, that this sequence has been historically true of the entire human family, up to the status attained by each branch respectively, is rendered probably by the conditions under which all progress occurs, and by the known advancement of several branches of the family through two or more of these conditions.

> An attempt will be made in the following pages to bring forward additional evidence of the rudeness of the early condition of mankind, of the gradual evolution of their mental and moral powers through experience, and of their protracted struggle with obstacles while winning their way to civilization. It will be drawn, in part, from the great sequence of inventions and discoveries which stretches along the entire pathway of human progress; but chiefly from domestic institutions, which express the growth of certain ideas and passions. (Morgan 1964:11; originally 1877)

The influence of Morgan's three-tiered view of human development would last well into the twentieth century. Vestiges of it can be seen in Émile Durkheim's *Elementary Forms of Religious Life* and in the writings of influential (but now largely vilified) conservative American sociologist Talcott Parsons, who, in his *Societies: Evolutionary and Comparative Perspectives*, divided societies into the supposedly less judgmental but nevertheless still misleading 'primitive', 'intermediate', and 'modern' (Parsons 1966).

From the nineteenth to the mid-twentieth century, a key aspect of modernism was the belief that science and technology would combine to create a material heaven on earth. Science would become a rational, hard evidence-based religion to supersede the traditional religions built on faith, on unproven and unprovable beliefs. Technology would free people from having to perform hard physical labour on the job and at home, while we humans, freed from tedious labour, would have plenty of leisure time to do with as we pleased. It's easy to smirk at the idealism of the 1950s and early 1960s, but how different is that from the message we hear in TV and radio ads today about how new time-saving technology, will keep us more 'connected' with the world?

Modernist theories of politics incorporate the idea that societies are constantly improving. In this view, societies are believed to be becoming more democratic, while respect for human

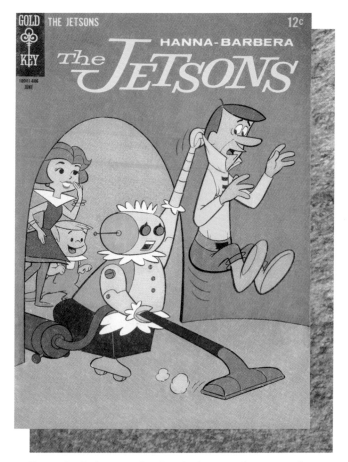

Rosie the Robot gets her hands dirty on the cover of a *Jetsons* comic book from 1963. Do you think the artist expected that by now every home would have its own domestic robot? (Colin Young-Wolff/Photo Edit Inc.)

rights is on the rise and the barriers between societies are falling, all of which will help to eradicate the threat of war. Indeed, this was the premise behind the founding of the United Nations after World War II (and its precursor, the League of Nations, after World War I). A glimpse of the spirit of that post-war feeling comes from the general introduction to a series of philosophical and religious works that was put together by liberal, religious-minded Oxford scholars during the 1950s:

> Read and pondered with a desire to learn, they will help men and women to find 'fulness of life', and peoples to live together in greater understanding and harmony. Today the earth is beautiful, but men are dis-illusioned and afraid. But there may come a day, perhaps not a distant day, when there will be a renaissance of man's spirit: when men will be innocent and happy amid the beauty of the world, or their eyes will be opened to see that egoism and strife are folly, that the universe is fundamentally spiritual, and that men are the sons of God. (The Editors 2002:8)

This view is one that is not likely to be echoed by their peers of the early twenty-first century.

It is easy for the leaders of developing empires to use modernist principles to justify their decision on the grounds that their latest achievement represents the culmination of progress and that whatever is in the best interests of their country is in the best interests of humankind. Noam Chomsky, in a number of best-selling publications, has expressed his concern that his country's presidents and policy makers and their supporters have taken this approach, wrapping American policy in the flag of modernism. In *Hegemony or Survival: America's Quest for Global Dominance*, he describes their modernist thinking of the American power elite:

> [T]here is a guiding principle that 'defines the parameters within which the policy debate occurs,' a consensus so broad as to exclude only 'tattered remains' on the right and left and 'so authoritative as to be virtually immune to challenge'. The principle is '*America as historical vanguard*': 'History has a discernible direction and destination. Uniquely among all the nations of the world, the United States comprehends and manifests history's purpose'. Accordingly, US hegemony is the realization of history's purpose, and what it achieves is for common good, the merest truism, so that empirical evaluation is unnecessary, if not faintly ridiculous. (Chomsky 2004:42–3)

Chomsky here identifies one of the flaws of the modernist model, namely its **narrow vision**, roughly cast as 'Whatever innovation benefits the dominant class is justifiable on the grounds of progress'. Today, we are often skeptical of modernism. Science and technology have enabled us to create problems of pollution that we need to solve more by how we live than by adding more technology. Commercials for SUVs promise personal freedom, yet if we in North America—currently the fasting-growing part of the car market—did not manufacture vehicles with such low fuel efficiency, our demands for oil and the damage to our environment would be less.

Meanwhile, human leisure time is not increasing. People with jobs seem to be working harder than in decades past in spite of labour-saving technology. The office is now a virtual space, as advances in telecommunications make it more difficult for people to leave their work at the end of the day. And in politics, governments with little respect for democracy, human rights, or peace abound in countries that talk of protecting those ideals.

So where might modernism apply? When I've asked this question in the classroom, the response I most often get is medical technology. Certainly medical technology has become more sophisticated, and in this sense it validates a modernist view of progress. At the same time, we must accept that reliance on this technology as an alternative to adopting preventative social practices is not a social improvement. The old saying 'an ounce of prevention is worth a pound of cure' would seem to hold.

Conservatism

Another interpretation of social change is **conservatism**. Conservative thinkers see social change as potentially more destructive than constructive, especially in emotionally charged areas of life such as family, gender roles, sexuality, and the environment.

It would be easy to dismiss conservatism as an 'unrealistic' interpretation of social change held by old-timers or religious fanatics romanticizing the past, by red-necked reactionaries gazing down the gun barrel at anyone attempting to interfere with their rights, or by anti-business, tree-hugging nature 'freaks'. It would, however, be often inaccurate to do so. Some values and customs, like community and 'neighbourliness', need to be preserved. Their loss is neither inevitable, nor desirable.

Conservatism as it relates to social change should not be confused with the political principles of right wing, large-'C' Conservative parties in Canada, Britain, Australia, and New Zealand. An excellent example may be seen in the nationalist sentiment of George Grant (1918–1988), one of the foremost conservative Canadian public intellectuals. Grant taught philosophy at a number of Canadian universities, including McMaster, Dalhousie, and

Queen's, and his *Lament for a Nation* (1965), recently republished on its fortieth anniversary, is widely recognized as a landmark of Canadian writing. His concern, expressed in *Lament* and in *Technology and Empire*, was that the technology, culture, and sense of progress emanating from the US would lead to the destruction of Canada as a place with an alternative vision. A man of deep religious convictions, he he inspired Canadian nationalists from the political left to the political right. Conservative Prime Minister Stephen Harper and NDP leader Jack Layton would both agree with points made by George Grant.

We mentioned in the previous section the modernist belief that science will ultimately replace traditional religion. So far this has not happened. Humans, it would appear, have spiritual needs, however they might be defined, that science cannot completely address. We see in the growing strength of conservative religion in the United States and in the battles that proponents of 'intelligent design' or 'scientific cre-ationism' are mounting against the basic scientific tenet of evolution that the modernist vision of the new religion of science has not overcome the old religions of faith.

One of the ideas closely associated with conservatism is that of the **cycle of civilization**. This is the belief that civilizations rise and fall in a somewhat predictable cycle. It is an old idea, one that was articulated, for example, by Greek historian Polybius (*c.*200–*c.*118 BC) in explaining to his fellow Greeks how the Roman Empire came to have dominance over them while warning the Romans about the potential for their collapse. In his words:

> [T]he destruction of the human race, as tradition tells us, has more than once happened, and as we must believe will often happen again, all arts and crafts perishing at the same time, then in the course of time, when springing from the survivors as from seeds men have again increased in numbers. (in Nisbet 1969:34)

While church attendance continues to decrease across North America, organized religion appears to be in no danger of dying out. (photo © Sophia Fortier)

Influential historian Oswald Spengler in his pessimistically titled *The Decline of the West* (1918–22), took a similar view when he wrote that civilization was passing 'through the age-phases of the individual man. It has its childhood, youth, manhood, and old age' (Nisbet 1969:8).

Adherents of conservatism are sometimes guilty of the logical fallacy known as a **slippery slope** argument. This occurs when they cite one instance of social change—say, gay and lesbian marriage—as evidence of the imminent collapse of the entire social order (including, to keep with this particular example, polygamy and bestiality). It amounts to an overreaction. As adapted to this model, this flaw consists of saying that if there is one small change I disapprove of (say gay and lesbian marriage) then huge negative changes will automatically take place (e.g., polygamy and sex with animals).

Another potential pitfall of the conservative position is a tendency to project backwards an idealized picture of social life from which the modern world is said to have fallen. For instance, people who decry what they consider the rampant sexual promiscuity occurring today speak in idealized terms of a time when couples would not—could not—engage in sex before the formal wedding ceremony. In holding this view, they would be rather misinformed, as British social historian Peter Laslett could attest. In his classic work *The World We Have Lost* (1971), he writes about how it was common in the late sixteenth century for couples to contract marriage (like our engagement) and then immediately live together for months, with full sexual benefits. In his conclusion to a discussion of the county of Leicester Laslett observes that 'Brides in Leiceistershire at this time must normally have gone to their weddings in the early, and sometimes in the late, stages of pregnancy' (Laslett 1971:150). He also points out that in Colyton, in Devon county, 46 per cent of first baptisms between 1538 and 1799 were recorded within the first eight months after the wedding ceremony of the parents (Laslett 1971:148).

Sometimes modernism and conservatism combine in theories that view signs of decline as indications that progress is on the horizon. In Marx's thinking, the worse capitalism got, with the shrinking of the bourgeoisie and the growth of the proletariat to include a falling middle class, the more likely capitalism would altogether collapse, leading to the ultimate social change, the communist revolution. With a similar perspective, albeit from a very different position, conservative Americans who believe in a fundamentalist form of Christianity often look upon environmental, economic, political, and social (i.e. moral) decline in their country as a sign that the world is on the verge of the apocalypse, which will bring the second coming of Jesus. Kirkpatrick Sale cites a survey, commissioned by Time and CNN, that indicates 59 per cent of Americans polled believe the apocalypse is just around the corner.

Case Study in Social Change and Conservatism: The Luddites

From spring 1811 to spring 1813, beginning in the industrializing area of Nottinghamshire—the fabled English territory of Robin Hood—and spreading to Yorkshire and Manchester, a group of independent textile workers took desperate measures into their hands by destroying what would today amount to millions of dollars' worth of property. In the words of American writer Kirkpatrick Sale, author of the book from which much of the following description will come, they were 'rebels against the future'. Part of a number of similar movements occurring about the same time in Britain, France, Germany, and the United States, they made nighttime raids to destroy machinery, sent anonymous threatening letters to known industrialists, stockpiled weapons, and participated in food riots in the marketplace.

They were called **Luddites**, named after a mythical, Robin Hood-like figure, Edward (Ned) Ludd, whose precise origin is not known. They were skilled tradesmen—croppers (finishers of wool cloth), wool combers (not as easy a job as it sounds), handloom wool weavers—who in the

Sociology in Action
The Impending Collapse of the American Empire?

A good example of modern conservatist thinking appears in 'Imperial Entropy: Collapse of the American Empire' (2005), by Kirkpatrick Sale. Sale regards the United States as an empire, and therefore subject to what he believes is the inevitable fate of empires: collapse. He explains:

> [T]hey all fell, and most within a few hundred years. The reasons are not really complex. An empire is a kind of state system that inevitably makes the same mistakes simply by the nature of its imperial structure and inevitably fails because of its size, complexity, territorial reach, stratification, heterogeneity, domination, hierarchy, and inequalities. (Sale 2005)

Sale points to four things that will help to bring about the collapse of the American empire, like all empires in his thinking: environmental degradation, economic meltdown (through excessive resource exploitation), military overstretch, and domestic dissent and upheaval.

What do you think?

1. Do you think that the United States can be considered an empire like the Greek, Roman, Mongol, Ottoman, British, and Soviet regimes were?

2. Do you agree with Sale that the decline or collapse of the United States is inevitable?

late eighteenth century worked out of their homes, often assisted by family members, and made good wages. They had leisure time probably similar to that of most Canadians today, and were part of strongly linked small communities.

But their jobs were becoming obsolete. While there were about 5,000 croppers in Yorkshire in 1812, within a generation there were virtually none. New kinds of machinery owned by the rising class of factory owners combined with new business practices were changing the working world and social world. Even with the earliest generation of machines, one man could do the work of five or six. It is important to note that contrary to the tradition surrounding the old-fashioned machine-hating Luddites, it was the social practices accompanying the machines that were just as much the enemy. A typical workday in the new factories averaged 12 to 14 hours in length, sometimes as many as 16 to 18, and there was at this time no five-day work week. Children as young as four and women were hired in preference to men and made up a great majority of the workforce (80 per cent, according to Sale). Women and children received about a third of a man's wages, and they were thought to be less likely than men to resist the oppression of the owners.

Desperate poverty for millions of people was the not unpredictable result. The life expectancy dropped drastically. In the rough statistics for 1830, it was reckoned that 57 per cent of the people of Manchester died before the age of five. While the life expectancy at birth for people throughout England and Wales was a lofty 40, for labourers in the textile manufacturing cities of Manchester and Leeds, it was reckoned to be about 18 (Sale 1995:48). Apparently the 'gentry' of those towns could expect to live to about 41.

Das Elend in Schlesien.

Hunger und Verzweiflung.

Offizielle Abhülfe.

The Luddites were part of a social movement occurring throughout Europe and parts of North America. This cover of a German pamphlet shows the plight of starving Silesian weavers displaced by cheap machine production, whose 1844 revolt was put down by the Prussian military. (The Granger Collection, New York)

Working conditions were not the only social change the Luddites were rebelling against. They also opposed the manufacturing of need. One of the most profound social changes accompanying the Industrial Revolution was the sudden creation of consumer goods creating a need where people had once been mostly self-sufficient. Food and clothing, for instance, now had to be purchased rather than produced at home. The social change this brought about was neatly summed up by nineteenth-century British writer Thomas Carlyle in *The Gospel of Mammonism* (1843), when he stated that, 'We have profoundly forgotten everywhere that *Cash-payment* is not the sole relation of human beings' (in Sale 1995:39). This trend, described by French historian Fernand Braudel as 'a revolution in demand', did not end at the borders of Britain. It extended to the colonies, particularly India, where millions of consumers were created by the dumping of manufactured cloth from Britain. It was not until the 1930s and 1940s, when Gandhi and the less lauded Muslim Pathan Badshah Khan (leader of the non-violent protest movement the Khudai Khidmatgar) intervened, that the people of India began to boycott British cloth and make their own, as had been their tradition.

A remarkable aspect of the Luddite social movement is its solidarity. Despite the rich rewards paid to those who would inform on their neighbours, despite the torture alleged to have been used on those who were caught, there were very few informers. In all, 24 Luddites were hanged, and about an equal number died in the raids; a similar number were put in prison, while at least 37 were sent to Australia.

And what did they ultimately achieve? There were a few short-term gains. Wages were raised slightly in areas where the Luddites had been the most active. Social reform got on the political agenda, although it would be a long time before changes of any consequence were made. And the 'poor laws', which administered what we might today call social welfare (although it would provide much less than what we are accustomed to now), received more attention and greater funding, although charities continued to carry the greater part of the welfare load.

Perhaps the main accomplishment of the Luddites lies in what they can teach us today about social change and what Sale calls the 'machine question'. We need to realize that machines are not socially neutral, and may be more likely to kill than to create jobs. The Luddites were not old-fashioned 'loonies' refusing to face the inevitability of technological 'progress'. They wanted an alternative future, an alternative modern. That progress can take many forms is perhaps the most important lesson of the Luddite movement.

Postmodernism

Postmodernism as a theory relates largely to voice. It challenges the notion that, for example, sociologists can speak for peoples that they study without letting the people studied have a voice, or speak in some way. Postmodernism challenges the notion that sociologists can, with any authority, talk of 'progress' or 'decline' across all society. Instead, a sociologist with a postmodernist perspective on social change might ask, 'Progress *for which group(s)?*' or 'Decline *for which group(s)?*'. The same sociologist, hearing conservatives complain about how Canadian values are eroding might wonder if what they really mean is that *their* ethnic group with *its* set of values is no longer dominating like it once was?

To take a more concrete example, think of how modernist media usually present computers and computer-related products and services as bringing about benefits to everyone. But how often do you hear or read the opinions of those, even within Canada, who cannot afford a (decent) computer or the education necessary to make use of one? This is creating what has been called a **digital divide**, a socio-economic gap separating those nations and groups within nations that are 'haves' from those that are 'have nots' where up-to-date computer technology and reliable Internet access are concerned. One person known for thinking this is way is futurist Arthur Kroker.

Arthur Kroker and the Virtual Class

Arthur Kroker, a member of the University of Victoria's political science department, is a Canadian 'futurist' who advanced the notion of the **virtual class** in the mid-1990s to articulate

What do you think?

1. Why can it be said that machines or technology are not neutral in terms of social change?

2. Why are the Luddites usually cast merely as people who destroyed machines because they could neither face nor understand 'progress'?

3. What do you consider the most important message of the Luddite movement?

his conservativist position. His innovative writing contains some Marxist discussion of class and a lot of postmodernist play with words (which can make him hard to read). His work is difficult to summarize in an introductory textbook because it depends on a great deal of jargon that would need to be explained in order for any summary to be intelligible. However, we can give you a taste of what Kroker has to say.

The virtual class, according to Kroker (1995:15–16), is a class of visionary capitalists, 'visionless-cynical-business capitalists, and the perhaps visionary, perhaps skill-oriented, perhaps indifferent techno-intelligentsia of cognitive scientists, engineers, computer scientists, video-game developers, and all the other communication specialists, ranged in hierarchies, but all dependent for their economic support on the drive to virtualization'.

We will briefly outline three ways in which this diverse group acts like a class. First, it is responsible, in Kroker's view, for the loss of jobs by those who do not belong to the class. To use a term we introduced in Chapter 11, this group supports the goals of neoliberalism. This is how Kroker accounts for the corporate downsizing that characterized the early 1990s in North America:

> Against economic justice, the virtual class practices a mixture of predatory capitalism and gung-ho technical rationalizations for laying waste to social concerns for employment, with insistent demands for 'restructuring economies', 'public policies of labor adjustment', and 'deficit cutting', all aimed at maximal profitability. (Kroker and Weinstein 1995:5)

Another instance of the virtual class's move for power has to do with its role in the way the the Internet, once democratic and freely accessible, became restricted by the authoritarian 'digital superhighway' ever more controlled by what Kroker calls 'privileged corporate codes'. To use an example familiar to the authors, online access to sociological journals is being more and

more limited to those who possess expensive memberships or those who are affiliated with universities and not community colleges.

The third reason for identifying the virtual class is the way this group, according to Kroker, restricts the freedom of creativity promoting 'the value of pattern-maintenance (of its own choosing)' (Kroker and Weinstein 1995:5). Have you ever noticed how computer-generated monsters, ghosts, and aliens all look remarkably alike? This is an example of pattern-maintenance: the tools of the trade are controlled by but a few companies. Compare that with the situation faced by the Luddites.

What do you think?

1. How does Kroker portray the virtual class as a class in the Marxist sense?

2. Do you think that Kroker leans a little too far towards conspiracy theory in his view?

Evolution

Evolution is perhaps the most misused of all scientific concepts. The biological term does not refer to general progress or improvement of a species. What it really means is adapting well to particular circumstances. Darwin's use of Spencer's phrase 'survival of the fittest' is best interpreted as 'survival of the *best fit*', in other words, the one best suited to the environment. It was not about the biggest, the meanest, the fastest, and so on.

Let's take an example from Jonathan Weiner's *The Beak of the Finch: A Story of Evolution in Our Time* (1995). Weiner explains that guppies swimming in the rivers of Venezuela come in two basic colour patterns. High in the hills, where the rivers are little more than just streams, the guppies are brightly coloured. They compete in terms of sexual selection, with the most colourful having the greatest chance of attracting a mate. The bright colours are the result of the competition. In the waters down in the valleys, the guppies share the environment with predators that feed upon those guppies that are easily seen. Not surprisingly, the guppies here are less brightly coloured. The competition here has more to do with not being seen. Neither colour pattern is a general improvement in the species; each is a better fit in a local environment.

How does this apply to social change? We can look at the history of the family structure in Canada as an example. At different times, the number of children born to parents has varied. In times and places where agriculture is the primary source of income, the number of children is relatively high, since children make good unpaid help to work the land. During the 1950s and early 1960s, the number of children went up, going against the trend of previous decades, because it was a time of prosperity: people could afford to have more children. What is the 'ideal' number of children? It's a number that will change with the circumstances—just like the colours of the Venezuelan guppies.

Fashion

Sometimes a change is just a change—change solely for the sake of change. We seek and discover novelty, and the result is neutral, neither an improvement nor a turn for the worse. It is not for everybody or anybody, and it does not reflect some deeper meaning, or a value shift. In this case, we have the **fashion** model of change. In *A Matter of Taste: How Names, Fashions and Cultures Change* (2000), Montreal-born, American-raised sociologist Stanley

In 1978 the NHL's Vancouver Canucks replaced their conservative blue-and-green sweaters with a new colour scheme meant to look more aggressive and intimidating. The unconventional and widely derided fashion was scrapped in the mid-1980s, and the original jersey, once considered plain and simplistic, is now worn on vintage nights and is popular among fans as well as consumers. How do you think sports merchandisers play to the fan's desire for fashion change? (Harold Snepts photo © Getty Images; Rory Fitzpatrick photo © Andy Clark/Reuters/Corbis)

In Our View
The F-Word and Social Change

I don't remember the first time I heard the 'f-word' used, but I do recall that in the suburban, middle-class junior high school that I went to in the early 1960s, there was one real tough guy, feared by everyone, who seemed to use it in every sentence he spoke. He was eventually expelled for hitting a teacher.

The first movie I heard the f-word uttered in was the 1970 film *Joe*. It was carefully and deliberately used for shock effect by Peter Boyle's character, a working-class guy who stuns his polite upper-middle-class companions by shouting 'F&%$ing right!'.

The one and only time I heard the word spoken in a university classroom was when a very well-spoken classmate of mine used it (with implied quotation marks around it) after the word 'mind', to refer to someone trying to psyche someone out. Her male classmates were dumbstruck.

As far as I can remember, the mores, or customs, surrounding the use of the word as I was growing up in my middle-class neighbourhood were these: I could, as a teenaged boy, use the word (but not too frequently) with my buddies, but never with my parents or teachers (no mat-

© Digital Vision

Lieberson argues that the change in North American baby names falls into the category of fashion. Consumer companies likewise profit from this desire for the new, and it's not just clothing companies, either. Tweaking an automotive design, or the 'look' of a team uniform, or the advertised attributes of a popular brand of beer can help a company make money on people's desire for the new.

Education can involve fashion changes as well. Buzzwords such as 'whole language', 'collaborative learning', and 'advanced learning' are used to promote new styles in education, but they merely reflect people's need to feel they have a fresh approach to an ages-old problem. Education fashions come and go, but real improvement or decline is hard to measure. The culture around education changes and has an impact on the scores that quantify educational 'excellence'. Declining marks in North American literacy scores may reflect educational changes, but they might also reflect an increase in students whose first language is not English, and a decrease in reading as a leisure activity. Increase in literacy may reflect being part of the 'Harry Potter cohort'.

ter how tempted I was on occasion to tell them all to 'f' off). I would not use the word in front of a girl or woman, ever. Generally, use of the f-word in front of a woman was considered a vile offence committed by a man too drunk, too stoned, or too angry to realize what he was doing. Use of the word by a woman would normally illicit shock and disgust.

That was a different time. Now, and in the Toronto college where I teach, use of the word seems to depend on social location. It was in the general concourse that I first started hearing the word regularly, between 10 and 15 years ago, and it is where I still hear it used most often. True it is on the premises of the college, but it isn't really a site of education; it is more of a public place. Recently I've begun to hear the f-word in the halls between classrooms. Five years ago I heard the word spoken for the first time in my classroom. It wasn't spoken in anger, but it was used for effect by someone with a reputation for brash attention-seeking behaviour.

Over the past five years, I've found that the f-word is relatively commonplace in the concourse and still not infrequent in the halls, used with no apparent concern that 'the teacher walking past might hear'. I have heard it in the classroom in general conversation during breaks, and used about as often by women as by men.

—J.S.

What do you think?

1. How have the rules, or mores, surrounding use of the f-word changed, according to the writer of the narrative?

2. What would it take for these mores to change back? Could they?

3. Could this kind of language use be considered a verbal 'fashion statement'?

The narrative in the narrative box on page 330 is a look at a social change that separates generations. When you read it, we want you to consider whether this follows a fashion model or has deeper sociological meaning.

Technology and Social Neutrality

As we can see from the situation of the Luddites, and from the ideas of George Grant and Arthur Kroker, it would be misleading to assume that technology is socially neutral. A change in technology always benefits some, and places others at a disadvantage. The beneficiaries can act like social predators, and the ones who lose out can become social prey. Imagine, for example, that you have been running printing presses for a major newspaper for 30 years and have developed an expertise with your machinery that is highly valued and (hopefully) well rewarded. One day your newspaper changes over to computer-run presses, creating a new company to do that work. Suddenly all of your expertise, knowledge, and seniority mean nothing. Either you are replaced by someone younger who is paid less, or else you accept a lower salary to start over.

Agricultural technology is biased against small farmers. The technology needs of the modern farm (some of which are mandated by governments with a poor sense of the technological bias) put small farm owners out of business. Education technology could pose a similar threat to college and universities instructors. It fosters a class system among instructors, with full-time, tenured professors providing the technological 'show' for large numbers of students, and graduate students and part-time faculty earning less to do the 'dirty work' of marking the massive number of papers generated.

Relative Deprivation, Absolute Deprivation, and Movements for Social Change

Situations like the ones just described tend to create in one group—the disadvantaged group—a feeling of **relative deprivation**, a sense of having less or enjoying fewer benefits than another group. Marshall defines the term in greater detail while introducing the related concept of **reference group**:

> The term relative deprivation refers to deprivations experienced when individuals compare themselves with others: that is, individuals who lack something compare themselves with those who have it, and in so doing feel a sense of deprivation. Consequently, relative deprivation not only involves comparison, it is also usually defined in subjective terms. The concept is linked with that of a comparative reference group—the group with whom the individual or set of individuals compare themselves—the selection of reference group being crucial to the degree of relative deprivation. (Marshall 1998:152)

As Marshall explains, the depth of a group's sense of relative deprivation will always depend on the particular reference group to which it compares itself. If the reference group is seen as comparatively quite well off, the group experiencing relative deprivation may be moved to protest. This is what happened with the Luddites, who watched the rising class of factory owners thrive under conditions that greatly threatened their own livelihoods.

The concept of relative deprivation is useful in looking at people's experience of poverty. As we saw in Chapter 2, on sociological research methods, poverty is difficult to define, in part because many sociologists believe that the subjective experience of 'feeling poor' should be considered a factor. If you are a teenager living in a relatively well-to-do bedroom community on the outskirts of a big city, it is easy for you to feel poor if your parents' income is less than that of many others in your town. Your reference group includes your peers in high school who have greater access to desired goods (for instance snowboarding equipment and associated branded clothing, along with a season's pass to the local slope). With these peers as your reference group, you may well feel relatively deprived, and therefore 'poor' (notwithstanding your parents' defence that 'most children your age don't have such things').

Social Change in China during the 1980s and 1990s

A good application of the theory of relative deprivation is social change in China during the 1980s and 1990s. As Joshua Harman explains, rapid social change led to Chinese workers' awareness of a new reference group, the existence of which sparked feelings of relative deprivation that eventually led to the 1989 Tiananmen Square protests:

> In order to understand how and why Chinese workers reached a state of relative deprivation, one must first examine Deng Xiaoping's rise to political preeminence.

Deng's rise brought with it the promise of a better material life for the general population as well as the potential for economic discord. Both of these aspects of the reform movement were recognized during the 1980s and the 1990s, and both are primary reasons for the Chinese workers' relative deprivation and political unrest.

Deng's reform coalition used a three-pronged approach to shore up its claim to legitimacy. First, it actively sought to increase the people's awareness of their own relative backwardness. Second, the coalition raised demand for new consumer goods and services. Finally, as it sought to raise consumer demand, it also promised to deliver these goods to the people.

Before the 1980s, there were few televisions and few foreign shows available in China. Most programming featured documentaries about the country's supposed economic progress. In 1979, the Chinese government loosened cultural restrictions on programming, and American and British television programs were suddenly let loose on the Chinese airwaves. By 1991, 12 per cent of total air time and more than 25 per cent of air time for entertainment (rather than news) was taken up by foreign shows. At the same time and at about the same pace, television ownership in China was growing. In 1979, there was 1 television set for every 240 people in the cities, and only 1 per 1,000 in rural areas. By 1988, 1 in every 2.6 city dwellers and 1 in every 15.2 rural citizens owned a TV. A new,

A Beijing man parks his bike in front of a billboard advertising televisions and washing machines in 1983. What message is the ad trying to convey to China's new consumer class? Why is the image of the iconic Great Wall used? (Photo © Kelly-Mooney Photography/Corbis)

foreign reference group had been created, with print media helping to promote this new reference group with increased advertising for Western consumer goods.

As workers' pay increased, there was a drastic increase in consumer spending on relatively 'big ticket' items, as can be seen in Table 12.1. But the late 1980s brought layoffs and growing job insecurity. The cost of living went up. On 20 April 1989, the Beijing Workers' Autonomous Union declared:

> The entire population of China now faces an intolerable situation. Long accustomed to bureaucratic-dictatorial forms of control, they now live with uncontrolled inflation and declining living standards. . . . We earnestly demand the following: a wage increase, price stabilization, and a publication of the incomes and possessions of government officials and their families.

In the spring of 1989 in Tiananmen Square, a growing number of protestors appeared, including thousands of college and university students and urban workers. The protest ended with the gunning down of the protestors; as many as 2,600 may have been killed. Despite the clampdown on worker protest, strikes and slowdowns occurred in previously unheard-of numbers throughout the early 1990s. Significant numbers of Chinese citizens now had reference groups that made them feel relatively deprived: their wealthier fellow citizens, themselves in earlier times, and the supposedly typical Westerners they watched on imported TV sitcoms.

Weaknesses in the Relative Deprivation Theory

One weakness in the theory of relative deprivation lies in the issue of how to distinguish, in practice, between absolute deprivation (however that is established) and relative depriva-

Table 12.1 >> Urban household possession of durable consumer goods (per 100 households)

	1981	1989
refrigerators	0.2	36.5
washing machines	6.3	76.2
electric fans	42.6	128.7
tape recorders	13	67.1
cameras	4.3	17.3
bicycles	135.9	184.7
watches	240.9	290.1
sofas	89.3	150
wardrobes	86.1	100

Source: Harman 1998.

tion? Take the earlier example of the teenager in the bedroom community. Say the teenager in question has access only to an outmoded computer with slow, inconsistent Internet access. Having an up-to-date computer and reliable Internet access is important, even essential, for achieving success in high school. Achieving good marks in high school might, in turn, determine whether or not she goes to college or university. Who is then to determine whether the teenager merely *feels* poor because the other kids have better computers or genuinely *is* poor because access to goods and services that enhance educational opportunities is part of determining class status in Canada?

Perhaps a more serious problem with the theory is that it can be used to conduct relatively superficial 'sociology-of-the-moment' that focuses on what is happening now without examining a current situation's roots in the past. In this sense, relative deprivation can trivialize both historical and contemporary grievances. Take the example of the 1990 Oka crisis, discussed in Chapter 5. The conflict surrounded a land rights issue that stretched back to the early 1700s. Causes included nearly 200 years of colonial oppression of the Oka Mohawk by federal and provincial policing agencies, as well as several decades of failing to recognize local Aboriginal political and policing agencies in several communities. To examine the Mohawk protest only through the lens of relative deprivation, as some recent sociology textbooks have done (see Steckley 2003), is to treat the matter in an overly simplistic way.

Understanding Social Change Through Cultural Norms and Statistical Norms

Oftentimes there are differences in a culture between **cultural norms**, which are the generally expected and *stated* rules of behaviour, and the **statistical norms**, which reflect what people actually do, since they are quantifiable and can therefore be measured by sociologists. In a way this pattern reproduces the distinction, noted in Chapter 3, between ideal and real culture. While a cultural norm may show little difference from its corresponding statistical norm, in many cases there are discrepancies. And as we will see from the following example, these discrepancies can sometimes be useful, as a group's discovery of a significant gap between expectation and action might spark social change in the cultural norm.

The Dobe !Kung: Differences in Cultural and Statistical Norms

The Dobe !Kung are a hunting society of the Kalahari Desert in southwestern Africa. As documented by anthropologist Lorna Marshall and corroborated with archaeological evidence from the 1940s found by John Yellen, the Dobe !Kung had observed a cultural norm of sharing—in particular, sharing meat. But in the 1960s, with the coming of a money economy to the people, especially to those working for their agriculturalist or farming neighbours, there was an increase in the production and supply of consumer goods. There was also a growing distance between houses (many enclosed in fences), and accompanying this came a gradual increase in hoarding. But even amid the locked metal trunks crammed full of unshared possessions, the Dobe !Kung continued to claim sharing as a cultural norm: 'Bushmen share things,' John Yellen was told. 'We share things and depend on each other, help each other out. That's what makes us different from the black people [i.e. their Bantu-speaking agriculturist neighbours]' (Yellen 1985 in Hanna and Cockerton 1990:74).

This kind of contradiction can be readily found in most cultures. Canadians raised in neighbourhoods with a reputation for a strong sense of community will often speak fondly of the importance of being close to their neighbours, though they controvert these statements when responding to simple questions such as *How many of your neighbours' homes have you been inside?*, *How many of your neighbours have you had inside your home?*, *How many of your neighbours do you know the phone numbers of?*, and *'Have you ever left your neighbours' phone numbers with your children when you are away from home for a long period of time?* It not that people are hypocrites. It is just that change takes place, driven by a number of factors that are beyond the immediate control of individuals (such as the fast turnover of homes when house prices are high and mortgage rates are low), and it affects behaviour before it does stated values.

Social Changes in Canada: Two Case Studies

Canadians have been and are experiencing social change in many forms. We touched in earlier chapters on the tremendous changes that occurred in the province of Quebec beginning in the 1960s with the Quiet Revolution, but other large-scale changes have been taking place across Canada. Farmers, especially those on the prairies, are finding that the family farm (as opposed to the corporate 'factory farm' and the foreign farm) is becoming more and more difficult to maintain. Cattle producers, who have been particularly hard hit, are still recovering from recent bans on exports to the US because of concerns about the spread of mad-cow disease. At the same time, Alberta is enjoying booming conditions because of the success of the oil industry. Immigration to the province is up sharply, and businesses in all sectors are racing to meet the needs of a consumer base that is growing in wealth and numbers. These are just two manifestations of social change in Canada. The following sections examine two striking, and very different, examples.

Fisheries Change on the Northern Peninsula of Newfoundland

One of the most devastating social changes to hit any part of Canada in recent decades is the loss of the longstanding cod fishery in Newfoundland and Labrador. A recent article by sociologists Lawrence C. Hamilton and Cynthia Duncan and biologist Richard Haedrich describes the ways that change has affected communities along the Northern Peninsula of Newfoundland (2004).

The most fisheries-dependent part of the province, the Northern Peninsula was hardest hit by the closure of cod fishery, which had sustained this area for centuries. The first signs of trouble appeared in the 1970s, when it became apparent that cod stocks were diminishing, owing largely to overfishing by foreign (mostly Russian and Portuguese) vessels and mismanagement of the resource. When, in 1976, the 200-mile economic exclusion zone was declared, reserving waters within 200 nautical miles of the shore for Canadian fishers, many in Newfoundland and Labrador thought that the troubles were over. People who had left the province returned, and the fishing population grew.

Sociologically and technologically, there were two different cod fisheries in Newfoundland: the dragger, or long-liner, fishery and the in-shore fishery. The first involved larger boats, more technology, and longer trips. Traditionally, both profited from the rich fishery, and the fishing community overall was very egalitarian. And in the 'glory years' following the establishment of the 200-mile line, the dragger fleet increased, as did the catch, which reached unprecedented levels. Dragger captains made huge profits, some as much as $350,000-600,000 a year, and even sharemen (often teenage sons of dragger boat owners) could earn $50,000 a year. But the in-shore fishery was suffering. In the words of one interviewed fisher, '"Guys were makin' big bucks and the other guys were just survivin'. Just livin' from day to day, where the other guys were drivin' fancy skidoos and two vehicles'" (Hamilton et al. 2004). The community was more financially divided than ever before.

Eventually, the cod fishery crashed, after a decade-and-a-half of harvesting groundfish, including cod, beyond their sustainable limits. In 1992, the federal government declared a two-year moratorium on the fishery from the Labrador coast to the southeastern tip of Newfoundland, temporarily suspending cod fishing in this part of the province; the following year the closure area was expanded to include the southern shore of the Island. Although it was supposed to be in effect for just two years, the moratorium has yet to be lifted.

In communities on the Northern Peninsula, as elsewhere in Newfoundland and Labrador and in the other Atlantic provinces, it was not just fishers and their families who were hit by the moratorium but others along the chain of the fishing industry. So at a local fish-processing plant in the Northern Peninsula, 400 workers were laid off. Different adaptations were made by the people in the area. For instance, as a general trend the birth rate went down, from one of the highest in Canada to slightly above the national average. Some of the dragger captains were well placed to shift their prey species from fish to invertebrates, such as snow crab, northern shrimp, and the more traditional lobster. Fortunately for them, government money was available to make the transition easier. This new fishery brought revenues comparable to those of the glory days of the cod fishery, but these were distributed across a much smaller segment of the local population. Many, forced out of their livelihood, had to leave the province to look for a new line of work. Others who remained could not afford to become involved in the new fishery, yet they refused to move off the island because they didn't feel they could leave their home. A growing per-

centage of the local income came from government transfer payments in the form of employment insurance and welfare.

Religious Change: Islam as a Canadian Religion

According to the 2001 statistics, Islam is the fastest-growing organized religion in Canada, with the number of Canadian Muslims rising by 128.9 per cent from 1991 to 2001, more than twice the increase for 1981 to 1991. In 2001 the Muslim population of 579,640 made up 2 per cent of the total Canadian population. Most of that population (352,525) was concentrated in Ontario, which over the same ten-year period had grown by 142.2 per cent. It was the sixth largest religion in the country, just a little behind the Baptist and Lutheran churches, and way behind the 'big three'—the Catholic Church, the United Church, and the Anglican Church. But in contrast to these, Islam was the religion with the youngest median age: its followers average just 28.1 years. Muslims come from a broad variety of ethnic backgrounds, including people from Iran, Iraq, Pakistan, India, Afghanistan, Turkey, Somalia, Bosnia, and Indonesia.

What do you think?

1. What were the adaptations made with the loss of the cod fishery?
2. Do you feel that the changes that took place were inevitable?

What do you think?

1. What do you think it would take for Canada to be considered, at least in part, a 'Muslim country?'
2. Do you think that the variety of ethnic backgrounds among Muslims has lead or will lead to the development of 'Canadianized' multicultural mosques?
3. Canadian introductory sociology textbooks often present Muslims, even those living in Canada, as 'them', an other. What are the effects on non-Muslim students of reading this treatment of Muslims?

In Other Words
Irshad Manji on the Gender Challenge for Canadian Muslim Women

Recently the Government of Ontario considered allowing sharia, or Islamic, law to be applied in family law cases involving Muslims. It was strongly opposed by most Muslim women as well as by more liberal Muslim groups. The Canadianization of Islam poses a considerable gender challenge, which the Muslim writer of the excerpt below, Irshad Manji, explains. Born in Uganda in 1972, Manji and her family emigrated to Canada when she was four, during the expulsion of Uganda's South Asian population under Idi Amin. As an activist and a lesbian, Manji has faced considerable opposition from within her Muslim community. In her provocative book *The Trouble with Islam: A Wake-Up Call for Honesty and Change* (2003), which has been a Canadian bestseller since it was published, Manji describes how she discovered, at the madressa, the Muslim school she attended on weekends, that the separation and inequality of the genders found in strict Muslim countries were being reproduced in Canada. That this was a situation that was not be challenged but obeyed without question conflicted with what she was learning about the importance of individuality and equality she was taught in the regular school system. In the following she describes the conflict that led her leaving the madressa:

The trouble began with *Know Your Islam*, the primer that I packed in my madressa bag every week. After reading it, I needed to know more about 'my' Islam. Why must girls observe the essentials, such as praying five times a day, at an earlier age than boys? Because, Mr Khaki [her nickname for her teacher] told me, girls mature sooner. They reach the 'obligatory age' of practice at nine compared to thirteen for boys.

'Then why not reward girls for our maturity by letting us lead prayer?' I asked.
'Girls can't lead prayer.'
'What do you mean?'
'Girls aren't permitted.'
'Why not?'
'Allah says so.'
'What's His reason.'
'Read the Koran.' (Manji 2003:13–4)

She did not find an answer there that satisfied her Western-trained (and somewhat Western biased) mind. Still, she remains a Muslim, and later in the book, she makes the following statement:

Had I grown up in a Muslim country, I'd probably be an atheist in my heart. It's because I live in this corner of the world, where I can think, dispute, and delve further into any topic, that I've learned why I shouldn't give up on Islam just yet. (Manji 2003:228)

While there isn't what could be called a 'Muslim tradition' in Canada, the faith is not entirely new to the country. There were 13 Muslims living in Canada in 1871, according to that year's census. The first mosque in Canada—in all of North America, in fact—was Al Rashid, built in Edmonton in 1938, funded by local Muslims, Arab Christians, and Jews.

Social Change and Sociology in Canada

Like all academic disciplines, sociology must change, and it must do so in a way that involves all four types of change. It needs to improve, to get better, in a modernist sense. But it also needs a touch of conservatism not to stray too far from the early vision that gave it perception; otherwise, it will diminish. It must constantly have postmodern eyes, using fly-like multi-dimensional perception to look at who has benefited and who hasn't from sociology as it has been traditionally practiced and written about. And it must adapt, evolve.

Concerning that last point, sociology in Canada, and probably elsewhere, is facing some serious challenges. One indication of this

was noted by Robert J. Brym in 2003. In an article in *The Canadian Journal of Sociology*, he remarked on the fact that, while the Canadian Sociology and Anthropology Association (CSAA) is the official organization of Anglo-Canadian sociology, it has been losing members, even while the number of faculty members in sociology and anthropology has been growing. Membership peaked at 1,165 in 1993, and within ten years had dropped by 39 per cent. Brym has his explanations for this phenomenon, including (a) external competition from American sociological organizations, (b) internal competition from the *Canadian Journal of Sociology*, (c) a changing organizational environment, and (d) unprofessionalism. Regarding the last point, he points to reform movements that are 'left-leaning' and 'feminist'. Those he names might argue that they left

Canada's growing cosmopolitanism is in evidence here as a Scottish Canadian enjoys Japanese sushi with his South Asian mother-in-law. Are multiculturalism and cosmopolitanism reflected throughout Canadian culture or is there a rural–urban split? How do you think this is changing? (Photo © Teena Aujla)

or never even joined because the organization had become an old boys' club that failed to represent their interests. Whichever way you interpret it, Canadian sociology needs to change. What follows is a personal narrative that suggests one aspect of that change.

Concluding Narrative: Where Does Sociology Go From Here?

We have had narratives throughout this textbook, so it is only fitting that the book ends with this final narrative. At the end of my doctoral dissertation on how Canadian introductory sociology textbooks present information about Aboriginal people, I argued that in order for textbook writers to present the information in a way that is worthy of the best aims and works of the discipline, they must engage in what can be called 'Aboriginal sociology'. We could generalize this approach to a broader category of 'minorities sociology', but here I will speak in terms of the minority I know best.

This Aboriginal sociology, as I envisioned it, must begin by recognizing the inadequacy of traditional methods of sociological knowledge production concerning Aboriginal people. The voices of the people need to be heard. I warned that if the writers of these textbooks continue to ignore Aboriginal voice in their knowledge production, they will continue to be complicit in the colonialist practices of governments. They are not being neutral, objective, or distanced. They are taking a side.

Equally important is the related realization that the non-Aboriginal cultural background of

'Enjoy Colonialism' is a Coast Salish parody displayed at the UBC Museum of Anthropology in Vancouver. What is the artist trying to communicate with this piece of work? (© Sonny Assu; photo by Guy Letts)

the writers of introductory sociology textbooks permits them but a limited perspective, as Dorothy Smith (1990) informs us, that will miss core concepts that are intrinsically important to understanding Aboriginal people from an Aboriginal standpoint. The important place of elders in Aboriginal society is one of these core concepts Elders are involved in all the social institutions of Aboriginal life—education, justice, religion, and politics, for example—and anyone in any way involved in Aboriginal society culture is aware of their significance. But people coming from other cultures that diminish the role of the elderly could easily miss this important point. Indeed, they have missed it. Spirituality is another such core concept, one that tends to be erased in sociology textbooks. The reserve is a spiritual centre, often (one can probably say usually) the location of a number of sacred sites of significance, and yet in sociology textbooks it is only a site for sorry statistics and horror stories.

More generally, the development of an Aboriginal sociology entails the recognition that non-sociologists have authority in talking about Aboriginal life. There are very few Aboriginal sociologists, something that the discipline should note and rectify. For the Aboriginal standpoint to be represented, the knowledge production of Aboriginal journalists, educators, filmmakers, elders, and literary writers should be sought out and respected. All of them have voices that are valued in Aboriginal society. That alone should guarantee their inclusion in introductory sociology textbooks.

In my first year of university, sociology opened my eyes to a world of understanding that changed my perception forever. Every semester I teach introductory sociology, I tell my students that my goal in teaching the course is to change how they think. I quote, with pride, a former sociology student of mine, a Brazilian nun, who said that my course had 'ruined her' by forcing (enabling?) her to question her previous perception of society. I am a believer in the discipline. I would neither teach the subject nor write about it if I weren't. But I strongly believe that it needs to change its textual presentation of Aboriginal people, and its presentation of other groups that do not belong to the dominant culture in ways as radical as how the discipline itself altered my viewpoint. It requires more voices to thrive in Canada in the twenty-first century.

Questions for Critical Review and Discussion

1. Compare and contrast the five different models of social change.

2. Outline the features of the cycle of civilization, and discuss the degree to which it might apply to the United States.

3. Identify who the Luddites were, and outline the social changes to which they were reacting.

4. Outline Arthur Kroker's idea of the virtual class.

5. Distinguish between cultural and statistical norms.

Suggested Readings

Freire, Paulo (1970). *Pedagogy of the Oppressed*. M.B. Ramos, trans. New York: Continuum.

Lummis, C. Douglas (1996). *Radical Democracy*. Ithaca: Cornell UP.

Schumacher, E.F. (1973). *Small Is Beautiful: Economics As If People Mattered*. New York: Harper/Perennial.

Alinsky, Saul D. (1971). *Rules for Radicals: A Pragmatic Primer for Realistic Radicals*. New York: Vintage Books.

Ronfeldt, David, et al. (1998). *The Zapatista Social Netwar in Mexico*. US Army, Rand Arroyo Center.

Merchant, Carolyn ed. (1994). *Ecology*. New Jersey: Humanities Press.

Suggested Websites

Citizenshift (Free Range Media for Social Change).
http://citizen.nfb.ca/onf/info

Green Peace.
http://www.greenpeace.org

Institute for Anarchist Studies.
http://www.anarchist-studies.org/publications/perspectives

Zapatistas Discussion Group.
http://www.zapatistas.org/

Glossary

Aboriginal visions meaningful inspirations, often experienced during a **vision quest** or dream. The individual may hear a song or chant in his or her head, see an animal that might take on a role as spiritual guardian, or in some other way perceive something that enables the individual to better understand his or her life and future.

absolute poverty poverty calculated in absolute material terms. To exist in absolute poverty is to be without sufficient nutritious food, decent and safe shelter, adequate access to education, etc. Compare **relative poverty.**

absolutist holding or having to do with the view that certain things are always right, good, moral, modern, or beautiful. Ethnocentrism is a negative example of an absolutist position.

age group a group composed of people of a particular age (e.g., teenagers, twentysomethings, etc.), considered over time.

agency the capacity to influence what happens in one's life. Compare **victimology.**

agents of socialization groups having a significant impact on one's socialization. Examples include family, **peer group**, community, school, mass media, the legal system, and culture generally.

American Dream the mostly unrealistic dream that any American can become rich if he or she just 'follows a dream' and works hard. A strong belief in the American Dream is sometimes used to justify punishing others for being poor.

anomie (as described by Durkheim) a societal state of breakdown or confusion, or a more personal one based on an individual's lack of connection or contact with society.

anti-colonialism (or **post-colonialism**) (as described by Fanon and Memmi) a theoretical framework that analyzes the destructive impact colonialism has on both the colonizer and the colonized.

anti-corporate globalization movement (as described by Buttelo and Gould) a movement opposing globalization by predominantly young, well-educated protesters in both **the North** and **the South**, supported by non-governmental organizations and affiliates, but having no readily identifiable political or organizational leaders.

archaeology of knowledge (as described by Foucault) the process of 'digging down' to find out how a piece of information or knowledge was constructed, especially as a means of discovering any flaws in the way the knowledge was constructed.

Arctic hysteria (as *pibloktuq*) a **cultural syndrome** that was conjured up by White colonizers of the Arctic to explain behaviour that might better be explained as a product of colonialism.

aristocrats (in Marxist theory) the landowner class of feudal times, who owned the land worked on by the peasants.

assimilation the process in which minorities, indigenous peoples, and immigrants lose their distinctive cultural aspects to become like members of the dominant culture.

authenticity the quality of being true to the traditions of a people. Authenticity is often **contested** by the modern representatives of the people themselves and 'experts' from outside the community.

barbarism (as described by L.H. Morgan in the nineteenth century) the second stage of social evolution on the way to modern civilization. It was identified as one of a series of stages all societies were thought to pass through in their natural development.

bar mitzvah (in the Jewish tradition) a **rite of passage** for a boy becoming a man.

bat mitzvah (in the Jewish tradition) a **rite of passage** for a girl becoming a woman.

behaviourism a school of thought in psychology, which emphasizes that behaviour can be studied and explained scientifically, not in terms of internal mental states (unlike **psychoanalysis**) but through observing how people's actions are supposedly conditioned by earlier actions and reactions.

best practices strategies with a proven history of achieving desired results more effectively or consistently than similar methods used in the past by a particular organization or currently by other organizations in the same industry.

biodiversity   the variety of plant and animal life in the world.

biomedicine   the application of standard principles and practices of Western scientific disciplines, particularly biology, in the diagnosis and treatment of symptoms of illness.

blaming the victim   (as described by W. Ryan) the process of assigning individuals responsibility for harmful events or circumstances that have broader social causes.

bodily stigma   (as described by Goffman) any of various physical deformities.

bopi   (in Mbuti culture) a playground that is almost exclusively the territory of children.

brain drain   the exodus of scientists, doctors, and other skilled professionals from a country.

broad socialization   socialization in which individualism and independence are promoted. Compare **narrow socialization**.

capital   (as described by Marx) the funds and properties necessary for the large-scale manufacture and trade of goods.

capitalists (also called: **bourgeoisie**)   (as described by Marx) the owners of the means of production, or capital, as these were known during the industrial era.

case study approach   a research design that takes as its subject a single case or a few selected examples of a social entity.

castes (also called: **varnas**)   social groups in South Asia that are traditionally born into the unequal possession of specific occupations, dharma (duty in life), rights to foods, colours in clothing, religious practices, and imputed personal qualities.

catharsis   emotional relief through the release of built-up energy or tension.

civilization (as described by L.H. Morgan in the nineteenth century)   the third and final stage of social evolution of all societies, thought by European and North American thinkers as best exemplified by Europe and North America.

class   (as described by Marx) a socioeconomic group defined either relationally—that is, in Marxist terms, with respect to their relationship to the **means of production** (e.g. owner, worker)—or absolutely, in terms of access to socially valued goods such as money, education, and respect (e.g., lower class, middle class, upper class).

class consciousness (as described by Karl Marx)

awareness of what is in the best interests of one's class.

class reductionism   the intellectual fallacy that all forms of oppression are just about class, which downplays the role of factors such as race, ethnicity, gender, and age.

clinical iatrogenesis   (as described by Illich) the ways in which diagnosis and cure cause problems that are equal to or greater than the health problems they are meant to resolve. An example would be catching a virus while in hospital for minor surgery.

cluttered nest   a situation in which adult children continue to live at home with their parents.

cohort   a group of people with a common statistical characteristic. Baby boomers, who were born in the same period, and the frosh of 2007, who entered college or university in the same year, are examples.

colonialism   the policy or practice of acquiring full or partial control over another country, occupying it with settlers, and exploiting it economically or culturally.

commodification   the treatment of something as an object that can be bought or sold. The commodification of medicine involves identifying certain conditions that might be considered normal (though slightly regrettable) as diseases that may be treated with 'commodity cures' (such as drugs or surgical procedures).

companionate roles   conjugal roles in which both husbands and wives work outside the home and do work around the house with their roles overlapping. Compare **complementary roles**.

complementary roles   conjugal roles in which men are the primary earners, doing paid work, while women do the unpaid work of childcare and housework. Compare **companionate roles**.

complex household   a household in which there are two or more adults who are related but not married to each other.

complicit masculinity   forms of masculinity that do not contribute to or embody male hegemony yet still benefit from it.

conservatism   a view of social change as potentially more destructive than constructive, especially in emotionally charged areas of life such as family, gender roles, sexuality, and the environment.

confirmation   (in the Christian tradition) a rite of passage in which a person—usually an adolescent—who has been baptized affirms his or her belief and is admitted as a full member of the Church.

conflict deviance   behaviour that is subject to

debate over whether or not it is deviant. Examples of conflict deviance include marijuana use and 'creative accounting' on tax returns.

conflict theory a sociological perspective involving the view that complex societies are made up of groups in conflict, with one or more groups dominating or oppressing the others.

conjugal roles the distinctive roles of the husband and wife that result from the division of labour within the family.

content analysis a study of a set of cultural artifacts (e.g., children's books, newspaper articles) or events by systematically counting them and interpreting the themes they reflect.

contested describing a practice whose moral goodness or badness, normalcy or deviance, etc., is disputed by some members of society.

corporate (or **organic**) **identity** the shared sense of common membership and common purpose that a social group can have.

corporate crimes (as described by Clinard and Quinney) offences committed by corporate officials for their corporation or the offences of the corporation itself.

countercultures groups that reject selected elements of the dominant culture, such as clothing styles or sexual norms.

counter ideology a set of beliefs that challenges or contests the **dominant ideology** put forward by the dominant culture and the ruling classes.

covert characteristics (**of deviance**) the unstated qualities that might make a particular group a target for sanctions. Compare **overt characteristics**.

critical sociology sociology that challenges both established sociological theories and the research that sociologists do.

crude marriage rate the number of marriages per 1,000 people in a population.

Crusades originally, military expeditions waged between the eleventh and thirteenth centuries by European Christians to claim land seen as holy by Christians, Jews, and Muslims. Today the term is often applied broadly, esp. by militant **Islamists**, to any peacekeeping or military campaign undertaken by Western countries; this use is comparable to the (mis)use, mostly by Westerners, of **jihad** to mean 'holy war'.

cultural globalization (as described by Manfred Steger) the intensification and expansion of the flow of culture across the world in a process that involves media and patterns of consumption.

cultural iatrogenesis (as described by Illich) a situation in which the knowledge and abilities of health professionals have become so mythologized that individuals lose the capacity to heal themselves.

cultural mosaic a metaphor for any society in which individual ethnic groups are able to maintain distinctive identities. Compare **melting pot**.

cultural norms generally expected and stated rules of behaviour. These may the **ideal culture** more than they do the **real culture**.

cultural relativism the view that any aspect of a culture, including its practices and beliefs, is best explained within the context of the culture itself, not by the standard or ways of another culture.

cultural studies a field drawing on both the social sciences (primarily sociology) and the humanities (primarily literature and media studies) to cast academic light upon the significance of and meanings expressed in popular culture.

cultural syndromes disorders supposed to afflict people of only certain ethnicities, often created to psychologize problems brought on by Western colonial control.

culture a system (sometimes **contested**) involving behaviour, beliefs, knowledge, practices, values, and material such as buildings, tools, and sacred items.

culture and personality (as described by R. Benedict) a now discredited school of thought that argued that every culture has a distinct personality that is encouraged by cultural practices and beliefs.

culture industry an industry that produces commodities and services that in some way express a way of life (such as the film and TV industry) or that occupy a special place in the social communications system (such as advertising or the media).

cultures of medicine the recognition that different cultures have different ways of practising medicine, including different **social courses of medicine**, different techniques, and different physical remedies.

cycle of civilization the supposed rise and fall of **civilizations** in somewhat predictable cycle. The term has been applied to the Roman Empire, the Mongol Empire, the Ottoman (Turkish) Empire, and the American Empire.

Dalits (also called: **Untouchables**) the lowest and most discriminated against group in the traditional caste system.

deciles ranked groups each making up 10 per cent of a total population, used for statistical analysis of such things as household income.

delinquent subculture (as described by A. Cohen) the **subordinate culture** of teenage gangs.

democracy a political system that involves a broad-based voting electorate, an opposition that is free to criticize the group in power without fear, freedom of the press and of speech, protection of the rights of minorities, and relative equality of men and women.

desensitization theory the idea that increased exposure to media violence (e.g., from television, movies, and video games) blunts, or desensitizes, natural feelings of revulsion at the sight or thought of violence.

developed nations the wealthier nations of the world, typically including the United States, Canada, the western European countries, and the more financially successful countries in Asia, Africa, and the Americas.

developing nations the poorer nations of the world. This term is **contested** by **skeptical globalizers**, who prefer the term 'underdeveloping nations', which they believe better reflects their status as they become poorer as a result of exploitation by **developed nations**.

dialect a version of a language, usually with a unique set of features (vocabulary, grammar, and pronunciation) and a socially identifiable group of speakers.

digital divide the situation in which citizens of the richer nations, as well as richer citizens of the poorer nations, have an access to computers and related technology that gives them an enormous social, economic, and political advantage over the poorer citizens of the richer nations and most people in the poorer nations.

discourse a conceptual framework with its own internal logic and underlying assumptions. Different disciplines, such as sociology and psychology, have their own discourse.

discourse analysis an approach to analyzing a conversation, a speech, or a written text. More recently the scope of discourse analysis has broadened, with **discourse** now including such things as entire academic disciplines, such as sociology and political philosophy.

discrimination acts by which individuals are differentially rewarded or punished based on their membership in a social group defined by class, sexual orientation, ethnicity, etc.

disjuncture a gap between knowledges produced from two or more different perspectives (e.g., those of management and employees).

dominant culture the culture that through its political and economic power is able to impose its values, language, and ways of behaving and interpreting behaviour on a given society.

dominant ideology a set of beliefs put forward by and in support of the dominant culture and/or ruling classes within a society, which helps to justify their dominant position and dominating practices.

dominants the group within a society that has the most political and social power, whose culture or subculture is seen as 'the' culture of a country.

Dragon Lady (as described by R. Tajima and T. Das Gupta) a stereotype of East Asian women as tough, ruthless, and mercenary. The stereotype is seen in film and TV portrayals of hardened prostitutes and madams, and women who fight with nasty, angry facial expressions.

dramaturgical approach (as described by Goffman) a way of approaching sociological research as if everyday life were taking place on the stage of a theatre.

dual colonialism a situation that occurs when the most oppressed groups (e.g., Rwanda's Hutu) are colonized both by the colonizing outsider group (the Belgians) and by a local group that is given privilege and power by the outsider group (the Tutsi).

dynamic denoting a social situation in which groups are subject to change. Compare **static**.

ego (as described by Freud) the conscious aspect of the individual personality.

embedded journalist a journalist who travels with and is protected by the military, but who is, in turn, authorized or led to express views sympathetic to the military's purposes.

empty nest a situation in which the children of an older couple have grown up and moved out of the family home.

endogamy marrying within one's class, 'race', or ethnic group. Compare **exogamy**.

epiphenomenal denoting a factor of secondary significance to a more significant cause. For Marx, race and ethnicity were epiphenomenal to economic structure.

eros (as described by Freud) the 'sexual' or 'life' instinct within the **id**.

ethnic class (as described by J. Dofny and M. Rioux) a class system that exists when members of different ethnic groups typically adopt occupations that are ranked differently (e.g., administration versus labourers). An ethnic class system has existed in Quebec for most of the twentieth century.

ethnic entrepreneurs individuals who manipulate symbols with strong meaning to their ethnic group in order to gain and wield personal power. Examples include Adolph Hitler and Slobodan Milosevic.

ethnocentrism the belief that one culture (often one's own, occasionally another considered more powerful) is the absolute standard by which other cultures should be judged.

ethnography a research method, shared by sociology and social anthropology, in which communities or groups are studied through extensive fieldwork. Ethnography requires the researcher to participate daily in the lives of the subjects, observing their actions and asking questions.

eugenics the science of improving a population by controlled breeding. The idea was especially popular in the early twentieth century, when people believed that 'good traits' and 'bad traits' were inherited, and that the poor, the colonized, and other marginalized people should be sterilized to prevent them from reproducing.

evolution (as described by Darwin) a model of **social change** in which change is seen as an adaptation to a set of particular circumstances (i.e., 'survival of the best fit').

exogamy marrying outside of one's class, 'race', or ethnic group. Compare **endogamy**.

exoticism the process of making peoples from other cultures seem more exotic or 'strange', more different from one's own culture than they actually are or were.

extended family the family beyond mother, father, and children. Use of this term implies that the **nuclear family** is the model of a 'normal' family.

fact something that has been observed, and that as far as can be proven is believed to be true.

false consciousness (as described by Marx) the belief that something is in the best interests of one's class (e.g., religion, racism) when it is not.

fashion a model of **social change** that promotes change for its own sake, not for better (**modernism**), not for worse (**conservatism**), not even for adaptation (**evolution**). Fashion change may occur because a manufacturer wants consumers to believe a product has been improved (though it hasn't), or it may occur because people desire something different.

fecundity a woman's ability to conceive, which changes with age.

feminist essentialism (or **essentialist feminism**) a feminist approach that involves looking at differences between the way women and men think while arguing for the equality—and sometimes female superiority—in that difference.

feminist liberalism (or **liberal feminism**) a feminist approach that typically involves working towards **pay equity** for women. This form of feminism is criticized as reflecting more the concerns of White middle-class Western women than the women of different ethnicities and classes.

feminist postmodernism (or **postmodernist feminism**) a feminist approach that involves looking at women more as subjects (i.e., people with **voices** and **standpoints** of interpretation) who guide research, rather than as objects being researched.

feminist socialism (or **socialist feminism**) a feminist approach that involves looking at the intersections of oppression between class and gender, focusing mainly on the struggles faced by lower-class women.

feminization the process whereby an occupational sphere becomes dominated by and associated with women (e.g., secretaries, clerical workers). Feminized occupations are usually rewarded with lower salaries and fewer benefits.

First World a term used prior to the collapse of the USSR in the late twentieth century to refer to the world's rich capitalist countries.

folk society (as described by R. Redfield) a rural, small-scale, homogeneous society imbued with a strong sense of the sacred and the personal, usually in contrast to an urban society.

folkways (as described by W. Sumner) **norms** that in the usual course of events one *should* not (rather than *must* not) violate. They are the least respected and most weakly sanctioned norms.

food bank a central clearing house run by a nonprofit organization to collect, store, and distribute food free of charge to the poor.

Frankfurt School a school of social philosophers (including Adorno, Horkheimer, and Marcuse) whose work began in the 1920s and applied the insights of Nietzsche, Marx, and Freud to their critical writing on fascism, communism, and capitalism.

free-floating statistic a statistic created in a particular context of time and place that is repeated outside of that context.

friendly (or **polite** or **smiling**) **racism** (as described by H. Codjoe) a form of racism that is subtle and seemingly (to the perpetrator) friendly in manner.

functionalism a sociological approach that involves explaining social structures in terms of 'what they do for' society (i.e., their functions).

game stage (as described by G.H. Mead) the third stage of intellectual development, in which the child considers simultaneously the perspective of several roles.

geisha a traditional occupation for Japanese women. Geishas are expected to be well trained in the arts and capable of intelligent conversation so that they can entertain well-to-do customers in the geisha house.

genealogy a form of **discourse analysis** that involves tracing the origin and history of modern **discourses** (e.g., the importance of light-coloured skin in South Asian culture). The term is sometimes considered interchangeable with the **archaeology of knowledge**.

gender (as described by A. Oakley) the socially constructed and socially unequal division of masculinity and femininity, as opposed to the biological division. Compare **sex**.

gendered denoting occupations or post-secondary programs dominated by either men or women. Examples include early childhood education and interior design for women, fire fighting and industrial design for men.

gender roles roles that a culture or society assigns as 'normal' for boys/men and girls/women.

general intelligence the largely mistaken idea that people have a single intelligence level that applies to many areas of life, skills, and abilities. Belief in general intelligence would lead one to conclude that a boy who does not earn high marks at school is stupid.

generalized others (as described by G.H. Mead) the attitudes, viewpoints, and general expectations of the society that a child is socialized into.

genocide a set of social practices designed to eliminate or exterminate a people. These practices include warfare, displacement from a homeland, enforced sexual sterilization, separation of family members, and banning languages and other culturally identifiable features; all of these practices were committed against Aboriginal people in Canada.

globalism (as described by M. Steger) an ideology that links globalization with neoliberalism.

globality (as described by M. Steger) a set of social conditions of globalization at a particular time and place.

globalization the worldwide process of making international the realms of communication and commerce.

globalization from above (as described by M. Steger)

processes of globalization that operate in the best interests of **transnational corporations** and the **power elite** of the North, rather than for people generally.

globalization from below (as described by M. Steger) processes of globalization that operate in the interests of global equality and the more marginalized peoples in the world.

glocalization (as described by R. Robertson) the process of tailoring globalization to local needs and tastes. Glocalization is done either by **transnational companies** bent on increasing their globalized sales and influence, or by the local culture filtering the effects of globalization.

government terrorism a form of terrorism in which the government of one country sponsors (through funding, military training, or providing a covert military presence) acts of terrorism to destabilize and change the political regime in another country.

habitus (as described by P. Bourdieu) a set of class-affected or culturally affected and socially acquired characteristics (e.g., opinions, definitions of 'manners' and 'good taste', leisure pursuits).

hallucination an image of something that is not considered to be 'objectively' there (not to be confused with an **Aboriginal vision**).

hegemonic masculinity (as described by R. Connell) practices and beliefs that normalize and naturalize men's dominance and women's subordination.

hegemony (as described by A. Gramsci) a set of relatively non-coercive methods of maintaining power used by the dominant class (e.g., through the various media and the legal system). Often the terms *hegemony* and *hegemonic* are used to refer just to the possession and exercise of power. See **hegemonic masculinity**.

high culture the culture deemed to be sophisticated, civilized, and possessing great taste within a society.

Highland Clearances the eviction by land-owning aristocrats of tenant farmers in the late eighteenth and early nineteenth centuries. The clearances, which were carried out to make room for sheep, helped aristocrats capitalize on the rapidly growing textile industry.

hijab an Arabic word for the veil or headscarf worn by women for religious and cultural reasons.

hyperglobalists people who are uncritical of globalization and dismissive of its negative effects. They champion the process of globalization as good for everyone.

hypothesis a statement that is verifiable/falsifiable (i.e., that can be proven true or false) that proposes a specific relationship between or among variables. An example of a hypothesis: 'Playing violent video games makes a person more violent or anti-social.'

iatrogenesis (as described by Illich) health problems that are supposedly caused by health professionals. See **clinical iatrogenesis**, **cultural iatrogenesis**, **social iatrogenesis**.

id (as described by Freud) the instinctive part of the subconscious. (Remember it by the term **i**nner **d**emons.)

ideology a relatively coherent set of interrelated beliefs about society and the people in it. Examples include **dominant ideology**, **counter ideology**, and **liberal ideology**.

ideology of fag (as described by G. Smith) the use of the negative label of 'gay' or 'lesbian' to make people conform to strictly proscribed gender roles (e.g., saying 'You're so gay' to a man who expresses interest in poetry, interior design, or figure skating).

impression management (as described by Goffman) the ways in which people present themselves publicly in specific roles and social circumstances. Goffman first used it to discuss the differences between how restaurant staff presented themselves to customers how they presented themselves to one another behind the kitchen door.

Indian Princess a portrayal of Aboriginal women as beautiful, submissive to White men, and ready to betray their nation for the love of a White man. Examples include Disney's Pocahontas.

indigeneity the product of the process of refashioning indigenous identities using alternative knowledges to those traditionally produced by outsider experts.

indirect rule a colonial policy in which a European nation uses members of a particular ethnic group as its intermediaries in ruling an area. The policy often leads to **dual colonialism** and **internal colonialism** (e.g., with Aboriginal people in Canada).

Indo-European (1) a language family that includes almost every language spoken in Europe in addition to the languages of Iran, Afghanistan, Pakistan, and India. (2) the prehistoric peoples that swept from a presumed location in the Ukraine to where the languages noted are spoken today.

informant a person knowledgeable in his or her own culture who provides his or her own view of the culture to an outside researcher (either a sociologist or an anthropologist).

insider perspective the viewpoint(s) of those who experience the subject being studied or written about. See **standpoint theory**, **subjective**.

institutional ethnography a form of ethnography that challenges the need for a neutral stance in sociological research, claiming instead that any institution or organization can be seen as having two sides: one representing the **ruling interests** of the organization, one representing the interests of those working for the organization (typically in a non-administrative capacity).

instrumentalism a sociological approach that focuses on situations in which ethnic leaders mobilize groups in order to develop the groups' political and social strength.

intelligences the idea that we have differing intelligence levels in different areas of life.

internal colonialism a situation that occurs when people within a country are colonized or put in a subordinate position (e.g., Aboriginal people in Canada; the Karen in Myanmar).

internalize incorporate the norms and values that one observes.

Inuit (singular: **Inuk**) a people indigenous to Canada, Alaska, Greenland, and Siberia, who have been in Canada for a shorter time (between 5,000 and 10,000 years) than earlier indigenous people. They speak related languages and share various aspects of an Arctic-adapted culture.

inverse care law (as described by J.T. Hart) the view that the availability of good medical care varies inversely with the need for it in the population served.

Islamists people who oppose globalization and Western culture generally with narrow-minded and distorted fundamentalist notions of Islam.

jihad a term generated from an Arabic word meaning 'to struggle, strive'; it has several different interpretations (see **jiha-i-akbar**, **jihad-i-asghar**, and **ummaic jihad**).

jihad-i-akbar the personal **jihad**, which represents the perpetual struggle to purge oneself of baser instincts such as greed, racism, hedonism, jealousy, revenge, hypocrisy, lying, and cheating.

jihad-i-asghar (lit. 'the smaller, lower, or lesser jihad') the struggle against aggressors who are not practising Muslims. **Islamists** practise a distorted version of this.

joint conjugal roles **conjugal roles** in which many tasks, interests, and activities are shared. Compare **segregated conjugal roles**.

Khudai Khidmatgar a Muslim peace movement of the Pathan of Pakistan and Afghanistan between 1930 and 1947.

liberal ideology a set of beliefs that focuses on the individual as an independent player in society, not as a member of a class or an ethnic group. Components of this set include a strong belief in the potential for **social mobility** in the individual (as seen in the **American dream**) and a tendency towards **blaming the victim**.

liberalism (as described by A. Smith) the belief that 'the market' should be completely free to expand and grow without any governmental interference. In the writing of nineteenth-century thinker John Stuart Mill, it referred to a belief in the freedom of the individual from both government and the dominant culture (the 'tyranny of the majority').

longitudinal study a study that continues over time as the subjects get older.

Lotus Blossom Baby (as described by R. Tajima and T. Das Gupta) a stereotype of East Asian women as childlike, sexually available, and respectful of men. Evidence of this stereotype may be found in the China doll and in Western notions of the Japanese **geisha**.

Low Income Cutoffs A measure of poverty derived by calculating the percentage of a family's income spent on food, clothing, and shelter.

Low Income Measure (LIM-IAT) a measure of poverty calculated by identifying those households with total incomes (after taxes) half that of the median income in Canada (with some adjustments made for family size and composition).

Luddites British members of an early anti-industrial movement in Europe, in which craftspeople who had lost their work with the introduction of labour-saving machines resisted by destroying the new machinery. The term is used today to refer to people who resist new technology.

Lumpenproletariat (as described by Marx) the group of people in capitalist society who neither own capital nor participate in wage labour. For the most part they get by with casual/occasional labour, scavenging for food and articles to sell, and crime.

macro-sociology an approach that involves looking at the large-scale structure and dynamics of society as a whole.

marginalized masculinity (as described by R. Connell) those forms of masculinity that, owing to class, race, sexual orientation, and ethnicity, are accorded less respect than other forms of masculinity.

marked term a term with a qualifying or distin-guishing label added to it (e.g., *field hockey* or *lite beer*), showing that it is not the usual form. Compare **unmarked term**.

Market Basket Measurement (MBM) an estimate of the cost of a specific basket of goods and services for a given year, assuming that all items in the basket were entirely provided for out of the spending of the household. Having an income lower than the MBM constitutes low income or poverty.

mass culture the **culture** of the majority, in so far as that culture is produced by big companies and powerful governments.

master narrative a story that a nation or a people constructs about itself. Master narratives typically make members them look heroic while casting other peoples, including minorities within their own countries, as bad or invisible.

matrilineal denoting kinship determined along the mother's line.

matrilocal denoting a situation in which a man and a woman live together in or near the mother's family residence(s).

means of production (as described by Marx) the main social means for producing wealth (e.g., land in feudal times; capital—wealth, machinery—during the industrial period).

medicalization the process by which certain behaviours or conditions are defined as medical problems (rather than, say, social problems), and medical intervention becomes the focus of remedy and social control.

melting pot a metaphor for a country in which immigrants are believed or expected to lose their cultural distinctiveness and assimilate with the dominant society. Compare **cultural mosaic**.

Métis a people of mixed Aboriginal and European ethnicity (usually Cree or Saulteaux and French) that developed in the late eighteenth century and grew to take on a sense of nationality as well as a distinct legal status.

micro-sociology an approach to sociology that focuses not on the grand scale of society but on the plans, motivations, and actions of the individual or a specific group. Compare **macro-sociology**.

minoritized denoting an identifiable social group that is discriminated against by mainstream society or the **dominants**.

misogyny (adj.: **misogynous**) practices or beliefs in a **patriarchal culture** that show contempt for women.

mobility sports sports such as soccer and boxing that provide access to socioeconomic mobility for the poorest groups in society. These sports do not require significant funds or access to resources, but can be played with little or no equipment.

modernism   an optimistic view of **social change** that envisions it as producing a world better than what preceded it.

moral entrepreneur   a group or individual that tries to convince others of the existence of a particular social problem defined by the group or individual.

moral stigma   (as described by Goffman) a perceived **stigma** or flaw in the character of an individual (e.g., a weak will).

mores   (as described by W. Sumner) rules that one 'must not' violate. Some of these are enshrined in the criminal code as laws; violation often results in shock or severe disapproval.

multiculturalism   the set of policies and practices directed towards the respect for cultural differences in a country.

narratives   stories that reflect the lives and views of the tellers.

narrow socialization   socialization in which obedience and conformity to the standards and expectations of the community are emphasized, and punishment for deviation is practiced. Compare **broad socialization**.

narrow vision   (as described by Chomsky) a shortsighted view, held by those who believe in **modernism**, that whatever innovation benefits the dominant class is justifiable on the grounds of progress.

national character   a belief, now discredited, belonging to the **culture and personality** school of thought, that people of different countries have distinct personalities unique to their country (e.g., Italians are passionate, Germans are cold).

negative sanctions   ways of punishing people who 'break the rules' of the cultural norms. Examples of negative sanctions include laughing at or isolating an individual.

neoliberalism (also called: **neoconservatism**)   policies that involve shrinking the public sector (through privatization of public enterprises, tax cuts, the reduction of public spending, and the downsizing of government) and increasing freedom for big business (through deregulation of the economy, control of organized labour, the expansion of international markets, and the removal of controls on global financial flows).

noble savage   the romantic belief that indigenous people, or 'savages', are superior in outlook and lifestyle because they don't live in the industrialized and urbanized environment of the person invoking the image.

non-utilitarian   denoting actions that are not designed to gain financial rewards or desired possessions.

normalized   made to seem 'normal', 'right', and 'good'.

norms   rules or standards of behaviour that are expected of a group, society, or culture.

North, the   the wealthiest nations of the world, previously termed the **First World** or the **developed nations**. It refers to the fact that the majority of rich countries are located in the northern hemisphere.

nuclear family   a family comprising a mother, a father, and children. The term is often used to describe what is often considered a 'normal' family.

objectivity (adj.: **objective**)   a supposed quality of scientific research that is not influenced by emotions, personality, or particular life experiences of the individual scientist. It better applies to the physical sciences—physics, chemistry, biology, etc.—than to the social sciences.

observational learning theory   the theory that children acquire 'aggressive scripts' for solving social problems through watching violence on television.

occupational crimes   (as described by Clinard and Quinney) offences committed by individuals for themselves in the course of their occupations, or by employers against their employees.

occupational segregation   (as described by R. Beaujot) the situation in which women choose (or end up in) occupations that afford them some flexibility and greater tolerance of childcare-related **work interruptions**.

oligarchy   rule of a country by a few powerful individuals or groups.

operational definition   the definition of an abstract quality (e.g., poverty, abuse) in such a way that it can be counted for statistical purposes.

Orientalism   (as described by Said) a **discourse** about the Middle East and the Far East constructed by outsider 'experts' from the West.

Other, the   an exotic, often fearful image conjured up by the dominant culture of a racialized subordinate culture, or by a colonizing nation of the colonized.

oversocialized   (as described by D. Wrong) a misleading conception of humans as passive recipients of socialization.

overt characteristics (of deviance)   actions or qualities taken as explicitly violating the cultural norm. Compare **covert characteristics**.

participant observation   a form of research in sociology and anthropology that entails both observing people as an outsider would and actively participating in the various activities of the studied people's lives. It is usually employed in undertaking an **ethnography**.

particularist protectionism an approach to opposing globalization by focusing on the economic, political, and cultural problems it causes in home country.

patriarchal construct a set of social conditions thought of or structured in a way that favours men and boys over women and girls.

patriarchy a social system in which men hold political, cultural, and social power. Patriarchy is visible in societies where only male political leaders are elected where the media and the arts are dominated by male views.

patrilineal kinship deteremined along the father's line.

pay equity compensation paid to women in traditionally female-dominated industries (e.g., childcare, library science, nursing, and secretarial work) where salaries and benefits have been lower than those given to employees in comparable (in terms of educational qualifications, hours worked, and social value) professions dominated by men.

peasants (in Marxist thinking) the people who in feudal times worked the land but did not own it.

peer group the social group to which one belongs, or to which one wishes to belong, as a more-or-less equal.

peer pressure the social pressure put on an individual to conform to the ways of a particular group that the individual belongs to or wishes to belong to.

petty bourgeoisie (as described by Marx) the sub-class made up of small-time owners with little capital.

play stage (as described by G.H. Mead) the second developmental sequence for child socialization, in which pretending is involved. See **role taking**.

political economy an interdisciplinary approach that involves sociology, political science, economics, law, anthropology, and history. It looks primarily at the relationship between politics and the economics surrounding the production, distribution, and consumption of goods.

political globalization (as described by M. Steger) the intensification and expansion of political connections across the world.

polyarchies (as described by R. Dahl) shifting coalitions of powerful interest groups that govern a country.

positive sanctions ways of rewarding people for following the norms of a society (e.g., inclusion into a desired group, career success).

postmodernism a model of **social change** that recognizes that change can benefit some while harming others (e.g., a **digital divide**).

Potlatch any of various traditional ceremonies of Aboriginal groups of the Northwest Coast. It involves reaffirming traditional values and stories through speaking, acting, dancing, and singing important stories, and reflecting the traditional value of generosity through large-scale giveaway of cherished items.

poverty a state of doing or being without what are considered essentials.

poverty line the arbitrary dividing point, usually based on household income, that separates the poor from the rest of society. It can differ according to the cost of living in the studied environment, and it may differ for urban and rural communities. It will also vary according to the political biases of the person drawing the line

power elite (as described by Mills) the people wielding significant economic and political power.

Powley test a set of questions used to determine whether Métis and other Native people can lawfully hunt without a licence.

prejudice the pre-judging of people based on their membership in a particular social group.

preparatory stage (as described by G.H. Mead) the first developmental sequence of child socialization, which involves pure imitation.

preventive war a military campaign justified on the grounds of preventing an attack on one's own country.

primary socialization the earliest socialization that a child receives.

primordialism (also called: **essentialism**) the view that every ethnic group is made up of a list of readily identifiable traits that have been passed down from the past to the present with little or no change.

professionalization the process of turning work done by volunteers into paid work.

professional sociology sociology that involves research typically designed to generate highly specific information, often with the aim of applying it to a particular problem or intellectual question. Its usual audience is the academic world of sociology departments, academic journals, professional associations, and conferences.

protestant (work) ethic (as described by Weber) a set of values embodied in early Protestantism, believed to have led to the development of modern capitalism.

psychoanalysis (as described by Freud) an approach to psychological study that involves hypothesized stages of development and components of the self (see **id**, **ego**, **superego**, **eros**, and **thanatos**). It is used by sociologists to look at individual relationships to society and at cultural expression.

public sociology (as described by H. Gans) sociology that addresses an audience outside of the academy. It is characterized by a language that can be understood by the college-educated reader, without the dense style of the academic paper or journal, and expressing concern for a breadth of sociological subjects.

qualitative research the close examination of characteristics that cannot be counted or measured.

quantitative research the close examination of social elements that can be counted or measured, and therefore used to generate statistics

queer theory (as described by J. Butler) an approach that rejects the idea that gender identity is connected to some biological essence, proposing instead that gender reflects social performance on a continuum, with 'male' and 'female' at opposite poles.

quintile each of five ranked groups making up 10 per cent of a total population, used for statistical analysis of such things as household income.

racial bigotry the open, conscious expression of racist views by an individual.

racialization a social process in which groups of people are viewed and judged as essentially different in terms of their intellect, morality, values, and innate worth because of differences of physical type or cultural heritage.

racializing deviance the creation of a connection, through various media (television, movies, textbooks), between a racialized group and a form of deviance or crime (e.g., Latinos and drug dealing, Blacks and prostitution).

racial profiling actions undertaken supposedly for reasons of safety, security, or public protection, based on racial stereotypes, rather than on reasonable suspicion.

radical monopoly (as described by Illich) a situation in which professional control work is deemed socially important (e.g., teachers in education; doctors/nurses in healthcare).

reductionist denoting any unrealistic statement or theory that attempts to explain a set of phenomena by referring to a single cause. In sociology, this includes **class reductionism**, or reducing all inequality to gender, race, or ethnicity.

reference group a group perceived by another group to be equal but better off.

registered Indian (formerly: **status Indian**) an Aboriginal person who bears federal government recognition of his or her legal right to the benefits (and penalties) of being 'legally Indian'.

relational denoting the relationship between a class and the means of producing wealth.

relational accountability an approach that balances the social portrayal of a people so that both strengths and weaknesses, problems and successes are seen.

relations of ruling (as described by D. Smith) the dominance of the individual or group by large government and large business. Smith argues that these are reinforced by uncritical sociological analysis.

relative deprivation a situation in which an individual or the members of a group feel deprived compared to a **reference group** that they see as having no greater entitlement to their relatively better situation.

relative poverty a state of poverty based on a comparison with others in the immediate area or country. Compare **absolute poverty**.

replacement rate the number of children born that is considered sufficient to replace the generation before them.

reproduction (as described by P. Bourdieu) the means by which classes, particularly the upper or dominant class, preserve status differences between classes.

residential schools a system of educating Aboriginal children that involved removing them from their homes and communities, isolating them from their culture, and often abusing them physically, emotionally, and sexually. Underfunded by federal government, the schools were run by a number of church groups, primarily the Roman Catholic, Anglican, and Presbyterian churches. The system, which began in the late nineteenth century and was formalized in 1910, ended slowly between the 1960s and the 1980s.

resocialization the process of unlearning old ways and learning new ways upon moving into a significantly different social environment.

reverse ethnocentrism a situation in which individuals set up a culture other than their own as the absolute standard by which to judge their own culture.

rhetoric the study of how people use language to persuade or put together an argument.

risk behaviour behaviour with a relatively high chance of harming an individual. Examples include driving at unsafe speeds, practising unsafe sexual activities, and abusing drugs and alcohol.

rite of passage (as described by Van Gennep) a ceremonial or ritualized passage from one stage of life to another. Examples include Christian **confirmation** and the Aboriginal **vision quest**.

ritual degradation a rite of passage in which the person is stripped of his or her individuality (e.g., hazing).

role taking (as described by G.H. Mead) the stage at which children assume the perspective of **significant others**, imagining what they are thinking as they act the way they do.

ruling interests the interests of the organization, particularly its administration, or the interests of those who are dominant in society

Sapir-Whorf Hypothesis (as described by Sapir and Whorf) the theory that language determines thought. A milder version argues for linguistic relativity, that language and culture have a unique relationship in each society.

savagery (as described by L.H. Morgan) the supposed first stage of social evolution toward modern civilization.

scientific classism the use of flawed, pseudoscientific ideas (e.g., eugenics) to justify discriminatory actions against poor people.

scientific racism the use of flawed, pseudoscientific ideas (e.g., eugenics, measuring brain sizes) to justify discriminatory actions against certain racialized groups.

scrips certificates issued to Métis in the latter part of the nineteenth century, which declared that the bearer could receive payment in land, cash, or goods. The legal status of these certificates was abused by government officials and land speculators.

secondary socialization any socialization that occurs later than the **primary socialization** in the life of a child.

Second World (prior to the collapse of the USSR in the late 1980s) a term used to refer to the Soviet Union and the eastern European countries under its power.

segregated conjugal roles **conjugal roles** in which tasks, interests, and activities are clearly different. Compare **joint conjugal roles**.

semiotics the study of signs and signifying practices.

sex the biological differences between boys/men and girls/women, as opposed to the sociological differences (which come under **gender**).

sick role (as described by T. Parsons) the set of expectations that go along with what a sick person can expect from society.

sign communication made up of a **signifier**, which carries meaning, and a **signified**, the meaning that is carried.

significant others (as described by G.H. Mead) those key individuals—primarily parents, to a lesser degree older siblings and close friends—whom young children imitate and model themselves after.

simple household a household consisting of unmarried, unrelated adults with or without children.

simulacra (as described by J. Baudrillard) cultural images, often in the form of stereotypes, that are produced and reproduced like material goods or commodities by the media and sometimes by academics.

Sixties Scoop the removal, between the 1960s and the early 1980s, of thousands of Aboriginal children from their families, communities, provinces (particularly Manitoba), and sometimes from their home country, to place them in non-Aboriginal homes.

skeptical globalizers those who see globalization as a process that is potentially dangerous to the environment and to the economies and social welfare of the 'have-not' countries.

slippery slope the logical fallacy that one small change will automatically snowball into the collapse of the entire social order. Slippery-slope arguments are often voiced by adherents of **conservatism**.

social change the set of adjustments or adaptations made by a group of people in response to a dramatic change experienced in at least one aspect of their lives.

social constructivism the idea that social identities such as gender, ethnicity, and 'race' do not exist 'naturally' but are constructed by individuals or groups for varying social purposes (e.g., **instrumentalism**).

social course of disease the social interactions that a sick person goes through in the process of being treated.

social darwinism the application, in the late nineteenth and early twentieth centuries, of the principle of **survival of the fittest** to human groups, used to justify the power held by Europeans and the upper classes on the grounds that they were the strongest and the best.

social gospel a movement in the late nineteenth and early twentieth centuries in Canada, the United States, and various European countries to apply the human welfare principles of Christianity to the social, medical, and psychological ills brought on by industrialization and uncontrolled capitalism.

social iatrogenesis (as described by Illich) the deliberate obscuring of political conditions that render society unhealthy.

social inequality the long-term existence of significant differences in access to goods and services among social groups defined by class, ethnicity, etc.

social mobility the movement from one class into another (usually higher) class.

sociolinguistics (as described by W. Labov) the study of language (particularly **dialect**) as a social marker of status or general distinctiveness, or the study of how different languages conceptualize the world (e.g., the **Sapir-Whorf Hypothesis**).

sociological imagination (as described by Mills) the capacity to shift from the perspective of the personal experience to the grander, societal scale that has caused or influenced that personal experience.

sociological poetry (as described by Mills) the writing of sociology in such a way that it is beautifully crafted and readily understood. See **public sociology**.

sociology the social science that studies the development, structure, and functioning of human society.

South, the the poorer nations of the world, previously termed **Third World** and the **developing nations**.

spurious reasoning the perception of a correlation between two factors, which are wrongly seen as cause and effect.

squaw a stereotype of the Aboriginal woman as lazy, drunken, and abused by Aboriginal men. Compare **Indian Princess**.

standpoint theory (as described by D. Smith) the view that knowledge is developed from a particular lived position, or 'standpoint', and that **objectivity** is thus impossible.

staples (as described by Innis) natural resources such as fish, fur, minerals, and crops, upon which countries such as Canada built their economy.

statistical norms **norms** that reflect, statistically, what people actually do, in distinction from **cultural norms**, which are what people say that they do.

statistics a science that, in sociology, involves the use of numbers to map social behaviour and beliefs.

status frustration (as described by A. Cohen) a feeling of failure to succeed in middle-class terms or institutions, leading to participation in **delinquent subculture**.

stigma (as described by Goffman) a human attribute that is seen to discredit an individual's social identity. See **bodily stigma**, **moral stigma**, **tribal stigma**.

strata social classes in ranked layers, with no specific relationship to the means of producing wealth.

subcultures groups organized around occupations or hobbies, engaged in no significant opposition to the dominant culture.

subjective denoting theories, beliefs, and opinions influenced by emotions, personality, and particular life experiences of the individual science. The term is used in opposing ways: some sociologists discredit observation as 'merely subjective', as opposed to 'objective fact'; others argue that all 'facts' are to some degree subjective but hide behind the mask of objectivity.

subordinate cultures groups who feel the power of the dominant culture and exist in opposition to it.

subordinate masculinity (as described by R. Connell) behaviours and presentations of self that can threaten the legitimacy of hegemonic masculinity. The usual examples given are gay or effeminate men, and those whose lives and beliefs challenge traditional definitions of male success.

superego (as described by Freud) the conscience or moral sense.

survival of the fittest (as described by Spencer) the principle, wrongly attributed to Darwin, that only the biggest and strongest survive, both in nature and in human society.

swaddling hypothesis (as described by J. Richman and G. Gorer) a hypothesis that attributed presumed 'moody' Russian behaviour to their being tightly swaddled or wrapped up as infants.

symbol an aspect of a culture that has many strings of meaning that are unique to that culture. Examples include the flag for Americans, hockey for Canadians, songs of the early fourteenth century for Scots.

systemic (or institutional) racism racist practices, rules, and laws that have become 'part of the system', or institutionalized. People who benefit from this type of racism tend to be blind to its existence.

taboo a **norm** so deeply ingrained that the mere thought or mention of it is enough to arouse disgust or revulsion (e.g., incest).

tabula rasa the idea that every human is born as a 'blank slate' upon which the culture writes or inscribes a personality, values, and/or a set of abilities.

terrorism the intentional use or threat of violence against civilians in order to attain political objectives (e.g., freeing 'political' prisoners, establishing an independent country, destabilizing a political regime in another country in order to produce a regime change).

thanatos (as described by Freud) the violent 'death instinct' within the id.

theory an attempt to explain what has been observed.

third variable a variable that causes two more variables to correlate.

Third World a twentieth-century term used to refer to the poorer nations of the world. Compare **First World**, **Second World**.

total fertility rate an estimate of the average number of children that a woman between the ages of 15 and 49 will have in her lifetime if current age-specific fertility rates remain constant during her reproductive years.

total institutions (as described by Goffman) institutions such as the military, hospitals, and asylums that regulate all aspects of an individual's life.

totalitarian discourse any **discourse** that makes a universal claim about how all knowledge and understanding can be achieved.

transnational corporations companies that are typically based in the North (particularly the United States, Japan, and Germany) but that have branches all over the world.

triangulation the use of at least three narratives, theoretical perspectives, or investigators to examine the same phenomenon.

tribal stigma (as described by Goffman) stigma that relate to being of a particular lineage or family that has been stigmatized (e.g., the family of a murderer or gang member).

tribalism a movement to promote the cause of a small nation that is usually not represented as having a country of its own.

trickle down the misleading social theory that if the rich are free to earn as much money as they can, the benefits will 'trickle down' to the poorer elements in society.

ummaic jihad the non-violent struggle for freedom, justice, and truth within the Muslim community.

universalist protectionism (as described by M. Steger) policies designed to promote **globalization from below** by representing the interests of the poor and other marginalized groups while advocating greater social, economic, environmental, political, and cultural equality worldwide.

unmarked term a term without any distinguishing term added; the usual form, as opposed to a **marked term**.

urban reserve a parcel of land within an urban area reserved for Aboriginal-run businesses and services.

values those features held up by a culture (though often **contested**) as good, right, desirable, and admirable.

vertical mosaic (as described by J. Porter) a metaphor used to describe a society or nation in which there is a hierarchy of higher and lower ethnic groups.

victimology either (1) the study of people who are victims of crime, or (2) an outlook that undervalues the victims of crime by portraying them as people who cannot help themselves, who cannot exercise **agency**.

virtual class (as described by A. Kroker) a **class** of people who are dependent for their jobs and general economic support on the virtualization industry.

vision quest (in traditional North American Aboriginal culture) the **rite of passage** in which an adolescent leaves the community for a brief period and goes without eating or sleeping in order to have a vision (see **Aboriginal vision**) that would teach him or her such things as what guardian spirit he or she may have and what songs he or she would have as personal songs.

voice the expression of *a* (not *the*) viewpoint that comes from occupying a particular social location (e.g., gender, 'race', ethnicity, sexual orientation, age, and class).

white collar crime (as described by E. Sutherland) crime committed by a person of the middle or upper middle class in the course of his or her occupation.

workers (also called: **proletariat**) (as described by Marx) the people who work for wages and do not own capital, the means of production, in an industrial, capitalist society.

work interruptions (as described by J. Baudrillard) time taken off work, especially by a woman, to care for an infant (i.e., during maternity or paternity leave) or a child who is sick.

xenocentrism a preference for foreign goods and tastes based on the belief that anything foreign must be better than the same thing produced domestically.

XYY males men and boys who differ from the 'normal' XY chromosome pattern. They are associated with above-average height, a tendency to have acne, and somewhat more impulsive and antisocial behaviour and slightly lower intelligence than 'normal' men and boys.

References

Abdo, Nahla, ed. (1996). *Sociological Thought: Beyond Eurocentric Theory*. Toronto: Canadian Scholars' Press.

Abu-Laban, Yasmeen (1986). 'The Vertical Mosaic in Later Life: Ethnicity and Retirement in Canada'. *The Journal of Gerontology* 41 (5), pp. 662–71.

Adachi, Ken (1976). *The Enemy That Never Was: A History of Japanese Canadians*. Toronto: McClelland & Stewart.

Adams, Howard (1975). *Prison of Grass: Canada From the Native Point of View*. Toronto: New Press.

Adams, Michael (2003). *Fire and Ice: The United States and the Myth of Converging Values*. Toronto: Penguin Canada.

Aguiar, Luis, Patricia Tomic, & Ricardo Trumper (2001). '"Whiteness" in White Academia'. In Carl James & Adrienne Shadd, eds, *Talking About Identity: Encounters in Race, Ethnicity and Language*, 2nd edn, pp. 177–92. Toronto: Between the Lines.

Allen, Richard (1971). *The Social Passion: Religion and Social Reform in Canada 1914–28*. Toronto: U of Toronto P.

Ames, Herbert Brown (1972 [1897]). *The City Below the Hill*. Toronto: U of Toronto P.

Anderson, Karen (1996). *Sociology: A Critical Introduction*. Toronto: Nelson.

Armstrong, Karen (2005 [1981]). *Through the Narrow Gate: A Memoir of Life in and Out of the Convent*. Toronto: Vintage Canada.

Arnett, Jeffrey (1995). 'Broad and Narrow Socialization: The Family in the Context of a Cultural Theory'. *Journal of Marriage and the Family* 57 (3), pp. 617–28.

Arnett, Jeffrey, & Lene Balle-Jensen (1993). 'Cultural Bases of Risk Behavior: Danish Adolescents'. *Child Development* 64, pp. 1842–55.

Aujla, Angela (1998). 'The Colour Bar of Beauty'. *The Peak* 1 (99), pp. 1–5.

Backhouse, Constance (1999). *Colour-Coded: A Legal History of Racism in Canada, 1900–1950*. Toronto: U of Toronto P.

Banerjee, Mukulika (2000). *The Pathan Unarmed*. Karachi & New Delhi: Oxford UP.

Barber, Benjamin (1992). 'Jihad vs McWorld'. *The Atlantic Monthly* March 1992.

Barnouw, Victor (1987). *An Introduction to Anthropology: Ethnology*, vol. 2, 5th edn. Chicago, IL: The Dorsey Press.

Barthes, Roland (1957). *Mythologies*. London: Paladin/HarperCollins.

Baudrillard, Jean (1983). *Simulations*. Trans. Paul Foss, Paul Patton, & Philip Beitchman. New York: Semiotext[e].

Beaujot, Rod (2000). *Earning and Caring in Canadian Families*. Peterborough: Broadview Press

Becker, Howard (1963). *Outsiders: Studies in the Sociology of Deviance*. New York: The Free Press.

Bellegarde-Smith, Patrick (2004). *Haiti: The Breached Citadel*. Toronto: Canadian Scholars' Press.

Benedict, Ruth (1946). *The Chrysanthemum and the Sword*. Boston: Houghton Mifflin.

Best, Joel (2001). *Damned Lies and Statistics: Untangling Numbers from the Media, Politicians, and Activists*. Berkeley and Los Angeles: U of California P.

Bezlova, Antoaneta (2002). 'Young Workers Toil to Churn Out Santa's Toys'. *Inter Press Service* 19 (23 Dec.), www.commondreams.org/headlines02/1223-01.htm.

Bibby, Reginald Wayne (1995). *The Bibby Report: Social Trends Canadian Style*. Toronto: Stoddard.

Bissell, Tom (2003). *Chasing the Sea: Lost Among the Ghosts of Empire in Central Asia*. New York: Pantheon.

Bolaria, B. Singh, & Peter S. Li (1985). *Racial Oppression in Canada*. Toronto: Garamond.

Bott, Elizabeth (1957). *Family and Social Networks: Roles, Norms of External Relationships in Ordinary Urban Families*. London: Tavistock.

Bourdieu, Pierre (1970). *La reproduction: Eléments pour une théorie d'enseignement*. Paris: Éditions de Minuit.

——— (1996). *On Television*. New York: New Press.

Boyd, Monica, & Doug Norris (1995). 'Leaving the Nest? Impact of Family Structure'. *Canadian Social Trends* 38, pp. 14–17.

Briggs, Jean (1970). *Never in Anger: Portrait of an Eskimo Family*. Cambridge: Harvard UP.

—— (1998). *Inuit Morality Play: The Emotional Education of a Three-Year-Old*. New Haven, CT: Yale UP.

Brym, Robert J. (2000). 'Note on the Discipline: The Decline of the Canadian Sociology and Anthropology Association'. *The Canadian Journal of Sociology* 28 (3), pp. 411–26.

Budgell, Janet (1999). *Our Way Home: a Report to the Aboriginal Healing and Wellness Strategy: Repatriation of Aboriginal People Removed by the Child Welfare System: Final Report*. Prepared by Native Child and Family Services of Toronto, Sevenato and Associates. Toronto: Native Child and Family Services of Toronto.

Burawoy, Michael (2004). 'The World Needs Public Sociology'. *Sosiologisk tidsskrift (Journal of Sociology, Norway)* 3.

Burnet Jean R., & Howard Palmer (1988). *'Coming Canadians'. An Introduction to a History of Canada's Peoples*. Ottawa: Ministry of Supply and Services.

Burton, Kirsteen R., & Ian K. Wong (2004). 'A Force to Contend With: The Gender Gap Closes in Canadian Medical Schools'. *Canadian Medical Association Journal* 170 (9) (17 April).

Bushman, Brad J., & L. Rowell Huesmann (2001). 'Effects of Televised Violence on Aggression'. In D. Singer & J. Singer, eds, *Handbook of Children and the Media*, pp. 223–54. Thousand Oaks, CA: Sage.

Butler, Judith (1990). *Gender Trouble: Feminism and the Subversion of Identity*. London: Routledge.

Buttel, Frederick, & Kenneth Gould (2004). 'Global Social Movement(s) at the Crossroads: Some Observation on the Trajectory of the Anti-corporate Globalization Movement'. *Journal of World Systems Research* 10 (1), pp. 51–2.

Campbell, Marie, & Frances Gregor (2002). *Mapping Social Relations: A Primer in Doing Institutional Ethnography*. Aurora: Garamond.

Canadian Association of Food Banks (2004). *Poverty in a Land of Plenty: Towards a Hunger-Free Canada*. Toronto.

Cardinal, Harold (1969). *The Unjust Society: The Tragedy of Canada's Indians*. Edmonton: New Press.

—— (1977). *The Rebirth of Canada's Indians*. Toronto: New Press.

Cavan, Ruth (1965 [1928]). *Suicide*. New York: Russell and Russell.

Certeau, Michel de (1984). *The Practice of Everyday Life*. Trans. S. Rendell. Berkeley, CA: U of California P.

Chaitin, Gilbert (1996). *Rhetoric and Culture in Lacan*. Cambridge: Cambridge UP.

Chang, Virginia, & Nicholas Christakis (2002). 'Medical Modelling of Obesity: A Transition from Action to Experience in a 20th Century American Medical Textbook'. *Sociology of Health and Illness* 24 (2), pp. 151–77.

Chen, Anita Beltran (1998). *From Sunbelt to Snowbelt: Filipinos in Canada*. Calgary: Canadian Ethnic Studies Association.

Chodrow, Nancy (1978). *The Reproduction of Mothering: Psychoanalysis and the Sociology of Gender*. Berkeley: U of California P.

—— (1994). *Femininities, Masculinities, Sexualities: Freud and Beyond*. UP of Kentucky.

Chomsky, Noam (2004). *Hegemony or Survival: America's Quest for Global Dominance*. New York: Henry Holt and Company.

Clark, S.D. (1962). *The Developing Canadian Community*. Toronto: U of Toronto P.

—— (1976). *Canadian Society in Historical Perspective*. Toronto: McGraw-Hill.

Clinard, M., & R. Quinney (1973). *Criminal Behavior Systems: A Typology*, 2nd edn. New York: Holt, Rinehart, and Winston.

Codjoe, Henry M. (2001). 'Can Blacks Be Racist? Further Reflections on Being "Too Black and African"'. In Carl James & Adrienne Shadd, eds, *Talking About Identity: Encounters in Race, Ethnicity and Language*, pp. 277–90. Toronto: Between The Lines.

Cohen, Albert K. (1955). *Delinquent Boys: The Culture of the Gang*. Glencoe, IL: Free Press.

Colapinto, John (2000). *As Nature Made Him: The Boy Who Was Raised as a Girl*. New York: HarperCollins.

Comte, Auguste (1830–42). *Cours de Philosophie Positive*. Paris: Librairie Larousse.

—— (1851–4). *Système de Politique Positive*.

—— (1853). *The Positive Philosophy of August Comte*. Trans. and ed. Harriet Martineau.

—— (1877). *The System of Positive Polity*. London: Longmans, Green.

Connell, R.W. (1995). *Masculinities*. Berkeley: U of California P.

Conrad, Margaret R., & James K. Hiller (2001). *Atlantic Canada: A Region in the Making*. Toronto: Oxford UP.

Craib, Ian (1989). *Psychoanalysis and Social Theory: The Limits of Sociology*. Amherst: U of Massachusetts P.

Crehan, Kate (2002). *Gramsci, Culture and Anthropology*. Berkeley: U of California P.

Curtis, James, Edward Grabb, & Neil Guppy, eds (1999). *Social Inequality in Canada: Patterns, Problems and Policies*, 3rd edn. Scarborough: Prentice Hall.

Dahl, Robert A. (1956). *A Preface to Democratic Theory: How Does Popular Sovereignty Function in America?* Chicago: U of Chicago P.

Dasgupta, Sathi (1992). 'Conjugal Roles and Social Network in Indian Immigrant Families: Bott Revisited'. *The Journal of Comparative Family Studies* 23 (3), p. 465.

Das Gupta, Tania (1996). *Racism and Paid Work*. Toronto: Garamond.

Dawson, Carl A., & Warren E. Getty (1948). *An Introduction to Sociology*, 3rd edn. New York: The Ronald Press.

Demerson, Velma (2004). *Incorrigible*. Waterloo: Wilfrid Laurier UP.

Dick, Lyle (1995). '"Pibloktoq" (Arctic Hysteria): A Construction of European–Inuit Relations?'. *Arctic Anthropology* 32 (2), pp. 1–42.

Dickason, Olive (2002). *Canada's First Nations: A History of Founding Peoples from Earliest Times*, 3rd edn. Toronto: Oxford UP.

Dofny, Jacques, & Marcel Rioux (1962). 'Les classes sociales au Canada français'. *Revue français de sociologie* 111 (3), pp. 290–303.

Dollard, John (1937). *Caste and Class in a Southern Town*. New Haven, CT: Yale UP.

Dosman, Edgar J. (1972). *Indians: An Urban Dilemma*. Toronto: McClelland and Stewart.

Du Bois, W.E.B. (1896). *The Suppression of the African Slave Trade in America*. New York: Longmans, Green.

——— (1903). *The Souls of Black Folk*. Chicago: A.C. McClurg.

——— (1935). *Black Reconstruction: An Essay toward a History of the Part which Black Folk Played in the Attempt to Re-construct Democracy in America*. New York: Harcourt Brace.

——— (1940). *Dusk of Dawn*. New York: Harcourt, Brace & World.

——— (1967 [1899]). *The Philadelphia Negro: A Social Study*. New York: Schocken Books.

Dumas, Jean, & Alain Bélanger (1996). *Report on the Demographic Situation in Canada, 1995*. Ottawa: Statistics Canada, cat. no. 91–209.

Dunfield, Allison (2005). 'Why Do Women Always Pay More?'. *Globe and Mail*, 15 March.

Dupuy, Alex (1997). *Haiti in the New World Order: The Limits of the Democratic Revolution*. Boulder, CO: Westview.

Durkheim, Émile (1938 [1895]). *Rules of the Sociological Method*. Chicago: U of Chicago P.

——— (1951 [1897]). *Suicide: A Study in Sociology*. Trans. John A. Spaulding & George Simpson. New York: The Free Press of Glenco.

——— (1965 [1912]). *The Elementary Forms of Religious Life*. New York: The Free Press of Glenco.

Eichler, Margrit (2001). 'Women Pioneers in Canadian Sociology: The Effects of a Politics of Gender and a Politics of Knowledge'. *Canadian Journal of Sociology* 26 (3) (Summer), pp. 375–404.

Elkind, David (2001). *The Hurried Child: Growing Up Too Fast Too Soon*, 3rd edn. Cambridge, MA: Perseus.

——— (2003). 'The Reality of Virtual Stress'. *CIO* Fall/Winter. www.cio.com/archive/092203/elkind.

Emke, Ivan (2002). 'Patients in the New Economy: The "Sick Role" in a Time of Economic Discipline'. *Animus: A Philosophical Journal for Our Time* 7.

Erlick, Larry (2004). Untitled speech to the Economic Club of Toronto. www.oma.org/pcomm/pressrel/economicspeech04.htm.

Esar, Evan (1943). *Esar's Comic Dictionary of Wit and Humour*. New York: Horizon.

Fadiman, Anne (1997). *The Spirit Catches You and You Fall Down. A Hmong Child, Her American Doctors, and the Collision of Two Cultures*. New York: Farrar, Straus and Giroux.

Fiske, John (1989). *Understanding Popular Culture*. London: Routledge.

Fanon, Franz (1965 [1961]). *The Wretched of the Earth*. New York: Grove.

——— (1967 [1952]). *Black Skin, White Masks*. New York: Grove.

Fleras, Augie, & Jean Elliott (1999). *Unequal Relations: An Introduction to Race, Ethnic, and Aboriginal Dynamics in Canada*, 3rd edn. Scarborough, ON: Prentice-Hall, Allyn & Bacon.

Foucault, Michel (1961). *Madness and Civilisation: A History of Insanity in the Age of Reason*. New York: Vintage.

——— (1975). *Discipline and Punish: The Birth of the Prison*. New York: Vintage.

——— (1978). *The History of Sexuality. Vol. 1: An Introduction*. New York: Pantheon Books.

——— (1980). 'Two Lectures'. In Colin Gordon, ed., *Power/Knowledge*, pp. 78–108. New York: Pantheon Books.

——— (1994 [1972]). *The Archaeology of Knowledge*. Trans. from *L'archéologie du savoir* (1969). London: Routledge.

Fowles, Jib (1999). *The Case for Television Violence*. London: Sage.

——— (2001). 'The Whipping Boy: The Hidden Conflicts Underlying the Campaign against TV'. *Reason* March.

Frank, David, & Nolan Reilly (1979). 'The Emergence of the Socialist Movement in the Maritimes, 1899–1916'. In Robert J. Brym & R. James Sacouman, eds, *Underdevelopment and Social Movements in Atlantic Canada*, pp. 81–106. Toronto: New Hogtown Press.

Freud, Sigmund (1977 [1916–17]). *On Sexuality*, vol. 7. London: Penguin.

Friedman, Thomas L. (2000). *The Lexus and the Olive Tree: Understanding Globalization*. New York: Anchor Books.

Gallagher, James E., & Ronald D. Lambert, eds (1971). *Social Process and Institution: The Canadian Case*. Toronto: Holt, Rinehart and Winston.

Gans, Herbert (1989). 'Sociology in America: The Discipline and the Public'. *American Sociological Review* 54 (February), pp. 1–16.

Garigue, Philippe (1964). 'French Canada: A Case-Study in Sociological Analysis'. *Canadian Review of Sociology and Anthropology* 1 (4), pp. 186–92.

Gephart, Robert (1988). *Ethnostatistics: Qualitative Foundations for Quantitative Research*. London: Sage.

Gerth, Hans, & C. Wright Mills (1958 [1946]). *The Sociology of Max Weber*. New York: Vintage Books.

Giles, Philip (2004). 'Low Income Measurement in Canada'. www.statcan.ca/english/research/75F0002MIE/75F0002MIE2004011.pdf

Gilligan, Carol (1982). *In a Different Voice: Psychological Theory and Women's Development*. Cambridge, MA: Harvard UP.

———— (1990). *Making Connections: The Relational Worlds of Adolescent Girls at Emma Willard School*. Cambridge, MA: Harvard UP.

Goffman, Erving (1959). *The Presentation of Self in Everyday Life*. New York: Anchor Books.

———— (1961). *Asylums: Essays on the Social Situation of Mental Patients and Other Inmates*. New York: Anchor Books.

———— (1963). *Stigma: Notes on the Management of Spoiled Identity*. Englewood Cliffs, NJ: Prentice-Hall.

———— (1976). *Gender Advertisements*. New York: Harper Torchbooks.

Goldscheider, Frances, & Regina Bures (2003). 'The Racial Crossover in Family Complexity in the United States'. *Demography* 40 (3), pp. 569–87.

Gomm, Roger, & Patrick McNeill (1982). *Handbook for Sociology Teachers*. London: Heineman.

Gorer, Geoffrey, & John Rickman (1949). *The People of Great Russia: A Psychological Study*. New York: Norton.

Gramsci, Antonio (1992). *Prison Notebooks*, vol. 1. Ed. Joseph A. Buttligieg. New York: Columbia UP.

Grant, George (1965). *Lament for a Nation: The Defeat of Canadian Nationalism*. Toronto: McClelland & Stewart.

———— (1969). *Technology and Empire: Perspectives on North America*. Toronto: House of Anansi.

Grattan, E. (2003). 'Social Inequality and Stratification in Canada'. In Paul Angelini, ed., *Our Society: Human Diversity in Canada*, 2nd edn, pp. 61–86. Scarborough, ON: Thomson-Nelson.

Griswold, Wendy (1994). *Cultures and Societies in a Changing World*. London: Sage.

Grygier, Pat (1994). *A Long Way from Home: The Tuberculosis Epidemic among the Inuit*. Montreal: McGill–Queen's UP.

Haedrich, Richard L., & Cynthia M. Duncan (2004). 'Above and Below the Water: Social/Ecological Transformation in Northwest Newfoundland'. *Population and Environment* 25 (3), pp. 195–215.

Hale, Sylvia (1992). 'Facticity and Dogma in Introductory Sociology Texts: The Need for Alternative Methods'. In William K. Carroll, Linda Christiansen-Ruffman, Raymond F. Currie, & Deborah Harrison, eds, *Fragile Truths: 25 Years of Sociology and Anthropology in Canada*, pp. 135–53. Ottawa, ON: Carleton UP.

Hall, Elaine J. (1988). 'One Week for Women? The Structure of Inclusion of Gender Issues in Introductory Textbooks'. *Teaching Sociology* 16 (4), pp. 431–2.

Hamilton, Lawrence, Cynthia Duncan, & Richard Haedrich (2004). 'Social/Ecological Transformation in Northwest Newfoundland'. *Population and Environment* 25 (3), pp. 195–215.

Hamilton, Roberta (1996). *Gendering the Vertical Mosaic: Feminist Perspectives on Canadian Society*. Toronto: Pearson Canada.

Hanna, William R., & Clive Cockerton (1990). *Humanities: A Course in General Education*. Toronto: Thompson Educational.

Harley, David (n.d.). 'Witchcraft and the Occult, 1400–1700: Gender and Witchcraft'. www. nd. edu/~harley/witchcraft/homepage.html.

Harman, Joshua (1998). 'Relative Deprivation and Worker Unrest in China'. 1998 Esterline Prize Winner, Asian Studies on the Pacific Coast.

Harris, Marvin (1987). *Cultural Anthropology*, 2nd edn. New York: Harper & Row.

Harrison, Deborah (1999). 'The Limits of Liberalism in Canadian Sociology: Some Notes on S.D. Clark'. In Dennis W. Magill & William Michelson, eds, *Images of Change*. Toronto: Canadian Scholars' Press.

Hart, Julian Tudor (1971). 'The Inverse Care Law'. *The Lancet* 27 Feb., pp. 405–12.

Hegel, Georg Wilhelm Friedrich (1956). *The Philosophy of History*. Trans. J. Sibree. New York: Dover.

Helmes-Hayes, Rick, & James Curtis, eds (1998). *The Vertical Mosaic Revisited*. Toronto: U of Toronto P.

Hill, Daniel (1960). *Negroes in Toronto: A Sociological Study of a Minority Group*. Unpublished doctoral dissertation.

———— (1981). *The Freedom Seekers: Blacks in Early Canada*. Agincourt: Book Society of Canada.

Hiller, Harry H., & Linda Di Luzio (2001). 'Text and

Context: Another "Chapter" in the Evolution of Sociology in Canada'. *Canadian Journal of Sociology* 26 (3), pp. 487–512.

Hiller, Harry H., & Simon Langlois (2001). 'The Most Important Books/Articles in Canadian Sociology in the Twentieth Century: A Report'. *Canadian Journal of Sociology / Cahiers canadiens de sociologie* 26 (3), pp. 513–16.

Hitchcock, John T., & Leigh Minturn (1963). 'The Rajputs of Khalapur'. In B. Whiting, ed., *Six Cultures: Studies of Child Rearing*, pp. 203–362. New York: John Wiley & Sons.

Hoebel, E. Adamson (1965 [1954]). *The Law of Primitive Man, A Study in Comparative Legal Dynamics*. Cambridge, MA: Harvard UP.

Hofley, John R. (1992). 'Canadianization: A Journey Completed?'. In William K. Carroll, et al., eds, *Fragile Truths: 25 Years of Sociology and Anthropology in Canada*, pp. 102–22. Ottawa: Carleton UP.

Hoodfar, Homa (2003). 'More Than Clothing: Veiling as an Adaptive Strategy'. In Sajida Alvi, H. Hoodfar, & Sheila McDonough, eds, *The Muslim Veil in North America: Issues and Debates*, pp. 3–40. Toronto: Women's Press.

Horowitz, Irving Louis, ed. (1971). *People, Power and Politics: The Collected Essays of C. Wright Mills*. New York: Oxford UP.

Huesmann, L. Rowell, & L.D. Eron (1986). *Television and the Aggressive Child: A Cross-national Comparison*. Lawrence Erlbaum Associates.

Huesmann, L. Rowell, & L. Miller (1994). 'Long Term Effects of Repeated Exposure to Media Violence in Children'. In L.R. Huesmann, ed., *Aggressive Behavior: Current Perspective*, pp. 153–86. New York: Plenum Press.

Huesmann, L. Rowell, J. Moise, C.P. Podolski, & L.D. Eron (2003). 'Longitudinal Relations between Childhood Exposure to Media Violence and Adult Aggression and Violence: 1977–1992'. *Developmental Psychology* 39 (2), pp. 201–21.

Hughes, Everett C. (1963 [1943]). *French Canada in Transition*. Chicago: U of Chicago P.

Husain, Mir Zohair (1995). *Global Islamic Politics*. New York: HarperCollins.

Illich, Ivan (1976). *Medical Nemesis: The Limits of Medicine*. London: Penguin.

Isajiw, Wsevolod W. (1999). *Understanding Diversity: Ethnicity and Race in the Canadian Context*. Toronto: Thompson Educational.

Iwasaki, Mineko (2002). *Geisha: A Life*. New York: Washington Square Press.

Jenness, Diamond (1932). *Indians of Canada*. Ottawa: King's Printer.

Jenness, Stuart (1991). *Arctic Odyssey: The Diary of Diamond Jenness, 1913–1916*. Ottawa: Canadian Museum of Civilization.

Jhally, Sut (1990). *The Codes of Advertising: Fetishism and the Political Economy of Meaning in the Consumer Society*. New York: Routledge.

Jocas, Yves de, & Guy Rocher (1957). 'Inter-generation Occupational Mobility in the Province of Quebec'. *The Canadian Journal of Economics and Political Science* 25 (1), pp. 57–68.

Johnston, Hugh (1989). *The Voyage of the Komagata Maru: The Sikh challenge to Canada's Colour Bar*. Vancouver: U of British Columbia P.

Kachuck, Beatrice (2003 [1995]). 'Feminist Social Theories: Themes and Variations'. In Sharmila Rege, ed., *Sociology of Gender: The Challenge of Feminist Sociological Knowledge*. New Delhi: Sage.

Kaizuka, Shigeki (2002 [1956]). *Confucius: His Life and Thought*. Mineola, NY: Dover.

Kane, P.R., & A.J. Orsini (2003). 'The Need for Teachers of Color in Independent Schools'. In P.R. Kane & A.J. Orsini, eds, *The Colors of Excellence: Hiring and Keeping Teachers of Color in Independent Schools*, pp. 7–28. New York: Teachers College Press.

Keay, John (2000). *India: A History*. London: HarperCollins.

Kehoe, Alice (1995). 'Blackfoot Persons'. In L. Klein & L. Ackerman, *Women and Power in Native North America*. Norman, OK: U of Oklahoma P.

Kimelman, Edwin C. (1985). *No Quiet Place: Review Committee on Indian and Metis Adoption and Placements*. Manitoba Community Services.

King, Alan, Wendy Warren, & Sharon Miklas (2004). 'Study of Accessibility to Ontario Law Schools'. Executive Summary (Social Program Evaluation Group, Queen's University).

Klein, Naomi (2000). *No Logo*. Toronto: Vintage Canada.

——— (2002). *Fences and Windows: Dispatches from the Frontlines of the Globalization Debate*. Toronto: Vintage Canada.

Kleinman, Arthur (1995). *Writing at the Margin: Discourse Between Anthropology and Medicine*. Berkeley: U of California P.

Klopfenstein, Kristin (2005). 'Beyond Test Scores: The Impact of Black Teacher Role Models on Rigorous Math-Taking'. *Contemporary Economic Policy* 23, pp. 416–28.

Knockwood, Isabelle (1992). *Out of the Depths: The Experiences of Mi'kmaw Children at the Indian Residential School at Shubenacadie*. Lockeport, NS: Roseway.

Koos, E.L. (1954). *The Health of Regionsville: What the People Thought and Did About It*. New York: Columbia UP.

Krause, Elliott (1980). *Why Study Sociology?* New York: Random House.

Kroker, Arthur, & Michael A. Weinstein (1995). *Data Trash: The Theory of the Virtual Class.* Montreal: New World Perspectives.

Langlois, Simon (1999). 'Empirical Studies on Social Stratification in Quebec and Canada'. In Y. Lemel & N. Noll, eds, *New Structures of Inequality.* Montreal: McGill–Queen's UP, and www.soc.ulaval.ca/corps/langlois/empirical.pdf.

LaRocque, Emma (1975). *Defeathering the Indian.* Agincourt, ON: Book Society of Canada.

——— (1993). 'Three Conventional Approaches to Native People'. In Brett Balon & Peter Resch, eds, *Survival of the Imagination: the Mary Donaldson Memorial Lectures*, pp. 209–18. Regina: Coteau Books.

Laslett, Peter (1971). *The World We Have Lost.* London: Methuen.

Lawrence, Bonita (2004). *'Real' Indians and Others: Mixed-Blood Urban Native Peoples and Indigenous Nationhood.* Vancouver: U of British Columbia P.

Leah, Ronnie, & Gwen Morgan (1979). 'Immigrant Women Fight Back: The Case of the Seven Jamaican Women'. *Resources for Feminist Research* 7 (3), pp. 23–4.

Le Bourdeau, C., & N. Marcil-Gratton (1996). 'Family Transformations Across the Canadian/American Border: When the Laggard Becomes the Leader'. *Journal of Comparative Family Studies* 27 (3) (Fall), pp. 417–36.

Leffingwell, William (1925). *Office Management: Principles and Practice.* Chicago: A.W. Shaw Co.

Leiss, William, Stephen Kline, & Sut Jhally (1988). *Social Communication in Advertising: Persons, Products, and Images of Well-Being.* Toronto: Nelson.

Lieberson, Stanley (2000). *A Matter of Taste: How Names, Fashions and Cultures Change.* New Haven, CT: Yale UP.

Lipset, Seymour Martin (1990). *Continental Divide: Values and Institutions of the United States and Canada.* New York: Routledge.

Lowe, Kevin, Stan Fischler, & Shirley Fischler (1988). *Champions: The Making of the Edmonton Oilers.* Scarborough: Prentice-Hall Canada.

Lundy, Katherina, & Barbara Warme (1986, 1990). *Sociology: A Window on the World.* Toronto: Methuen.

McKay, Ian (1998). 'Changing the Subject(s) of the "History of Canadian Sociology": The Case of Colin McKay and Spencerian Marxism, 1890–1940'. *Canadian Journal of Sociology* 23 (4).

MacLean, Annie Marion (1897–8). 'Factory Legislation for Women in the United States'. *American Journal of Sociology* 3, pp. 183–205.

——— (1898). 'Two Weeks in a Department Store'. *American Journal of Sociology* 4, pp. 721–41.

——— (1899–1900). 'Faculty Legislation for Women in Canada'. *American Journal of Sociology* 5, pp. 172–81.

——— (1903–4). 'The Sweat Shop Summer'. *American Journal of Sociology* 9, pp. 289–309.

——— (1908–9). 'Life in the Pennsylvania Coal Fields'. *American Journal of Sociology* 14, pp. 329–51.

——— (1909–10). 'With the Oregon Hop Pickers'. *American Journal of Sociology* 15, pp. 83–95.

——— (1910). *Wage-Earning Women.* New York: Macmillan.

——— (1923). 'Four Months in a Model Factory'. *Century* 106 (July), pp. 436–44.

Maclean, John (1970 [1889]). *The Indians of Canada: Their Manners and Customs.* Toronto: Coles.

McLeod, Linda (1980). *Wife Battering in Canada: The Vicious Circle.* Hull, PQ: Canadian Government Publishing Centre.

McQuaig, Linda (2004). 'Closed Shop Gives Doc the Hammer in New Brunswick Strike'. *Straight Goods.* www.straightgoods.com/McQuaig/010122.shtml.

Maines, D.R. (1993). 'Narrative's Moment and Sociology's Phenomena—Toward a Narrative Sociology. *Sociological Quarterly* 34 (1), pp. 17–37.

Maioni, Antonia (2004). 'New Century, New Risks: The Marsh Report and the Post-War Welfare State in Canada'. *Policy Options* August 2004, pp. 20–3.

Mandell, Nancy, & Ann Duffy (1995). *Canadian Families: Diversity, Conflict and Change.* Toronto: Harcourt, Brace & Company.

Manji, Irshad (2003). *The Trouble with Islam: A Wake Up Call for Honesty and Change.* Toronto: Random House Canada.

Maracle, Brian (1996). *Back on the Rez: Finding The Way Home.* Toronto: Viking Penguin.

Maracle, Lee (1992). *Sundogs.* Penticton, BC: Theytus Books.

Marcuse, Herbert (1964). *One Dimensional Man.* Boston: Beacon.

Marshall, Gordon (1998). *Oxford Dictionary of Sociology.* New York: Oxford UP.

Martineau, Harriet (1962 [1837]). *Society in America.* Garden City, NY: Doubleday.

——— (2005 [1838]). *Retrospect of Western Travel.* Honolulu: UP of the Pacific.

——— (1848). *Eastern Life Past and Present.* London: Moxon.

Marx, Karl (1967 [1867]). *Capital: A Critique of Political Economy*. Ed. F. Engels. New York: International Publishers.

Marx, Karl, & Friedrich Engels (1967 [1848]). *The Communist Manifesto*. New York: Pantheon.

———— (1970 [1845–6]). *The German Ideology*, part 1. Ed. C.J. Arthur. New York: International Publishers.

Mazón, Mauricio (1984). *The Zoot-Suit Riots: The Psychology of Symbolic Annihilation*. Austin: U of Texas P.

Mead, George Herbert (1934). *Mind, Self, and Society*. Chicago: U of Chicago P.

Memmi, Albert (1991 [1957]). *The Colonizer and the Colonized*. Boston: Beacon.

Merton, Robert K. (1968 [1949]). *Social Theory and Social Structure*. New York: The Free Press.

Milan, Anne, & Kelly Tran (2004). 'Blacks in Canada: A Long History'. *Canadian Social Trends* Spring 2004, pp. 2–7.

Miller, J.R. (1996). *Shingwauk's Vision: A History of Native Residential Schools*. Toronto: U of Toronto P.

Mills, C. Wright (1948). *The New Men of Power: America's Labor Leaders*. Harcourt Brace & Company.

———— (1951). *White Collar: The American Middle Classes*. New York: Oxford UP.

———— (1956). *The Power Elite*. New York: Oxford UP.

———— (1958). *The Causes of World War Three*. London: Secker & Warburg.

———— (1959). *The Sociological Imagination*. New York: Oxford UP.

———— (1960). *Listen Yankee: The Revolution in Cuba*. New York: Ballantine Books.

———— (1962). *The Marxists*. New York: Dell Publishing.

Mills, Kathryn, ed. (2001). *C. Wright Mills: Letters and Autobiographical Writings*. Berkeley and Los Angeles: U. of California P.

Miner, Horace (1963 [1939]). *St Denis: A French Canadian Parish*. Chicago: U of Chicago P.

Montagu, Ashley (1942). *Man's Most Dangerous Myth: The Fallacy of Race*. New York: Columbia UP.

Monture-Angus, Patricia (1995). *Thunder in My Soul: A Mohawk Woman Speaks*. Halifax: Fernwood.

Morehead Phillip, & Albert Morehead (1981). *Roget's College Dictionary*. New York: Penguin.

Morgan, Lewis Henry (1964 [1877]). *Ancient Society or Researches in the Lines of Human Progress from Savagery through Barbarism to Civilization*. Cambridge, Mass: Harvard UP.

Murphy, Emily (1973 [1922]). *The Black Candle*. Toronto: Coles.

Muzzin, Linda J. (2001). 'Powder Puff Brigades: Professional Caring vs Industry Research in the Pharmaceutical Sciences Curriculum'. In Eric Margolis, ed., *The Hidden Curriculum in Higher Education*, pp. 135–54. London: Routledge.

Myers, S.A., trans. (1862). *Martin's Natural History, First Series*. New York: Blackeman & Mason.

Nakhaie, M. Reza (1995). 'Housework in Canada: The National Picture'. *Journal of Comparative Family Studies* 23 (3), pp. 409–25.

Nanda, Serena (1994). *Cultural Anthropology*, 5th edn. Belmont, CA: Wadsworth.

Newbury, Catharine (1993). *The Cohesion of Oppression*. New York: Columbia UP.

Nietzsche, Frederick (1968 [1901]). *Will to Power*. Trans. Walter Kaufmann. New York: Vintage.

———— (1996 [1878]). *Human, All Too Human*. Trans. Marion Faber & Stephen Lehmann. Cambridge, MA: Cambridge UP.

———— (2003 [1887]). *The Genealogy of Morals*. New York: Dover.

———— (2006 [1882]). *The Gay Science*. New York: Dover.

Nihmey, John (1998). *Fireworks and Folly: How We Killed Minnie Sutherland*. Ottawa: Phillip Diamond.

Nisbet, Robert A. (1969). *Social Change and History: Aspects of the Western Theory of Development*. Oxford: Oxford UP.

Nock, David. A. (1993). 'Star Wars in Canadian Sociology': Exploring the Social Construction of Knowledge. Halifax: Fernwood.

———— (2001). 'Careers in Print: Canadian Sociological Books and Their Wider Impact, 1975–1992'. *Canadian Journal of Sociology / Cahiers canadiens de sociologie* 26 (3), pp. 469–85.

Ontario Human Rights Commission (2003). 'Paying the Price: The Human Cost of Racial Profiling'. www.ohrc.on.ca/english/consultations/racial-profiling-report.pdf.

Ontario Medical Association (2002). 'Position Paper on Physician Workforce Policy and Planning'. Document addressing concerns of the Ontario Medical Association (OMA).

Park, Robert, & Ernest Burgess (1921). *Introduction to the Science of Sociology*. Chicago: U of Chicago P.

———— (1967 [1925]). *The City*. Chicago: U of Chicago P.

Parsons, Talcott (1951). *The Social System*. New York: Free Press.

———— (1966). *Societies: Evolutionary and Comparative Perspectives*. Englewoods Cliff, NJ: Prentice-Hall.

Patai, Raphael (2002). *The Arab Mind*. New York: Random House.

Payer, Lynn (1992). *Disease-Mongers: How Doctors, Drug Companies, and Insurers Are Making You Feel Sick*. New York: John Wiley & Sons.

Philp, Margaret (2006). 'Cancer in the Mind's Eye'. *Globe and Mail*, 9 Dec. www.theglobeandmail.com/servlet/story/RTGAM.20061208.cover09/BNStory/cancer/home

Pohlmann, Lisa (2002). 'Inequality is Bad for your Health'. www.mecep.or/MEChoices02/ch_029.htm.

Porter, John (1965). *The Vertical Mosaic: An Analysis of Social Class and Power in Canada*. Toronto: U of Toronto P.

Rajulton, Fernando, T.R. Balakrishnan, & Zenaida R. Ravanera (1990). 'Measuring Infertility in Contracepting Populations'. Presentation, Canadian Population Society Meetings. Victoria, BC, June.

Rege, Sharmila (2003). 'Feminist Challenge to Sociology: Disenchanting Sociology or "For Sociology"?'. In S. Rege, ed., *Sociology of Gender: The Challenge of Feminist Sociological Knowledge*, pp. 1–49. London: Sage.

Reid, Anna (2002). *The Shaman's Coat: A Native History of Siberia*. London: Weidenfeld & Nicolson.

Reiman, Jeffrey (1998). *The Rich Get Richer and the Poor Get Prison: Ideology, Class and Criminal Justice*. Boston: Allyn & Bacon.

Reinharz, Shulamit (1992). *Feminist Methods in Social Research*. New York: Oxford UP.

Riesman, David (1950). *The Lonely Crowd: A Study of the Changing American Character*. New Haven, CT: Yale UP.

Ruddick, S. (1989). *Maternal Thinking: Towards a Politics of Peace*. Boston: Beacon.

Robertson, Roland (1997). 'Comments on the "Global Triad" and "Glocalization"'. In Inoue Nobutaka, ed., *Globalization and Indigenous Culture*. Institute for Japanese Culture and Classics, Kokugakuin University.

Ross, Aileen (1962). *The Hindu Family in Its Urban Setting*. Toronto: U of Toronto P.

——— (1976). 'Changing Aspirations and Roles: Middle and Upper Class Indian Women Enter the Business World'. In Giri Raj Gupta, ed., *Main Currents in Indian Sociology*, 103–32. Bombay: Vikas Publishing House Pvt Ltd.

——— (1977). 'Some Comments on the Home Roles of Businesswomen in India, Australia and Canada'. *Journal of Comparative Family Studies* 8 (3), pp. 327–40.

——— (1979). 'Businesswomen and Business Cliques in Three Cities: Delhi, Sydney, and Montreal'. *Canadian Review of Sociology and Anthropology* 16 (4), pp. 425–35.

——— (1982). *The Lost and the Lonely: Homeless Women in Montreal*. Montreal: Canadian Human Rights Commission.

Ryan, William (1976 [1971]). *Blaming the Victim*. New York: Pantheon.

Said, Edward (1978). *Orientalism*. New York: Pantheon.

Sale, Kirkpatrick (1980). *Human Scale*. New York: Coward, McCann & Geoghegan.

——— (1996). *Rebels Against the Future: The Luddites and Their War on the Industrial Revolution—Lessons for the Computer Age*. Cambridge, MA: Perseus.

——— (2005). 'Imperial Entropy: Collapse of the American Empire'. *CounterPunch* 22 Feb. 2005.

Sargent, Paul (2005). 'The Gendering of Men in Early Childhood Education'. *Sex Roles: A Journal of Research*, Feb.

Seeley, John, R. Alexander Sim, & Elizabeth Loosely (1956). *Crestwood Heights: A Study of the Culture of Suburban Life*. Toronto: U of Toronto P.

Saussure, Ferdinand de (1966). *Course in General Linguistics*. New York: McGraw-Hill.

Simmel, Georg (1890). *On Social Differentiation*. Leipzig: Duncker & Humbolt.

——— (1990 [1900]). *The Philosophy of Money*. Ed. David Frisby. New York: Routledge.

——— (1908). *Sociology: Investigations on the Forms of Socialization*. Lepizig: Duncker & Humbolt.

Smith, Dorothy (1987). *The Everyday World as Problematic: A Feminist Sociology*. Boston: Northeastern UP.

——— (1990). The Conceptual Practices of Power: A Feminist Sociology of Knowledge. Toronto: U of Toronto P.

Smith, George W. (1998). 'The Ideology of "Fag": The School Experience of Gay Students'. *The Sociological Quarterly* 39 (2), pp. 309–35.

Smits, David D. (1982). 'The "Squaw Drudge": A Prime Index of Savagism'. *Ethnohistory* 29 (4) (Autumn 1982), pp. 281–306.

Spencer, Herbert (1862). *First Principles*. http://praexology.net/HS-SP-FP-pref1.htm.

——— (1896). *Social Statics, Abridged & Revised Together with Man Versus the State*. New York: D. Appleton & Company.

——— (1896 [1880]). *The Study of Sociology*. New York: D. Appleton & Company.

Spengler, Oswald (1918–22). *The Decline of the West*. New York: Alfred A. Knopf.

Steckley, John L. (1999). *Beyond Their Years: Five Native Women's Stories*. Toronto: Canadian Scholars' Press.

——— (2003). *Aboriginal Voices and the Politics of*

Representation in Canadian Sociology Textbooks. Toronto: Canadian Scholars' Press.

Steckley, John, & Bryan Cummins (2001). *Full Circle: Canada's First Nations.* Toronto: Prentice-Hall.

Steckley, John, & Brian Rice (1997). 'Lifelong Learning and Cultural Identity: A Lesson from Canada's Native People'. In Michael Hatton, ed., *Lifelong Learning: Policies, Programs & Practices,* pp. 216–29. Toronto: APEC.

Steger, Manfred B. (2003). *Globalization: A Very Short Introduction.* Oxford: Oxford UP.

Stewart, Walter (2003). *The Life and Political Times of Tommy Douglas.* Toronto: McArthur & Company.

Stiglitz, Joseph E. (2003). *Globalization and Its Discontents.* New York: Norton.

Sutherland, Edwin (1940). 'White Collar Criminality'. *American Sociological Review* 5 (1), pp. 1–12.

——— (1949). *White Collar Crime.* New York: Holt, Rinehart and Winston.

Tajima, E. Renee (1989). 'Lotus Blossoms Don't Bleed: Images of Asian Women'. In Asian Women United of California, ed., *Making Waves: An Anthology of Writings by and About Asian American Women,* pp. 305–9. Boston: Beacon.

Talbot, Yves, E. Fuller-Thomson, F. Tudiver, Y. Habib, & W.J. McIsaac (2001). 'Canadians Without Regular Medical Doctors: Who are They?'. *Canadian Family Physician* 47 (January), pp. 58–64.

Tepperman, Lorne, & Michael Rosenberg (1998). *Macro/Micro: A Brief Introduction to Sociology,* 3rd edn. Scarborough, ON: Prentice Hall, Allyn & Bacon Canada.

Thomas, W.I., & Florian Znaiecki (1996 [1918–20]). *The Polish Peasant in Europe and America.* Urbana: U of Illinois P.

Thorndike, Edward (1999 [1911]). *Animal Intelligence: Experimental Studies.* Piscataway, NJ: Transaction Publishers.

Turnbull, Colin (1961). *The Forest People.* New York: Simon & Schuster.

Urmetzer, Peter, & Neil Guppy (1999). 'Changing Income Inequality in Canada'. In J. Curtis et al., eds, *Social Inequality in Canada,* pp. 56–65. Scarborough, ON: Prentice Hall.

Veblen, Thorstein (1904). *The Theory of Business Enterprise.* New York: Charles Scribner's Sons.

——— (1912 [1899]). *The Theory of the Leisure Class.* New York: Macmillan.

Walton, John (1984). *Reluctant Rebels: Comparative Studies of Revolution and Underdevelopment.* New York: Columbia UP.

Warner, Jessica (2003). *Craze: Gin and Debauchery in an Age of Reason.* New York: Random House.

Watson, John B. (1925). *Behaviorism.* New York: Norton.

Weatherford, Jack (2004). *Genghis Khan and the Making of the Modern World.* New York: Crown Publishing.

Weber, Max. (1930 [1904]). *The Protestant Ethic and the Spirit of Capitalism.* Trans. Talcott Parsons. New York: Charles Scribner's Sons.

——— (1968 [1914]). *Economy and Society: An Outline of Interpretive Sociology.* New York: Bedminster Press.

Weiner, Jonathan (1995). *The Beak of the Finch: A Story of Evolution in Our Time.* New York: Alfred A. Knopf.

Weyer, Edward M. (1962 [1932]). *The Eskimos: Their Environment and Folkways.* Hamden, CT: Archon Books.

Whiting, Beatrice B. (1963). *Six Cultures: Studies of Child Rearing.* New York: John Wiley.

Whyte. William F. (1955). *Street-Corner Society: The Social Structure of an Italian Slum,* 2nd edn. Chicago: U of Chicago P.

Williamson, Judith (1978). *Decoding Advertisements: Ideology and Meaning in Advertising.* London: Marion Boyars.

Willis, Paul E. (1977). *Learning to Labour: How Working Class Kids Get Working Class Jobs.* New York: Columbia UP.

Wilson, Stan, & Peggy Wilson (1998). 'Relational Accountability to All Our Relations'. *Canadian Journal of Native Education* July.

Woolf, H. Bosley (1974). *The Merriam-Webster Dictionary.* New York: G & C Merriam Company.

Wrong, Dennis (1961). 'The Oversocialized Conception of Man in Modern Sociology'. *American Sociological Review* 26 (2), pp. 183–93.

Yalnizyan, Armine (1998). *The Growing Gap: A Report on Growing Inequality between the Rich and Poor in Canada.* Toronto: Centre for Social Justice.

Yellen, John (1985). 'Bushmen'. *Science* 85 (May).

Young, Egerton R. (1974 [1893]). *Stories from Indian Wigwams and Northern Campfires.* Toronto: Coles.

Acknowledgements

The authors gratefully acknowledge their use of the following material:

Excerpt from *Al Muqaddimah*, from *Sociological Thought* by Nahla Abdo (Toronto: Canadian Scholars' Press/Women's Press, 1996). Reprinted by permission of Canadian Scholars' Press Inc.

Excerpt from 'Narrative's Moment and Sociology's Phenomena' by D.R. Maines, *Sociological Quarterly*, Vol. 34, no. 1 (1993): 17–37. Published by Blackwell Publishing Ltd.

Excerpts from 'More Than Clothing: Veiling as an Adaptive Strategy' by Homa Hoodfar, in Sajida Alvi, Homa Hoodfar, and Sheila McDonough, *The Muslim Veil in North America: Issues and Debates* (Toronto: Canadian Scholars' Press/Women's Press, 2003. Reprinted by permission of Women's Press.

'I Lost My Talk' by Rita Joe, from *Son of Eskasoni* (Charlottetown, PE: Ragweed Press, 1988).

Excerpt from *Cultural Anthropology*, 5th edn by Serena Nanda (Belmont, CA: Wadsworth, 1994): 138–40. Adapted from John T. Hitchcock and Leigh Minturn, 'The Rajputs of Khalapur' in *Six Cultures: Studies of Child Rearing* by Beatrice B. Whiting (New York: John Wiley & Sons, 1963).

Excerpts from *Arctic Odyssey: The Diary of Diamond Jenness, 1913–1916* by Diamond Jenness © Canadian Museum of Civilization.

Excerpts from *The Hurried Child: Growing Up Too Fast, Too Soon*, 3rd edn, by David Elkind (Cambridge, MA: Perseus Publishing, 2001).

'Boys Must Read to Catch Up to Girls' by Marney Beck, ed., *Caledon Enterprise* 26 January 2005.

Excerpt from *Incorrigible* by Velma Demerson. Wilfrid Laurier University Press, 2004. Reproduced by permission.

Excerpts from *Writing at the Margin: Discourse Between Anthropology and Medicine* by Arthur Kleinman (Berkeley, University of California Press, 1997). Copyright © 1997 by The Regents of the University of California.

Excerpt from 'Paying the Price: the Human Cost of Racial Profiling by Ontario Human Rights Commission, Government of Ontario, © Queen's Printer for Ontario, 2003. Reproduced with permission.

Excerpt from *Crestwood Heights: A Study of the Culture of Suburban Life* by John R. Seeley, Alexander Sim, and Elizabeth Loosley (New York: Basic Books, 1956): 159–60.

Excerpt from *Globe and Mail*/CTV poll, *Globe and Mail*.

Excerpts from *A Long Way from Home: The Tuberculosis Epidemic Among the Inuit* by Pat Grygier (Montreal: McGill-Queen's University Press, 1994): 55, 96.

'Alternative 10 Tips for Better Health' by David Gordon, from http://www.bris.ac.uk/poverty/health%20inequalities.html. Reprinted by permission of the author.

Excerpts from 'Can Blacks Be Racist? Further Reflections on Being "Too Black and African"' by Henry M. Codjoe, in Carl E. James and Adrienne Shadd, eds, *Talking About Identity: Encounters in Race Ethnicity and Language* (Toronto: Between the Lines, 2001): 286.

Excerpt from 'The Sikhs in Canada', an address delivered by Dr. Sundar Singh to the Empire Club of Canada on January 25, 1912. The Empire Club of Canada.

Excerpts from *The Cohesion of Oppression* by Catherine Newbury. Copyright © 1993 Columbia University Press. Reprinted with permission of the publisher.

Excerpt from *The Souls of Black Folk* by W.E.B. Du Bois, introduction by Donald B. Gibson, notes by Monica E. Elbert (London: Penguin Classics, 1989). Copyright © the Estate of W.E.B. Du Bois 1903. Introduction copyright © Viking Penguin, a division of Penguin Books USA Inc., 1989. Reproduced by permission of Penguin Books Ltd.

Excerpts from *Haiti: The Breached Citadel* by Patrick Bellegarde-Smith (Canadian Scholars' Press/Women's Press, 2004). Reprinted by permission of Canadian Scholar's Press.

Excerpts from *The Lexus and the Olive Tree: Understanding Globalization* by Thomas L. Friedman (New York: Anchor Books, 2000): 295.

Excerpts from *Globalization: A Very Short Introduction* by Manfred Steger (Oxford: Oxford University Press, 2003):13, 41, 53–4, 105, 114. By permission of Oxford University Press, Inc.

Lyrics from 'Take the Power Back' by Rage Against the Machine, from *Rage Against the Machine*, Epic Associated Records, 1992.

Excerpts from *Social Change and History: Aspects of the Western Theory of Development* by Robert A. Nisbet (Oxford: Oxford University Press, 1970): 3, 39, 159. By permission of Oxford University Press, Inc.

Excerpt from *Ancient Society* by Henry Lewis Morgan, edited by Leslie A. White (Cambridge, MA: Harvard University Press, 1964): 11. Copyright © 1964 by the President and Fellows of Harvard College. Reprinted by permission of the publisher.

Table 2.4, 'Correlation between divorce and suicide rates in four countries, 1870–1889', from *Suicide: A Study in Sociology* by Emile Durkheim, trans. John A. Spaulding, ed. and intro George Simpson (New York: Free Press, 1966): 259.

Table 3.1, 'Percentage of respondents agreeing with the statement "The father of the family must be master of his own home"' and Table 3.2, 'Percentage of respondents agreeing with the statement "Men are naturally superior to women"', from Michael Adams, *Fire and Ice: The United States and the Myth of Converging Values* (Toronto: Penguin Canada, 2003): 50–1. Copyright © Michael Adams, 2003. Reprinted by permission of Penguin Group (Canada), a division of Pearson Canada.

Table 6.3, 'Support for Changing the Definition of Marriage to Include Same-Sex Unions, By Region, 2003', from 'Public Divided About Definition of Marriage: Results of a Public Opinion Poll on Same-Sex Marriage September 5, 2003', TNS Canadian Facts. The study was conducted by TNS Canadian Facts (formerly NFO Cfgroup), one of Canada's leading full-service marketing, opinion, and social research organizations.

Table 6.4, 'Canadians' Approval of Intergroup Marriage (%), 1975–1995', from Reginald W. Bibby, *The Bibby Report: Social Trends Canadian Style* (Toronto: Stoddart Publishing, 1995).

Table 7.2, 'Photographic treatment of SARS in the national media, 2003', from Carrianne Leung and Dr. Jian Guan, 'Yellow Peril Revisited: Impact of SARS on the Chinese and Southeast Asian Canadian Community', (Toronto: Chinese Canadian National Council, 2004).

Table 8.1, 'Percentage of total before-tax income going to families and unattached individuals, by quintile, 1951–1996', adapted from Statistics Canada, *Income distributions by size in Canada, 1997*, Catalogue no. 13-207-XPB.

Table 8.2, 'Percentage of total 1995 income going to families before transfers and after taxes, by quintile', adapted from Statistics Canada, *Income after tax, distributions by size in Canada, 1997*, Catalogue no. 13-210-XPB.

Table 8.3, 'Percentage of total after-tax income going to families, by quintile, 1995', from The World Bank, *World Bank Development Report 1997: The State in a Changing World* (New York: Oxford University Press, 1997).

Table 8.4, 'Total family income, 1st and 10th deciles compared, 1973, 1996', from Armine Yalnizyan, *The Growing Gap: A Report on Growing Inequality Between the Rich and Poor in Canada* (Toronto: Centre for Social Justice, 1999). Reprinted by permission of the publisher.

Table 9.1, 'Salmon Gill Net Licences Issued 1922–1925', from *Report on Oriental Activities within the Province*, British Columbia Archives NW 305.895R425.

Table 9.2, 'French and British in the Professional and Financial Occupations', from John Porter, *The Vertical Mosaic: An Analysis of Social Class and Power in Canada*, (Toronto: University of Toronto Press, 1965): 94. Reprinted by permission of the publisher.

Table 12.1, 'Urban household possession of durable consumer goods (per 100 households)', *Chinese Statistical Yearbook 1988* and *Chinese Statistical Yearbook 1997*, China Statistics Press.

Index

2006 Census Update

Society never stops changing, and neither does sociology, the discipline that charts society's changing and emerging trends. But a textbook—even one that covers sociology—is a different matter. There comes a point, once the final proofs have been checked and all of the photos are in place, when a textbook cannot change any further.

So it was with *Elements of Sociology*. But the world keeps turning, and there have been significant developments in many of the areas covered by this textbook since its first printing. In particular, Statistics Canada has released an abundance of information, not just in the wake of the 2006 census but as part of its ongoing efforts to collect and disseminate important data about Canadian society. The question arose: how best to incorporate at least a sampling of this vital information without having to wait the three or four years that usually pass before a new edition is issued?

The solution, we decided, was to add this supplement, with a brief selection of interesting data that has come to light since the book's first printing. We hope that by including the material here in the text itself, rather than on a separate website, readers and instructors will find it convenient to flip back and forth between the main text and this addendum to see how aspects of society have changed in the short period time since the original version of the text was printed.

Canada's Native People and Census Statistics

Statistics on Canada's Aboriginal population have been notoriously misleading over the years, although they are much more reliable now than they used to be. Census figures generated by the federal government in the late nineteenth and early twentieth centuries tended to overestimate the Native population in the North, thereby distorting Aboriginal population counts for the country as a whole. When more realistic figures were used in subsequent censuses, it created the false impression that there had been a dramatic decrease in the number of Canada's Aboriginal inhabitants. This is important to keep in mind when looking at, for instance, the data for 1891–2, when it appears as though Canada's Native population fell from 121,638 to 109,205, though in fact much of this drop can be attributed to a change in estimating procedures. Another factor that has complicated the Native population count is Bill C-31, which provided a mechanism for restoring official Indian status lost through marriage. Prior to 1985, when the bill was introduced, Indian women who married men without official Indian status lost their own status, as did their children. (Paradoxically, a non-status woman could gain status by marrying a man with official Indian status.) Bill C-31, by enabling people with Native ancestry to regain their Indian status, artificially increased the size of Canada's Native population, allowing many people who prior to 1985 were Indian in every way but legal status to once again claim that identity in census polls.

It remains difficult to obtain accurate statistics about some First Nation bands, as certain communities, rightly suspicious of the ends to which outsider researchers and government agencies are using the statistics, will not give their numbers to Statistics Canada. However, the situation is improving. In 1996 there were 77 non-enumerated reserves in Canada; in the 2001 census, that number had fallen to 30, and was down to just 22 in 2006. Still, it is important to recognize that these 22 non-enumerated reserves include some of Canada's largest bands.

On-Reserve and Off-Reserve

It is also important to bear in mind that census statistics reflect the way people choose to report their identity. As a result, the number of people reporting 'Indian' status is higher than the number of 'status Indians' legally registered under Canada's Indian Act. This discrepancy shows up prominently in the figures for on-reserve and off-reserve populations for each First Nation. The Statistics Canada data for 2006 asserted that roughly 60 per cent of First Nations (not including Métis and Inuit) people lived off-reserve, with just 40 per cent living on-reserve. This would suggest that Canada's Native people

Table A.1 >> Canadian Aboriginal people living in cities, 1996–2006

	2001	2006	1996 ESTIMATE[1] (fn1)
Atlantic Provinces			
St. John's	1,195	2,015	1,000–2,000
Halifax	3,525	5,320	7,795
Saint John	945	1,255	2,000–3,000
Quebec			
Montreal	11,085	17,865	43,675
Quebec	4,130	4,000	6,000–10,000
Trois-Rivières	730	1,210	2,000–3,000
Sherbrooke	280	1,145	9,000–10,000
Ontario			
Toronto	20,300	26,575	39,380
Ottawa–Gatineau	13,485	20,590	29,415
St Catharines–Niagara	4,970	6,650	9,000–10,000
Windsor	3,965	5,590	7,000–10,000
Thunder Bay	8,200	10,055	8,600
Kitchener	3,235	4,645	6,000–10,000
Prairie Provinces			
Winnipeg	55,760	68,385	52,525
Regina	15,685	17,105	14,570
Saskatoon	20,280	21,535	18,160
Calgary	21.915	26,575	23,850
Edmonton	40,930	52,100	44,130
British Columbia			
Vancouver	36,855	40,310	46,805
Victoria	8,695	10,905	10,000–15,000

Sources: www12.statcan.ca/english/census01/products/highlight/Aboriginal/Page.cfm?Lang=E&Geo=PR&View= 1a&Table=1&StartRec=1&Sort=2&B1=Counts01&B2=Total; /www12.statcan.ca/english/census06/data/highlights/ Aboriginal/pages/Page.cfm?Lang=E&Geo=CMA&Code=01&Table=1&Data=Count&Sex=1&Age=1&StartRec= 1&Sort=2&Display=Page; Frideres 2005:165

Table A.2 >> Canadian Aboriginal population by province/territory, 2001–6

	2001	2006	INCREASE NUMBER	PERCENTAGE
Canada	976,305	1,172,790	196,485	20.0
Newfoundland and Labrador	18,775	23,455	4,675	23.8
Prince Edward Island	1,345	1,730	385	28.6
Nova Scotia	17,010	24,175	7,165	42.1
New Brunswick	16,990	17,655	665	3.9
Quebec	79,400	108,430	29,030	37.7
Ontario	188,315	242,495	54,180	28.7
Manitoba	150,045	175,395	25,350	16.8
Saskatchewan	130,185	141,890	11,705	9.0
Alberta	156,225	188,365	32,140	20.6
British Columbia	170,025	196,075	26,050	15.3
Yukon	6,540	7,580	1,040	15.9
NWT	18,730	20,635	1,905	10.2
Nunavut	22,720	24,920	2,200	9.7

Sources: www12.statcan.ca/english/census01/products/highlight/Aboriginal/Page.cfm?Lang=E&Geo=PR&View= 1a&Table=1&StartRec=1&Sort=2&B1=Counts01&B2=Total; www12.statcan.ca/english/census06/data/highlights/ Aboriginal/pages/Page.cfm?Lang=E&Geo=PR&Code=01&Table=1&Data=Count&Sex=1&Age=1&StartRec=1& Sort=2&Display=Page

are leaving the reserves, a trend that could affect federal policies and monies directed towards reserves. (It also serves the agenda of some policy makers who would like to see Aboriginal people integrated into mainstream society so that they can 'be like everyone else'.) According to Canada's official registry of status Indians, there were, at the end of 2006, 763,555 registered Indians in Canada, of whom 404,117 were living on reserves (roughly 53 per cent), 24,320 were living on Crown land (where they have special rights), and only 335,109 were living off-reserve (about 43 per cent).

Urban Statistics

Precise statistics on urban Aboriginal populations are also difficult to obtain, owing in part to the same suspicion of enumeration that causes some bands and individuals not to report, and also to the transient lives of many urban Native people, who may have both reserve and non-reserve addresses and may not be in the city all year. As well, with the growth of the Aboriginal number based on those who have obtained official status since 1985 (roughly 100,000 by 2001), there is an upward distortion in the statistics measuring the increasing urbanization of the Aboriginal population. Sociologist James Frideres, in a textbook whose influence has lasted more than three decades, used estimates he obtained from city officials. Notice how the 1996 estimates published in Frideres are typically higher than 2006 Statistics Canada figures for large urban centres in the East and in British Columbia, but are more like the StatsCan numbers for smaller urban centres in the East and on the Prairies. We suspect that when Statistics Canada figures are lower than the other estimates, the StatsCan figures are farther from the actual figure.

Immigration Statistics

With total fertility levels currently well below the replacement rate of 2.1, Canada is increasingly dependent on immigration as a source of population growth. As Table A.5 shows, immigrants to Canada have made up an increasing share of the national population since the mid-twentieth century, coinciding with declines in the total fertility rate from its post-war, baby boom highs.

Table A.3 >> Distribution of immigrants and recent immigrants in total population, by province/territory, 2006

PROVINCE OR TERRITORY	PERCENTAGE OF CANADIAN POPULATION	PERCENTAGE OF IMMIGRANTS[a]	PERCENTAGE OF RECENT IMMIGRANTS[b]
Newfoundland and Labrador	1.6	0.1	0.1
Prince Edward Island	0.4	0.1	0.1
Nova Scotia	2.9	0.7	0.6
New Brunswick	2.3	0.4	0.4
Quebec	23.8	13.8	17.5
Ontario	38.5	54.9	52.3
Manitoba	3.6	2.4	2.8
Saskatchewan	3.1	0.8	0.9
Alberta	10.4	8.5	9.3
British Columbia	13.0	18.1	16.0
Yukon Territory	0.1	0.0	0.0
Northwest Territories	0.1	0.0	0.1
Nunavut	0.1	0.0	0.0

Notes

[a] 'Immigrant population' is defined in the 2006 census as people who are, or have been, landed immigrants in Canada. Another term with the same meaning is 'foreign born'.

[b] A recent immigrant for the 2006 census is someone who came to Canada between 1 January 2001 and 16 May 2006.

Source: www12.statcan.ca/english/census06/analysis/immcit/tables/table2.htm

But as tables A.3 and A.4 show, immigrants to Canada continue to settle in the country's three most populous provinces: Ontario, British Columbia, and Quebec. Ontario, in particular, appears to receive a disproportionately high percentage of immigrants.

Is it natural for newcomers to Canada to want to settle in parts of the country that already have large immigrant populations, where they may even have friends or relatives who have preceded them? Should the government regulate the distribution of immigrants, forcing larger numbers to settle in provinces with lower populations, such as Saskatchewan or Nova Scotia? What problems could that kind of approach create both for the immigrants and for the existing residents of those provinces?

Population Statistics

The term 'cluttered nest'—opposite of 'empty nest'—refers to situations in which adult children are living at home with their parents, either having returned after a short time away (at college or university, for example) or never having left. As Table A.6 shows, this phenomenon is on the rise in Canada, with 60 per cent of those aged 20–24 living at home

Table A.4 >> Distribution of immigrants and percentage of provincial/territorial population, 2006

PROVINCE OR TERRITORY	NUMBER OF IMMIGRANTS	PERCENTAGE OF PROVINCIAL OR TERRITORIAL POPULATION	NUMBER OF RECENT IMMIGRANTS
Newfoundland and Labrador	8,385	1.7	1,440
Prince Edward Island	4,785	3.6	855
Nova Scotia	45,190	5.0	6,900
New Brunswick	26,400	3.7	4,300
Québec	851,560	11.5	193,905
Ontario	3,398,725	28.3	580,740
Manitoba	151,230	13.3	31,190
Saskatchewan	48,155	4.9	8,090
Alberta	527,030	16.2	103,680
British Columbia	1,119,215	27.5	177,840
Territories	6,275	6.2	1,040
Total	6,186,950	19.8	1,109,980

Sources: www12.statcan.ca/english/census06/analysis/immcit/atlantic.cfm; www12.statcan.ca/english/census06/analysis/immcit/quebec.cfm; www12.statcan.ca/english/census06/analysis/immcit/ontario.cfm; www12.statcan.ca/english/census06/analysis/immcit/prairies/cfm; www12.statcan.ca/english/census06/analysis/immcit/bc.cfm; www12.statcan.ca/english/census06/analysis/immcit/territories.cfm

Table A.5 >> Total number of foreign-born or immigrants to Canada and percentage of total population, 1901–2006

CENSUS YEAR	NUMBER	PERCENTAGE OF TOTAL POPULATION
1901	684,671	12.7
1911	1,586,961	22.0
1921	1,955,736	22.0
1931	2,307,525	22.0
1941	2,018,847	17.5
1951	2,059,911	14.7
1961	2,844,263	15.6
1971	3,295,530	15.3
1981	3,843,335	16.0
1991	4,342,890	16.1
1996	4,971,070	17.4
2001	5,448,480	18.4
2006	6,186,950	19.8

Source: 5) www12.statcan.ca/english/census06/analysis/immcit/charts/chart1_summ.htm

Table A.6 >> Living arrangements among Canadians aged 20–24 and 25–29, 1986 and 2006

	1986	2006
Living with parents		
20–24	49.3	60.3
25–29	15.6	26.0
20–29	32.1	43.5
Living as a Couple		
20–24	28.4	17.9
Common law	9.3	12.6
Married	19.1	5.3
25–29	62.3	48.5
Common law	10.2	22.6
Married	52.1	25.9

Note: 'Couple' refers to those living on their own or with the parents of one partner.

Sources: www12.statcan.ca/english/census06/analysis/famhouse/charts/chart14_summ.htm; www.12.statcan.ca/english/census06/analysis/famhouse/charts/chart15_summ.htm

and 26 per cent of those aged 25–29 living with their parents. (Note that roughly the same percentage of 25–29-year-olds—25.9 per cent—are married.) What conditions in society do you think have led to the increase in the number of adult children living with their parents? Do you think that most young adults who still live at home do so by choice or by necessity?

The second part of Table A.6 shows the number of young adults living as couples, either formally married or cohabiting (i.e., living in a common-law relationship). Do you find it surprising that the number of young married and common-law couples has declined since 1986? Take a close look at the breakdown in married and common-law couples aged 20–24. What do you notice? What do you think accounts for the change over the 20-year interval?

Tables A.7 and A.8 give an overview of how Canada's population has grown since the 1960s. At first glance, it would appear that Canada's population growth over the early part of the twenty-first century, compared with earlier periods, has been slight (see Table A.7), yet compared with growth in other G-8 nations (Table A.8), Canada's population increase looks strong. (The G-8, or 'Group of 8', nations are the 8 countries that together make up most of the world's economy.) Why might growth rates in Western industrialized countries be slowing?

Table A.7 >> Population Growth in Canada, 1961–2006

	POPULATION NUMBER	POPULATION GROWTH	PERCENTAGE GROWTH
1961	18,238,000	1,157,000	13.4
1966	20,015,000	1,777,000	9.7
1971	21,568,000	1,553,000	7.8
1976	22,993,000	1,425,000	6.6
1981	24,343,000	1,350,000	5.9
1986	25,309,000	966,000	4.0
1991	27,297,000	1,988,000	7.9
1996	28,847,000	1,550,000	5.7
2001	30,007,000	1,160,000	4.0
2006	31,613,000	1,606,000	5.4

Note: All numbers have been rounded off to the nearest thousand.

Source: www12.statcan.ca/english/census06/analysis/popdwell/charts/chart2_summ.htm

Table A.8 >> Population growth rate in Canada compared with growth in other G8 countries, 2001–6	
Canada	5.4
United States	5.0
Italy	3.1
France	3.1
United Kingdom	1.9
Japan	0.4
Germany	0
Russia	–2.4

Source: www12.statcan.ca/english/census06/analysis/popdwell/charts/chart 3_summ.htm

Employment Statistics

Tables A.9 and A.10 give a snapshot of which Canadian industries are growing fastest. Table A.9 looks at percentage increases, while Table A.10 looks at industry growth in terms of overall numbers of employees. Employment statistics are a good indicator both of a country's overall economic health and of which sectors of the economy are strongest. What do these two tables tell you about the state of Canada's economy? Are you surprised by any of the trades and professions that show up in the two tables? Are there any occupations you're surprised not to see here among Canada's fastest growing jobs?

Table A.9 >> Largest percentage workforce increases in Canada by occupation, 2001–6

	2006 EMPLOYMENT	GROWTH FROM 2001 (%)
oil and gas well drillers, servicers, testers, and related workers	11,500	77.8
production clerks (e.g., preparing production schedules for construction)	24,100	73.3
postsecondary teaching and research assistants	61,500	65.7
loan officers	35,400	64.5
construction inspectors	13,700	61.8
estheticians, electrologists, and related occupations	36,500	57.4
construction trades helpers and labourers	143,900	57.4
administrative clerks	101,700	53.9
refrigeration and air-conditioning mechanics	21,400	53.6
petroleum engineers	9,000	53.5

Source: Statistics Canada, Catalogue no. 97–559: Table 1, p. 12.

Table A.10 >> Largest numerical workforce increases in Canada by occupation, 2001–6

	2006	CHANGE FROM 2001
Retail salespersons and sales clerks	685,800	+132,200
male	285,800	63,600
female	400,000	68,600
construction trades helpers and labourers	143,900	52,300
male	133,600	47,500
female	10,300	4,800
truck drivers	286,100	44,000
male	276,200	40,900
female	9,900	3,100
cashiers	299,200	43,000
male	43,700	7,500
female	255,500	35,500
nurses aides, orderlies and patient service associates	169,700	37,100
registered nurses	265,900	37,000
male	16,500	3,200
female	249,400	33,800
customer service, information and related clerks	191,600	36,300
administrative clerks	101,700	35,600
information systems analysts and consultants	138,400	35,300
carpenters	145,000	33,900
male	133,600	32,900
female	11,400	1,000

Source: Statistics Canada, Catalogue no. 97–559: Table 2, p.13; Table 3, p. 14.